*Scales of
Resistance*

Scales of Resistance

Indigenous Women's Transborder Activism

Maylei Blackwell

DUKE UNIVERSITY PRESS
Durham and London   2023

© 2023 DUKE UNIVERSITY PRESS
The text of this book is licensed under a Creative Commons AttributionNonCommercial-NoDerivatives 4.0 International License: https://creativecommons.org/licenses/by-nc-nd/4.0/

Designed by Courtney Leigh Richardson
Typeset in IBM Plex and Portrait by Typesetter, Inc.

Library of Congress Cataloging-in-Publication Data
Names: Blackwell, Maylei, [date] author.
Title: Scales of resistance : indigenous women's transborder activism / Maylei Blackwell.
Description: Durham : Duke University Press, 2022. | Includes bibliographical references and index.
Identifiers: LCCN 2022029792 (print) |
LCCN 2022029793 (ebook)
ISBN 9781478017967 (paperback)
ISBN 9781478015352 (hardcover)
ISBN 9781478022602 (ebook)
ISBN 9781478092742 (ebook other)
Subjects: LCSH: Mexican American women—Political activity. | Indigenous women—Politicalactivity— Mexico.| Women political activists—Mexico. | Women political activists—United States. | BISAC: SOCIAL SCIENCE / Ethnic Studies / American / Native American Studies | SOCIAL SCIENCE / Gender Studies
Classification: LCC E184.M5 B533 2022 (print) | LCC E184.M5 (ebook) | DDC 305.48/86872073—dc23/eng/20220622
LC recordavailableathttps:/ /lccn.loc.gov/2022029792
LC ebookrec ordavailableathttps:/ /lccn.loc.gov/2022029793

Cover art: Indigenous women activists across Abiayala at the opening ceremony of the seventh Continental Network of Indigenous Women, Guatemala City, November 15, 2015. Photo by Maylei Blackwell.

This book is freely available in an open access edition thanks to TOME (Toward an Open Monograph Ecosystem)—a collaboration of the Association of American Universities, the Association of University Presses, and the Association of Research Libraries—and the generous support of Arcadia, a charitable fund of Lisbet Rausing and Peter Baldwin, and the UCLA Library. Learn more at the TOME website, available at: openmonographs.org.

Contents

LIST OF ILLUSTRATIONS • vii

ABBREVIATIONS • xi

PRELUDE:
Walking Together: The Politics of Acompañamiento • xv

INTRODUCTION • 1

1 THE MULTISCALAR PRACTICE OF AUTONOMY IN MEXICO • 41
2 ABIAYALA AS SCALE • 96
3 REBELLION AT THE ROOTS • 143
4 TRANSBORDER GEOGRAPHIES OF DIFFERENCE • 193
5 TRANSLOCAL GEOGRAPHIES OF INDIGENEITY • 230

CODA:
The Subterranean Life of Seeds • 258

NOTES • 297   REFERENCES • 313   INDEX • 349

Illustrations

FIGURE I.1. CONAMI Activist Tomasa Sandoval speaking at the Congreso Nacional Indígena, 2001 • 2

FIGURE 1.1. María de Jesús Patricio at CONAMI's Second National Encuentro, 2000 • 48

FIGURE 1.2. Margarita Gutiérrez speaking at the founding encuentro of CONAMI, 1997 • 60

FIGURE 1.3. CONAMI workshop participants, 1997 • 66

FIGURE 1.4. National Encuentro of Indigenous Women, Oaxaca City, 1997 • 69

FIGURE 1.5. CONAMI activist Cándida Jimenez and CONAIE leader Blanca Chancoso, 2001 • 74

FIGURE 1.6. Second Encuentro of CONAMI, Chilpancingo, Guerrero, 2000 • 75

FIGURE 1.7. Group photo from the Second National Encuentro of CONAMI, 2000 • 77

FIGURE 1.8. Nellys Palomo, Tomasa Sandoval, and Martha Sánchez, Mexico City, 2001 • 85

FIGURE 1.9. Selfie of participants in the CONAMI Workshop on Documenting the Violence Against Indigenous Women, Mexico City, 2018 • 88

FIGURE 1.10. CONAMI march to call attention to uncounted feminicides of Indigenous women, 2013 • 92

FIGURE 2.1. March at ECMIA's 5th continental gathering in Quebec, Canada, July 2007 • 97

FIGURE 2.2. Jennie Luna, Margarita Gutiérrez, and Cándida Jimenez at the UN World Conference against Racism, Durban, South Africa, 2001 • 99

FIGURE 2.3. Activists from across Abiayala at the Seventh Gathering of the Continental Network of Indigenous Women, 2015 • 114

FIGURE 2.4. After the organizing meeting of the First Indigenous Women's Caucus, Tenth Latin American and Caribbean Feminist Encuentro, 2005 • 122

FIGURE 2.5. Members of the Amazonian Indigenous Women's Network at the Tenth Latin American and Caribbean Encuentro, 2005 • 123

FIGURE 2.6. Preparing to read the statement from the Indigenous Women's Caucus, Tenth Latin American and Caribbean Encuentro, 2005 • 123

FIGURE 2.7. Reading the Indigenous Women's Caucus Statement, Tenth Latin American and Caribbean Encuentro, 2005 • 124

FIGURE 2.8. Martha Sánchez Nestor at the Eleventh Latin American and the Caribbean Feminist Encuentro, Mexico City, 2009 • 125

FIGURE 2.9. Session on Indigenous women's activism at the Eleventh Latin American and the Caribbean Feminist Encuentro, Mexico City, 2009 • 125

FIGURE 2.10. Indigenous women reading their declaration at the Eleventh Latin American and the Caribbean Feminist Encuentro, Mexico City, 2009 • 127

FIGURE 2.11. Tarcila Rivera Zea leading an ECMIA event • 137

FIGURE 2.12 Martha Sánchez Nestor and Margarita Gutiérrez of CONAMI at the Seventh Continental Network of Indigenous Women, 2015 • 140

FIGURE 3.1. New leadership team including newly elected municipal president Sofía Robles, Tlahuitoltepec, Mixe Region, Oaxaca, 2012 • 171

FIGURE 3.2. First assembly of the Network of Mixe Women (REDMMI), Ayutla Mixe, October 2009 • 183

FIGURE 4.1. FIOB Otros Saberes workshop, Los Angeles, California, 2005 • 198

FIGURE 4.2. Isabel Reyes, FIOB member, Oaxaca, 2007 • 199

FIGURE 4.3. Doña Matilde and her gastronomical products, Juxtlahuaca, Oaxaca, 2007 • 200

FIGURE 4.4. FIOB Otros Saberes workshop in Huajuapan de León, Oaxaca, 2007 • 209

FIGURE 4.5. Rosie Mendez Moreno, Ana Ruth Mendez Mendez, and Maura Díaz, Huajuapan de León, 2007 • 209

FIGURE 4.6. Maura Díaz and Odilia Romero Hernández lead the discussion about findings from the Otros Saberes study, Binational General Assembly, Juxtlahuaca, Oaxaca, 2009 • 213

FIGURE 4.7. Mujeres Indígenas in Leadership (Indigenous Women in Leadership, MIEL) logo • 214

FIGURE 5.1. Mayoral proclamation of Oaxacan Heritage Month in Los Angeles • 238

FIGURE 5.2. Maritza Sánchez, 2014 Queen of the Vela Muxe LA • 239

FIGURE 5.3. FIOB LA after a protest in solidarity with the APPO at Macarthur Park, Los Angeles, 2006 • 241

FIGURE 5.4. Odilia Romero Hernández • 245

FIGURE 5.5. Monserrat Bernardino, May 1 March, Los Angeles, 2012 • 251

FIGURE C.1. Consulta on Indigenous and Afro-descendant Reform of the Mexican Constitution, Los Angeles, 2019 • 273

FIGURE C.2. Janet Martinez, Indigenous Literatures Conference • 277

Abbreviations

AMIO

Asamblea de Mujeres Indígenas de Oaxaca (Assembly of Indigenous Women of Oaxaca)

ANIPA

Asamblea Nacional Indígena Plural por la Autonomía (National Plural Indigenous Assembly for Autonomy)

APPO

Asamblea Popular de los Pueblos Oaxaca (Popular Assembly of Oaxacan People)

AZACHIS

Asamblea de Autoridades Zapotecas y Chinantecas de la Sierra (Assembly of Zapotec and Chinantec Authorities)

CAMI

Casa de Mujer Indígena (Indigenous Women's House)

CBDIO

Centro Binacional para el Desarrollo Indígena Oaxaqueña (Binational Center for Oaxacan Indigenous Development)

CDI

Comisión Nacional para el Desarollo de los Pueblos Indígenas

CEDAW

Convention on the Elimination of All Forms of Discrimination against Women

CGMI

Coordinadora Guerrerense de Mujeres Indígenas (Guerreran Coordinator of Indigenous Women)

CHIRLA

Coalition for Humane Immigrant Rights of Los Angeles

CIELO

Comunidades Indígenas en Liderazgo (Indigenous Communities in Leadership)

CIG

Concejo Indigena de Gobierno (Indigenous Governing Council)

CMPIO

Coalición de Maestros y Promotores Indígenas de Oaxaca

CNI

Congreso Nacional Indígena (National Indigenous Congress)

COCOPA

Comisión de Concordia y Pacificación (Commission on Concordance and Pacification)

CODREMI

Comité de Defensa de los Recursos Humanos y Culturales Mixes (Committee in Defense of Mixe Human and Cultural Resources)

CONAIE

Confederación de Nacionalidades Indígenas del Ecuador (Confederation of Indigenous Nationalities of Ecuador)

CONAMI

Coordinadora Nacional de Mujeres Indígenas de México (National Coordinator of Indigenous Women)

CONAMIE

Confederación Nacional de Mujeres Indígenas del Ecuador (National Confederation of Indigenous Women of Ecuador)

CONAYA

Comisión Nacional de Intermediación (National Intermediation Commission)

CRAC-PC

Coordinadora Regional de Autoridades Comunitarias—Policía Comunitaria (Regional Coordinator of Community Authorities—Communitarian Police)

ECMIA

Enlace Continental de Mujeres Indígenas de las Americas, formerly Enlace Continental de Mujeres Indígenas de Abya Yala (Continental Network of Indigenous Women of the Americas, formerly of Abya Yala)

EZLN

Ejército Zapatista de Liberación Nacional (Zapatista Army of National Liberation)

FIOB

Frente Indígena de Organizaciones Binacionales (Indigenous Front of Binational Organizations), formerly Frente Indígena Oaxaqueña Binacional (Binational Oaxacan Indigenous Front)

FIPI

Frente Independiente de Pueblos Indios (Independent Front of Indigenous Peoples)

HTA

hometown association

ILO

International Labor Organization

MIEL

Mujeres Indígenas en Liderazgo (Indigenous Women in Leadership)

NAFTA

North American Free Trade Agreement

NGO

Nongovernmental organization

ORO

Organización Regional de Oaxaca (Regional Organization of Oaxaca)

PAN

Partido Acción Nacional (National Action Party)

PRD

Partido de la Revolución Democrático (Party of the Democratic Revolution)

PRI

Partido Revolucionario Institucional (Institutional Revolutionary Party)

REDMMI

La Red de Mujeres Mixes (Network of Mixe Women)

SER

Servicios del Pueblo Mixe (Services of the Mixe Pueblo)

UCIZONI

Unión de Comunidades Indígenas de la Zona Norte del Istmo (Union of Indigenous Communities of the Northern Zone of the Isthmus)

UN

United Nations

UNDRIP

United Nations Declaration on the Rights of Indigenous People

Prelude

Walking Together: The Politics of Acompañamiento

I live in and teach on the unceded territory of the Tongva (Gabrielino) people and honor them as the traditional caretakers of Tovaangar, the land now known as Los Angeles and the South Channel Islands. As a two-spirit Thai Cherokee relative, I recognize and honor them as the stewards of the land and water and offer my gratitude to these ancestors past, present, and emerging. I dedicate this book to all those Indigenous women and their allies who fight colonial, feminicidal, structural, institutional, and political violence and work to heal themselves and their communities. *Scales of Resistance* is inspired by so many fellow travelers, luchadoras, and dreamers who are now ancestors, including Nellys, Marya, Tatiana, Horacio, Policarpo, Irma, and Martha. It is an offering in honor of the world we are building together and the future generations who will inherit it.

This book is a gift of the collective knowledge of Indigenous women activists in what is now Mexico and its diaspora in the United States. This knowledge was generated and shared with me while accompanying Indigenous women's organizing for over twenty years. It draws from seventy oral histories I conducted and more than eighty events I attended, including local, national, and transborder/transnational meetings, encuentros (gatherings), marches, workshops, and shared projects. This project's path has been guided by community-based, activist research and shaped by the deep collective conversations it engendered—a research process that changed as I traveled a shared path with others. Research undertaken in this way opens a journey created by rich connections, relationships, and commitments, all of which have taken me on unforeseen paths I could have never imagined when I set out. In this way, the research processes at the center of this book are rivers that flow through and have shaped much of my adult life.

I came to intellectual life and academia through politics and activism. On January 1, 1994, during the first year of my doctoral studies in the History of Consciousness program at the University of California (UC) Santa Cruz, an Indigenous rebellion led by the Zapatista Army of National Liberation, or the

EZLN (the acronym formed from its Spanish name, Ejército Zapatista de Liberación Nacional), sparked a global movement organized around the alternative to the ravages of the neoliberal economic order gripping the planet envisioned by the EZLN. A few years earlier, in 1992, I participated in the cross-border Indigenous networks formed throughout Turtle Island—what is known as the Americas—to refuse the five-hundred-year celebration of Christopher Columbus's so-called discovery of the Americas and to forge an Indigenous, Black, and popular front of resistance. In Mexico in the early 1990s, Indigenous people created a national movement, breaking out of the peasant and class-based organizing of prior generations to challenge anew, through mass mobilizations and uprisings, their own economic, political, and social marginalization. Indigenous women were at the center of these movements for Indigenous autonomy and continue to be. As the most marginal of the marginalized, they devised new strategies and discourses of political participation, equity and inclusion, and autonomy by weaving in and between household, community, municipal, regional, national, and international scales of power. Yet the promise and hope of the 1990s and Mexico's precarious transition to democracy aimed at transforming authoritarian populist nationalism forms of governance, undergirded by the coloniality of power, were undermined by the mass social inequality of neoliberal reforms and later, large-scale violence of an emerging narcostate and drug cartels.

I began working with Indigenous activists and organizers in Mexico in 1998, initially accompanying their organizing as an activist. Later, as we built trust and long-term relationships, we created activist research and collaborative research practices. These forms of accountability and knowledge production have begun to transform the historically uneven, and often exploitative, relations of power that university researchers have practiced in their research with Indigenous peoples. I have researched, written, and even published with the Indigenous women activists I write about. As a doctoral student in my twenties, I was called to Mexico to understand the role of difference in women's organizing in Mexico and the United States. I sought to study lesbian, Indigenous, and working-class organizing or questions of difference in women's organizing. Yet the urgency and vibrancy of Indigenous women's organizing eclipsed other aspects of my original project. Guided by ethics of Indigenous self-determination, autonomy, and my activist commitments, my conversations around decolonizing methodologies and collaborative and community-based research grounded in Indigenous protocols of knowledge production, permission, respect, and reciprocity evolved along with the work.

I started work with CONAMI (Coordinadora Nacional de Mujeres Indígenas de Mexico/National Coordinator of Indigenous Women) in the late 1990s in

Mexico City. As a relatively young scholar-activist the same age as the younger women in the founding cohort of CONAMI activists, including Martha Sánchez Nestor (Amuzgo from Guerrero) and Cándida Jimenez (Ayuujk [Mixe] from Oaxaca), who provided the backbone of early organizational labor, I fell in with them, hauling huge pots of beans, photocopying materials and making carpetas (folders) for national trainings for members that CONAMI hosted every other month in Mexico City, for which activists from all over the country came into the capital. I often met with activists in the apartment office the organization shared with K'inal Antesetik DF, under the leadership of Afro-Colombian socialist feminist Nellys Palomo, where CONAMI organizers would often stay. I fell into accompanying and working alongside organizers because I came from a working-class, activist background and political organizing came to me easier than the research I was conducting for my dissertation. That was how I began on the path of acompañando (accompanying) Indigenous women's organizing in Mexico, and I did not know where it would lead. We sometimes remembered to turn on a tape recorder or to sit down to conduct a formal oral history interview after long meetings or early in the mornings before activists would depart the capital on their long journeys back home to the mountains of Oaxaca, as was the case with Cándida Jimenez; to the rich P'urépecha homelands in Michoacán like Tomasa Sandoval of the Nación P'urépecha Zapatista; or to the states of Veracruz, Chiapas, and Guerrero, like other activists.

Over time, I realized that the process of accompanying Indigenous women's organizing and thus my research process followed the multiscalar nature of Indigenous women's resistance, weaving in and between local, national, international, continental, and transborder organizing. I lived in Mexico City in the late 1990s and met many Indigenous women activists who came into the capitol regularly for those national meetings. I conducted some early interviews during national meetings or the bimonthly national trainings CONAMI organized in its early years. Other times, I sat and waited for appointments with activists who were caught up in endless meetings, like the day I spent waiting in the Party of the Democratic Revolution (PRD) offices in Mexico City for an interview with Margarita Gutiérrez, a Hñahñú activist who worked in the PRD's Secretariat of Indigenous Peoples and was one of two Indigenous women who worked on the women's sessions of the San Andrés Peace Accords. On other occassions, I rode the bus for days to attend meetings or conduct oral histories, like the one I conducted with Zapotec/Ayuujk (Mixe) leader Sofía Robles at the offices of Servicios del Pueblo Mixe (SER) in Santa Maria Tlahuitoltepec, the Southern Mixe region in the southwest of the state of Oaxaca.

In those heady days of the Indigenous movement, much activity and organizing occurred. After I moved back to California, I returned often to Mexico and was honored and inspired to attend the Second National Encuentro of Indigenous Women in Chilpancingo, Guerrero, in 2000. Hundreds of Indigenous women gathered to demand justice for women who suffered under the increased militarization of their communities, due to increased political repression of their movements. Together they analyzed the gendered racialized violence against Indigenous women forging the early movement against feminicide and the heightened violence enacted by the state and narcotraffickers in the War on Drugs—which all too often looked like a war on Indigenous communities. I had been in women of color feminist organizing circles that initiated INCITE! Women of Color Against Violence and as an early member in the Bay Area and Los Angeles chapters, I saw the interconnection between colonial and state violence and intimate partner violence and the challenges of seeking solutions that did not rely on and reinforce structures of policing founded on racial violence, settler colonial occupation, and class oppression. I immediately recognized these connections in Indigenous women's fight against gendered and state violence in Mexico.

CONAMI's second encuentro represented the growth of a multigenerational struggle of Indigenous women. In Chilpancingo, Guerrero, I continued interviewing founding members of CONAMI who were of an older generation, including María de Jesús Patricio, a Nahuatl healer known as Marichuey who became the spokesperson for the Indigenous Govering Council of the National Indigenous Congress that, as a collective, ran to become a presidential candidate in the 2018 elections. I met Doña Rufina Villa from Masehual Siuamej Mosenyolchicauani (Women Who Support Each Other), one of the oldest Indigenous women's organizations in the country, formed in 1985 in Cuetzalan, Puebla. Tomasa Sandoval, a powerful leader from the Nación P'urépecha Zapatista of Michoacán, spoke on one of the plenary panels delivering a persuasive analysis that debunked the dichotomy between individual and collective rights that pits women's rights against Indigenous rights in Western legal thought. These leaders comprised a different generation in CONAMI whose leadership and social authority was grounded in their experience as mothers and as leaders and organizers of their families, communities, and local organizations. The second encuentro also included a dynamic generation of younger activists who were forged in the fire of Indigenous autonomous struggles, including Hermalinda Turbicio, a Mixtec leader from Guerrero who had stepped into leadership when the men of her community were arrested because of state repression in response to the community declaring themselves autonomous, and "Lorena," a leader from a weavers collective in Chiapas whose empowerment and consciousness shifted along with the EZLN's women's revolutionary law and the historic community deliberation of women during the San Andrés Peace Accords following the 1994 Zapatista uprising.

Some of the oral histories and collaborative research were conducted at multiple "local" and regional scales, such as hometowns and organizations' offices in municipal centers. For example, the first oral history I conducted with Zapotec/Ayuujk (Mixe) leader Sofía Robles at the offices of Servicios del Pueblo Mixe (SER) in Santa Maria Tlahuitoltepec, the Southern Mixe region in the southwest of the state of Oaxaca. I rode the bus for a day to meet Sofía for that first interview in Tlahuitoltepec. Over the years I conducted return interviews with her in the SER offices in the state capital of Oaxaca City, where she coordinated women's rights work in the Mixe region, across the state and internationally. I continued to meet and interview her as she traveled to Los Angeles as part of the rich connections of the Indigenous diaspora from Oaxaca in California. I conducted other research at the continental scale across solidarity networks of Indigenous people that span Abiayala, a scale of solidarity anchored in land epistemologies of the Guna people of Panama and Colombia. Invoked by Indigenous organizers across the continent that is now called the Americas, Indigenous women conjure this scale of organizing based on Indigenous relationships and commitments to land in ways that disrupt settler colonial nation-state borders of what scholars call "transnational" organizing. By organizing across multiple borders, Indigenous women foreground their Indigenous nations and territories based on their cosmovisions, notions of place, and responsibilities, weaving them into the scales that are conjured, traversed, interwoven, and trans-ed through this organizing. This research included accompanying activists from Mexico who helped to form the Enlace Continental de Mujeres Indígenas de Abya Yala (Continental Network of Indigenous Women, ECMIA); the group later changed *Abya Yala* to *the Americas* as activists learned which Indigenous epistemologies translated across scales and which were not effectively scalable.

In this way, I accompanied activists at continental and international meetings and transnational scales of activism that organizers use to cross colonial scales created by and between nation-states as well as scales conjured by Indigenous epistemologies and advocacy networks for Indigenous and women's rights activists globally. For example, although I missed Margarita Gutiérrez that afternoon in the PRD offices when I lived in Mexico City, I eventually sat down with her in 2001 in Durban, South Africa, at the NGO Forum of the World Conference against Racism, where we conducted our first of many oral histories. In chapter 2, I document how the scale of Abiayala was conjured, to use Anna Tsing's word (2012), and map Indigenous women's multiscalar activism within diverse transnational sites such as the Latin American and Caribbean Feminist Encuentros, ECMIA gatherings, hemispheric Indigenous gatherings, and UN meetings.

My role as researcher and participant in these spaces was richly layered and complex, and it often shifted. It was informed by my own identities and political commitments as an urban native, mixed-race, two-spirit/queer, feminist researcher formed in women of color feminist and anti-imperialist politics. I was a researcher accompanying Mexican Indigenous women and ECMIA activists and a member of women's native rights networks and two-spirit communities from the North. Unlike other researchers who were positioned as observers or guests, I sometimes was invited as a guest or observer, and other times was positioned as an activist/member of the organizations and networks I was accompanying and documenting. For example, Indigenous activists from Mexico invited me to speak as a native feminist activist at a session they organized at one of the Latin American and Caribbean Feminist Encuentros and invited mestiza feminist researchers to participate as allies. At other times Northern native women's organizers and friends positioned me as part of our regional formation, particularly when I attended Northern meetings as a participant rather than as an observer accompanying women to the Mexico and Central America meetings. I attended the World Conference of Indigenous Women in Lima, Peru, to catch up with friends and activists from all over Latin America, all members of ECMIA. During each meal, elders and knowledge holders from Northern Indigenous women's organizations in the United States would sit next to me and regale me with their powerful histories and stories of organizing. After a time, they told me that some of the founding members had shared their histories because they wanted to collaborate with me to document the origins of one of the older networks of Indigenous women's organizing, which I thought was a beautiful project I am honored to do. I may have been in that space to do return interviews with organizers from the South, but native women from the North had plans, too, and they positioned me within their own agendas—and of course, I was a willing coconspirator.

I kept in touch with activists over the years by traveling to Mexico and international meetings and, between meetings, by connecting through social media, email, and WhatsApp. After I returned to California and finished my PhD, I moved to Oakland to undertake a UC President's Postdoctoral Fellowship under the mentorship of Norma Alarcon at UC Berkeley. There I organized forums and tours to bring activists like Nellys Palomo from K'inal Antsetik and Martha Sánchez of CONAMI to the United States to give talks (for example, at an event called "Rebellion at the Roots," which I organized at the San Francisco Women's Building) or to attend meetings with other Indigenous women to build the Northern Network of Continental Network of Indigenous Women. Cherríe Moraga and Celia Herrera hosted these visitors at their home in Oakland to bring them together with members of the Red Xicana Indígenas. Martha Sánchez and I later traveled to Chicago to attend the INCITE! Women of Color Against Violence Conference and to meet up with other Northern native women to build the northern region of ECMIA. This was before Mexico broke off to become a separate region, thereby illustrating how activists not just weave in and between existing scales, but conjure new ones. Despite the fact that they are geopolitically located in North America within hegemonic geographies, Mexico created their own region within the network by arguing that, even though they are only one country, they are so large and diverse and yet, too linguistically and culturally different from the United States and Canada, that organizationally Mexico should operate as one of the regions within the network, which not only expanded the North, Central, South regional scalar organization of the network but exemplified the flexibility in conjuring new scales of resistance. After that tour, Martha and I finished our second and longest, oral history interview at the San Francisco International Airport. I have met up with her many times over the years at Indigenous gatherings and meetings. I have continued to interview her, even when our time was short because we had meetings, were drafting declarations, or were just catching up on life. This is why it was devastating to learn that Martha died of COVID-19 complications in 2021 (Burgete Cal y Mayor 2021), as had many other Indigenous activists, including Los Angeles-based Maya K'iche, spiritual leader, interpreter, and founder of Mayavision Policarpo Chaj (Solis 2021). Other times I was able to invite ECMIA members such as Tarcila Rivera Zea, Margarita Gutiérrrez, and Sonia Henríquez to visit UCLA. While Tarcila's schedule did not permit her to come, both Margarita and Sonia joined me in 2014.

Over the years, I continued to return to Mexico to attend events with CONAMI. In 1999, I traveled with Nellys Palomo, an advisor to the CONAMI who also tragically died in an accidental fall in 2009, to the mountains of Guerrero to do a training workshop on Indigenous autonomy and women's rights. Riding in the back of a camioneta (a pickup truck) with people headed home from the market with their turkeys and crops, we became ensnared at a checkpoint the Mexican state used to repress Indigenous social movements by using the War on Drugs as a pretext. This is part of what Aida Hernández Castillo (2018) calls the continuum of violence where the Dirty War of state repression against organized resistance movements between the 1960s and 1980s merged with the repression of Indigenous autonomy movements in the 1990s and later connected the use of the Mexican military to occupy Indigenous communities in resistance under the guise of the Drug War in the 2000s. We were detained and had to wait hours before we were allowed to move on; by then it was too late to make it to the community. I have vivid memories of this trip because I started smoking again after quitting six months after I finished my dissertation—one of seven attempts to quit before it finally stuck.

There were other negotiations to consider while doing fieldwork. In those years that I lived and traveled back and forth to Mexico frequently I had short hair and presented as less feminine so I had to navigate different gender, sexual, and racial conventions as a queer, mixed-race urban native feminist who stood out as wearing "men's" shoes. Over time my presentation became more femme, and some negotiations became easier, whereas others became differently complex—as when I was propositioned at political meetings and conferences or had to turn down marriage proposals with some grace and humor. My being queer/two spirit meant becoming a parent relatively late in life, so I was often regarded as a perpetual señorita—a young, unmarried woman—even when I was the same age as the grown women we addressed with the respectful *Doña*. Class and racial differences have always been indexed by how I am addressed. I noticed the rigidity of the class structure in Mexico and that I had little in common with other academics and researchers I met due to differences in our class backgrounds. They were referred to by their academic titles (with the forms of social distance that implies), whereas I was not. Nor did I need to be. These negotiations became even more intense as the "field" became more integrated with daily life and activism as I began organizing and working with migrant Indigenous women in California.

Other scales of accompaniment and research include the translocalities or transregions created by the Indigenous migrant routes that link, through dense diasporic ties, the Sierra Norte, the Central Valleys, and the Mixteca regions of Oaxaca to Mexico City, Baja California, and the California cities of Oceanside, Los Angeles, Fresno, and Santa Maria—so much so that these locations form a transborder scale. In 2005, Odilia Romero was elected as the Binational Coordinator of Women's Affairs. She invited me to become an advisor to FIOB. Later, as FIOB members wrote a research proposal to study ways to diversify FIOB's binational leadership, they invited Laura Velasco, of the Colegio de la Frontera Norte, and me to join the team. The proposal won the group the Latin American Studies Association's Otros Saberes Grant, which funds Indigenous and Afro-descendant knowledge producers. For many years,

I worked in solidarity with the FIOB and supported its members as they built leadership development programs for women. I met with the team of facilitators and supported them with documentation and resources as we built the Mujeres Indígenas en Liderazgo (MIEL) workshops held in Oaxaca and California. I met Janet Martinez, Odilia's daughter, when she was fifteen in their small studio apartment jammed with shelves of books, in the Pico Union district of Los Angeles. During that meeting, we made food as they shared their plan to reinitiate *El Tequio*, FIOB's magazine, by modeling it on the feminist magazine *Bitch*. After Janet went to college at UC Berkeley, Poncho joined Odilia as her life partner, and I have fond memories of bringing their son his favorite Cookie Monster cake for one of his first birthdays. A highlight of working in collaboration with Odilia and Janet are the many working sessions over Oaxacan, Thai, and Korean food.

Another long-term relationship that has informed this work is with Dr. Gaspar Rivera-Salgado, Mixtec scholar and founding member of the FIOB, who I met in graduate school in Santa Cruz. We have shared many political and research collaborations as fellow travelers journeying, for example, to the Mixteca for research and staying at his family's home or to the fields of San Quintin to bring mutual aid and solidarity to striking Oaxacan Indigenous agricultural workers. Accompanying the base building and leadership development of Indigenous migrant women has been a great honor. I've witnessed the joys and sorrows of these strong women, including Monserrat, who learned to fight for herself as a young girl in the Central Valleys of Oaxaca and who uses this strength and resilience as an organizer of tenants and domestic workers. As we sat in the park to do our interview, she told me about getting up at 3 or 4 a.m. to do all the "women's work," which fell on her shoulders when her mother passed away, and then walking miles to school—all to show her dad that her dream of going to school would not interfere with the labor she was charged with completing. As she shared the struggle and exhaustion of those years trying to access education, the waves of memories swept over us, and we wept together on the park bench. Reflecting on her fight to go to school, she shook her head and shared how challenging it was to animate her kids to want to pursue their educations, as they were often consumed by video games and did not understand her arduous struggle for what they take for granted.

Yet, another courageous woman I met was Doña Mari, who told me how she crossed the border while carrying an infant to join her husband working in the United States. Before she would let me interview her, she thanked me for mentoring her son—that same baby who had been my student at UCLA: the talented Zapotec historian Luis Sánchez-López, who went on to earn a PhD in

History and become a professor at the University of California, Irvine. Many of these collaborations grew into friendships and other shared projects of Indigenous women's empowerment, Indigenous survivance across colonial borders, and digital storytelling that spanned years of meetings, marches, fundraisers, ceremonies, solidarity tours, and parties in the Los Angeles neighborhoods of Korea Town, Pico Union, Westlake, and the city of Long Beach. These relationships crossed Oaxacan migrant geographies including the communities of Oceanside, Santa Maria, Fresno, Ventura, and San Diego in California; San Quintin and Tijuana in Baja California; and Oaxaca City, Huajuapan de León, Santiago Juxtlahuaca, Tlacolula de Matamoros, Zantatepec, or the Isthmus of Juchitán in Oaxaca; and in Mexico City.

While working on this project, I lived in many Indigenous homelands, including Awaswas Ohlone, Chumash, Tewa, and Tongva territories. I've also visited many other Indigenous territories where Indigenous women are weaving their scales of activism, including Hñähñú (Otomí), Zapotec, Ñu Savi (Mixtec), Triqui, Ayuujk (Mixe), Amuzgo, Mexica, Maya, Nahuatl, and Guna in Fresno, Oceanside, and Los Angeles, California; Morelos in the State of Mexico; Michoacán, Guerrero, Oaxaca, Chiapas, Tijuana, and the San Quintin Valley of Baja California; and other nation-states including Peru, Guatemala, Mexico, the United States, Brazil, Costa Rica, Dominican Republic, Canada, and South Africa.

In 2011, I received the Lillian Robles (Juaneno/Acjachemen) Award for Leadership and Action from the Women's, Gender, and Sexuality Studies Department at California State University Long Beach (CSULB) for community-engaged research. I received this great honor with Georgiana Sanchez, a Chumash storyteller and scholar and one of my beloved college teachers. As the Robles family sang honoring songs during the award ceremony, I was struck by the convergence of an American Indian scholar-activist who works with Mexican Indigenous movements and their diasporas on Native California Indian territory, holding the stories of displaced Indigenous peoples on the lands of those who have been dispossessed of their lands and are struggling to survive. I had been working with students and with Dalit transmedia storyteller Thenmozhi Songdaragan, one of the original creators of digital storytelling, to create digital storytelling projects with organizers of the FIOB women's leadership program called Mujeres Indígenas en Liderazgo (MIEL). We began to write grants to build a storytelling platform for this multiple and layered Indigenous Los Angeles. After the evening at the Robles Awards, with the multiple layers of Indigenous LA present together in one space but often kept from knowing each other's histories, I was even more inspired to create this digital storytelling platform we called Mapping Indigenous LA. I applied for an initial seed grant and invited UCLA professors Mishuana Goeman, Wendy Teeter, and Keith Camacho to serve as co-principal investigators for a story-mapping project that uncovers the histories of sedimented layers of Indigenous LA, including the original inhabitants of the Los Angeles basin and islands, the Tongva/Gabrielino, relocated American Indians, Pacific Islanders, and the Latin American Indigenous diaspora. Although Keith did not stay on with us as we built the Mapping Indigenous LA platform (mila.ss.ucla.edu), throughout the autumn of 2012 we met weekly to design the project based on digital story maps and the digital platform in collaboration with Tongva community members and cultural educators. We each continued to build, and in the summer of 2016 I worked intensively with six community researchers from the Zapotec, Mixtec, and Mayan communities of Los Angeles to design the Latin American Indigenous Diaspora map, which informs my thinking in chapter 5 of this book. I conceptualized the original proposal, wrote the language used on the platform, and managed grants and staff on multiple projects for our collaborative project, including the Crossroads and Currents, Pacific Islander, and Two-Spirit Maps. Many other colleagues and friends went on to build storymaps and this hub for Indigenous stories of place and teaching resources, as when Tongva cultural educators came together to build resources and train schoolteachers in the LA Unified School District. Even more important, many communities, tribes, collaborators, and organizations went on to build their own storymaps that show the transformative histories they are weaving.

I thank all the Indigenous women activists who generously shared their insights, dreams, knowledge, and visions with me. I appreciate the longtime friends and collaborators who made this work possible, including Margarita Gutiérrez, Tomasa Sandoval, Paty Sandoval, Martha Sánchez, Fabiola Jurado, Norma Don Juan, Odilia Romero, Janet Martinez, Dr. Gaspar Rivera-Salgado, the late Rufino Dominguez, Centolia Maldonado, and many, many others. I thank Angela Davis, who served as my PhD advisor and mentor as I began this project as a first-generation doctoral student. She taught me how to walk the activist-scholar path. Pat Zavella modeled the best of critical feminist ethnography, humor, and decades of mentorship and ultimately friendship. Sonia Alvarez and Jonathan Fox guided my work as I completed my intial fieldwork and doctoral thesis. Many others generously read iterations of chapters and versions of the manuscript as it worked its way through the writing and publication process including Lynn Stephen, Shannon Speed, Josie Saldaña, Pat Zavella, Nadine Naber, Tony Lucero, Grace Hong, Horacio Roque Ramirez, Gloria Chacon, Gaye Theresa Johnson, Leisy Ábrego, Juan Herrera, Mauricio

Magaña, Gaspar Rivera-Salgado, Holly Worthen, Sherene Razack, Monisha Das Gupta, and Judy Wu. I thank Lise Nelson for our early conversations, which directed me to theorizations of scale by feminist geographers. I learned early on to survive the academy to break its solitude and competitiveness by building community. For many years I have written in community, in writing groups and with many writing friends. I am especially grateful for the writing accountability group that has supported me with their wisdom and humor during the past six years while writing this book: Tiffany Willoughby-Herard, Michelle Habell-Pallan, Julia Fogg, and Lynn Fujiwara. What a gift to be in community with these talented, powerful women. I wrote with another "get the book done club" that included Pat Zavella and Nadine Naber and thank them for their grit and insight. I have had the privilege to build writing communities and have writing dates with many friends along the way, including Tiffany Willoughby-Herard, Lilith Mahmud, Alicia Carroll, Mauricio Magaña, Juan Herrera, Floridalma Boj Lopez, Josh Guzmán, Micaela Diaz, Audrey Silvestre, Rafael Solorzano, Nadia Zepeda, Brenda Nicolás and Eddie Alvarez.

I workshopped an early draft of the book and thank the UCLA Center for the Study of Women for the early protoype of the Research Excellence Award. I thank Grace Hong for her advocacy to create spaces such as these on campus; Tony Lucero for reading an early version of the manuscript; and those UCLA colleagues who read chapters, including Grace Hong, Shannon Speed, Flori Boj Lopez, Leisy Ábrego, Gaye Theresa Johnson, Gaspar Rivera-Salgado, and Brenda Nicolás. I was generously invited to workshop the manuscript for chapter 4 at the University of Connecticut and later at the Institute for Research on Women and Gender at the University of Michigan as part of the Rethinking Transnational Feminisms Working Group and as a fellow at the School for Advanced Research in Santa Fe, New Mexico. I also workshopped the chapter 2 manuscript as part of that same group's UCI Humanities Center Faculty-in-Residence Seminar and the chapter 5 manuscript as part of the Critical Latinx Indigeneities LA Writing Group. I thank members of the LOUD collective, the Critical Latinx Indigeneities Working Group, most especially Floridalma Boj Lopez, Luis Urrieta, Gloria Chacon, Bianet Castellanos, and Lulu Alberto. When I lived in New Mexico, I was lucky to write and discuss work with Corinne Sanchez, Laura Harjo, Susan McKinnon, Karin Fredric, and Brian Burke. I have been blessed to work with the next generation of Indigenous scholars who are emerging as an emphatic force that will reshape multiple conversations. It has been a pleasure to work in community and conversation with Flori Boj Lopez, Brenda Nicolás, Luis Sánchez, Daina Sánchez, and Michelle Vasquez Ruiz in our critical Indigenous studies reading group. I have worked at the intersection of Indigenous, Chicano/a/x, and Latinx studies for many decades, founding and helping to build spaces of convergence, such as the Women's Indigenous/Native Caucus of Mujeres Activas en Letras y Cambio Social (MALCS), attending the founding meeting of the Native American Indigenous Studies Association (NAISA), and helping to build the Abya Yala Working Group in subsequent meetings, Otros Saberes within the Latin American Studies Association, and finding spaces of affiliation and collaboration in the American Studies Association (ASA). Ines Hernandez-Ávila and Ines Talamontes are forerunners who opened the space for multiple indigeneities across these fields.

For accompanying me in the last stages of this project and for their research assistance, I thank Audrey Silvestre for her clarity, strength, grace, and friendship; Rafael Ramirez Solorzano for his insights, perpetually positive outlook, and merging of movement work and scholarship; Rose Simons for her work translating, annotating, and reflecting on the work with me; and Chantiri Resendiz Ramirez for her critical engagement and timely assistance. Finally, my deepest gratitude to Michelle Vasquez Ruiz for her steadfast research, intrepid spirit, and commitment to community-engaged Indigenous digital humanities. Over the years, I have benefitted from many sources of support over the multiple stages of research for this project, including the UC Institute for Mexico and the United States, a UC President's Postdoctoral Fellowship, a Woodrow Wilson Fellowship, the School for Advanced Research, and the Latin American Studies Association Otros Saberes Initiative. At UCLA I thank the Institute for American Cultures, especially Chon Noriega and the Chicano Studies Research Center for years of unwavering support. Many other research centers have been important community hubs, including the American Indian Studies Center, thanks to the powerful leadership of Angela R. Riley and Shannon Speed; the Latin American Institute, under the leadership of Kevin Terriciano; and the Center for Mexican Studies, under the leadership of Ruben Hernández. I have received critical support from two key colegas in the UCLA Department of Chicana/o and Central American Studies. I thank Leisy Ábrego and Gaye Theresa Johnson. The UC Academic Senate's Committee on Research and the dean of social sciences have supported my research in key phases.

This project manifested alongside many political struggles, en camino to building family and community, and during life transitions that span accompanying my mom through end-stage lung cancer to the birth of my daughter, and the rise of authoritarianism in the United States and renewed uprisings to end white supremacy—all while surviving a global pandemic (it's not our first as Indigenous people). Friends have surrounded me with love and solidity. Thank you Dre, Joan, Josie, Alice, Deb, Erica, Lilith, Juliet, Raja, Queen, Dean, Iyatunde, and especially my family: Gary, Alphonce, Rubi, Jose, Cosme, and Luna. Mostly, I am ever grateful for the light that is Juniper Nayeli.

Introduction

The third National Indigenous Congress, held in 2001 in Nurio, Michoacán, took place in the lead-up to a historic debate in the Mexican Congress. Many in attendance were traveling with the Zapatista caravan to Mexico City, including Comandante Esther, who would make history by being the first Indigenous woman to speak on the floor of the Mexican Senate. Numerous leaders had called for a women's session during the gathering and so, at the designated time, hundreds of us sat and stood in concentric circles, waiting for the session to begin. When, or even if, the women's session "began" is not really clear. At first, the discussion centered on whether a women's session should be held at a gathering of the national Indigenous movement in Mexico at all. Two hundred women stood at the ready while a couple of male activists moved to the center of the circle to argue against the idea of a separate women's session. As I sat in the circle, I was initially annoyed that the right to have a women's session was being debated yet again, but as I looked around me, I saw hundreds of women leaders and members of Indigenous organizations throughout Mexico, like Tomasa Sandoval of la Nación Purépecha Zapatista of Michoacán and Martha Sánchez of 500 Años de Resistencia of Guerrero (see figure I.1). Among the leaders from Indigenous regions throughout Mexico, I saw Zapatista women from Chiapas, including several comandantas who were attending as part of the 2001 Zapatista caravan. Leaders of other international Indigenous movements were there, too, such as Blanca Chancoso, one of the founders of la Confederación de los Pueblos de Nacionalidad Kichua del Ecuador, former president of the Confederación de Nacionalidades Indígenas del Ecuador (CONAIE), one of the organizations that hosted one of the first gatherings of the Continental Indigenous Women's Network in 1995. Blanca stood, spread out the rainbow-colored flag of the Indigenous movement of Ecuador, and spoke in solidarity with and in support of women having their own space for deliberation. About an hour into the debate, I realized that the women's session was actually happening despite being denied a formal space. Women spoke in between the decreasing arguments that a women's session divides the movement or is unnecessary because Indigenous cosmovisions are already complementary in terms of gender. Between the counterarguments, I realized that a power-

Figure I.1. CONAMI activist Tomasa Sandoval speaking to the women gathered at the Congreso Nacional Indígena (National Indigenous Congress), Nurio, Michoacán, 2001. Photo by author.

ful discussion was continuing regardless of the opposition being voiced against it. As that opposition slowly dissipated, the interstitial conversation began to gain momentum. I was witnessing the way in which Indigenous women, organized at multiple levels and scales, could weave together the power and momentum of "in-between." The threads of their organizing linked remote, rural communities to networks that spanned Mexico, came together to form the national Indigenous women's movement, and connected across the continent to the global stage. That day, I got to see how Indigenous women used the threads, networks, and knowledge from multiple scales to work around resistance to their organizing at the national level.

The 1990s witnessed the emergence of mass Indigenous rights movements in Mexico—indeed throughout Latin America. The roots of Indigenous struggles, many of which had been organizing below the surface at the community or the regional level, surfaced into the public eye after the Zapatista rebellion in 1994 in Mexico, and then out across the world. As these local struggles for dignity and social justice began to grow into national networks, Indigenous women who had been active locally in community radio, in Indigenous assemblies, or within weaver's collectives began to meet with other women activists—first in their own regions and then nationally and internationally. In 1997, they came together to form a national network of Indigenous women activists, the Coordinadora Nacional de Mujeres Indígenas de Mexico (CONAMI), the first national Indigenous women's organization in Mexico's history. Some were established leaders in their own communities, some had been participating in Indigenous assemblies with their fathers since they were children, whereas others were young women thrown into leadership when the male leaders in their community were imprisoned. Some were already members of Indigenous women's organizations in the community, whereas others still were brand new to social activism. But all felt the shift in the winds and were called to commit their lives to organizing themselves and their communities to stand up for the rights of Indigenous peoples and, together, to revitalize Indigenous cultures.

In the late 1990s, I had the great privilege of accompanying CONAMI members during the early years of the organization. I returned to interview them ten years later. I start with the vignette at the beginning of this chapter to illustrate just one instance of how, despite blockages, Indigenous women organizers built a vibrant national network that spanned Mexico. Many think of the Zapatista rebellion as isolated to the state of Chiapas, but this view ignores the extent to which the uprising only brought to the surface local Indigenous rights movements that were operating just out of view of dominant society but within Indigenous communities throughout Mexico. Once these efforts coalesced, they quickly formed into a broader national movement after 1994, and women were pivotal in building this momentum at each step. Women met at numerous local and regional meetings to debate Indigenous autonomy and discuss which parts of Indigenous communal practices they liked and, just as important, which they did not—all vital conversations about women's rights in what would form the basis of Indigenous normative systems (known as usos y costumbres). As the Indigenous rights movement and other sectors of civil society mobilized as the EZLN negotiated with the Mexican government culminating in the 1996 San Andrés Peace Accords, these workshops and meetings focused on Indigenous autonomy flourished all over the country—so much so that organizers began to leverage these conversations to gain access to greater women's participation in local mixed-gender organizations or collective Indigenous governance structures. They were able to point, for example, to other communities where women did participate in community decision-making or argue that their organization was out of step with the national Indigenous movement. The early 1990s were also critical in the coalescence of a hemispheric solidarity among Indigenous peoples in the Americas as they rose up with Black and popular sectors to protest the five-hundred-year celebration of the arrival of Christopher Columbus to the Americas. As this grounded transborder activism spread across Abiayala, Indigenous migrants also began to organize as political subjects who crossed colonial borders, such as the 1992 formation of the Zapotec/Mixtec Front, whose organizing raised questions about indigeneity in diaspora, challenging the ways it is often fixed by settler colonial strategies of containment while often being displaced and dispossessed as part of the settler colonial logic of elimination (Speed 2019).

What I share in this book is the result of my participation and research accompanying Indigenous women's organizing efforts for more than twenty years across local, national, continental, transnational, international, and transborder scales of activism. *Scales of Resistance* includes Indigenous women's organizing in Mexico and their work building advocacy networks across Abiayala,[1] a concept of the Kuna people of Panama and Colombia used by activists to name an Indigenous scale of interconnection and responsibility to land. The book also explores the ways they (re)grounded this activism and localized it into their own pueblos, municipalities, and territories. It then joins the organizing within the migrant stream that is building (trans)local ways of being and belonging that form Indigenous transborder scales of cultural continuity and political mobilization among Zapotecs and Mixtecs from Oaxaca and among members of the Latin American Indigenous diaspora who spatialize geographies of indigeneity on the unceded territories of the Tongva/Gabrileño peoples, which include the Los Angeles basin and southern Channel Islands. The insights I share are part of collective knowledge forged through the experience of many Indigenous women activists and several generations of organizers across different communities and multiple scales.

Scales of Resistance: Transborder Indigenous Women's Organizing shows how Indigenous women activists developed a strategy of weaving in and between multiple scales of power to create new spaces of participation and new forms of consciousness and discourse and how their organizing conjures, reimagines, and rethinks scale. The Chiapas uprising opened new political spaces for Indigenous women and increased social movement networking, not only between various regions within Mexico but also across different kinds of sectors and movements, or scales of organizing across the globe. Indigenous women, one of the most marginalized sectors of Mexican society, effectively learned to move within the limited social and political spaces allowed them, thereby creating new forms of identity and social meaning in the crevices of discourses that excluded them, and building new forms of political subjectivity and new spaces of political engagement. Out of the most restrictive locations, activists developed this political skill of moving in and between different scales of political representaion and negotiating, in turn, the distinct configurations of power at each level. And with this skill came a new form of political consciousness, one that facilitated new kinds of conversations and led to new kinds of practices, analyses, hopes, and commitments. Importantly, these developments helped sustain the work of the Indigenous women's movement in times of attempted neoliberal incorporation or co-option, subsequent demobilization, and political repression, and during an unprecedented wave of state and narco violence in the decades that followed. This book tells the story of how organized Indigenous women were able to revitalize and, in some cases, redefine women's role in community decision-making and create discourses that addressed women's rights within Indigenous rights frameworks. Indigenous women activists began conversations about their own cosmovisions and the gendered nature of social organization in their own communities, leading some to decolonize gender hierarchies and identities, and others to argue that Indigenous women are the heart of family and community structures and therefore are at the heart of Indigenous resistance and autonomy.

The book highlights the creativity and agency central to Indigenous women's organizing strategies in what is now Mexico and its diaspora in what is now the United States. It demonstrates, through extensive multisited, multiyear, and multiscalar ethnography, how Indigenous women activists have navigated exclusions of and blockages to their participation at one level by moving to another, and then leveraging the skills, knowledge, experience, and discourses gained in one political space to effect change in the other. Such strategies have multiplied the places in which Indigenous women's demands are engaged and have helped them to create new organizational spaces and visions of inclusion for themselves and their communities. I map how the linkages between these scales of power shape the way in which Indigenous women articulate themselves as political subjects and influence the discursive strategies they employ. By using their own interstitial positioning to create new sites for participation, new visions for (other) world making, modalities of organizing, and discursive strategies, Indigenous women have transformed various scales of power—instances of governance and authority in which they are ignored—into scales of resistance.

Analysis of multiscalar movements is hardly new, of course, and a number of scholars have shown the benefits of being able to scale *up*, from feminist to human rights movements to the struggle to pass the UN Declaration of Indigenous Peoples to the Zapatistas becoming a global force against neoliberalism (Brysk 1993; Escárcega 2013; Keck and Sikkink 1998; Olesen 2005). Others have called attention to how activists have successfully localized, vernacularized, or retrofitted political projects and imaginaries from transnational, national, and translocal scales to their lived realities (Blackwell 2014; Hernández Castillo 2016; Levitt and Merry 2009; Thayer 2001). Building and expanding on earlier work (Blackwell 2006), I analyze a strategy of interweaving scales by which organized Indigenous women in Mexico have used the momentum of local movements to build a women's network within the national Indigenous movement and even to demand women's formal leadership in national organizations. *Scales of Resistance*, however, also reveals the importance and efficacy of being able to scale not only *up or down* but also *across* different *types* of scale—connecting formal political arenas with specifically gendered bodies, for example, and contrasting colonial divisions of scale itself with Indigenous conceptions of scale, space, solidarity, and connection. In chapter 1, for example, I examine how Indigenous women scaled the concept of Indigenous autonomy down from the formal claim for legal rights afforded by the state to demand women's autonomy over their own bodies and within their own homes in their local communities. This scaling down translated rights discourse into a practice of autonomy that, along with their organizing work with other Indigenous women horizontally across other translocalities and vertically to other scales, became an important strategy of resistance to neoliberal state incorporation and the shortcomings of state-based forms of recognition (Coulthard 2014). Organized Indigenous women weave scales of power not only horizontally but vertically to influence and organize other (trans)localities on the same scale.

Furthermore, rather than exploring a fixed set of demands, strategies, or identities that are scaled in one direction or another, this book examines how Indigenous women activists and social movements traverse and negotiate vastly different terrains of power at each scale, what I have been calling *geographies of difference*.[2] Transnational social movement scholars Keck and Sikkink (1998) theorize the importance of scaling up with their concept of the "boomerang effect," whereby movements blocked at the national level can take their work to international nongovernmental organizations (NGOs) or other international solidarity organizations that then exert pressure back on the national scale. What many fail to acknowledge, however, is that marginalized actors have to navigate relationships of power that disenfranchise them in order to scale up. Indeed, most theories of transnational organizing do not account for how intersectional entrapments of power are configured and exerted differently at each scale and across scales. Political actors who are marginalized, often in multiple ways, at one scale have to navigate those different configurations of race, class, gender, indigeneity, and citizenship at each level (Blackwell 2000, 2014, 2015). The analytic I call "geographies of difference" is attentive to how even within differential relations and flows of power that constitute networked scales of activism, not only is power configured differently between each scale, but social movement actors are differentially situated by these power configurations within each scale. Geographies of difference names how the political landscape of each region, not to mention each country or scale, at which Indigenous women organize in is quite distinct, so that activists at each scale navigate the different terrains of social, political, and economic power as they move. Further, based on decades of work accompanying transnational and transborder organizers, the concept of geographies of difference accounts for the way different transborder political actors are situated by intersections of race, class, gender, sexuality, and citizenship status differently as they cross borders. It centers the complex and creative ways differently situated transborder actors navigate power in and between scales.

What I have called geographies of difference bridges central tenets of women of color feminist praxis, including an intersectional understanding of power and the practice of building solidarity and power from difference, with feminist and critical geographers and Critical Indigenous Studies. In his 1996 book *Justice, Nature, and the Geography of Difference*, David Harvey called for a theory of justice that not only accounts for social and ecological issues at local and global scales but one that attends to questions of difference and commonality. In light of the challenge decolonization movements across the globe lodged against the ways European rationalities of enlightenment thinking had become universal and the demands of radical social movements of people of color, feminists, and queers in the US and Europe to dismantle the white supremacist, capitalist and patriarchal logic underpinning those universalisms, many theorists on the left challenged, avoided, or just outright ignored these challenges by conflating them with poststructuralist preoccupations with difference. Harvey argued that only through a "critical re-engagement with political-economy, with our situatedness in relation to capital accumulation, can we hope to re-establish a conception of social justice as something to be fought for as a key value within an ethics of political solidarity built across different places" (360). In his thinking about "differentiated construction embedded in processes operating at quite different spatio-temporal scales," he asserts that "the task of progressive politics is to find an equally powerful, dynamic, and persuasive way to relating the universal and particular at different scales in the drive to define social justice from the standpoint of the oppressed" (362). Women of color theory and praxis does not rely on universals that imagine the oppression of women, for example, based on sameness, but builds an understanding of power and solidarity based on difference (Moraga and Anzaldúa 1981; Alexander and Mohanty 1997; Cohen 1997; Hong and Ferguson 2011; and Hong 2006, 2015).

Doreen Massey's (1993) early work foregrounded this "complex social differentiation" (62) in what she called the "power-geometry of time-space compression," which illustrated how globalization, not only a set of processes driven by capital but as a set of social relations, can produce uneven geographies. (68) She argued that "different social groups have distinct relationships" to time and space and as a result also have a "differentiated mobility" for different social groups and different individuals are placed in very distinct ways in relation to these flows and interconnections. The point concerns not merely the issue of who moves and who doesn't, although that is an important element of it; it is also about power in relation *to* the flows and the movement" (61). As Massey built on this (1994, 1999) argument that places are constituted through 'power geometry,' she theorized the interconnections between local, regional, national, and global processes by refusing "to see this differing scaling of time-space as a simple hierarchy," which complicates the view of "the 'global' being something above, or determinate of, the local" (Latham 2002, 124). If these power geometries are configured differently not only in different locales but at differing scales, then we can see more clearly the ways these power geometries shape how social movement actors negotiate those specific configurations of power.

What I call geographies of difference marks not only these differentiated terrains of power that social movement actors navigate but how actors within those terrains are also complexly and differentially situated in relation to the intersectional ways power operates through categories such as class, gender, race, sexuality, and indigeneity. Indeed, others have taken Massey's power geometries to analyze the way social location and geographic scale play into transnational migration in what Pessar and Mahler (2003) call "gendered geographies of power." Building on an intersectional analysis, they consider what the multiple scales of those power hierarchies might mean or how "hierarchies are not built just at the national or supra-national level. Rather, hierarchies of class, race, sexuality, ethnicity, nationality and, of course, gender operate at various levels that affect an individual or group's social location" (816). This framing is useful in understanding that gender, race, class, and sexuality, for example, operate simultaneously on different scales and how to account for social location or how a person is located within a gendered, racialized, classed, and colonial hierarchies. While theorists of transnational feminism discussed the notion of scattered hegemonies (Grewal and Kaplan 1994) to name how systems of power at one level may operates at different scales to collude and compound gendered oppression, in chapter 4 I examine how these systems collide and hybridize. Before turning to the specific historical, regional, and political context of Indigenous women's organizing in Mexico, it is important to elaborate on and clarify my use of the term *scale*. In Chicana literary theorist Mary Pat Brady's brilliant work *Scales of Captivity* (2022), she defines scale as "a fundamental grid structuring the Western imaginary, one of the operative, taken-for-granted principles of the coloniality of power (3)." Brady argues that what she calls a "scalar imaginary" is a tool that maps and secures empires as well as the nation-state and its borders. Simultaneously, scalar logics justify carceral and other forms of state sanctioned captivity, including enslavement, incarceration, internment, detention, family separation, and constrained lives. Precisely because it has been so historically imbricated with colonial logics and projects, we must unpack the conventional concept of "scale" to reveal the assumptions that underlie it and that it serves to naturalize. I triangulate notions of scale with Marxist, feminist, and Indigenous understandings that highlight the mutual constitution of space and social relations.

Decolonizing Scale, Weaving Scale

Western ideas of scale are rooted in colonial governance and epistemological structures, with a long history of colonial spatial projects being imposed over Indigenous ceremonial, political, and economic spatial structures such as market spaces or trade routes (Vicenti Carpio 2011). This imposition is dramatically illustrated throughout Mexico, where colonial churches and government buildings are built directly on top of precolonial temples and Indigenous civic, political, spiritual, and cultural centers, often using the same stones. Pre-Hispanic and early colonial Indigenous mapping sought to represent social and spatial relationships to the landscape. Elizabeth Boone's (2000) study of Aztec cartographic histories and Mixtec screen folds, lienzos (sheets), and tiras (rolls), documents how pictorial codices "held explanatory keys to the Mexican social order . . . [showing] how the present and previous worlds were created and organized. Like community charters, they explained how the people came to occupy and control the lands they did and how their government was established. The books [maps] explained the relationships between peoples, their neighbors, and their enemies. These painted histories of the past held the evidence that supported the rights of the governing families to rule, and they kept true the stories of the heroic deeds of the ancestors" (27).

Indigenous notions of scale can be illustrated by how Nahuatl speakers in the Valley of Mexico organized themselves into a political and communal unit called an altepetl, which Charles Gibson (1964, 9) identifies as an Indigenous city-state. In *The Mapping of New Spain: Indigenous Cartography and the Maps of the Relaciones Geográficas* (1996), Barbara E. Mundy writes: "Politically, altepetl were somewhat like Russian nesting dolls, holding within them smaller and smaller subunits; most comprised numerous calpolli (house[s]), each with its own leader, which in turn comprised family-centered households" (105). Yet, we can imagine the ways these scales were not linear but were often a form of mediation between precolonial Indigenous land and water epistemologies and graphic traditions and the emerging colonial reality. Pictorial histories of the Aztecs and Mixtecs recorded events through the lens of the local scale (local polity/stories), through their coverage of altepetls/community kingdoms, rather than recording regional histories/polities. These Indigenous archives stressed "supernatural origins, others focusing on long migrations and others detailing events that affected the polity after it was established" (Boone 2000, 2). Using postconquest accounts of "Indigenous forms of sociopolitical and economic organization" between 1550 and 1650, Rebecca Horn (1989), unlike previous authors writing about cartographic maps, draws on primary sources such as Indigenous landholdings, descriptive accounts, and colonial litigation records written in Spanish in the sixteenth century to argue that any regional study concerning Indigenous communities in the Valley of Mexico "must take into account the nature of Indigenous forms of sociopolitical organization" (9). The altepetl (*alt*: water; *tepetl*: mountain) referred to both a people and a territory, and they were ruled by a dynastic lineage (18). Horn explains that the altepetl was "subdivided into smaller units called *calpulli* or *tlaxilacali*, and these units were often organized into groups within the altepetl, group which in most cases were not recognized by the Spaniards or explicitly described in Spanish sources" (10). She notes that their organization "was cellular rather than hierarchical, each subunit being equal . . . each with its own sense of separate origins, each a microcosm of the whole [altepetl]" (18).

In the Mixtec region, these political and social units were called ñuu and, after the arrival of the Spanish, colonists referred to such communities as cacicazgos to describe the lands they perceived an Indigenous leader or cacique to rule over. Even notions of territory and governance were shaped by colonists' interpretations of Indigenous precolonial spatial and political categories. In fact, *cacique* comes from the Taíno word *kassiquan*, meaning to "to keep house" (Dove 2004, 136), and was thought to be earned by a democratic process; whereas *cacicazgo* is the Spanish transliteration of the Taíno word for lands ruled over by a cacique, which the Spanish apparently understood as minikingdoms. The lienzos grounded historicity to tiras to map territory in order to record how territory is linked to a sacred past, a specific history, and a genealogy of rule. "This union of place, history, and rule thus formed a kind of community charter, such that many towns in Oaxaca and southern Puebla relied on their lienzos to function as community land titles throughout the colonial period and into the nineteenth century, some even into the twentieth century" (Boone 2000, 128). Hidalgo's (2019) cartographic study of the region that is now the state of Oaxaca between 1573 and 1778 reveals the function of maps in the multilayered, complex, and even contradictory relations between Indigenous communities and Spanish colonialists (judges, magistrates, hacendados). Maps were the cultural collision of meaning making in relation to spatial, geographic, and cartographic knowledges where Indigenous map makers wove in their own epistemes and representational strategies with colonial ones to create a double consciuousness (2). The work of historian Stephanie Wood (1997) actually shows the presence of women in Mixtec codices and other maps, marking the importance of women in Mixtec genealogies. Haudenosaunee literary scholar Mishuana Goeman (2013), however, cautions that although women participated in the exchange and production of native mapping and spatial knowledge, "Native women ... were doubly excluded from the realm of a seemingly objective and masculine world of science and cartography. These erasures have had an enormous impact on the archives of colonial maps" (24).

Scale was a colonial project of conquest. The logics embedded in scale, according to Brady (2022), facilitated the colonial endeavor through epistemic and spatial violence, enforced, of course, through military violence and Christianity.

> Francisco López de Gómara, Hernán Cortés's confessor and apologist, sought to shift away from a plurivocal multiverse to gain a sense of perspectival possession that could enact the terms and architecture for empire and form a monovocal, monofocal universe. He turned to the idea of scale to produce the possibility of empire; scale enables rationalized abstraction (the world is one), transforming and authorizing indistinction and defining possessions claimed and carved and narrated from the ejido to the rancho, from the local to the regional to the hemispheric to the global, the planetary, and beyond. The many belong to the one (a king, a pope), articulated as his, as mappable and mapped, as for sale, a source of tribute and point of pride, articulated within a nested hierarchy, a new geoimaginary. (18)

Given the ways in which the discipline of geography was constituted through colonial surveys, descriptions, representations, and Western understandings of space designed to eradicate, displace, or contain Indigenous peoples, Kwagu'ł (Kwakwaka'wakw Nation) geographer Sarah Hunt (2014) asks, "How might Indigenous geographic knowledge, or knowledge rooted in Indigenous worldviews, be situated in relation to the discipline and its hegemonic ontologies?" (30). On the basis of her analysis of the interconnection between colonial and interpersonal violence, Hunt (2015) reminds us of the settler colonial function of scale: "Just as reconciliation discourse requires us to create a temporal divide between past wrongs and current colonial realities, this framing creates a scalar division which positions everyday legal and state violence out of view. Because in order to buy into the notion that state violence 'no longer constitutes the regulative norm of settler colonialism,' we have to view gendered violence, police brutality, carcerality of everyday life, death of kids in care and willful negligence of our communities as not politically significant" (4).

Yet, Maya K'iche theorist and public intellectual Gladys Tzul Tzul (2015) conceptualizes Indigenous resistance through Indigenous communal systems of government in ways that engage gender and scale in important ways. "Strength and power lies in the ability to disrupt and sabotage domination projects, but this capacity draws from a communal network of men, women, girls and boys who produce government and defend a territory, which I will call in this text: indigenous communal system of government" (128). Her analysis is scalar as she goes on to locate the locust of resistance at the communal within the scale of Indigenous territory and at the scale of the household, or what she calls the unit of reproduction of daily life. "When I say the concrete means for the reproduction of life, I mean the territory and everything that contains it, namely: Water, roads, forests, cemeteries, schools, sacred places, rituals, feasts; in sum the concrete and symbolic richness that communities produce and govern through a series of strategies developed from a specific space and time that are structured from each reproduction unit. To make what I say more intelligible, I clarify that the reproduction unit is the space where everyday life takes place; that is, houses inhabited by nuclear and/or extended families that enjoy water service, that make use of the road, that feed on the mushrooms that occur in the forests, among several more" (129). While Tzul Tzul has discussed forms of Indigenous self-governance through what she calls "tramas comunales" (communal plots or weaves) and "tramas de perentesco" (plots or weaves of kinship), each of these plots or weaves is a scale of communal belonging or building relations. Tzul Tzul further elaborates that the struggle for Indigenous communal governance is structured through three strategies: kinship alliances, k'ax k'ol (communal labor), and the assembly as the political form of collective decision making. Finally, she argues theses scalar forms of Indigenous self-determination meet the force of colonial scales of exploitation: "Thus, from indigenous communal government systems, emerges a series of practices and strategies that organize and dynamize ways to limit and/or disrupt capitalist state domination in their local forms, municipalities and other local ways of state power. Indigenous communal government systems have known how to read that the exploitative, colonial paradigm that continues to operate; specifically the strategies of meaning making in indigenous community politics and the local composition of statehood (or state formation)" (131).

Chicana scholar María Josefina Saldaña-Portillo (2016) examines how contemporary racialized geographies of the US-Mexico borderlands are products of differing British and Spanish colonial logics and legacies—what we could call the coloniality of spatial organization. After independence, governance in Mexico not only identified regions according to colonial logics but also, as Zapotec historian Luis Sánchez-López (2018) argues, established its own hegemony by recognizing Indigenous regions and limited forms of Indigenous territorial and spatial autonomy as a way to establish a settler state. Indeed, Chickasaw anthropologist Shannon Speed (2017, 2019) argues that settler colonialism in Mexico and Guatemala is a structure established during the independence era. The contemporary organization of power into scale includes colonial and Indigenous notions of scale. In Latin America, the colonial imprint on structures and relations of power has been termed the *coloniality of power* (Quijano 2000). But whereas the coloniality literature has been challenged in relation to gender and intersectionality, the spatial arrangements of the coloniality of power and the gendered nature of those colonial imprints has yet to be fully examined (Pérez 2010; Pratt 2008; Rivera Cusicanqui 2012). In Sarah Radcliffe's work thinking about decoloniality and geography (2020), she reflects on the coloniality of power in relation to knowledge production and policy. Her earlier work accompanying Kichwa and Tsáchila women as theorists of development (2015) examines how they disrupt academic and policy analysis and shift the geopolitics of knowledge production. Despite the deep flaws of Andean state policies meant to align with Indigenous concepts of *sumac kawsay* or *Buen Vivir*, she notes that these policies represented a "decolonizing political possibility, combining collective and individual rights, Indigenous epistemologies, [and] challenges to (intersectional) patriarchy" (2020, 585). Hernández Castillo (2019) examines how these colonialites of power shape racialized geographies of the war on drugs produced by an onslaught of violence and dispossession where "women's bodies have become territories to be invaded, violated, and incarcerated" (2). Indigenous women activists navigate these local, national, transnational, and transborder colonialities of spatial power but they also move in bodies, homes, families, pueblos, and municipalities guided by Indigenous cosmovisions that overlay Indigenous regions and territories which can be life affirming spaces of dignity as well as oppression.[3] In dominant representations throughout Latin America, Indigenous women are often symbolically bound to the local, seen as rural, uneducated, and low class, on the one hand, and as bearers of culture and embodiments of the authentic (dress, foodways, etc.), on the other. Yet, as Indigenous women activists have collectively worked across Abiayala, they have forged their own Indigenous political imaginary that has created alternative forms of transnational, transboder and hemispheric solidarity, connection, and responsibility in their continental network, which I explore further in chapter 2.

In following these organizers in and between sites of power, I turn to the way geographers understand scale in the social construction of space. In naming these levels of political representation and new sites of struggle, the rich literature on scale elaborated by Marxist and feminist geographers is useful (Braman 1996; Marston 2000; N. Smith 1992; Staheli 1994). Scale is "the embodiment of social relations of empowerment and disempowerment and the arena through which they operate" (Swyngedouw 1997, 169). Scale, at its most basic level, is a scale of representation (Gregory 2009; Marston 2000). In this project, *scale* means the levels through which power is organized and how activities enacted and political interests articulated, contested, and negotiated produce those levels. Rather than fixed platforms for social activity and economic and political processes that "connect up or down to other hierarchical levels, "scales" are instead outcomes of those activities and processes, to which they in turn contribute through a spatially uneven and temporally unfolding dynamic" (Gregory 2009, 665; see also Swyngedouw 1997). Or, as Neil Brenner concisely puts it, scales are "the temporarily stabilized *effects* of diverse sociospatial processes" (2011, 31).[4]

Scholars have used scale to analyze the effects of capitalism, gender relations of re/production, and social movement resource mobilizations. For example, they have theorized the multiplicity of scale in the socio-spatial organization of capitalism, identifying possibilities of resistance and opportunities to create linkages across scale (N. Smith 1992). Others have importantly critiqued the literature on the social construction scale for its overreliance on modes of production in the public sphere, with the goal of calling attention to the scales of gender and social reproduction (Marston 2000). This work richly illustrates other systems of domination besides capitalism and its effects on the social construction of scale in the organizing of political parties, unions, and AIDS politics. Others have used scale to understand social movements. For example, Lynn Staheli argues, "To the extent that oppositional movements can move across scales—that is, the extent that they can take advantage of the resources at one scale to overcome the constraints encountered at different scales (in the way that more powerful actors do)—they may have greater potential for processing their claims" (1994, 388).

But as I emphasize, the processes and networks of Indigenous women's activism, in which scales are established and collapse, depend on differing configurations of power, movement flows, and Indigenous visions of scale, relation, connectivity, solidarity, and responsibility, such as Abiayala. In addition, not all networked scales stay equally connected—some tear away from each other, and others re-form around alternate visions of region or around various spatial logics of political urgency or strategy. While some scholars think of networks as "the overlapping and contested material, cultural and political flows and circuits that bind different places together though differentiated relations of power" (Featherston, Phillips, and Waters 2007, 386), others theorize them as meshworks to capture not only a vertical organization but a horizontal one: The concept of meshwork is meant to suggest that place-based groups "engage in dynamic vertical and horizontal networking, connecting among themselves and with others in places far and near, across cultural, political, racial, and ethnic divides" (Harcourt and Escobar 2005, 14). Meshworks, Escobar, and Harcourt (2005) argue, involve parallel strategies of localization and interweaving. Localization requires reading the geographies of difference or the different ways power is configured for differentially situated actors at each scale. *Interweaving* names the strategy that activist Indigenous women I have accompanied use to weave scales by reading power differential across scales and geographies of difference.

Although my work was not originally part of the spatial turn, because the Indigenous women organizers I work with weave in and between local, national, transnational, transborder, and land-based scales of power to create new spaces of participation, I decolonize social geography's concept of scale to describe how they used these nodes of power. The scope of *Scales of Resistance* includes those scales created by Indigenous women's organizing at the local, pueblo (town or village/people), or municipal level, or across Indigenous regions—territory that might include several pueblos, municipalities, and settler colonial juridical borders. It analyzes how their organizing creates scales of resistance across various conceptualizations of scale, such as settler nations, states, and geopolitical regions (across Latin America and Caribbean); across hemispheric, transnational, and international scales; and across trans-Indigenous scales like Abiayala. Finally, the project includes transborder scales produced by the way Indigenous migrants build translocal, transborder lives and politics with such density that some scholars have called them "transregions" (Jonas and Rodríguez 2015; Stephen 2007, 2012). Sofía Robles, a Zapotec/Mixe activist whose long history of organizing forms part of this book, described to me the levels or scales of organizing that situate her political work. When I asked her about the relationships between the levels or scales of activism, Sofía said,

> The levels, there are a lot of levels [of activism]. For example, in Mexico, speaking just in Mexico, the local level is the community. Then comes the regional that includes various communities. Then the state level that already includes different regional places, or different regions of the state. Later, at the national level . . . there might be two or three from each state represent[ing] us [within national organizing]. Now at the continental [level], which is all of Latin America, Canada, the United States, all of Central America and South America. The network includes super regions like South America that is the southern region [of the Continent], Central America is the central region and there is Mexico, United States, and Canada, right? We are the northern region . . . language is difficult but those are the levels [of activism]. Then at the international level we organize with others, but we relate mostly to the continental level. The worldwide level is more difficult, more complex. (Sofía Robles, interview with Maylei Blackwell, August 31, 1999)

Moving in and between scales is a form of weaving. Weaving knowledges, weaving spaces, strategies, and discourses. This mode of organizing is specific to Indigenous women, who weave worlds to produce modes of social change relationally. In her 2010 book, which topples racialized geopolitical hierarchies of knowledges and colonial circuits of theory, Aymara scholar-activist Silvia Rivera Cusicanqui examines Indigenous proposals for engaging in mestizo modernity and citizenship. In subsequent work, she critiques the masculinized notion of identity as territory as "still marked by the colonial seal of the exclusion of women" (2012, 106). She continues:

> The notion of the identity of women, however, is similar to a fabric. Far from establishing the property and the jurisdiction of the authority of the nation—or the people, the autonomous indigenous—the feminine practice weaves the fabric of the intercultural through women's practices as producers, merchants, weavers, ritualists, and creators of languages and symbols capable of seducing the "other" and establishing pacts of reciprocity and coexistence among different groups. This seductive labor, acculturated and surrounding women, allows for the complementing of the territorial homeland with a dynamic cultural fabric that reproduces itself and spreads until it reaches the mixed and frontier areas—the *ch'ixi*

areas—and there contributes its vision of personal responsibility, privacy, and individual rights associated with citizenship. (107)

This act of weaving from the inside to meet the outside, creating a third space in the middle, is also used to create the Cherokee doubleweave basket woven with rivercane. Two spirit Cherokee scholar Qwo-Li Driskill (2010, 2016) theorizes how this form of weaving creates bridges between multiple knowledges, practices, and epistemologies. Whereas from the outside the basket appears one way or has one face, on the inside there is another weave, held by various splints, which serves as a metaphor of how, for example, the queer and the Indigenous knowledges in Driskill's Asegi theory, when doublewoven, create a new, interwoven epistemology. Driskill argues that "by looking to doubleweave as a Cherokee theory and practice, we can theorize a third space that materializes through the process of doubling. Doubleweaving privileges the voices and stories that colonial projects have attempted to destroy but that, hidden in the third space forgotten about by colonial cultures, survive" (Driskill 2016, 24). This inter- or doubleweaving describes how Indigenous women's organizing moves in and between both colonial and Indigenous scales, as well as conjures new ones to produce interstitial or third space knowledges, practices, and scales of resistance.

Even the translocal ways Indigenous migrants are weaving localities and scales when they are deterritorialized calls attention to how those weavings become an embodied mobile Indigenous archive that has the possibility of resisting settler colonial logics. Maya K'iche scholar Floridalma Boj Lopez argues that Mayan clothing worn in the diaspora functions as an embodied Indigenous geography that marks the body with spiritual epistemologies and spatial cartographies that preceded, and now exceed, the nation of Guatemala. Boj Lopez theorizes wearing Mayan weaving as a form of continuity and rupture across the generations and spaces within the diaspora has the possibility of contesting settler colonialism. Those weavings "embody difference" representing Maya cosmovision, localized histories, and landscapes on the body. "Whether it is the sacred numerical values that are present in the technique of weaving, which correspond to numbers of key significance in the sacred calendars of the Mayas, or the actual figures and designs that speak to important landmarks in the area (lakes, mountain ranges, or volcanoes)" (Boj Lopez 2017b, 196). Indeed, weavings are just one of many cultural and political formations that are embodied mobile archives of indigeneity, according to Boj Lopez (2017a).

Scales of Resistance moves along these interwoven, networked activist scales to show how Indigenous cosmovision, knowledges, discourses, identities, and epistemologies are woven into and with those forms found in and across scales. Building from Cusicanqui's woven fabric of Indigenous women's land epistemologies and world building, Driskill's theorization of doubleweave, and Boj Lopez's mobile archives of indigeneity, I examine how Indigenous women's organizing interweaves scales to create third spaces and what Chicana feminist theorist Chela Sandoval (1991, 1998) calls "differential consciousness" to describe the tactical shifts in consciousness produced by reading and responding to multiple contexts, and I would add scales, of power, or *geographies of difference*. Differential consciousness describes the ways in which Indigenous women in Mexico and its diaspora move within and between forms of consciousness, epistemologies, and discourses as they travel the circuits and scales that structure power and meaning in their lives.[5]

Driskill theorizes the ways in which "Cherokee Two-spirit and queer people are reimagining our pasts and futures through a practice of re-storying in the present" (2016, 3). This project examines how the spaces of connection between interwoven scales creates third spaces from which to envision and create new worlds and, as Driskill invites us, to weave the past and future. Indigenous women activists struggle to create a new world where many worlds fit by weaving together ancestral knowledge, dreams, and instructions with visions for future generations. This re-storying is at the heart of the innovation and embodiment Mayan youth enact in their use of ancestral weaving in Los Angeles that can "blur the boundaries between settler, Native, and migrant in ways that may challenge what it means to be an indigenous migrant in a settler society" (Boj Lopez 2017b, 200) creating what Boj Lopez calls, with a nod to Audra Simpson, Indigenous geographies of refusal. Indeed, the National Movement of Maya Weavers of Guatemala refuses the appropriation of their territories and their bodies by insisting that their weavings have been, for millennium, protected in a communitarian and collective manner in their book, *Our Weaving Are Books the Colony Could Not Burn* (2020).

Yet weaving scales also produces frictions. Anna Tsing (2005, 2012) calls our attention to the important ways scales are produced by global capital, how they produce frictions, and how they can fail. These conceptual tools help map how Indigenous women activists in Mexico and its diaspora create, use, and weave scales of resistance and how they also learn to tie threads off when their projects, visions, or epistemologies are revealed to be "unscalable" (Tsing 2012, 523). Tsing argues that "scalability, again, is this ability to expand without distorting the framework. But it takes hard work to make knowledge, landscapes, and projects scalable. What I have tried to show is how that work, by its design, covers up and attempts to block the transformative diversity of social relations. From this perspective, the history of scalability must be considered in relation to both its moments of success and its sometimes-happy failures" (2012, 523). In the project of weaving scales, strategies, epistemologies, and movement discourses, new scales are conjured, as Tsing suggests, but, critically, some elements of Indigenous knowledges and practices are unscalable and must be valued for their inability to be deterritorialized, universalized, and scaled (which, ironically, is why they are often dismissed as backward, unmodern, quaint, local, specific, etc.). Brady (2022) calls for the refusal of the seduction of scale and the scaffold imaginary "as the vision of the world as understandable through a set of nested hierarchies that privilege a vertical plane. Most clearly articulated as the stretch from body to home to city to region to nation to hemisphere, scale names mass and relation, while insisting on the fundamental logic of abstraction, containment, categorization, and comparison folded into a vertical, hierarchical orientation" (19). The Indigenous women activists I have accompanied scale down and across to create new communities of resistance and practices of autonomy, conjure new scales, navigate the unscalable, bypass colonial scale with Indigenous epistemologies that reground scale into the Earth, challenge the scaffold imaginary by centering and connecting their own locales and territories, disrupt scalar confinement, and rescale Indigenous belonging through diaspora. They engage in Brady's alternatives to scale—queer horizontality and density—to "shirk the violence of the scaffold imaginary that scalar thought enforces" (3). Throughout the book, I describe these densities of connection, solidarity, and relation making as well as the multidirectional reorganization of scales from hierarchal and vertical to horizontal, translocal, transregional and transborder. For example, in chapter 1 Indigenous women activists in Mexico practice Indigenous autonomy through what could be called a density of autonomous practices and communal connections located not in the State, but in the embodied and community scales of autonomy. Practicing another of Brady's alternatives to scale, queer horizontality, I illustrate how Indigenous women's continental activism conjured the scale of Abyiayla, a horizontal scale of connection to each other and to land, that shifts the geopolitics of international diplomacy and transnational activism that had erased them and their epistemologies. In chapter 3, I explore how Indigenous women's multilocal organizing interrupts the verticality of scale through meshworks that not only interweave the vertical and horizontal notions of scale but create new relations across horizontal planes by weaving Indigenous epistemologies and communalities. These strategies of density and connection are manifest through Indigenous transborder organizing and transborder community that rescale Oaxacan Indigenous belonging in chapters 4 and 5. Drawing on more than twenty years of ethnographic research and seventy oral histories, *Scales of Resistance* examines how Indigenous women activists are navigating, rejecting, localizing, interweaving, and remaking ideas of scale.

Contesting Gender as a Discourse of Governmentality

Mexico has the largest population of Indigenous peoples in the Americas, representing 15.1 percent of the population (IWGIA 2021). About 6.2 percent of the total population of Mexico speaks an Indigenous language (INEGI 2020) and Mexico has the largest number of native languages spoken: 68 languages with 364 recognized dialects of those languages (Jacquelin-Andersen 2018, 77). The seventy-year single-party rule of the PRI (Partido Revolucionario Institucional, or Institutional Revolutionary Party) began to be increasingly challenged by forces of democratization and ended in 2000. In the early 1990s, Indigenous movements across the continent united to protest the 1992 quincentennial celebration of Columbus's so-called discovery of the Americas. Mexico surprised many by adopting policy measures that addressed Indigenous peoples and recognized the nation's pluricultural nature. In 1990, it became the second country in the world and the first in Latin America to ratify Convention 169 on Indigenous and Tribal Peoples of the UN International Labor Organization (ILO), a critical tool for Indigenous social movements around the world that recognizes the collective economic, cultural, social, and political rights of Indigenous people. Mexico adopted the UN Declaration on the Rights of Indigenous Peoples (UNDRIP) in 2007.

While purportedly positive in nature, the signing of Convention 169 and Mexico's subsequent passage in 1992 of Article 4 of its constitution, which recognized the pluricultural nature of Mexico as a nation as well as Indigenous peoples' cultural rights, were regarded warily by many skeptics. It seemed all too possible that such moves were yet another strategy to address mounting international pressure without meaningful reform during a critical juncture in Mexico's alignment with a hemispheric neoliberal agenda carried out through free trade, deregulation, and privatization. Such suspicions were confirmed, for example, in 1992 when, in preparation for the North American Free Trade Agreement (NAFTA), then President Salinas de Gotarri dismantled the Ejido system, a collective land tenure system that was one of the remaining victories of the Mexican Revolution affecting some 61 percent of the land within Indigenous communities, effectively undercutting rural and Indigenous farmers' ability to survive (Hernández Navarro and Carlsen 2004). Ultimately, neoliberal reforms have had a profound and detrimental impact on Indigenous communities throughout Mexico, leading to displacement, migration, and greater marginalization.

Such effects, however, are obscured by celebratory accounts of arguably superficial symbolic gestures. On the one hand, for the first time in Mexico's history, the constitutional reform to Article 4 (which is now Article 2 after being renumbered) acknowledged the pluricultural nature of Mexico as a nation recognizing Afro Mexicans and Indigenous peoples' cultural rights surrounding the protection of their own languages, cultures, customs and traditional practices, and forms of social organization. On the other hand, the article lacked enforcement mechanisms and failed to recognize the collective rights of Indigenous peoples, thereby bounding Indigenous rights within a cultural rights frame whose meaning and parameters are determined by the state, rather than recognizing collective rights to self-determination codified in international law. Critics pointed out how the underlying minimalist, neoliberal notion of state responsibilities defanged any effort to redistribute wealth or power, watering the article's implications down to become virtually meaningless (Hindley 1996). Neil Harvey noted that the state's limited interpretation of Convention 169 "had the effect of not only ignoring the social and economic factors that prevented Indigenous peoples from truly exercising their rights, but also reproduced the authority of the state (and specifically the executive branch) over the acceptable practices of Indigenous peoples" (1998, 201–2).

The Chiapas uprising on January 1, 1994, the day NAFTA went into effect, brought many of these tensions to public light, disrupting the myth of progress and exposing the devastating poverty, racism, and neglect that Mexico's sixty-eight Indigenous pueblos continue to experience. In November 1996, the Commission on Concordance and Pacification (COCOPA) proposed their initiative for constitutional reform based on the San Andrés Peace Accords on Indigenous Rights and Culture, which the Zapatista Army of National Liberation (EZLN) and government representatives signed in February of that year. Despite being designed by government representatives and receiving mass approval after widespread deliberation convened by the EZLN and the National Indigenous Congress, then President Ernesto Zedillo rejected the plan. A stalemate ensued until the next presidential sexenio (six-year term), when the PAN (National Action Party) candidate, Vicente Fox, promised to introduce the COCOPA initiative to congress and resolve the problem in Chiapas in twenty minutes. In 2001, the EZLN traveled by caravan through twelve states to the Mexican capital for a historic appearance on the floor of the lower house of the Mexican Congress. But despite broad support for the COCOPA proposal, both houses of the legislature chose instead to pass the Law on Indigenous Rights and Culture, a counterreform that fails to meet the basic agreements of the San Andrés Peace Accords (Mora 2017b).

Those analyzing state responses to the rise of Indigenous and women's mobilization in Latin America have observed that states, instead of denying or repressing social movement demands, use a strategy of selective co-option, whereby minimal recognition of rights leads to an increased role for the state in constituting and regulating identities through its administrative and technocratic power (Hale 2002; Schild 1997). Charles Hale (2005) argues that state recognition of cultural rights and limited Indigenous autonomy as states rolled back their social welfare policies became a cultural logic of neoliberalism or what he called "neoliberal multiculturalism." Addressing the ways in which the discourse of gender equity has been co-opted by successive elected governments in Latin America, Verónica Schild states that "increasingly, the advancement of women's rights—a political goal—is being transformed into a technical task that leaves unchallenged the exploitative capitalist relations that enable the successful global economic integration of countries in the region, and may even deepen the problem of the feminization of poverty" (2000a, 25). Instead of being seen as contradictory to neoliberalism, gender and Indigenous cultural rights were increasingly seen as part of neoliberal governmentality (Hale 2002, 2005; Postero 2007).[6] Indeed, Sarah Radcliffe examined how Ecuador established administrative and discursive biopolitical power to form both governmentalities of race and gender in her analysis of the State's reproductive and sexual health policy and the use of gender rights and intercultural multiculturalism (2008).

While some analysts examine how demands for Indigenous autonomy fit into the cultural logic of neoliberalism and feminist scholars critique the selective co-optation of some of the most liberal elements of the feminist movement (Schild 2015), I have called attention to the ways in which Indigenous claims are engaged and managed by the neoliberal state *through* the discourse of gender (Blackwell 2012). Bridging the ways scholars have looked at both the co-optation of gender and Indigenous rights through neoliberal governance in Latin America, I examine how gender has been used by the state as a discourse of governmentality to regulate Indigenous subjects. When we examine closely how the Mexican state has understood and denied Indigenous claims, we see that much of its opposition to claims for Indigenous autonomy ultimately revolves around questions of gender and hegemonic constructions of Indigenous culture (Blackwell 2004). This response stems from the gendered logic of racism that the government has deployed in response to women's rights and

Indigenous communities. The Mexican government first claimed that the Zapatista uprising was not truly Indigenous (and was led by outside agitators and feminist infiltrators) because, among other reasons the movement was too well organized and executed or started too early in the morning as the uprising started in the dawn hours of January 1, 1994. Further evidence of this supposed outside influence was that women comprised some 30 percent of the EZLN and the rights of women to equality, a life free of violence, equal pay, and the right to choose their partner and when and whether to bear children were codified in the Women's Revolutionary Law. In direct contradiction, when the Indigenous movement did make a claim for Indigenous peoples' autonomy, the government justified its denial of the right of autonomy to Indigenous people on the claim that women's rights are not protected within Indigenous customs and practices (I unpack this assertion in chapters 1 and 3).

A gendered logic of racism has often served as the lynchpin of the debate in the sense that much of the government's argument against Indigenous self-governance has hinged on the question of gender. In fact, this governmental tactic has been deployed so often that we might consider how gender has become a discourse of governmentality that is used to define what counts as "authentically indigenous" and to regulate indigenous subjects. Foucault (1991) turned toward governmentality as a way to understand how neoliberal governance acts on populations through the logic of the market so that subjects become self-regulating individuals in a context where power is decentered and where regulation and control are not limited to state institutions but include a wide range of civil society (NGOs, for example) (Alvarez 2010).[7] This is linked to the political rationality that shifts responsibility for services formally provided by the state in social welfare, education, and social services onto the individual. Neoliberal withdrawal of the state is tied to personal responsibility and new technologies of the self whereby subjects must become self-managing (Gil-García 2015).[8] As a new relation of rule between the state and Indigenous communities was consolidated through a watered-down multiculturalism, the Mexican state used a gendered logic of racism to define and regulate Indigenous subjectivity and rights (Speed 2008). Whereas Hale (2004) warns against forms of selective governmental co-optation that define which activists are appropriate Indigenous subjects (or the Indio Permitido), I have argued that gender has become a discourse of governmentality used to regulate and define "good" and "bad" Indigenous subjects, those worthy of rights and autonomy as peoples and those not (Blackwell 2012).

This gendered governmentality came into play in the debates leading up to the 2001 constitutional reform of articles 1, 2, 4, 18, and 115. Legislators called into question the right to Indigenous self-determination on the basis of the (disingenuous) premise that Indigenous normative systems (usos y costumbres) do not protect the rights of women. This premise, of course, ignores the patriarchal norms of the Mexican state and the widespread work of Indigenous women to transform Indigenous laws and cultures in order to recognize gender diversity, create equity, and stop violence. The law that was implemented instead of the San Andrés Accords, negotiated between the government and the EZLN in 1996, are better understood as "counterreforms" because they fail to implement the collective right of Indigenous people to self-governance (Mora 2015; Stavenhagen 2001). Starting in 2003, the members of the EZLN and the Congreso Nacional Indígena (CNI) began to implement the San Andrés Accords, starting in their own autonomous communities outside of the state's purview. Indigenous movements have navigated the perils of selective co-optation and the ways in which the state restricts Indigenous demands for autonomy to cultural rights by largely bypassing state forms of recognition. Although several states have gone on to pass provisions recognizing Indigenous peoples in state constitutions, Indigenous jurisprudence and governance have yet to be fully recognized. In the context of Oaxaca where three-fourths of all municipalities hold elections through Indigenous law, Worthen has found that women's rights are often constructed as a colonial "rescue narrative" where the state is positioned as the savior, especially in relation to recent legislation on gender equity in election law in Oaxaca. Increasingly, in a context of Mexico's democratic tradition and the war on drugs, Indigenous peoples' political and legal frameworks of self-governance were portrayed as not only as nondemocratic but illegal. Worthen (2021) argues "By creating new hegemonic ways of conceptualizing indigeneity within a legal/illegal binary, it helped promote an agenda of state securitization that portrayed Indigenous people as a threat to national security (Hernández et al. 2013)" (2).

It is important to note, however, that Indigenous women activists have played a critical role in contesting the government's use of gender to deny collective Indigenous rights. Chapter 1, for example, explores how their grassroots practices of construction and consultation have sustained the movement beyond the claim for rights in the face of military repression and governmental recalcitrance. At the same time, Indigenous women activists face a significant challenge in the form of the state's gendered logic of racism. Yet by creating a strategy of scaling down rights discourse into a decolonial practice of autonomy, Indigenous women activists have devised, implemented, and sustained a long-term movement for self-determination. Along with scaling down the right to Indigenous autonomy to the practice of autonomy embedded in multiple scales of the home, the body, and the community, the work of interweaving in and between scales became more strategic with the passage of the Law on Indigenous Culture and Rights, which undermined the basic guarantee for Indigenous self-determination in Mexico at the national scale. The strategies Indigenous women have developed in response are instructive to other social movements given the neoliberal state strategy of co-opting selected rights discourses without implementing real change (Schild 2000a).

While activists and critics decried the conjunction of neoliberalism and a watered-down multiculturalism, what Mariana Mora and Jaime García Leyva (2020) call attention to is the simultaneous growth of the state security apparatus, specifically during the undeclared war on drug trafficking by the administration of President Felipe Calderon (2006-12), and carried on by the subsequent Peña Nieto administration. For example, Mora and García Leyva underscore that while historically the state divested resources dedicated to education and health with the rise of neoliberal regimes, it made a corresponding biopolitical investment in the state security apparatus. From 2000 to 2012, for example, while spending on education increased only 54 percent, the Mexican state's investment in the security apparatus increased 334 percent. The increased militarization of Mexico has been justified by the war on drugs, and linked to increased repression, but Mora and García Leyva highlight the racialized nature of who came to occupy the category "criminal" in these processes. They argue that the state security apparatus and the increased militarization of social spaces led to the criminalization of social actors who were racialized, such as political activists, many of whom were environmental and anti-extractivist organizers, teachers, and students, throughout Indigenous and Afro-descendent communities in Mexico (Mora and García Levya 2020, 219). In fact, Aída Hernández Castillo had already analyzed the ways increased state violence and criminalization of social movements had begun to specifically repress activist women through gendered forms of violence. She wrote widely on what happened in Atenco in 2006 when the community was protesting their dispossession by a megadevelopment project and police forces violently entered the community, detaining 207 people—including children, women, and elders—by extralegal means; 2 people died; 20 people were injured and 26 women were sexually assaulted while detained (Hernández Castillo 2013b).

The power of her 2016 book, *Multiple InJustices: Indigenous Women, Law, and Political Struggle in Latin America*, is that it brings together an analysis of the latest phase of capitalist extraction and Indigenous dispossession with an understanding of gender and sexual violence, specifically how these forms of violence are being used against Indigenous women and organized Indigenous communities. Specifically, Hernández Castillo condemns sexual torture by governmental agencies, which she argues is part of the "patriarchal semantics of violence and impunity" (2016, 22) across Indigenous regions of Latin America that are undergoing a process of accumulation by dispossession (see Harvey 2003). Critically, Hernández Castillo finds that "we are before a new onslaught of capital that appropriates the territories and resources of native peoples through neocolonial strategies that criminalize social movements and use sexual violence as a repressive strategy in the processes of dispossession" (2016, 22–23). This new onslaught of capital, then, produces continuities and layers onto the gendered forms of racism in the earlier neoliberal moment I previously described, creating devastating effects.

Shannon Speed's book *Incarcerated Stories* (2019) critically analyzes this shifting context. She argues: "In the span of a little more than a decade, we have seen a significant shift in the state itself and its forms of governance. Since the 1990s, Mexico and Central America quickly expanded and grew out of the control of legal regimes. Meanwhile, the nascent democratic tendencies and fledgling rights regimes, however limited, were quickly sucked into the vortex of the mass-scale illegal economies . . . fed by the wide-scale corruption of the government and military and the deregulated flows of capital" (4). Her analysis of Indigenous women refugees from Central America centers on what she calls "neoliberal multicriminalism" created by the structural forms of neoliberalism, drug cartels that found a reserve army in those impoverished by neoliberal reforms, and the emergence of the national security state as both state and nonstate actors carried out obscene levels of bloodshed with impunity (5). Speed examines how these forms of violence extend the genocidal and patriarchal logics of settler colonialism within Latin America, and how these logics create overlapping and interrelated dynamics that exponentially increase the forms of violence that Indigenous women experience. In the introduction to their 2021 edited volume, she and her colleague Lynn Stephen write: "The racial and gender logics that underpinned native dispossession, slavery, and successive waves of labor exploitation are structuring logics, inherent to those systems. Today these structuring logics—and the forms of intersectional violence inherent to them—are driving processes of criminalization and victimization of Indigenous men and women, leading to escalating levels of murder, incarceration, or transnational displacement of Indigenous people, and particularly affecting Indigenous women" (2021, 4).

Collaborative Methods and Other Knowledges

Scales of Resistance is the result of nearly twenty-five years of collaborative research conducted while accompanying Indigenous women activists in Mexico, into their continental networks, and throughout the Mexican Indigenous diaspora in the United States. Collaborative work and collective conversations have not only guided the methodological design of this study, but these forms of collaboratively produced and shared knowledge guide the book's arguments. The methodology includes ethnography, seventy oral histories, and community-based digital storytelling projects and story maps. The project follows the multiple scales of Indigenous women's organizing and sees them as interconnected rather than divided by national contexts or easily divided by the policy or political arena in which they make their claims. That is, the collaborative research and ethnographic strategy center the activists themselves as the point of connection linking their lives, scales of organizing, and multiple sites of increasingly networked activism. This approach addresses the challenge of bringing together different levels or scales of analysis—in other words, how to analyze changes in international and state institutions while paying due attention to actors' agency in everyday spaces and their organizational and political dynamics. I devised this methodological strategy by following the network logics of activist organizing and being attentive to how globalization produces tensions within and across the multiple "sites" of activism. Following Juris and Khasnabish (2013) and "against overly romanticized views of transnational activism" (4), I use ethnography to highlight that "inevitable, yet productive, 'friction' (Tsing 2005) that ensues in the encounter between activists from diverse movements, political contexts, and cultural backgrounds" (4).

Whereas ethnographers of globalization, transmigration, and transnational social movements call for multisited ethnography, this project moves along scales of political organizing to illuminate the complex, cross-border, and transnational dialogues that are reshaping local ideals of justice as well as national and international policies. Although I might traditionally describe this project as multisited ethnography, that depiction does not accurately reflect how the field "sites" are not just bounded spaces of "here" but places constituted by other scales of power and the simultaneity of how "here" exists with usually one but often more "theres." These sites are not discrete spaces easily separated from each other; they are scales of power and place. Understanding this requires seeing how Indigenous women activists use their "peripheral vision" (Zavella 2000) to understand how changes they advocate for at the National Indigenous Congress, for example, might play at home in their community assemblies; how continental women's politics might leverage more influence for them at the national level; or how, when they organize in local "sites" such as Los Angeles, Fresno, or Huajuapan de Leon, Oaxaca, they are also organizing—usually quite explicitly—with other points on the migrant route and the transborder communities that span those spaces. As Juris and Khasnabish (2013) have argued, "Grasping such dynamics requires not so much an ethnographic strategy that is multisited (although that can be a critical component) as one that is networked: attuned to the complex place-based meanings, flows, and sensibilities that interact within momentary spaces of encounter" (5). Each site within these networked and scaled organizing strategies happen, like globalization, "in place," as Escobar (2008) has argued. As much as these struggles are products of globalized flows of people, capital, and movement discourses, they are also in defense of collective Indigenous places, worlds, and projects: "Place-based struggles more generally link body, environment, culture, and economy in all their diversity" (7).

I began my earlier research, focused on Indigenous women's movements in Mexico, during a year of fieldwork in Mexico City in 1998; I initially sought to examine questions of difference within women's organizing. Yet, as with much engaged research, working with movements and communities shifts research agendas, subjects, and approaches, and forces the ethnographer to ask how the research is both accountable to those communities and useful to them. At that time, I began documenting the formative years of the CONAMI, attending meetings, conducting interviews, and assisting with organizational tasks such as getting materials photocopied and picking up food for the meeting. I continued to attend national gatherings of CONAMI and continental meetings of the Enlace Continental de Mujeres Indígenas de las Américas (ECMIA), and to meet up with Indigenous organizers at several Latin American and Caribbean feminist encuentros. In 2009, I began returning to Mexico to reinterview several of the founding members of CONAMI; during the next ten years, I met subsequent generations of leaders who shared their reflections on the Indigenous women's movement and their organization over the past two decades.

In 2005, during my research with CONAMI and ECMIA, I was approached by Odilia Romero Hernández, then the newly elected binational coordinator of women's affairs and a member of the Los Angeles office of the Frente Indígena de Organizaciones Binacionales (FIOB), who invited me to serve as an advisor to the organization. We had a series of meetings, and our conversations eventually led us to begin designing a set of workshops designed to empower women in the community and develop their leadership skills in FIOB. We developed a curriculum that was part consciousness-raising, part skills-building, and we applied for an initial collaborative grant. A few months later, the FIOB applied to the Otros Saberes Initiative of the Latin American Studies Association, which funded Indigenous and Afro-descendant organizations and communities to partner with academics to design and carry out a collaborative research project. They were awarded the grant for a project entitled "Developing Binational Indigenous Leadership: Gender, Generation and Ethnic Diversity within the FIOB." The research team included Rufino Domínguez-Santos, then the General Coordinator; Centolia Maldonado, the coordinator of the Juxtlahuaca region of Oaxaca at the time; Odilia Romero Hernández; Laura Velasco, a sociologist from the Colegio de la Frontera Norte; and myself. Over the next year and a half, we designed and implemented statewide workshops on gender, generation, and ethnic diversity with leaders of the FIOB across three states in the United States and Mexico.

Sixty-three activists participated in the workshops in Tijuana, Baja California; Los Angeles, California; and Huajuapan de León, Oaxaca. Among the participants, 59.5 percent were men and 40.5 percent were women. Participants' mean age was 32.2 years. They spoke any of seven languages: Mixtec, Zapotec, Triqui, P'urépecha, Mixe, Spanish, and English; 56.8 percent spoke an Indigenous language (Romero Hernández et al. 2013). Interestingly, the Los Angeles workshop had the most linguistic diversity among Indigenous-language speakers, and though many people spoke some Spanish, English fluency was most prominent among migrant youth of the 1.5 and second generations. In addition to this initial work, chapters 4 and 5 draw on the many years of collaborative research and over twenty oral histories I conducted while accompanying women in the FIOB as they organized leadership programs and worked to be heard at all levels of FIOB. I served as a binational advisor to the organization for six years. After that project, I spent another ten years attending more events and forging relationships with FIOB members in Oaxaca City, Zanatapec, Juxtlahuaca, Fresno, Los Angeles, and Oceanside. That research included participant observation, oral history, and digital storytelling.

In 2013, I began a large-scale public humanities project creating digital story maps with Indigenous communities in Los Angeles. Honoring Indigenous protocol, we consulted with Tongva communities to build the project and create a prototype of a story map; we worked with community educators to build the first story map. Mapping Indigenous LA has been a platform for collaboration, communication, and dialogue between the Tongva and Tatavium, relocated native communities, Pacific Islanders, and the Latin American Indigenous diaspora and the spring board for many other community-led story mapping projects. In 2018, I started the archivo móvil de las comunidades indígenas

(Mobile Indigenous Community Archive, MICA) as an Indigenous memory project that works to rematriate Indigenous women activists' knowledge and stories of resistance back into Indigenous communities and movements. Conceptualized as a seed bank, the mobile digital archive is a community controlled platform where rich histories of Indigenous organizing in Mexico and the Latin American Indigenous diaspora are gathered, preserved, and shared, often with younger organizers. Centering on Indigenous women who are often left out of the documenting and archiving process, guided by community designed protocols and a commitment to replant the knowledges that are gathered, MICA provides training and labor for Indigenous organizations and community members to collect and digitize their documents, videos, photos, and ephemera as well as to create exhibitions and popular education modules guided by the movement's needs and desires.

Theoretical Inspirations and Conversations

Scales of Resistance builds on rich political and intellectual traditions of Indigenous activists and scholars throughout the hemisphere, along with literatures in Indigenous feminisms, Critical Indigenous Studies, Indigenous migration, and Critical Latinx Indigeneities. It is inspired by intellectual, epistemological, and political conversations with many Indigenous activists, social thinkers, and Indigenous scholars whose work dismantles the legitimacy of settler colonial borders and empire such as Inés Hernández-Ávila, Inés Talamontez, Gloria Chacon, Margo Tamez, Jodi Byrd, Hokulani Aikau, Audra Simpson, and Shannon Speed; those whose work emerges from and centers Abiayala including Silvia Rivera Cusicanqui and Emil Keme; those whose thinking transforms colonial systems of gender and sexuality like Gladys Tzul Tzul, Aura Cumes, Emma Chirix, Cristina Cucurí, Joanne Barker, Irma Velásquez Nimatuj, J. Kehaulani Kauanui, Dian Million, Deborah Miranda, Renya Ramirez, Jennifer Denetdale, Maile Arvin, Qwo-Li Driskill, to name a few; and the numerous collaborators building Critical Latinx Indigeneities including Indigenous scholars Floridalma Boj Lopez, Luis Urrieta, Lourdes Alberto, Brenda Nicolás, and Luis Sánchez. This works builds on prior conversations on comparative and hemispheric Indigeneities including those who contributed to and edited the groundbreaking collection *Comparative Indigeneities of the Américas*.

Feminist journalists, activists, and anthropologists have engaged the transformative role of women in the Zapatista rebellion (Eber and Kovic 2003; Klein 2015; Lovera and Palomo 1997; Ortiz 2001; Rovira 2000; Speed, Hernández Castillo, and Stephen 2006). Other scholars have focused on forging new forms of Indigenous gendered political claims on autonomy (Millán 1996, 2014a; Speed, Hernández Castillo, and Stephen 2006), human rights and community organization (Speed 2008), healing (Forbis 2003), violence (Hernández Castillo 1998b, 2014), building the Zapatista caracoles, epistemologies, and pedagogies (Klein 2015; Mora 2017a), and the role of women in the Consejo Indígena de Gobierno (Indigenous Governing Council; CIG) (Muñoz Ramírez 2018). There is a rich tradition of scholarship on Indigenous women's activism in Mexico (Bonfil Sánchez and del Pont Lalli 1999; Espinosa Damien 2009a, 2009b). Bonfil et al. (2008) highlight how Indigenous women's participation and leadership engages in two parallel systems in which they have faced gender, racism, generational, and other forms of discrimination (116): the national political system and Indigenous normative systems. Aída Hernández Castillo (2001, 2016) called attention to how Indigenous women's gendered demands were triangulated between feminist ethnocentrism and Indigenous ethnonationalism, concerns that have been echoed widely by Indigenous feminist scholars in the United States and Canada. Indigenous women's organizing has been critical in scaling down political claims to Indigenous autonomy into daily lived realities (Blackwell 2000, 2006; Forbis 2003; Speed 2008). Indigenous women activists and thinkers have envisioned shared frames of resistance based on Indigenous cosmovisions, asserting their role in the balance, responsibilities and right relationships embedded in their millennial cultures in a wide arrange of struggles from land and water defense in the fight against extractivism, to those resisting state and narco violence, to those who have fought for Indigenous autonomy, territory and communal decision making in ways that challenge sexual and gender violence, discrimination and exclusion (Cumes 2014; Cunningham 2006; Enlace Continental de Mujeres Indígenas 2010; Sánchez 2005; Tzul Tzul 2015) Other social thinkers have formed a powerful gendered critique from an Indigenous perspective, which has led some to begin questioning the basis of feminism predicated on individual western rationality (Cumes 2021; Gargallo Celentani 2012; Marcos 2005; Millán 2014b). Analyzing how "organized Indigenous women are developing diverse forms of cultural politics from within organizations where women's rights are central to their political agenda, and also from those where local demands are the priority," Hernández Castillo maps the complex project of Indigenous women's organizing in Mexico and beyond (2016, 8). Indigenous women's political agenda "decenters not only the discourse of power about law and custom but also hegemonic discourses on indigeneity gender, modernity and tradition" (8). Over decades, Lynn Stephen's work on Indigenous women (1991, 2005, 2011), social movements (1997, 2002, 2009), migration (2007, 2012, 2014a), and testimonio (2013) has reshaped the way the field has been understood. In just one instructive example, her work on the 2006 Oaxacan uprising examines how Oaxacan Indigenous women gendered human rights discourse to challenge the ways they are stigmatized as "short, fat, and brown" insisting on the right to speak and be heard as the face of Oaxaca (Stephen 2011). Others have sought to understand Indigenous women's rights within legal pluralities and struggles for justice (Picq 2012; Sieder 2008, 2017; Sierra 2004, 2005, 2006, 2007, 2009, 2012; Sierra and Speed 2005; Terven Salinas 2005). Finally, Berrio Palomo (2006) offers a rich comparison of Mexico and Colombia and Rousseau and Rosales Hudson (2016, 2018) offer a unique comparative perspective on Indigenous movements in Mexico, Peru, and Bolivia. The latter argue that "the fact that most Indigenous women leaders have first mobilized within mixed-gender organizations sets the frame for understanding autonomy as relationally constructed in the context of the broader dynamics of Indigenous movements" (Rousseau and Rosales Hudson 2016, 59).

Scales of Resistance combines and contributes to the scholarship on transnational social movements, transnational migration, and translocality—phenomena that are often studied as distinct but that are, in fact, often interrelated. Indigenous migrants navigate the complexity of what earlier transmigration scholars called transnational community, families, and identities to describe the ways sending and receiving communities influenced each other in a circular nature (Glick Schiller, Basch, and Black-Szanton 1994). Glick Schiller (2005) argues that migrants produce transnational social fields that cross the boundaries of various nation-states. As a political stance, the late Mixtec organizer Rufino Dominguez, one of the founders and leaders of FIOB, refused the term *transnational*, saying on numerous occasions that "we [Indigenous migrants] are not goods capitalism imports and exports for profit." In seeking to understand Indigenous migration, I complicate transnationalism, arguing that it must be approached from a perspective that denaturalizes the colonial borders of the nation-state and recognizes Indigenous peoples and nations as transnational actors. This perspective insists that migration scholarship cease replicating the settler colonial logic of terra nullius and understand that the territories being transited are not empty spaces but are Indigenous territories and homelands (Blackwell, Boj Lopez, Urrieta 2017). This move unmasks the "settler move toward innocence" (Tuck and Yang 2012) embedded within the notion that the US is a "country of immigrants" as a settler colonial narrative (Dunbar-Ortiz 2021). This approach to migration studies forges a more complex interplay of multiple colonialities, Indigenous transnationalisms, transregions, and translocalilties, thereby opening up a conversation about transindigeneity for Indigenous migrants (Blackwell 2017a).

Indeed, scholars of Indigenous transnational migration call attention to the complexities of social, cultural, and political spatial relations within deterritorialized indigeneity and to efforts to retain Indigenous social, economic, cultural and political norms in transborder communities. Early scholarship on Indigenous cross-border politics called attention to the presence of binational (Indigenous) civil societies (Fox 2005; Rivera-Salgado 2006). Velasco Ortiz and París Pombo argue that Indigenous migration articulates "the duality of origin and destination and of modernity and tradition in a new field of multiterritorial integration and differentiation" (2014, 10). Similarly, Lynn Stephen notes that within transborder lives, the "ability to construct space, time and social relation in more than one place simultaneously is part of the daily framing of life in . . . extended families" (2007, 5). Much work on Indigenous migration from Mexico draws on the groundbreaking work of anthropologist Michael Kearney (1995), who coined the term *Oaxacalifornia* to explain the migratory patterns, cultural, social, and political identities of thousands of Oaxacans in California. In the words of Gaspar Rivera-Salgado, from his essay on "The Right to Stay Home," "'Oaxacalifornia' is a transnationalized space in which migrants bring together their lives in California with their communities of origin" (2014b, 99). This "space" has enabled Oaxacan migrants in California to engage in collective action and cultural enrichment while away from their communities of origin. Oaxacalifornia is a way in which Indigenous migrants maintain their connection to their Oaxacan origin. As they work in California to raise money for their families back home, these largely Zapotec, Mixtec, and Triqui migrants find it important to retain their Oaxacan identity. To maintain ties with their communities of origin, some migrants have formed hometown associations to fundraise and carry out community rituals, like holding feast days, transborder communal care, and teaching and continuing Indigenous cultural forms. There is also a rich tradition of mutual aid and civic organizing where coalition projects that focus on "translocal" ties enable migrants to "bring people together from a broader, regional, ethno-geographic sphere," according to Rivera-Salgado (2014b, 98). Some examples of these types of coalitions are FIOB and the Organizacion Regional de Oaxaca (ORO) discussed in chapters four and five.

Although conceptions like Oaxacalifornia signal the notion of transregional social, cultural, and political worlds and projects of community belonging, we still must attend to the fact that the lands upon which transregional Indigenous belonging are constructed belong to other Indigenous nations. Ideas like Oaxacalifornia make space and home for Oaxacan Indigenous migrants in California, which already is structured by Spanish and Mexican colonial arrangements overlaid by US settler colonial ones (Blackwell, Boj Lopez, and

Urrieta 2017; Blackwell 2017a). Crafting a place of belonging amid structural violence and hostility is part of what scholars have called Latino cultural citizenship (Flores and Benmayor 1998), yet these forms of belonging being created on the homelands and territories of native California communities. Zapotec scholar Brenda Nicolás (2020) critiques the concept of Oaxacalifornia for the ways it aligns Oaxaca to the Spanish colonial frame of California, erasing Indigenous peoples whose homelands are settled on thereby creating a new settler project.

Some notes toward the use of terms may be necessary, as this project crosses disciplines and fields (political science, anthropology, and ethnic, gender, and Latin American studies) as well as academic and activist borders and Indigenous and non-Indigenous worlds. *Transnationalism* has been used to talk about the movement of cultures, peoples, and capital across borders under neoliberal capitalism. Scholars of social movements often use *international* to describe formal state-to-state relationships to distinguish transnational actors and processes that occur across nation-state borders but do not necessarily involve state actors. For example, Francesca Miller (1990), in her study of early transnational women's organizing in the Americas (the Pan-American Scientific Congresses of the 1890s and the First International Feminist Congress in 1910 in Argentina) distinguishes between internationalism as "formal intergovernmental activities carried on at the international level" and the transnational arena where women organize not as representatives of their governments but as those who are marginalized by them (225). Add to this complexity an Indigenous perspective that sees relationships between Indigenous people and states as nation-to-nation relationships, especially in the North American context. For example, Chickasaw scholar Jodi Byrd (2011) has argued that the homogenization of more than five hundred Indigenous nations through US settler colonialism is a process of minoritization that makes racial what is truly international. Whereas the state has attempted to manage indigeneity via racial/ethnic categories (Barker 2006), others have argued that Indigenous people have radically different goals than a civil rights agenda or pluralist discourses of inclusion that misconstrue Indigenous claims as being race based (Kauanui 2008). Yet not all Indigenous groups who recognize themselves as a distinct people refer to themselves as nations; for example, in Mexico, many Indigenous peoples refer themselves in relation to their pueblos (people/places) even though in official discourse they are referred to as ethnicities.

Federico Besserer's (2004) work mapping transnational topographies of the Mixtec diaspora in terms of culture, politics, economics, and labor shows the multiple borders that migrants cross. For me, Stephen's (2007) notion of transborder is an important tool in this toolbox or analytic repertoire, and her work on transborder lives (2007, 2012) introduced the theoretical complexity of borders, border crossing, and borderlands (Anzaldúa 1987; Segura and Zavella 2007) to cross-border migration and the complex social, cultural, political, and economic ties Indigenous migrants forge. In this formulation Stephen argues that migrants cross nation-state borders and the national racial hierarchies that others have called "coloniality of power" (Quijano 2000), which means Indigenous and Afro-descendent migrants face discrimination for being not only part of a national group but also part of a racially subjugated group within that nation. For me, the concept of transborder is also useful to call attention to the multiple colonial, racial, class, and gendered borders that transborder migrants and organizers navigate.

I build on transborder as a tool to disrupt and open up what *transnational* means—to include transindigenous or Indigenous nation-to-nation relationships and to account for the multiple configurations of power within nations. For example, I use the term *transborder* rather than *transnational* to denaturalize multiple colonial borders, colonialities of power (systems that have colonial arrangements of meaning and power at their center), and settler colonial structures (designed to eliminate the native). Immigration scholars overlook the idea that the US-Mexico border is not only a colonial border that migrants—and their translocal cultures and binational civil societies—cross, but also a border that is mapped over other Indigenous nations' territories, which are also crossed, divided, and traversed, though far less frequently acknowledged (Tamez 2013). I have contributed these perspectives to building a framework called Critical Latinx Indigeneities that I argue later in chapter five is part of understanding how Indigenous migrants navigate Indigenous geographies of difference. This perspective allows us to (1) rethink and unsettle colonial borders; (2) grapple with the role of migration in settler colonial projects, and (3) challenge state-generated racial projects of Indigenous erasure, as do mestizaje and notions of indigenismo.

One of the challenges of Indigenous migration is the often-obscured fact that multiple colonialities may be at play in any given space, and that those colonial projects are not isolated from one another but have historically colluded to create the power relationships, indeed the geographies of difference, that Indigenous women navigate, especially in migration. These multiple and divergent colonialities have produced conflicting notions of indigeneity. Indigenismo was part of a mestizo intellectual and cultural movement in Latin America in which national elites imagined and constructed national unity by recognizing the grandeur of the Indigenous civilizations on which Latin American societies have by and large been built, and which they have surpassed.

The way indigenismo was deployed in the nation-building project of post-revolutionary Mexico celebrated the grandeur of an Aztec past while denying the present and future of the sixty-eight Indigenous groups of Mexico, which comprise the largest Indigenous population in the hemisphere. In *Blood Lines* (2008), Contreras defines *indigenismo* as "the stylistic appropriation of Indigenous cultural forms and traditions by non-Indigenous artists and intellectuals" (24). Although recognizing the power of Mesoamerican Indigenous civilizations may seem like a positive development, it was tied to cultural projects of modernism and state projects of modernity. In the hands of state institutions, indigenismo as an ideology and set of policies allowed mestizo elites to regulate not only the meaning of indigeneity but which cultures were worth preserving and under which terms. Portraying Indigenous people only in the past is part of a genocidal logic that locks Indigenous people in a temporal frame of extinction or disappearance.

Mestizaje has been understood as the mixture of Indigenous, African, and European roots. Yet its historical origins are not so innocent; they buttress racial projects of whitening in the region including in countries such as Brazil and Mexico. In 1920s Mexico, then Minister of Education José Vasconcelos wrote that the country was populated by a cosmic race, by which he imagined indigeneity and Africanness to be eradicated via whiteness (Saldaña-Portillo 2003). Uncritical deployments of mestizaje and indigenismo in the Chicano movement and by Chicana feminisms have recycled the Mexican state project of eugenics based on whitening and on Indigenous/African erasure (Blackwell 2017a, 2017b; Contreras 2008, Guidotti Hernandez 2011). Following Gloria Anzaldúa's retheorization of mestiza consciousness (1987) as a facultad to break down dichotomies between first and third world, Mexican and American, straight and queer, many critical theorists took up the liberatory possibilities of hybridity in her writings. Scholars were disturbed by the way her work seemed to embrace the hybridity of mestizaje while overlooking how it had historically been deployed to erase, eliminate, and ultimately whiten Black and Indigenous communities in Mexico. Others argued that she, along with other Chicana scholars, "appropriated this concept to construct a new mestiza cultural identity that resists racial, sexual, and other forms of structural oppression" (Gutiérrez Najera, Castellanos, Aldama, 2012, 7). Sandy Grande (2000) cautions critical theorists who take up the mantle of mestizaje "as the basis of a new cultural democracy [because it] does not fully consider Indigenous struggles to sustain the cultural and political integrity of American Indian communities" (469). She asks if mestizaje can be reconciled with Indigenous imperatives of self-determination and sovereignty (474).

In terms of Indigenous migration and transborder organizing, I have argued that multiple colonialities have produced different state-managed boundaries of indigeneity, which, under conditions of neoliberal globalization, have collided and hybridized. This process is what I call elsewhere "hybrid hegemonies" to describe how one racial system migrates and gets mapped onto US white supremacist and settler state projects through the process of migration. I have argued that Indigenous migrants are learning to navigate not only multiple racial hegemonies but also the intersection of local, national, and transnational systems of power that shift, overlap, and hybridize during the process of migration (Blackwell 2010). These migrating meanings of race in relation to indigeneity are both historic and new and signal the ways in which racial power is signified and utilized to create structures of disempowerment. For example, the anti-Indian prejudice in which Mexican racial hierarchies are embedded facilitates labor segmentation and the hyperexploitation of Indigenous migrants in the increasingly global economy. These historical racial hegemonies from Mexico that have marginalized Indigenous peoples are not just imported; they are hybridized and get mapped on American race, class, gender, and sexual relations. Further, these hybrid hegemonies create conflicting boundaries of who is considered Indigenous by the US and Mexican states and dominant societies, thereby creating the erasures, invisibilities, and, ironically, new possibilities for Indigenous identity and consciousness. Thinking through how racial logics are marshaled by the coloniality of power and settler colonialism, and the ways they hybridize, pushes us to consider the ways meanings of US Latinidad and indigeneity are shifting because of Latin American Indigenous diasporas.

Overview of the Book

Each chapter of *Scales of Resistance* focuses on a different set of scalar relationships. Chapter 1 examines how women activists in the national Indigenous movement in Mexico scaled the concept of autonomy down into the multiple scales of their daily lives, such as their homes, bodies, and communities. It highlights the lessons gleaned from how Mexico's Indigenous autonomy movement navigated the selective co-optation of neoliberal multiculturalism in Latin America. The chapter analyzes how Indigenous women activists have, through their participation in the Indigenous rights movement since the 1994 Zapatista uprising, and before, refigured the right of Indigenous autonomy as a lived practice that is embedded in multiple spaces of their lives. As Indigenous women began to enunciate themselves as autonomous political subjects in Mexico in the 1990s, they not only looked to the state to demand their rights as citizens/subjects but also turned their attention to *where* those rights are practiced. By scaling autonomy down into their homes, communities, and communal Indigenous social customs and governance practices, they have essentially created a *practice* of autonomy as a vital strategy that moves beyond rights discourse and the ways in which neoliberal states have selectively co-opted social movement demands (Blackwell 2004; Forbis 2003).

Chapter 2 is based on oral histories with the founders and subsequent leaders of the Continental Network of Indigenous Women of Abya Yala (later the Continental Network of Indigenous Women of the Americas, ECMIA), a hemispheric network that formed to protest the ways Indigenous women were excluded from the Latin American NGO forums held in preparation for the Fourth World Conference on Women in 1995. It examines how Indigenous epistemology was used shift the conversation, decolonize "transnational" consciousness, and create solidarity among Indigenous rights organizers to name the interconnected struggles of Indigenous peoples on the land of what is now called the Americas. The research on ECMIA involves documenting not just the articulation of collective identities and spaces of resistance but also the critical strategy of weaving in and between scales of power—even creating new scales when existing ones do not reflect Indigenous women's political needs and cosmovisions. The chapter follows activists from Mexico who helped to found the organization and who hosted the second continental encuentro in 1997, as well as other activists from the United States, Bolivia, Canada, Panama, Brazil, and Guatemala who have participated in the leadership of the network. My thinking is shaped by my observations at three of the continental encuentros in 2004, 2007, and 2011—the latter in Hueyapan, Mexico—and by seeing members participate in other transnational regional formations such as the Latin American Feminist Encuentros and the First International Encuentro of Politics, Art, Sport, and Culture for Women Who Struggle, organized and hosted by the Zapatista in 2018.

Critically, the place-based struggles that Escobar has called "multi-scale, network oriented subaltern strategies of localization" (2001, 139) are at the heart of many of these transnational networks, regional movements, and transborder organizations. With this in mind, in chapter 3 I explore how work at other scales both emerges *from* and is localized *to* Indigenous pueblos, municipalities, and regions—the local scales where Indigenous women organize for communal defense or against their own exclusion from community decisions. Within the scales created by Indigenous regions/territories and states within Mexico, Indigenous women have created networks of women's organizing, linking multiple movements, congresses, marches, caravans, and workshops across hundreds of communities and municipalities in order to better their lives and those of the people in their communities. Thus, chapter 3 returns to Mexico and the local politics in the states of Jalisco and, more deeply, Guerrero and Oaxaca in order to understand the impact and interrelationships of the other scales of organizing on local realities. These locales and the forms of organizing across them became even more important as activists scaled down coordinating efforts at the state and local levels after the Mexican government betrayed earlier commitments to Indigenous rights at the national level. On the basis of initial interviews with many activists I met in the 1990s who have since returned to build local organizations, and subsequent interviews with them conducted more than a decade later, I trace the ways in which political mobilization at the national level draws from and nourishes the local as well as the way migration has shaped local/global dynamics.

Although many Indigenous migrants originate from the Sierra Norte, the Central Valleys, and the Mixtec regions of Oaxaca, one of the poorest states in Mexico, they are settling and working across the migrant stream that runs from Oaxaca through Mexico (Mexico City and Baja California) to California and north through the Pacific Northwest. Thus, chapter 4 examines women's roles in shaping transborder politics within Indigenous communities, in this case largely Mixtec and Zapotec women. It is based on collaborative research with the Women's Commission of FIOB and on the work of activist Indigenous women as they organize along the Oaxacan Indigenous diaspora in Juxtlahuaca, Huajuapan de León, and Zanatepec (Oaxaca); Tijuana (Baja California); and Los Angeles and Fresno (California). It examines the transregional scale created by the dense networks of Oaxacan Indigenous migrant organizing and communal life—much of which relies on the labor, imagination, and dreams of Indigenous migrant women who create transboder Indigenous life worlds for themselves, their families and their communities. The chapter analyzes how these organizers learn to articulate their demands, identities, and campaigns (trans)locally while creating resonance binationally within this transregional Indigenous scale and beyond.

Finally, chapter 5 focuses on Los Angeles as a "transnational hub" (Ramirez 2007) for many Indigenous cultures and migrant streams, specifically examining how Indigenous groups from Mexico and Guatemala interact with multiracial Los Angeles creating multilayered geographies of indigeneity within the traditional, unceded territories of the Tongva/Gabrielino people. The chapter responds to the estimated 250,000 Oaxacan Indigenous immigrants settling and working in Los Angeles, whose presence, along with the diaspora of Mayans (largely Kanjobal and K'iche) from Guatemala, challenges us to see immigration from Mexico and Central America as a multiracial process (Fox 2006; Vankin 2017), shaking loose some of our received notions of who is "Latina/o," "Mexican," and "Indian." Although Los Angeles has a rich Latino immigrant history and the largest urban Native American population—thanks to the "relocation days" of the 1950s when the US government enacted its specific policy of termination and "detribalization" by relocating reservation-based populations to urban centers and large Indigenous diasporas from Oceania and Latin America—social services fail this growing population because these migrants and refugees are often non-Spanish-speaking monolingual speakers of their own Indigenous languages. Chapter 5 examines Indigenous mobility, translocal community formation, and political organizing among the Latin American Indigenous diaspora in Los Angeles. It explores how community organizing, labor circuits, sacred geographies, and the spatial projects created by the Oaxacan Indigenous culinary and musical soundscapes are forms of Indigenous place-making that are reorganizing socio-spatial relations in Los Angeles. By proposing a Critical Latinx Indigeneities framework by which to understand Latin American Indigenous migration, this chapter explores how Indigenous migration and place making come into complex play with the region's multiple colonialities and considers the conflicts, responsibilities, and opportunities to build solidarity with the native communities upon whose land these translocal Indigenous social worlds and transregional ways of being are being forged.

1. The Multiscalar Practice of Autonomy in Mexico

We believe that autonomy of our peoples includes all areas of our lives—the home, family, community, region—and that it has to do with the respect and recognition of our culture, our territories, our traditional medicine. For us, autonomy means parity, democracy, and equity between men and women, Indigenous and non-Indigenous, between all human beings, and, above all, that our rights be recognized as the original peoples we are.[1]

In Chilpancingo, Guerrero, Mexico, I participated in small breakout sessions and sat with hundreds of Indigenous women activists in the plenaries at Second National Gathering of Indigenous Women held by Coordinadora Nacional de Mujeres Indígenas (CONAMI) in 2000. I was moved by how they were collectively forging a multifaceted, multiscalar concept of autonomy, as illustrated above in the final declaration of the gathering. Although Indigenous autonomy is a shared discursive and political terrain of struggle within the broader Indigenous movement in Mexico, women activists have multiplied the meaning of autonomy beyond a right the state grants to a set of multiscalar practices of Indigenous freedom and survival that have the potential to democratize and empower Indigenous women in their communities and in the world. The demand for autonomy is part of a larger framework of basic rights for Indigenous people that includes the right to be a pueblo, the right to land and protection of territory, the right to self-determination and autonomy, the right to cultural traditions and forms of political representation and jurisprudence, and the right to protect and use the land's natural resources.[2] The Indigenous women's movement has supported juridical, territorial, and cultural claims to autonomy. Yet, during the 1990s and early 2000s, in both large and small venues from intimate workshops to national gatherings across Mexico, including the ones I attended in Chilpancingo and many others such as the 1999 National Workshop of Indigenous Women in Autonomy Processes in Mexico City, women in the Indigenous movement expanded the meaning of these claims by scaling them down to the levels at which they are practiced in their daily lives. These lived daily scales of women's bodily, political, and economic autonomy thereby create a lived *practice* of autonomy that is situated in the multiple and gendered scales of sociality and politics in their communities.[3] These intimate, grounded autonomies are practiced by those who have declared themselves autonomous municipalities and by Indigenous women across Mexico as a way of advancing Indigenous autonomy, despite the government's failure to implement the San Andrés Accords (Hernández Navarro and Carlsen 2004; Hernández Navarro and Vera Herrera 1998).[4]

Autonomy is part of a broader social movement repertoire that allows political actors to move beyond rights discourse, especially in a context where the government has backtracked on its commitment to Indigenous rights. I refer to Indigenous autonomy as a terrain of struggle to signal how it is used both as a language of contention with the state in order to gain collective rights to self-determination and, beyond formal political and juridical claims, as a decolonial practice that has, through a process of communal deliberation, transformed it into a pedagogy of empowerment. Through that process of community discussion, or consulta, Indigenous autonomy has been debated, expanded, and scaled down to the more intimate scales of community, family, home, and body. Women activists have used Indigenous forms of consultation so that would-be practitioners of rights interrogate "tradition" and the cultural basis of Indigenous law (usos y costumbres), thereby democratizing the meaning-making practice of autonomy. Nationally, translocally across regions, and in their own Indigenous territories and pueblos, women's participation in community deliberations has helped to shape the meaning of Indigenous autonomy and how it is practiced in the multiple spaces and scales of political and communal life, creating a form of community consciousness-raising and direct democracy.

This chapter examines how Indigenous women activists shifted the Indigenous movement's struggle for autonomy from a discourse of rights to a practice of autonomy by scaling down to levels of the community, the home, and the body. This shift has been critical in a context where neoliberal states throughout Latin America have selectively co-opted the demands of the Indigenous rights movement before Indigenous communities in Mexico confronted the massive rise in corruption and violence associated with the drug war and an increasingly repressive state or what Speed (2019) calls "neoliberal multicriminalism." Here I emphasize that scale is constructed not only by states and the international system but also by Indigenous epistemologies, geographies, knowledge projects, organizing practices, and political strategies. Because power is configured differently at each scale, Indigenous women as marginalized actors have developed a multiscalar strategy to avoid blockages by state and nonstate actors and maintain forward momentum.

With the emergence of the Indigenous rights movement along with multicultural constitutional reforms in Mexico—and, indeed, throughout Latin America in the 1990s—Indigenous people became "both the agents and the subjects of this new discourse of citizenship," participating in what Nancy Postero (2007, 176) characterizes as the "push from below" and "incorporation from above." When the state reversed its course in fully implementing the San Andrés Peace Accords, it prompted the Zapatistas and many other sectors of the Indigenous rights movement to take their demands for autonomy largely outside of the state. With the passage of the Law on Indigenous Culture and Rights, a 2001 counterreform that undermines the basic guarantee for Indigenous self-determination that was set forth in the San Andrés Peace Accords, Indigenous women's efforts to put autonomy into practice in every sphere of life experience became ever more important for implementing and sustaining a long-term movement for self-determination. Their grassroots practices of construction and consultation sustained the movement beyond the claim for rights in the face of military repression and governmental recalcitrance. Given what Dagnino (2007) calls this "perverse confluence" between a new form of citizenship claimed by social actors fighting for their "right to have rights" and the state's neoliberal efforts to roll back its role as the guarantor of those rights, part of my work here is to explore the strategies Indigenous women activists in Mexico deployed to confront neoliberal governmentality and devise strategies of autonomy in the context of increased narco violence and state repression, extractivism, and criminalization through the "War on Drugs."[5]

Beyond engagement with the state, the innovation of the Indigenous rights movement in Mexico has been to call attention to Indigenous lifeways, belonging, and self-governance as a set of rights encapsulated in Indigenous autonomy—enacting "cultural citizenship."[6] Latina/o scholars have called attention to the ways in which historically marginalized groups create an alternative sense of nonstate belonging in the context of racism and exclusion as enacting a form of cultural citizenship. Aihwa Ong, however, cautions that subject-making is a two-way process in which one must consider not only the elaboration of a collective subjectivity by an aggrieved group but also the state's role in that subject-making, or what she calls "subject-ification" (1996, 737).[7] Ong's formulation offers a counterbalance to understanding the formulation of dissident subjectivities and projects of belonging. She defines cultural citizenship as "cultural practices and beliefs produced out of negotiating the often ambivalent and contested relations with the state and its hegemonic forms that establish the criteria of belonging within a national population and territory" (Ong 1996, 734). With this in mind, I examine how organized Indigenous women grounded the practice of Indigenous autonomy, first through community consultation by scaling down rights claims within and through the gendered practice of their daily lives. This allowed them to create a pedagogy of autonomy that allowed them, in effect, to shift the understanding of autonomy from a right granted by the state to a lived, decolonial practice that is part of everyday life and community sociality (Blackwell 2000, 2004). Taking their struggles for autonomy beyond the state has thus enabled Indigenous women to destabilize and resist the "subject-ification" described by Ong by unfixing the meaning of autonomy and the monopoly of the state to define, grant, and adjudicate it. Further, the strategy of moving in and between scales has allowed Indigenous women to continue their political project even when blocked at various levels, which has contributed to the long-term vitality of Indigenous social movements and resistance.

The chapter first examines how a national scale of organizing was constituted by interweaving translocal activism in new ways that resulted in the founding of a national network of Indigenous women. It illustrates how Indigenous women's political consciousness often emerged at the scales of home, territory, and municipality, when as girls Indigenous women first learned to navigate geographies of difference—how power was configured differently at and between each of those scales—in their efforts to gain education and deal with labor migration. It then examines the San Andrés Peace Accords as a site in which a broader consciousness of Indigenous women's rights was forged both in the working sessions of the negotiations and in consultas across Mexico about Indigenous rights and usos y costumbres. Within these widespread consultas, Indigenous autonomy was vernacularized and scaled down from political claims of autonomy to include demands for autonomy within Indigenous women's homes, communities, and bodies. In the latter sections of the chapter I examine how the founding of the Coordinadora Nacional de Mujeres Indígenas de México (CONAMI) created a national space in which to talk about and denounce the violence occurring at more intimate scales and to make visible the scale of the regional. Finally, I explore how reframing Indigenous autonomy as a practice resists co-optation by the Mexican federal government, which uses gender as a discourse of governmentality to deny Indigenous peoples their collective right to self-determination. The conclusion reflects on the demobilization and resurgence of CONAMI as a new generation of activists collaborates with the founding generation in a new campaign around Indigenous women's autonomy and bodily integrity.

Lived Roots of Struggle: Learning from Experiences of Mobility and Shifts in Scale

Formed as a national network at the First National Gathering of Indigenous Women in Oaxaca in 1997, CONAMI has called for Indigenous autonomy based on Indigenous jurisprudence, self-governance, and usos y costumbres while simultaneously critiquing and transforming those practices in relation to their own gendered understanding of power (Blackwell 2004, 2006, 2009, 2012; Hernández Castillo 2016; Sánchez Néstor 2005). The gathering that formed CONAMI was historic because it brought together seven hundred women to create an Indigenous women's rights agenda based on their experiences as participants in mixed-gender Indigenous and popular organizations, such as 500 Years of Indigenous, Popular and Black Resistance in Guerrero; the Union of Indigenous Communities of the Northern Zone of the Isthmus (Unión de Comunidades Indígenas de la Zona Norte del Istmo, UCIZONI) and Services of the Mixe Pueblo (Servicios del Pueblo Mixe, SER)—both from Oaxaca; and in Indigenous rights organizations in Jalisco and Veracruz, and weavers' collectives from Chiapas. In addition, a good number of activists were from local Indigenous women's organizations such as Erandi (meaning "dawn," a P'urépecha Women's group in Michoacán) or Casa de Mujer Indígena (Indigenous Women's House, CAMI) in Cuetzalan, Puebla. Inspired by this experience, others went on to form statewide Indigenous women's organizations in Oaxaca, Guerrero, and Jalisco, as I discuss in chapter 3. This founding generation of CONAMI leaders historically participated in the women's commissions of the national Indigenous organizations in Mexico at that time, including the Congreso Nacional Indígena (National Indigenous Congress, CNI) and the Asamblea Nacional Indígena Plural por la Autonomía (National Plural Indigenous Assembly for Autonomy, ANIPA). Over time, members of CONAMI went on to hold leadership positions in ANIPA and the CNI.

I began accompanying CONAMI in 1999, two years after the organization was founded. What follows is based on ethnography and twenty-five oral histories that I conducted with past and current members. I gathered the ethnographic data while conducting fieldwork during the year I lived in Mexico in 1999 and at dozens of local, national, and transnational meetings and gatherings between 1999 and 2002. In addition, ten years after the initial interviews, I returned to Mexico to attend national and continental encuentros, or gatherings, and to interview the first and subsequent generations of founders and leaders to understand how activists from the Indigenous rights movement of the 1990s think about their current work.

My oral histories with members of CONAMI illustrate that Indigenous women had walked many paths of community organizing before coming together to build a national movement. CONAMI, as a political formation, was built on a wealth of organizing experiences in both mixed-gender and Indigenous women's organizations. Members' early organizing revolved around liberation theology and community-based organizing, campesino or rural peasant organizations, economic collectives and productive projects that developed out of the economic crisis in Mexico in the 1980s, and traditional Indigenous governing structures such as community assemblies and early Indigenous rights organizations. While Indigenous women emerged as new political subjects in the 1990s by drawing on those prior organizing experiences, the gendered insurgency of Indigenous women in Chiapas, and the convening of the broader Mexican and Indigenous civil society for the San Andrés Peace Accords, was a catalyst for building a national Indigenous women's movement. It was not until 1994 that women's mass participation and leadership within the Zapatista Army of National Liberation (EZLN) made Indigenous women visible and gender equity a crucial component of the struggle for Indigenous rights and autonomy (Hernández Castillo 2001).

The historical impact of the EZLN uprising drew on prior Indigenous organizing across Mexico (N. Harvey 1998) and while that was the case for women, the uprising, especially women's role in it, amplified and called women forward in new ways. Indeed, the reverberations of women's gendered demands in Chiapas helped to empower women translocally throughout Mexico (Blackwell 2006; Stephen 2002). The mobilization of Indigenous women in Chiapas created a wider conversation that legitimated organizers in other regions who had long histories of participating in political and community organizing (an issue I explore further in chapter 3). The visibility of women's leadership and the demands of Indigenous women also helped local organizers to leverage greater participation in their own communities throughout Mexico. Indigenous women organizers developed a translocal strategy to open new spaces for other women's participation, community leadership, and empowerment. The mobilization of an Indigenous women's political subjectivity made grassroots women's leadership visible to the broader Indigenous movement and to Mexican society in general. For example, Lorena, a Tzotzil weaver from Chiapas using a pseudonym she chose for herself, described how the uprising resulted in a shift in how women saw themselves:

> We had a cooperative, but we did not get to manage it. It was the men who decided, the men who gave their opinions on how they wanted the cooperative to function. Since '94, we have begun to take on more strength and valor. It's not just in the cooperative; it is in different events that we have attended as women. Now we can make the decisions, we can also be in the decision-making process that only men had ruled. After '94 various organizations emerged, the women organized, began to work collectively in ways they had not before. We always had had a lot of fear.... We were always dependents of our fathers, or our husbands.... We were not able to speak of things that we felt. Now we feel a bit more free, because we can think, and it was this [organizing] that gave us courage so that we could express our feelings too. (Lorena, interview with Maylei Blackwell, April 1, 2000)

As Lorena makes clear, the shift was not one of getting women to participate—they were already active participants—but in *how* they viewed their own roles. Seeing other women in decision-making roles in the EZLN, and at national gatherings after the uprising, set a powerful example that inspired women translocally to become more vocal in their own organizations.

In the late 1990s, I met María de Jesús Patricio, known as Marichuey, who was already an established Nahua community leader and traditional healer, and an early member of CONAMI and the CNI. She would go on to speak, in addition to the EZLN's comandanta Esther, on the floor of Congress during the historic 2001 debates on the Law on Indigenous Rights and Cultures. In 2017 she was named by the EZLN and the CNI as their vocera, the one elected to carry the message of the Indigenous movement across Mexico and beyond. The CNI formed the Consejo Indígena de Gobierno (Indigenous Governing Council or CIG) by selecting one female and one male representative from each community active in the CNI. Surprising many by adopting an electoral strategy after long criticizing the corruption of electoral politics in Mexico, the CNI decided to run the CIG, as a collective body, as the Indigenous movement's candidate for the 2018 presidential election. Marichuey served as the vocera of that body, a process I explore in the coda of this book. Many learned of the story of Marichuey when she became the vocera during the CIG's presidential candidacy but she, of course, has a much longer and formative history. I interviewed Marichuey in 2000 in Chilpancingo during CONAMI's Second National Encuentro, where she led workshops and worked tirelessly with the hundreds of other Indigenous women gathered there to envision Indigenous autonomy from the perspective of Indigenous women (see figure 1.1). When we sat down to do an

Figure 1.1. María de Jesús Patricio leading a workshop at the Second National Encuentro of CONAMI, Chilpancingo, Guerrero, 2000. Photo by author.

oral history, we spoke in lowered voices at the side of the room while her infant slept in her rebozo. Marichuey began her story by recounting how she came to political consciousness and began her path in the struggle for Indigenous rights:

> Well, [when] I began to acquire consciousness, I remember that it was when I was young when I began to feel the problematic at home. I began to see the social problems existing in the community and that these were beginning to impact the family. I come from a numerous family. There are eleven siblings and, well, the basic needs were in terms of education, health.... And all of this made me think why some people had more and some others had less. And that made me realize that I had to do something, that I did not want the rest of my sisters and brothers from other pueblos to also suffer the same way I suffered as a woman.
>
> I felt that I had to do something, but I asked myself, how? What was missing was seeing or discovering where to begin. I remember that a priest arrived to my community where he began work that was liberating, not a traditional, conservative pastoral. Well, I liked that a lot and he began

inviting people to come give us training workshops on human rights, on educational projects, on health. It was then that I started to learn more, and to get to know other types of organizations, and that made me see that we had to work not only at the local [level], but also with other organizations in other communities, from other states. (Maria de Jesús Patricio, interview with Maylei Blackwell, April 1, 2000)

When I asked her about the conditions that led her to work with Indigenous women, she described the crucial scale of the home in a powerful way:

All the injustice that there is against women, mainly at home. At home, well . . . a woman is not considered a person, but an object. [Even though] we see that she is a great . . . a great contributor to the development of Indigenous Peoples, she is not considered as such. Her participation with her own voice is not valued. So, we saw that it was necessary to create our own space, because there are many particular women's issues that cannot be talked about just like that [so easily] in the organizations, or in assemblies, where the majority are men. So, for this, we feel the need to create our own space. (Patricio, interview, April 1, 2000)

Marichuey was not the only woman to specifically name the home as a scale at which Indigenous women's empowerment is necessary. Throughout my years accompanying CONAMI activists, I began to recognize how activists linked scales, leveraging the spaces and skills gained in one to create opportunities in another. As I learned more about their life histories, I saw that this strategy emerged from their daily lived experiences of literally moving back and forth between socio-spatial and political scales—for example, traveling from their home in the pueblos to municipal centers and markets; moving to receive an education or to work in urban centers; and crossing various types of social, spatial, and scalar borders. Further shattering assumptions that Indigenous women are somehow bounded by the local, the women I have interviewed, along with their families, have long histories of internal labor migration in Mexico. This echoes Karen Kampwirth's (2002) study of women in guerilla movements, which identifies the experience of labor migration and working in mestizo homes as one of the precursors to Zapatista women's political consciousness. Indigenous people, especially Indigenous women, often are imagined as fixed in place, as static people who do not travel and whose pueblos are bounded in time and space (Hernández Castillo 1994b). Yet their lives are shaped by multiple forms of mobility, from multiple generations of internal labor migration to pick cane or coffee in Veracruz or to work in state and national capitals; or, as young women—especially those from rural areas—to attend secondary school or college in municipal centers where they often have to work as domestic workers and nannies to earn their room and board. Their lives and those of their families and communities are shaped by mobility and by traversing scales where they learn to read shifts in racial, class, and gender power arrangements. This is not even to mention those whose families have crossed international and settler-state borders to travel to the United States to work, and who live transborder Indigenous lives even if they still live in their hometowns (Stephen 2007), as I explore in chapters 4 and 5.

Most CONAMI activists I interviewed began organizing in the 1980s, so that by the time I started my research, there were two distinct generations of activists with two sets of generational experiences.[8] One generation began to participate when they were already married women, many with children; in response to the severe economic crisis of the 1980s they joined women's community-based productive projects aimed at increasing their family income or began organizing through the church. Others began working in Indigenous community radio, peasant organizations, or early organizations of Indigenous authorities and then married partners within the movement. The second, younger generation of activists often began to participate in Indigenous organizing as young girls with their fathers, and they quickly became organizers in their own right. Others worked as secretaries or technicians of rural development within Indigenous communities and were cast into leadership roles during the crisis of political repression whe traditional leaders were imprisoned for their defense of Indigenous territories.

Although married or widowed women and mothers negotiated their activism with partners and family members, they had some degree of social legitimacy and mobility in terms of social and cultural gendered expectations. Many were politically active alongside their husbands, while others stayed in the struggle even after becoming widowed or separated. Others still negotiated abusive relationships with their husbands who were movement leaders while they worked to organize Indigenous women. The organization of women in Chiapas and the mobilization of women at national Indigenous meetings gave visibility and legitimacy to many women who were among the first generation to move into leadership of the national Indigenous movement and of local organizations. The women of this generation whom I met include Sofía Robles of SER in Oaxaca; Doña Rufina Villa of the Nahua Indigenous women's collective Masehual Sihuamej Mosenyolchicauani in Cuetzalan, Puebla, one of the oldest existing women's organizations in Mexico (founded in 1985); Margarita Gutiérrez, a Hñahñú activist from Hidaldo; Tomasa Sandoval of the Nación

P'urépecha Zapatista and Erandi; and María de Jesús Patricio, whom I mentioned earlier. Many of this founding generation, such as Ernestina Ortiz Peña, a Hñähñú activist from Santiago Tilapa in the state of Mexico, became active in the 1980s. Ernestina, following in her father's footsteps, became active in youth organizing; she admired him for living a life of service through participation in ancestral traditions and the traditional community authority or Indigenous normative systems. In 1992 she attended the Continental Encuentro of Indigenous Peoples, where she began down the path of fighting for her rights as an Indigenous woman. She took a year off in 1993 for the birth of her first child, but she continued to work politically through the emergence of the EZLN and accompanied the formation of ANIPA, the CNI, and the CONAMI. With the birth of her second child, she dedicated herself more to organizing in her community and at the state level. She was respected for this work and was nominated as the national coordinator of the CONAMI; she also participated in the Continental Network and served as the general coordinator of ANIPA. She also continued to work in her pueblo and was elected as a community authority. Yet she reflects that

> there is something important here, that with all this leadership that I had and [the work] we began to do in my pueblo. Unfortunately, because I am a woman, the caciques of the pueblo did not let me. I mean, they started putting all the locks on me and I didn't last long. Only four months they let me work and they themselves talked to the authority in Santiago to have me step down. Unfortunately, this is still something to overcome in the pueblo, where women themselves do not accept women as a [traditional] authority . . . it is still very difficult. It doesn't exist. It is not easy. So that is how we started the path as a CONAMI formation, participating at the national and international levels. (Ernestina Ortiz Peña, interview with Maylei Blackwell, August 17, 2017)

Ernestina's reflection illustrates the painful blockages to Indigenous women's leadership and how her own life journey and her parenting responsibilities shaped her ability to interweave between scales of participation. She moved from her pueblo to continental organizing to national organizations, including the CONAMI, to return to work on local organizing when her children were young, before she rejoined the other scales of movement organizing when her children got older.

Many of the younger women of that founding generation began to organize with their fathers, like Mixe activist Cándida Jiménez, whom I met in the late 1990s. Others were secretaries of Indigenous rights organizations, like

Martha Sánchez Néstor of the 500 Años of Resistencia Indígena, who went on to become a national and international leader in her own right, or Hermalinda Turbicio, who worked as a secretary and was thrust into leadership when the male leaders were incarcerated for an occupation in defense of Indigenous territory and autonomy in Rancho Nuevo, a Mixtec community of Guerrero. From there, the younger members of this first generation went on to become human rights and community leaders, community educators, or promoters of Indigenous rights, Indigenous women's reproductive health, and women's rights within the struggle for Indigenous autonomy.

When I first interviewed them in the late 1990s, many of these activists were in their early twenties and confronting the paradox that fighting to defend Indigenous rights and cultures simultaneously led them to challenge community expectations that they marry. Although some of their fathers agreed and supported their pursuit of education, as I discuss below, many Indigenous women activists faced both censure from their families for not marrying at the typical age like other girls in their pueblos and harassment from men in their communities for this decision. For example, Mixe organizer Cándida Jiménez shared the painful experiences she negotiated as a young woman.

> My situation as a youth was the same. My dad wanted me to marry when I was thirteen years old. I said, "I won't marry at thirteen years old!" But that was disobedience. For 5 years my dad did not speak to me. I wrote to him, I asked him for forgiveness, I said "Aye! Forgive me. Forgive me, I can't. I do not want to marry." He said, "You are not my daughter, I do not know you, I do not want to see you." And I couldn't see him. I kept going [to the pueblo] because I had to see them, to see my mom.
>
> At the same time, men they saw me as free. I was somewhat protected because of my role in the church so I was not seen as so normal but they didn't accept it [my decision] either. They were always bothering me to marry them. Two, three men at a time would follow me, "You need to marry. Let's get married," and all that. I would say, "I don't want to marry, I don't even love you" and with all that how are we going to work and have political participation [as Indigenous women]. (Cándida Jiménez, interview with Maylei Blackwell, August 23, 1999)

In their new roles as community leaders, many Indigenous women activists are required to move between Indigenous municipalities, among different regional centers, to state capitals, to the nation's capital, and even within continental and international circuits of Indigenous activism, and then to return to their home communities. Subsequent generations of CONAMI leaders include both mothers like Fabiola Jurado, who navigated her role as general coordinator of CONAMI and as a mom, and younger women like Paty Torres, who grew up in the Indigenous rights movement with both of her P'urépecha parents and became a youth member of CONAMI in the 2000s, and Ether Trujillo, a Triqui organizer who advocates for the workers in the agricultural fields of San Quintin, Baja California, part of the Oaxacan Indigenous diaspora.

As the narratives below illustrate, navigating scale is something that many Indigenous people learn early in their daily lives, as they regularly confront the vertical and horizontal organization of power as they transit from their pueblo to markets, to larger towns that serve as regional commercial centers, and to administrative and political centers such as municipal cabeceras (heads). Moving between scales revealed the spatial relations that are imbued with racial, classed, and gendered meanings in place. Indeed, it is often when they traveled as girls to municipal heads/centers that Indigenous women first became explicitly conscious of the racial, classed, colonial, and gendered codes of spatial power. Only by crossing from one scale to another did they learn, for example, that being Indigenous was equated with being rural, poor, backward, uneducated, and uncivilized. The very process of struggling for an education while negotiating family and community expectations is, for many Indigenous women activists, their introduction to navigating different scales.

When I first interviewed Hermalinda Turbicio in 2000, she was a powerful young organizer and a member of 500 Years of Indigenous Resistance and CONAMI who went on to found K'inal Antestik (Women's Land in Tzetzal) Guerrero and helped to start CAMI. Born in Yoloxóchitl, the heart of the Mixtec mountains of the Costa Chica region of Guerrero, at the young age of eleven she fled to Ometepec, the municipal capital, to avoid an arranged marriage. There she found work as a domestic worker to eke out a living so she could study and go to high school. She described the physical and emotional journey she went through not only to gain an education and survive but also to begin working on behalf of her community at the local level documenting human rights abuses by the military:

> I left the house very young. We lived . . . well, my father was very poor. I had to run away from my house in order to go study because my father did not want to allow me to go study. He told me, "No, you have to marry, all your sisters already married." Then, one day, I had to escape . . . it was the 9th of June . . . and I went like un tipo [a guy] to study in the city. I arrived and began to search for work. . . . I became trained as a technician of community development. . . . I had to run away from my home. . . .

> I did not return to my home because my father wanted me to marry. I had to seek out a living not knowing how to live nor where, but I enjoyed my autonomy because I was not dependent on my parents, or anyone. I just worked and studied. I never really knew what autonomy meant or if daughters were allowed to study. I thought it was only my father who did not allow me to study, but when I traveled in the communities [later working as an organizer] I saw that nobody studied.
>
> It was very difficult. We women live a very difficult life because many times we are afraid to leave. We don't know what we'll find, how we'll eat or what we'll encounter. So we are always afraid, but when I left, I lost this fear. Even though I felt very, very alone . . . little by little I recovered and after a while saw that I had a future and had to seek out that future. I worked at a market, and I washed people's clothes and later I learned to iron. . . . So my work and my autonomy has cost me a lot, but thank God I learned so many things. It's as if I have lived eighty years and really I have barely lived twenty-three. I learned many things about how to take care of myself. (Hermalinda Turbicio, interview with Maylei Blackwell, March 31, 2000)

While many pueblos have traditions of women's leadership and political participation, some communities in resistance are undergoing cultural, social, and political revitalization as community structures change because of economic, labor, and migratory patterns. The transformation of gender roles can be a source of conflict. Whereas some parents still fear for the lives and personal safety of their daughters, especially in zones that became increasingly militarized—first in order to repress Indigenous movements in the 1990s and later because of the so-called War on Drugs—others have come to respect the work their daughters are doing. Meanwhile, more and more daughters now resist the idea that they must live in community exile in order to be part of the struggle for Indigenous rights. Other leaders are working to bring the changes home by linking the struggle for women's human rights to Indigenous autonomy and structures of traditional authorities. I vividly recall Hermalinda telling me this story of her struggle to earn a living and for education as her tears erupted and started streaming down her face. Over the years, I was deeply affected by three similar stories that were shared with me, and I witnessed the struggle of young Indigenous girls who yearned for an education—some whose tears came because they, like Hermalinda and Monserrat, whose story appears in chapter 4, challenged their fathers. Even when fathers supported their education like Felicitas, whose story I tell next, others endured family separation and abuse in the mestizo homes in which they worked as live-in domestic workers while attending school.

Felicitas Martinez Solano is a Me'phaa leader of la Coordinadora Regional de Autoridades Comunitarias—Policía Comunitaria (the Regional Coordinator of Community Authorities—Communitary Police), also known as the "Comunitaria." She is the daughter of campesinos who grow corn, beans, coffee, and jamaica (hibiscus for tea). Her father encouraged her to go to school because he wanted his daughter to have the same opportunities as everyone else. Their small community of Potrerillo Coapinole had no secondary school, so when she was ten years old, she and her father embarked on a journey to take her to live in a mestizo household where she could attend school for a few hours in the afternoon. She recalled walking "to the next town, Horcasitas, four or five hours [in order] to catch a car down" to the municipal head of San Luis Acatlán, in the state of Guerrero, so she could go to secondary school. Felicitas recalls the major life changes that accompanied this shift:

> All the people who live in the [municipal] head are mestizos. But for me it was a big change because they gave me food that I was not accustomed to. For example, we never drink milk in my pueblo. Because there is a lot of cattle in the municipal head/center, they gave us milk, not from a carton, but from a real cow.... I said "I am not a cat or dog.... In my pueblo, we are not used to this, we eat quelite, ocote, things like that." My dad came to see me ... [and] my godmother [the title given to the woman who let Felicitas live in her house, where she cooked and cleaned in exchange room and board] said, "Your daughter does not want to eat, she does not know how to do anything." ... My dad explained, "I am poor, comadre, my daughter does not know. She is just a girl, she is not grown ... she doesn't know how to use a stove because we cook by wood fire. There we collect wood." Those were the big changes. So I changed places. Leaving, there was shouts [and] crying as I left the house. Can you imagine?! The problem was that there was so much discrimination, racism as well as marginalization because people always called us [in a derogatory tone] "those Indians from the hills."[9] The town was all mestizos and [for food] they gave us only their leftover food to eat. What they had to eat one day was what we would have to eat the following day. The food was hard but, you know, that with hunger, you don't play, you have to eat. (Felicitas Martinez Solano, interview with Maylei Blackwell, November 19, 2015)

Having survived this transition to go to secondary school, at age fourteen, Felicitas made another long journey with her father to the capital of Guerrero,

Chilpancingo. "It was such a long stretch, I felt it was so far because there was no car that could take us directly to Chilpancingo so we passed pueblo, after pueblo, after pueblo." At this point in her story, Felicitas cried as she recounted the memory. I asked why remembering it made her sad.

> Because my dad went to leave me and he returned [to our pueblo] but I could no longer return because it was such a long distance. My dad took the trip just to leave me there but he never knew if I was good, or bad, or if I got sick. Nothing. At fourteen, I was completely alone. In Acatlán, my uncles and my brothers would come down but Chilpancingo was very far [from our pueblo]. We were at a great distance. Also, it was different because it was a city with many cars and buses. That was the other thing that was different from San Luis Acatlán because there are no buses, you walk. You travel to take care of all your business by walking. I arrived at the city, enrolled in high school. The first day I skipped school until the afternoon class because I had to work and the man said he would pay me $100 pesos ... for me, that was *a lot* of money because in secondary school [where I lived before] they never paid us. We were like slaves working all day to do whatever had to be done, go to river to bring water whenever there were dishes to wash. But they did not pay us anything because they gave us a roof—[leftover] food and a roof over our heads. There, at least I had a roof over my head, [and] what's more is that they were also going to pay me. For me that was like being in heaven that they would give me 100 pesos per month and I would go to school in the afternoon shift.
>
> But, there it was also like being a slave because I had to prepare the whole meal and table before going to school at three exactly and I started school at four. Sometimes they would eat at three but sometimes I would miss class [because the family would dine late]. And sometimes I got nothing all month. ... Sometimes el señor would give me ten or twenty pesos because I had asked for an advance for school, for the bus, to make copies in the library. Because sometimes la señora got mad that I would stay late going to the library to make copies or that at night I would do my homework. I stayed about six years in that house and I finished high school working there. (Martinez Solano, interview, November 19, 2015)

Indigenous women activists drew from these often painful life experiences to navigate the differential organization of power at different scales—what I call geographies of difference to name the intersectional ways power is organized—once they began organizing. This shifting between pueblo and municipality, between contexts where power is organized differently—where racial and class power are articulated together and gendered labor is racialized—allowed many Indigenous women to gain the skill of not only moving in and between different scales but also of learning to read how power is organized in each, a form of differential consciousness. Understanding this history and the relevance of Indigenous women's early life experiences is crucial as we turn, next, to the strategies they developed in more explicitly political spaces. Far from encountering completely new, unfamiliar struggles when they began to organize formally, Indigenous women activists drew on existing skills and knowledge from their daily lives. Their formative experiences navigating different scales of power as girls would prove essential to their own efficacy as activists and to the survival of the broader movements of which they are part.

Consulta: Collective Deliberation and the Creation of Indigenous Women's Rights within the Struggle for Indigenous Autonomy

"[Indigenous] autonomy for us women implies the right to autonomy for women, [where] we make ourselves capable to search for spaces and mechanisms to be heard in community assemblies and to have positions of responsibility [cargos]. Similarly, it implies facing our own fears and daring to make decisions and to participate, to seek out economic independence, to have independence in the family, to continue informing ourselves, because knowledge gives us autonomy."[10]

A national Indigenous movement mobilized in the wake of the Zapatista uprising by building on the process and political methodology of consulta, or community consultation, based on Indigenous notions of collective deliberation and civic participation. Consulta not only created links between Indigenous communities and Mexican civil society at large; the articulation of gender-specific demands by Indigenous women was a result of women's mass participation in the process of consultation. For example, the excerpt above emerged from the first national Women's Conference of ANIPA in December of 1995, which gathered together 270 women in San Cristóbal de las Casas, Chiapas, where activists clarified women's demands in relation to the call for Indigenous autonomy through the process of consulta. It shows how, during their communal deliberations about Indigenous autonomy, they scaled down the notion of Indigenous autonomy from a right granted by the state to a practice that women engaged in within community assemblies and in their homes, and they analyzed the multiscalar violence they faced. For example, their final declaration read:

> As Yaqui, Mixe, Nahuatl, Tojolabal, Tlapenec women, each, and every, one of us come from far away to give our palabra (word) in these lands of Chiapas.... In these two days of work, we have talked about the violence that we live within our communities, by our spouses and husbands; by the caciques; the military; of the discrimination that we suffer for being women and Indian; of how the right to land is denied to us and of how we want today to establish that women's opinions be taken into account. We want an autonomy that has a voice, face, and consciousness of women and as such, we can reconstruct the feminine half of the community that has been forgotten. (Declaration of the National Encuentro of Women of ANIPA, 1995)

Organized Indigenous women recognized that forms of self-governance and recognition of cultural and traditional norms based on Indigenous normative systems are positive, but they broke with the uncritical celebrations of tradition to identify both "good and bad customs" during their deliberations about how the right to Indigenous autonomy would function in their lives. There "are customs that can be counterproductive or contrary to the dignity or liberty of women," remarked Juliana Gómez, a Mixtec representative of the Editorial Center of Indigenous Literature in Oaxaca (Santamaria 1996, 7).

These forms of deliberation were also a form of consciousness-raising that produced collective subjectivities and new horizons of women's inclusion and equity, sending reverberations throughout many local community organizations. One of the earliest outcomes of women's consulta was the Women's Revolutionary Law itself, which was deliberated and passed by EZLN base communities on March 8, 1993, and was described as the first Zapatista uprising in a letter published by Subcomandante Marcos in *La Jornada*, describing the process of how the EZLN Women's Law came to be (Marcos 1994). The law very publicly created a space in which women working in mixed-gender organizations could have a voice. The visibility of women's demands and the central role of women in the EZLN empowered other women to create new forms of gender consciousness, articulate their own political demands, and develop a new political language for expressing their agency and sense of cultural belonging. Below, Margarita Gutiérrez, one of the founders of CONAMI, speaks to how her consciousness as an Indigenous woman was born at the negotiation tables between the government and the EZLN to produce the San Andrés Peace Accords. The impact rippled across Mexico—the idea not just of Indigenous autonomy enshrined in the accords, but of Indigenous women activating their autonomy through Indigenous notions of consulta, which in turn deepened and transformed the claim to autonomy into a pedagogy of liberation.

The EZLN convened many actors within the Indigenous movement to negotiate the peace agreement, known as the San Andrés Accords. Women's participation was key to articulating an Indigenous women's political agenda. Initiated in February 1994, the San Andrés Accords were the first of what were supposed to be several rounds of negotiations between the EZLN and the federal government.[11] The accords were eventually signed on February 16, 1996, in San Andrés Larrainzar, renamed by the Zapatistas as San Andés Sacam ch'en (San Andrés of the Poor in Tzotzil). Although the government did not fulfill its side of the negotiations, the Accords on Indigenous Rights and Culture were historically important because they recognized Indigenous pueblos as legal subjects and legitimated the concepts of self-determination and autonomy, thus laying the groundwork for cultural and political autonomy, greater self-determination, and legal claims to Indigenous rights (Hernández Navarro and Vera Herra 1998). The accords guaranteed not only access to political representation within governing state structures but also the validity of internal structures of Indigenous self-government.

Margarita Gutiérrez, a Hñähñú (Otomí) organizer from the state of Hidalgo, who later moved to Chiapas to start a family, came to Indigenous organizing via community radio and went on to participate as a member of two early national Indigenous organizations, the Frente Independiente de Pueblos Indios (FIPI), formed in Mexico in 1987, and CONAMI (see figure 1.2). She later served in the executive leadership of the Secretaría de Pueblos Indígenas of the PRD (the center-left Party of the Democratic Revolution), provided key leadership for Mexico's Indigenous women's movement, and led efforts to train other women in Indigenous law and the workings of the UN so they could participate at the international level, such as in the UN Permanent Forum for Indigenous People. As I prepared to leave for fieldwork in the 1990s, I was falsely warned by an Indigenous male scholar that Indigenous women organized *only* as a way to gain access to international funding. Contrary to this notion, Margarita described to me how Indigenous women came to gendered consciousness and articulated themselves as political subjects *through* the process of Indigenous mobilization: "It was the collective space of coming together that allowed us to clarify our consciousness as Indigenous women and the profound historical knowledge of our pueblos. We suffer double discrimination as Indigenous people and women outside of our communities, in addition to being denied full participation in our own pueblos and the right to speak in community forums. It was our common history that brought us together to consider proposals for

Figure 1.2. Margarita Gutiérrez speaking at the founding encuentro of CONAMI, Oaxaca City, 1997. Photo courtesy of Margarita Gutiérrez.

Indigenous autonomy from the voice of women" (Margarita Gutiérrez, interview with Maylei Blackwell, September 3, 2001). The San Andrés Accords represented a critical shift in consciousness, shaping Margarita's political formation and commitment to working for Indigenous women's rights:

> The EZLN invited me to be an advisor and only two Indigenous women were invited by the EZLN. Bartola, a Chinantec Indigenous compañera from Oaxaca and myself. We are the two that arrived to advise the EZLN [all the way] to the end of the San Andrés Accords. I was in the COCOPA (la Comisión de Concordia y Pacificación/Commission of Concordance and Pacification) that was comprised of *los diputados* (representatives of the lower house of Congress) of all the political parties and later I was in CONAYA (la Comisión Nacional de Intermediación/National Inter-

mediation Commission) that represented various academics and leaders of Mexico including Bishop Samuel Ruiz, Juan Bañuelos, as well as many more including the Rosarios Castellanos group, a group of mestiza women that worked with us [Indigenous women] as an interlocutor with Indigenous advisors and the Zapatistas, but we as Indigenous women, we had a lot of voice.

Also, it was very interesting that there was a plenary during the women's session. Everyone from the other working sessions participated in an open plenary with us. It was like a huge, collective a brainstorm about what should be done, an analysis and proposal [of Indigenous women's rights] discussed by all four hundred to five hundred Indigenous people there, as well as some non-Indigenous people who worked on those issues. But the role of Indigenous people was very important.

[Participating] was my privilege. It was a teaching and a learning. It built on my formation within the struggle for cultural rights to recover the language, to strengthen [Indigenous] languages in young people and in older people who speak but do not know how to write their language. Later came the Convention 169, a tool the Indigenous movement could use to assert that Indigenousness is part of an identity, a way of life, a way of being [that is recognized] through Convention 169 [established in 1989]. (Margarita Gutiérrez, interview with Maylei Blackwell, October 20, 2014)[12]

"Situation, Rights, and Culture of Indigenous Women" was one of the working sessions during the peace dialogues between the EZLN and the government in which Indigenous women, nineteen invited guests, and twelve advisers from Indigenous communities and women's organizations throughout Mexico participated. During this working session, participants recognized that Indigenous women live in the same dire situation as their pueblos, that both men and women are oppressed and discriminated against, and that the Mexican state has demonstrated a racist and sexist attitude of extermination. Ultimately, the invited advisers from both the government and the EZLN reached a consensus recognizing the triple oppression of Indigenous women and their marginalization both inside and outside their communities, the urgent need for greater participation on the part of women under conditions of equality with men, and the need to address different levels of representation and power both within and outside their pueblos (Gutiérrez and Palomo 1999, 65).

One of the key issues to come out of Indigenous women's participation in the dialogues at San Andrés Sacam ch'en, as it had been renamed by the Indigenous participants, was an articulation of women's demand for autonomy.

Women from the Tzotzil, Tzetzal, Tojolabal, Chinantec, Chol, Mixtec, and Hñahñú pueblos deliberated and presented their list of demands despite language barriers. Article E of the San Andrés Accords calls for "legislation about rights of Indigenous pueblos to elect their own authorities and to exercise the authority in accordance to their own norms in the interior of their autonomous environments, guaranteeing the participation of women in conditions of equality" (Palomo 1998, 5). Although the COCOPA did not ratify the women's document, dismissing the struggle for women's rights in the negotiations as a failure would be an oversimplification. Often, we measure the success of social movements by whether they exerted enough pressure for the state to adopt their claims, but it is also critical to note shifts in the discursive terrain and that such struggles create new norms and open a new horizon of meanings (Alvarez, Dagnino, and Escobar 1998). Indeed, the San Andrés Accords reverberated out to several other women's meetings and served as a model for fusing demands for Indigenous autonomy and respect for women's rights. The EZLN members themselves recognized formally that the accords fell short in the area of women: "In reference to the theme, Situation, Rights and Culture of Indigenous Women, the EZLN delegation considers insufficient the actual points of the accords. Due to the triple oppression suffered as women, as Indigenous, as the poor, they demand the construction of a new national society, with a different economic, political, social, and cultural model that would include all (both women and men) Mexicans" (Palomo 1998, 5). The way the Indigenous movement embedded Indigenous women's rights as a central feature of the struggle for Indigenous autonomy in Mexico from the earliest moments is critical to remember. Later, in efforts to deny Indigenous claims to self-governance, the Mexican government sought to cleave the two apart, arguing that Indigenous law discriminates against women. I have argued that this use of gender functioned as a discourse of governmentality to regulate indigeneity and which Indigenous subjects deserve rights, which I have explored elsewhere (Blackwell 2012) and discuss further later in the chapter.

I interviewed Margarita Gutiérrez in 2001 during the UN World Conference Against Racism and again in 2014 in Los Angeles when I conducted extended series of return interviews; we edited those interviews in her home in San Cristobal de las Casas in 2018, days before the EZLN'S first Encuentro internacional politico, artístico, deportivo y cultural de mujeres que luchan (International Gathering of Politics, Art, Sport, and Culture for Women in Struggle).[13] In 2014, reflecting on more than twenty years of Indigenous women's activism, Margarita discussed one of the most unexpected surprises of the negotiations between the government and the EZLN:

To me, my consciousness as an Indigenous woman was born at the *mesa* [working session of Indigenous women] at San Andrés because [before that] I had never known.

It's like something you feel.

When you are struggling for cultural or global rights but [then you are asked by a male comrade], "You say Indigenous women now have rights. What is that?" For me, that was the challenge of San Andrés, to confront it face on; to recognize that we have particular and specific rights as Indigenous women. And this also gave me the strength to struggle when Indigenous compañeros told me, "You are a traitor because you are dividing the struggle of Indigenous pueblos [by calling for women's rights]."

Throughout the years, I have undergone transformations. I think we should work where we feel the best—for example, many Indigenous or women's organizations have invited me [to join] but it just doesn't feel right. I feel at home, like a fish in water within organizations of Indigenous women and when I am in [Indigenous] communities. I know it is there where I belong. I don't have to close myself off because making alliances is also very important. Being with other Indigenous women reinforces my identity and my belonging to that collective. (Gutiérrez, interview, October 21, 2014)

For Margarita, one of the unexpected outcomes of the struggle at the San Andrés Accords was a shift in political consciousness that led her to embrace a collective subjectivity with other Indigenous women that then shaped her lifelong commitments and organizing. Just as prior roots of local Indigenous movements came to the surface to shape the EZLN and its demands, the political force of the Chiapas uprising allowed other Indigenous organizations to generate the momentum to build national Indigenous networks. This vibrant national movement drew from diverse political sectors, and women accompanied the process at each step of its construction, from the surge in regional women's meetings to the women's caucuses and committees at national gatherings. In fact, these two levels of participation, or scales of power, became intertwined and mutually reinforcing. Indigenous women used local and municipal structures to call more women to participate; as they gained a voice and articulated a national agenda, they used those developments to encourage local organizations and Indigenous municipal structures to become more open to women. By responding to the EZLN's charge to spread the word and deliberate the San Andrés Accords, Indigenous women gathered together in collective deliberation or consulta, which I outline below, and began to scale down claims for Indigenous rights to the level of their homes, their communities, and their life choices, merging and vernacularizing collective, individual, Indigenous, and gender rights claims.

Beyond Chiapas, a first step in creating space for women within the broader mobilization of Indigenous peoples in Mexico was in the Zapatista's first National and International Consulta in 1994. The consulta, a form of informal popular deliberation or plebiscite, was developed at the National Democratic Convention in Aguascalientes in August of 1994 as a way to ignite and engage civil society in relation to the Zapatistas' demands and future role as a political entity. The consulta included six questions that were accompanied by a video of Subcomandante Marcos explaining the purpose of each, distributed in print and electronic forms nationally and internationally. It circulated widely from street-level interviews in Mexico City to countries throughout the world, including among Mexican delegates to the UN Conference on Women in Beijing, who distributed the questions. The EZLN gathered more than 1.3 million responses in what is now a widely renowned example of an early, effective, and innovative use of the internet by a social movement (Downing 2000). The sexta pregunta (sixth question) asked whether women should have parity in all cargos (positions) of responsibility and participation; the response was a resounding yes. As Lorena mentioned, Indigenous women began to construct their own collective consciousness and political subjectivity through their participation in a larger civil society mobilization. Unique in Latin American insurgencies and guerilla warfare, the EZLN created a broader alternative vision for democracy. Recognizing that a change in the regime would not be enough to initiate a process of democratization, the EZLN attempted to bring together sectors that previously found little commonality and involve them in the larger project of building a democratic civil society in Mexico. In the years following the uprising in Chiapas, the mobilization of Indigenous peoples continued, spread, and coalesced on the national level, and women made themselves quite visible in this movement by constructing a specific space in which to articulate their own demands, critiques, and hopes as fully participating members of their communities (Bonfil Sánchez and del Pont Lalli 1999, 239).

As detailed by movement pamphlets, memorias, and documents, gendered consciousness within the Indigenous movement was the result of thousands of women activists attending events and collectively deliberating what autonomy means for them and for their communities.[14] Through these grassroots meetings and workshops throughout Mexico, Indigenous women came together, discussed their role in Indigenous cultures, and deliberated what they liked and disliked about usos y costumbres (Hernández Castillo 1994a, 2016; Olivera Bustamante 1994). In Chiapas alone, approximately twenty-four women's organizations met in August 1994 and held a second session in October that brought together five hundred women from one hundred organizations (Palomo, Castro, and Orci 1999).[15]

Workshops and meetings of this nature served as consciousness-raising sessions in which Indigenous women drew from their daily lived experience to analyze the structures that oppressed them and the cultural, economic, and political processes that excluded them. Specifically, these early workshops began conversations that would spread across the nation in relation to the consultation process initiated by the San Andrés Accords and to national and regional meetings organized to discuss Indigenous normative systems and the role of women's rights in the fight for Indigenous autonomy. In their deliberations, many women reaffirmed Indigenous cultural practices that empowered them as women and their collective self-determination and autonomy as Indigenous peoples: traditional dress, knowledge of traditional medicine, juridical systems, and their own cosmovisions. But women also began to challenge collectively some "traditional" cultural practices; in doing so, they reaffirmed that Indigenous cultures are living and that traditions change (Stephen 2005). In Chiapas, many women began to question forced marriage, lack of access to reproductive health care, and lack of control over their own reproduction. They agreed that autonomy for Indigenous women includes having control over one's body and that women must make their own decisions about life partners and when and if to bear children, and how many to have. This early strategy of scaling down to the body has had other outcomes such as a resurgence in Indigenous birthing practices and the midwifery movement that has emerged to fight the high rate of Indigenous infant and maternal mortality. These translocal meetings became the catalyst for consensus among women nationally and regionally that Indigenous customs and practices should be honored only when they respect "the human rights of Indigenous women" and when they do not "threaten their dignity."[16]

The strategy of collective consulta shared by actors in many Indigenous social movements throughout Mexico is critical for women because of their historical exclusion from structures of governance and decision-making within the Mexican government and many Indigenous communities. Indigenous women activists have emphasized practices of autonomy, rather than the state discourse of rights, by scaling autonomy down to daily lived realities and a gendered analysis of power. In this way, autonomy has become a practice of decolonization that furthers the goals of the Indigenous movement with or without state approval. The point is not to supplant or substitute state engagement but rather to multiply the scales at which autonomy can be practiced. These alternative strategies that social movement actors elaborate have broad implications for rights discourse and Indigenous autonomy in the era of neoliberalism.

The work of organized Indigenous women on the question of autonomy addresses the proposal for state reform but also moves beyond engagement with the state. They have expanded the process by engendering the Indigenous movement's call for autonomy to include Indigenous women's bodily, political, and cultural autonomy. Through grassroots consultation in numerous local, municipal, and national forums, workshops, meetings, and gatherings throughout the country during the decades since the Zapatista uprising, activist Indigenous women have developed an analysis of Indigenous autonomy as a practice that occurs largely at the level of daily life and often outside the state's purview (Blackwell 2006; Hernández Castillo 1997; Lovera and Palomo 1999; Palomo, Castro, and Orci 1999) (see figure 1.3). These forums created a grassroots pedagogy of autonomy for women in Indigenous communities, allowing the most marginalized actors within marginalized communities to make decisions about the parameters and practices of Indigenous autonomy, rather than waiting for the state, or even their leaders, to define its limits (Blackwell 2004; Gutiérrez and Palomo 1999; Speed, Hernández Castillo, and Stephen 2006). Women have used the practice of giving one's opinion or perspective, *dar su palabra*, to add their own innovations to the conversation

Figure 1.3. CONAMI workshop participants at the First National Encuentro of CONAMI, Oaxaca City, 1997. Photo courtesy of Margarita Gutiérrez.

about how and where Indigenous autonomy is practiced. This has transformed how women experience themselves as community members and political actors, how they participate in community assemblies and political congresses, and how their ideas are heard. It has also shaped a new sense of collective identity that empowers Indigenous women in their own communities and builds momentum toward a national movement, as Lynn Stephen (2011) has explored in relation to women's participation in the Oaxacan popular uprising of 2006.

Nunca Más un México Sin Nosotras/Never Again a Mexico with Us: Forging a National Indigenous Women's Movement in Mexico

Consulta is a form of deliberation that allowed organized Indigenous women in Mexico in the 1990s to create a shared agenda and multiscalar strategy of autonomy. If consulta was important to building local and regional scales of resistance for Indigenous women as I explored in the last section, it was also crucial to their work in creating organizational networks at the scale of the national. Activists used the scale of the national as a platform to give visibility to and expand the notion of autonomy for Indigenous women at the scale of the body, the home, and the community thereby interweaving scale. At the national level in Mexico, several gatherings were key sites for convergence and dialogue in forging an Indigenous women's rights agenda after the San Andrés Peace Accords, including the National Democratic Convention, the National Indigenous Forum, and the Seminar on Reforms to Article 4 of the Constitution. In each national political formation that grew out of the Indigenous movement of the 1990s, women constructed internal structures of participation and representation, such as the Women's Commissions of ANIPA and the CNI.[17] As the Indigenous movement grew at the national level, activist Indigenous women also created a parallel structure of political participation when they began convening, organizing, and attending national Indigenous women's meetings as early as 1995. The structure and the need to have an Indigenous women's national space in turn served as the organizational impetus to build their own network, CONAMI, in 1997. In perhaps an unexpected way, the construction of the national network of Indigenous women in Mexico was also the result of organizing around the international arena, such as preparations for the Fourth World Conference on Women and the UN Decade of Indigenous Peoples, as well as transnational organizational processes—specifically, hosting a meeting of the Continental Network of Indigenous Women, as I explore further in chapter 2. Indeed, it can be argued that in Mexico, the national scale of organizing came into being to bridge and weave together local/regional organizing and transnational organizing.

In August 1995 at the third ANIPA, held in the city of Oaxaca, Josefa González Ventura, a Ñu Savi women well respected for her long history of struggle, was successful in calling for a working session on the rights of women. In one of the first statements of women to emerge from the Indigenous movement outside of Chiapas, participants at this session devised a multiscalar strategy that explicitly called for women's political participation "in the home, the community, the municipalities, in autonomous regions, and at the national level." Further, a "national meeting of Indigenous women was proposed in order to have more in-depth discussion and analysis of the initiative for a law of autonomous regions" (Gutiérrez and Palomo 1999, 64). A group of 270 women from different parts of the country and diverse pueblos came together at the Encuentro Nacional de Mujeres de la ANIPA in San Cristóbal de las Casas, Chiapas, in December 1995, two days before the fourth assembly. To continue building a larger space of participation for Indigenous women, they agreed to search for forms of organization that they hoped would grow into a national network. The Special National Forum on Indigenous Rights and Culture, convened by the EZLN to forge dialogue on the San Andrés Accords, held its first working session, "Indigenous Culture and Rights," on January 3–8, 1996.

Over the next six months, three hundred delegates met in Oaxaca, Jalisco, Veracruz, San Luis Potosí, Puebla, Tabasco, Campeche, Quintana Roo, and Michoacán. In July 1996, the delegates met again in Chiapas, but on August 29, the EZLN left negotiations with the federal government to demand the release both of Zapatistas who were detained in northern Chiapas and of other political prisoners. They made it clear, however, that they were not breaking off the negotiations, only demanding minimal conditions before they would continue. It was in the context of increasing militarization that organizations within the Permanent National Indigenous Forum convened an urgent meeting in Mexico City in October 1996 to plan a large encuentro of all Indigenous organizations in the country (Hernández Navarro 1999). Although a stalemate occurred between the EZLN and the government, which would not grant the right of free transit, the EZLN selected Comandanta Ramona, a respected member of the EZLN, to be their representative at the meeting. Ramona and one thousand delegates came to the meeting, where the National Indigenous Congress was formalized. The formation of the CNI was a unifying moment in the Indigenous movement. There, María de Jesús Patricio, one of the founding members of CONAMI whom we met earlier, read the final declaration.

During this period, the Indigenous women's movement was also growing and consolidating. In the Women's Commission of the National Indigenous Forum in January 1996, participants further considered the accords approved in San Andrés. Through the Women's Commission of the CNI and a national meeting of Indigenous women, the First National Encuentro of Indigenous Women was planned. Called "Constructing Our Own History," the encuentro was held in Oaxaca in 1997 (figure 1.4). With more than seven hundred Indigenous women in attendance from diverse states, organizations, and most of Mexico's sixty-eight pueblos, as well as Comandanta Ramona and a women's delegation from the EZLN, the formation of CONAMI was seen as a historic mandate. Cándida Jiménez, a Mixe promotora (community educator) from Oaxaca, stated, "In this great event, we agreed that it was the moment to unite forces and to work together toward the respect of our rights that have been violated. The Coordinadora Nacional de Mujeres Indígenas was given formality and a representative from each state was chosen" (Jiménez, interview, August 23, 1999). CONAMI, formed August 30, 1997, focused its early agenda on human rights, reproductive health, stopping family and military violence, and collective

Figure 1.4. The First National Encuentro of Indigenous Women, Oaxaca City, 1997. Photo courtesy of Margarita Gutiérrez.

self-education on international and national treaties, pacts, accords, and conventions concerning the rights of Indigenous peoples, specifically from the perspective of Indigenous women. The objectives of CONAMI were to

> construct a space for analysis [of] and reflection on the problems confronting Indigenous women in Mexico; to sensitize Indigenous pueblos and national society to respect the human rights of Indigenous women, including a vision of gender; to influence in an organized manner the political, social, and cultural processes that affect Indigenous women; to fortify and consolidate the Coordinadora Nacional de Mujeres Indígenas as a site of coordination between all organizations, networks, and projects as a plural and inclusive space of indigenous women throughout the country; and to fortify the processes of autonomy and self-determination of Indigenous pueblos, with conscious and true participation of women. (*Construyendo nuestra historia* 1997)

CONAMI's goal was to operate as a representative coordinating body of the organized Indigenous women's movement in Mexico, consisting of approximately one hundred organizations. They defined themselves as "a space of Indigenous women who struggle against forms of social domination and exclusion, and who revendicate a communal identity, specific territories and autonomy; where a debate is produced about their rights as women and as Indigenous peoples" (*Construyendo nuestra historia* 1997). Members participated as representatives of their own pueblos' traditional governing structures as well as community and rural organizations, regional associations, and peasant collectives. Whereas a good number of the participants belonged to independent Indigenous women's groups, most belonged to mixed-gender organizations of men and women, so CONAMI functioned as a vital space of participation, reflection, and strategy for Indigenous women's organizing. Some of these organizations include UCIZONI and SER from Oaxaca and the Consejo Guerrerense 500 Años de Resistencia Indígena, as well as the Consejo de Pueblos Nahuas del Alto Balsas from Guerrero, Consejo de la Nacionalidad Nauhautl from the state of Mexico, and the Nación Purhéphecha Zapatista from Michoacán. An impressive number of Indigenous women's organizations also exist, such as Grupo de Mujeres Indígenas and Masehual Siuamej Mosenyolchikaunij (meaning women who work together and support one another) from Puebla; Mujeres Indígenas en Lucha and Mujeres Independientes, both from Guerrero; Mujeres Olvidadas del Rincón Mixe from Oaxaca; Grupo Erandi (*erandi* means "dawn" in P'urépecha) from Michoacán; and Grupo de Mujeres de San Cristóbal de las Casas Chiapas. A large cross section came to CONAMI from peasant organizations, both mixed and women's groups, such as the Consejo Estatal de Organizaciones Indígenas y Campesinas, the Asociación Rural de Interés Colectivo, and the Central Independiente de Obreros Agrícolas y Campesinos—all from Chiapas—as well as women's rural and peasant organizations such as the Unión de Mujeres Campesinas de Xilitla from San Luis Potosí, the S. S. S. Titekititoke Tajome Sihuame from Guerrero, and the S. S. S. Maseualsiuamej Mosenyolchikaunij from Puebla. Women from groups organized around productive projects such as small coffee producers from Veracruz and Puebla, and women's weaving collectives such as J'Pas Lumetik and Jolom Mayaetik of Chiapas, also participated.

The original structure of CONAMI included three representatives from each state in Mexico, all of whom attended bimonthly national meetings and served on the five commissions that were set up to address financing, human rights, international organizing, training, and capacity-building. CONAMI held several national workshops and trained promotoras in areas ranging from reproductive health and human rights to the prevention of violence against women and Indigenous women's autonomy. The national workshops scaled down Indigenous autonomy by centering on internal community issues such as reproductive health, violence against women and intrafamilial violence, greater participation of women in pueblos' decision-making structures, a reconsideration of Indigenous normative systems so they do not violate women's dignity, and women's right to inherit land. Training on and discussion of issues external to pueblos included demands for human, cultural, collective, and territorial rights of Indigenous peoples; a stop to violence against Indigenous women carried out by police and military forces as well as state agencies; and enforcement of international conventions on labor, discrimination against women, intellectual property rights, and biological diversity. Further, one of the three representatives from each state attended monthly meetings in Mexico City throughout the year in addition to workshops, forums, and talks organized in the capital and in regions where CONAMI was active in the early years, such as Chiapas, Michoacán, Morelos, Mexico City, Guerrero, Hidalgo, Jalisco, State of Mexico, Puebla, Queretaro, San Luis Potosí, Sonora, Veracruz, and Oaxaca. The work of the early organizing of CONAMI was accompanied by the feminist NGO K'inal Antsetik Distrito Federal, in particular by Nellys Palomo, an Afro-Colombian socialist feminist and psychotherapist specializing in healing trauma whose team supported CONAMI by systematizing the work of the organization, housing the office, and providing administrative support for the organization's financial resources.[18]

Although most women in CONAMI came from their local or regional organizations, they represented the ideological diversity of various approaches and organizational sites of the national Indigenous movement in Mexico in the 1990s. Several women participated in both ANIPA and the CNI. Margarita Gutiérrez has been a member of ANIPA since its founding and has served as executive president. Martha Sánchez, former general coordinator of ANIPA, is an Amuzgo from Xochistlahuaca, Guerrero; former secretary of 500 Años de Resistencia Indígena; and a leader of CONAMI. Many women, including María de Jesús Patricio, Sofía Robles, Ernestina Ortiz, and Cándida Jiménez, have been on CONAMI's coordinating team and were active in the CNI. While some male activists from these organizations were unable to work together, diverse elements of the Indigenous sector worked to build CONAMI, which established and maintains its autonomy from both the CNI and ANIPA. When I first interviewed her in 1999, Sofía Robles explained this history and the importance of Indigenous women's organizational autonomy and their strategies of moving in and between organizational spaces to create new modes of articulation for themselves:

> Well, the CNI named a women's commission, and I am part of this CNI women's commission with other women. But then we continued, in addition to the CNI commission, parallel to this, we continued to maintain a small women's space. This was where we talked and we gained strength. It was like being in dialogue with the CNI. And this is where the Coordinadora originated.... [It] was born after the First National Encuentro of Indigenous Women, already the most inclusive encuentro where several organizations participated. The CNI has had its lows, it has had its difficult times.... But the important part is that women's issues are maintained, right? Independently from the CNI.... And I think that this was a good thing because if the CNI falls, the women are still there. It's like a CNI working group, but it is not the CNI, nor is it because of the CNI that we meet, but rather it is because of the desire to maintain a Coordinadora Nacional, to make it possible for women. (Robles, interview, August 31, 1999)

This organizational autonomy from the members' organizations and the conflicts and blockages members faced in those organizations illustrates the importance of CONAMI to the Indigenous women's movement—in particular to those women who were activists in mixed-gender organizations. Despite women's participation at every step of building the national Indigenous movement in Mexico, they have been blocked at the national level at a few critical junctures. For example, at the CNI in Mexico City in October 1996, Indigenous women activists who were members of the organization mobilized to hold a working session dedicated to discussing Indigenous women's issues. Building on and working to protect the advances organized Indigenous women had made, specialists in gender, jurisprudence, and Indigenous law analyzed the San Andrés Accords, strategies for implementation, and multicultural state reform in a series of monthly meetings convened as the Seminar on the Legislation and Women, focusing on article 4 (now article 2 after renumbering) of the constitution, and brought the results to the CNI.[19] Yet there was opposition to the proposal to create a women's session at the 1996 CNI and the motion to consider the proposal was defeated by fifty votes (among the five hundred delegates). Whereas some activists saw this as a devastating blow that signaled a lack of support for women's rights in the national Indigenous movement, others adopted a different stance: "The women won our first battle. Because, even though some leaders supported our proposals and others opposed [them], we had some male allies in favor of our organization as women" (Gutiérrez, interview, September 3, 2001). Working quickly, the women came up with an alternative plan; the resolution that passed established that the document outlining the results of the seminar on Indigenous women's rights in the San Andrés Accords and multicultural state reform would have to be discussed during each of the working sessions. Some viewed this blockage as a defeat, whereas others reframed it as a victory, claiming that their initial proposal to have a women's working session was successful in guaranteeing that women's concerns were to be taken up during each of the working sessions of the CNI that year.

Indigenous women's voices and issues were denied space at yet another critical juncture five years later at the Third National Indigenous Congress held in March 2001, where the proposal to dedicate one of the simultaneous working sessions to women's concerns was blocked. As I describe at the beginning of the prelude, there was a proposal to have one of the many working sessions of the meeting dedicated to discussion of Indigenous women's rights. Although many sectors of the Indigenous movement, including the EZLN, gave an outpouring of support, there was also resistance. The proposed women's session overflowed with participants. At the beginning of the discussion, each woman who stood to propose the women's session and defend the importance of the issues advanced for discussion met with several men who argued that there should not be a separate space for Indigenous women's issues. Gathered in a big room in which participants sat in concentric circles, the delegates debated furiously. After about an hour, the opposition receded into the ocean of voices of those activists who had new proposals, debates, and ideas about women's rights, Indigenous law, and women's participation in the Indigenous movement and community assemblies. Eventually the tide turned solely to discussing Indigenous women's issues. Members of CONAMI and CNI, including Tomasa Sandoval from Erandi, a P'urépecha women's organization from Michoacán, and Mixe activist Cándida Jiménez, an early CONAMI organizer, spoke in favor of a women's session. This current was supported both by delegates of the EZLN joining the session, who spoke out in favor of supporting women's rights, and by Blanca Chancoso, a principal leader of the Confederation of Indigenous Nationalities of Ecuador (known as CONAIE, an acronym from its Spanish name) who made a statement of solidarity (figure 1.5).

As I chronicled the emergence and early years of CONAMI over the years, I found that part of what inspired these women to form a national network was actually a desire to have a national organized presence that would allow them to be able to host the Second Continental Network of Indigenous Women (ECMIA), which I explore in chapter 2; early blockages within the CNI only underscored the need for that space. The multiple scales of Indigenous women's organizing within national organizations, along with the powerful organizing of women in local spaces such as EZLN base communities, had long-term success. This is evident in the centrality of women's rights within CNI proclamations in recent years that routinely demand an end patriarchy, a victory for Indigenous women's organizing I touch on in the coda of this book.

Figure 1.5. CONAMI activist Cándida Jimenez and leader Blanca Chancoso speaking to those gathered for the Women's Session of the CNI, Nurio, Michoacán, 2001. Photo by author.

Scaling Up Indigenous Regions, Communities, and Bodies in the Struggle Against Violence

In the spring of 2000 at the Second National Encuentro of Indigenous Women, I gathered with five hundred participants from twelve states—representing more than fifty organizations, a wide array of Indigenous women's groups, and mixed Indigenous organizations, organized and convened by CONAMI—to discuss the theme of the gathering: "¡Construyendo la Equidad, Democracia y Justicia!" (Constructing Equity, Democracy, and Justice) (see figure 1.6). There I saw how activists used this national platform to bring attention to the gendered violence linked to the increased militarization of Chiapas, Oaxaca, and Guerrero. For example, Hermalinda Tiburcio from Rancho Nuevo a la Democracia discussed the importance of Indigenous women speaking for themselves: "[We need women] with their own voice to state what they are experiencing in the Indigenous zones because much of the time it is from the desks [those who have the power to write] who say that nothing is occurring in the Indigenous zones." Other activists from Guerrero used the encuentro to draw media attention to the increasing number of human rights violations within and growing militarization of that state. Although there was a formal meeting

Figure 1.6. Opening plenary at the Second National Encuentro of CONAMI, Chilpancingo, Guerrero, 2000. Photo by author.

with working sessions during which specific themes were discussed at length, denunciations of human rights violations were strategically presented to the media and effectively captured the attention of the press and of officials from various governmental agencies who were present. The documented cases and denunciations centered on human rights violations in the Indigenous zones of Oaxaca and Guerrero. Other activists called attention to the practice of forced sterilization (without informed consent) by employees of the Secretariat of Health and a demand for an end to government antipoverty programs that promote the sterilization of Indigenous women, illustrating how activists used the national scale to call attention to the scale of the body as a site of colonial violence. Other women from the municipalities of Ayutla and Acatepec were present to give testimony about their experiences. The four Indigenous groups of Guerrero—Amuzgo, Mixteco, Tlapaneco, and Nahua—joined to denounce the militarization of their communities. Libni Iracema Dircio, speaking on behalf of Titekititoki Tajome Sihuame, an organization in Chilapa, stated, "We have been trying to push for the defense of human rights for Indigenous people, and we know [that,] above all, it is the woman who is discriminated against, harassed and repressed, and for that reason, we are struggling."

Many women gave reports on human rights from the perspective of their communities, and several individual cases, such as two cases of rape the previous year in Barrio Nuevo San José in the municipality of Tlacoachistlahuaca, were also discussed. The women who suffered these attacks gave their testimonies, as did women from Santíago Mixquetitlán and San Ildefonso, both spaces that were overrun with military and police at the time. Cándida Jiménez, the Mixe organizer from Oaxaca, stated, "There is repression against Indigenous pueblos and even more against the poor, where violations of our rights as women [exist], because we have little backing from anyone, let alone from the institutions." Many women noted that the military entered their communities on the pretext of reforestation programs or anti-narcotrafficking activities, but the end result was political repression and violence against women. A theme of the testimonies given in Chilpancingo was that the responsible governmental agencies have consistently denied that such violations occur, signaling a longer state strategy that CONAMI would later challenge in a social media campaign, which I discuss at the end of this chapter. As Martha Sánchez stated at the event, "Even though [the government] says that there are no abuses against Indigenous women, we say that there are, and for this reason we will present testimonies [from the victims,] and included [at this Encuentro] will be women who have been subjected to humiliating situations of having their human rights violated."

Several women gave testimony about specific kinds of violations occurring in their regions and communities. Doña Rufina Villa, a leader of the historic Indigenous women's organization Masehual Siuamej Mosenyolchicauani, founded in 1984, recognized the many kinds of violence that Indigenous women face both within and outside their homes, which constitute violations of their right to bodily autonomy. Rufina Villa is from Cuetzlan in the Sierra Norte of Puebla, and she put it like this: "There is no violence from the Mexican military [in my region], but there is violence from the police who beat and violate the rights of the youth. In addition, there is more intrafamilial violence against women and children." Part of CONAMI's work has been to recognize the various forms of violence in Indigenous women's lives, and much of that work—learning about violence and what it means to live in families and communities that are free of violence as the pedagogy of Indigenous autonomy—that happened in workshops, allowing women to scale down these forms of analysis and visioning into their own homes, families, and bodies (see figure 1.7).

The early work of CONAMI was critical in legitimating women community leaders and providing them with a national stage from which they could analyze and articulate the intersection of Indigenous, women's, and economic

Figure 1.7. Group photo at the Second National Encuentro of CONAMI, 2000, featuring Sofía Robles (*top row, far left*), Rufina Villa (*top row, second from left*), Cándida Jimenez (*top row, third from left*), and María de Jesús Patricio (*bottom row, far left*). Photo by author.

rights. For example, Hermalinda Turbicio, the Mixtec activist from Guerrero whose history I shared earlier, was unexpectedly catapulted into a leadership role as she began coordinating denunciations and calling media attention to the increasing number of human rights violations and the growing militarization that occurred in the sierra of Guerrero after el Rancho Nuevo a la Democracia declared itself an autonomous Indigenous region. In the heart of the mountains, the Indigenous municipalities of Tlacoachistlahuaca, Metlatonoc, and Xochistlahuca declared themselves autonomous, breaking from the government and forming an Indigenous municipality in rebellion on December 16, 1995. This event occurred after approximately one hundred people from thirteen villages walked nearly thirty-five miles to take part in a seven-month occupation of the Municipal Palace in Tlacoachistlahuaca, where their demands included the completion of a development plan for the region (to include paved roads, running water, and electricity) and recognition of elected municipal commissioners from their communities. After seeing no results from their action, a remote village of approximately seven hundred Mixtecs joined together to declare themselves an autonomous Indigenous municipality and change their name from Rancho Viejo (Old Ranch) to Rancho Nuevo a la Democracia (New Ranch for Democracy). This declaration of autonomy was just one of many happening throughout Indigenous communities across Mexico at that time—including in Chiapas, Michoacán, Guerrero, Hidalgo, and Yaqui territory—that spans several states and, indeed, crosses settler colonial borders. When they began their struggle, Mixtec activists witnessed incursions from the Judicial State Police, the Mexican army, and paramilitary groups; increases in threats, disappearances, torture, and murders have been documented. Specifically, human rights activists have decried the murder of at least thirteen Indigenous peasants in the region, Rancho Nuevo witnessed the incarceration of their leaders, and numerous rapes occurred—conditions that initially thrust Hermalinda into leadership when she was the secretary of the organization.

Participation in national organizations such as CONAMI has helped validate women's local leadership and support and deepen the work of leaders like Hermalinda. From her humble beginnings as a secretary, she began to participate in the struggle and provided leadership in the community by organizing the denunciations of the human rights violations and repression. Hermalinda described how she began, how the community slowly changed their view of her leadership, and how CONAMI played a role in her work:

> My life, I've dedicated many years of my life to the empowerment capacity building of Indigenous women. It cost me a lot to get here, but it

has been a space that I have been earning, and ... well, I am [still] very young in this struggle. In 1998 I came as the secretary in the autonomous [Indigenous] municipality of Rancho Nuevo a la Democracia. I arrived there as a secretary in the municipal government ... and I began to live in another world. I saw the community members' struggle, and then I had to join the struggle.... There were many deaths before I arrived.... They've been struggling for five years, [but] the municipality has not been recognized yet.

... Life like this [in the struggle] has been very difficult, in part because I am a woman, and it is very difficult to travel through the communities. The community members have attacked me a lot; those who think that they are the only ones with the moral authority to do things. So during those years I've lived, kind of in that crisis, they tell me, "No, but it's that you're a woman, you can't govern." ... [During the] six months when one of the community leaders was put in jail, then we did everything we could, thanks to the community members, who supported me a lot. We took several measures and then, well, the people recognized my capacity to resolve issues, to solve problems, to take the necessary measures, and to bring in women so that they too are empowered. Joining with the coordinadora [CONAMI] helps me to find other ways that women can participate [so that] it won't just be me who comes out to speak, but that in time there will be more and more women [speaking].... Because I would want all of my knowledge and my ideas to be transmitted to other women. (Turbicio, interview, March 31, 2000)

In addition to working to found K'inal Antsetik and Casa de Mujer Indígena in Guerrero, and participating in the Guerreran Coordinator of Indigenous Women, one of the state networks established by CONAMI (discussed in chapter 3), Hermalinda continued to work against violence against women and to demand access to reproductive health, specifically to accompany pregnant Indigenous women, which included educational work and walking with them to make sure they can access health services and midwives in remote rural settings to prevent maternal death. She was among the first activists to denounce sexual violence on the part of the military, including the rapes of Francisca Evarista Santos Pablo and Victoriana Vásquez Sánchez of Barrio Nuevo San José, Municipio de Tlacoachistlahuaca, who, while searching for a missing family member the women arrived at a milpa, where the found their family member killed and where they were raped by soldiers. For her denunciation, false charges were fabricated against her and a warrant was issued for her apprehension; neither was dismissed until there was a formal demand for protection in 2003. She continues to work on human rights for Indigenous youth, women, and men and regularly receives death threats; she was shot at in 2010 and survived a kidnapping attempt in 2012 (García Martínez 2015). She went on to get a degree in psychology and continues her work with K'inal Antesetik Guerrero, running programs such as Protected Sexuality for Indigenous Girls and Youth for Holistic Development. The Human Rights Commission of the Distrito Federal honored her in 2015 with the Ponciano Arriaga Award, in recognition of her lifelong work. Hermalinda, along with the others mentioned earlier, are just some of the Indigenous women activists who used CONAMI's second encuentro to scale their local human rights struggle to the national spotlight and begin to call attention to violence against Indigenous women and the massive multiscalar corruption and impunity that let perpetrators of this violence continue. They were the first to signal the wide-scale violence against Indigenous communities, and women in particular, in a way that foreshadowed the devastating violence of the drug war and the state violence that have consumed communities more recently.

At the Second National Gathering of Indigenous Women, I was in the audience when something Tomasa Sandoval said struck me. She argued that the seeming tension between the autonomy of Indigenous women and the autonomy of Indigenous pueblos is "dos rostros de un mismo problema" (two faces of the same problem). She noted that autonomy has two dimensions: first, the individual rights of each human being, into which the call for autonomy for Indigenous women fits; and second, a corresponding collective right to autonomy for Indigenous peoples. Cutting through the ways in which these two issues have been called contradictory, Sandoval stated, "An Indigenous women's right to autonomy cannot exist without the guarantee of autonomy for Indigenous peoples. The individual right and the collective right do not contradict one another; they are complementary. That is why we insist that both individual and collective autonomy be strengthened. This will require creativity and initiative because it is a very difficult and long task." Sandoval noted that it is important to see autonomy as a faculty that historically has emerged out of relations of domination and inequality. Indigenous pueblos have sought out autonomy based on the historic cultures of their peoples and the fact that many pueblos have practiced forms of community autonomy for centuries, with their own traditional structures operating outside of the state. Sandoval claimed that whereas autonomy is largely thought of as a juridical question, calls for various levels of autonomy—individual, communal, municipal, and regional—are interlinked and vital to one another. She even suggested that without a consideration of women, the political and cultural project of Indigenous autonomy would not be "a complete autonomy because women's right to land and to equality with men is not recognized." This idea, echoed in many other forums, is a key feature of the political vision that emerged from Indigenous women's organizing at the time. It builds on the idea that Indigenous women's rights are inalienable and inextricably linked to both Indigenous peoples' rights and women's rights. This perspective was much needed in debates on multiculturalism and women's rights, which often viewed women purely as individuals who can somehow be isolated from other determining social, cultural, and economic factors (Moller Okin et al. 1999). Despite Sandoval's insights and the collective understanding of the interwoven nature of women's rights and Indigenous rights forged by the Indigenous women's movement, the year following the CONAMI's Second National Encuentro, the Mexican congress revealed its own gendered form of racism during the deliberations of the COCOPA law that was the result of the San Andrés Peace Accords negotiations.

Between a Rock and a Hard Place in the Struggle for Autonomy: The Debate over Indigenous Governance and the Gendered Logic of Racism in Mexico

The 2001 congressional debate on passing the proposed COCOPA law, which would have recognized Indigenous peoples' right to autonomy and respect for Indigenous rights and culture, became embroiled in a form of racism that uses gender in a duplicitous way to deny Indigenous rights. Mexican legislators used a false concern for women's rights to deny the full range of Indigenous rights agreed to at the San Andrés Peace Accords. Indigenous women activists were right there on the front lines demanding that their struggle for women's rights within Indigenous cultures—by then more than a decade long—not be erased. EZLN Comandanta Esther's 2001 historic speech to the Mexican legislature and comments from other Indigenous rights movement activists passionately called attention to the strides they had made and the irony that no one else in Mexico is denied their cultural rights because patriarchy and gender discrimination are rampant (Hernández Castillo 2002a; Marcos 2005). They addressed legislators who continued to use a gendered form of racism to perpetuate the stereotype that Indigenous communities are backward and unmodern, and thus inherently more sexist. This gendered logic of racism locks the question of Indigenous rights into externally imposed Western notions that split gender from race/indigeneity. For example, when the Zapatistas first recognized women's rights as part of the agenda during their January 1, 1994, uprising, the newspaper *El Despertator* printed the EZLN's Revolutionary Women's Law, pundits held that up as evidence that the movement was not truly Indigenous and must be the result of foreign, outside influence or feminist infiltrators. On the other hand, despite a decade of Indigenous women's activism that brought together Indigenous and women's rights, when Indigenous rights were debated and codified into law in 2001, full autonomy was denied because legislators claimed Indigenous normative systems violate women's rights—though Mexico's own track record on women's rights leaves much room for improvement. Yet organized Indigenous activists who have insisted on the simultaneity of Indigenous and women's rights have troubled the legitimacy of the state's gendered logic of racism against Indigenous autonomy.

One of the clearest responses to the state's gendered logic of racism came in Comandanta Esther's powerful 2001 speech, one of the first times an Indigenous woman had spoken from the floor of the Congress:

> We, in addition to being women, are Indigenous and as such, we are not recognized. We know which are good and which are bad traditions and customs. The bad ones include hitting or beating women, the selling and buying [of women], marriage by force against her will, not being allowed to participate in assembly, not being permitted to leave the house. This is why we want the Indigenous Rights and Culture Law to be approved. It is very important to us, Indigenous women all over Mexico. It will mean that we are recognized and respected as the women and the Indigenous people we are. This means that we want to have our form of dress, speaking, governance, organization, prayer, healing, our form of working in collectives, of respecting the earth, and understanding life, that is the natural world we are part of. Our rights as women are also included in this law, so that no one will be able to prevent our participation, our dignity or [the] integrity of our work, the same as men. This is why we tell the Deputies and Senators to carry out their duties, to be true representatives of the people.[20]

Serving as a delegate of the women's commission of the CNI, María de Jesús Patricio, who participated in the formation of CONAMI, also spoke to the legislature that day. She responded to questions posed by deputies about women's rights within Indigenous autonomy. She said:

> Retaking the issue of whether [Indigenous] customs and practices injure Indigenous women in the pueblos, in the communities, we feel that it is

not only a problem of Indigenous people. No, it goes beyond that, it is all of civil society as well. Yet only the negative is attributed to Indigenous peoples. The problem is [the perception] that if the COCOPA initiative is approved, it is going to damage women. We say no. To the contrary, it will fortify the equitable participation of both men and women. Of course, there are problems that we are eliminating and refining, but it's not only Indigenous pueblos, it is everyone. I believe this implies that we need to be united as Indigenous pueblos, civil society and all those who want to create an alternative response to this situation we are living in now.[21]

On the one hand, Indigenous women activists, who have waged a grassroots challenge to have the full right to participate in Indigenous movements they helped create, forged a new political project that upholds both the rights of women and of Indigenous people. Yet, on the other hand, the state's use of gender as a discourse of governmentality redeploys the historic construct of Indigenous people as stubborn roadblocks to modernity and progress. The gendered logic of racism in Mexico has a long history, as illustrated by the way the Malinche complex functions to lay the responsibility for colonization of Indigenous people at the feet of one woman, Malintzin Tenepal, an enslaved noblewoman who served as interpreter for Christopher Columbus. The gendered logic of racism in the contemporary moment views Indigenous communities as somehow more sexist by positing Indigenous people as premodern, uncivilized, and perpetually stuck in a temporal frame of "pastness." In a circuitous formulation, Indigenous peoples are seen as backward, nonmodern subjects who are unable to govern themselves precisely because they are situated temporally always in the past, which is measured, in part, by Western liberal notions of gender and modernity. This dominant view ignores the diversity of sex/gender systems of Indigenous peoples in Mexico, the role of colonialism in imposing a patriarchal and dualistic gender system, and the role of the Mexican state in making Indigenous governance and normative systems more patriarchal, as I explore in chapter 3. Finally, by continuing to refuse to see Indigenous women's fight for their own rights, Mexican legislators enact a settler logic that casts Indigenous people pertually in the stereotypically premodern past.

As neoliberal governance selectively co-opts gender and cultural rights throughout Latin America, as I discussed in the introduction, the case of CONAMI signals the strategies that women and Indigenous social movements use to articulate their demands in contexts where there is a limited politics of recognition and where gender, rather than a tool to understand relationships of power, is used as a technocratic language of modernity meant to limit rather than extend their ability to seek justice. Through its development schemes,

Mexico's advancement as a nation is now measured in part by gender as a main indicator of modernity and progress through the neoliberal co-optation of the gender-technocratic language of the World Bank and the International Monetary Fund. Although constitutional reform represented a historic departure, it nevertheless reinscribed the Indigenous problem as a cultural problem (Hindley 1996). Staged on the terrain of culture, gender has become a signifier in discursive struggles about rights and has been mobilized in the new (resurrected but reconfigured) racism. This gendered logic of racism functions despite overwhelming evidence that the Mexican government can hardly be called a protector of women's rights in this era. Further, it flies in the face of the broad visibility gained by Indigenous women activists who have demanded that gender justice must be included in Indigenous law over the past two decades (Newdick 2005).

The mere presence of Comandanta Esther was historic; she was the first Indigenous woman to address the Mexican Congress. Indigenous women activists not only advocated for the passage of Indigenous rights legislation; they also took the opportunity to refute the government's negation of Indigenous autonomy based on gendered claims. This was not accidental. It was the result of a decade of political work and organizing, in both local and national movements, by Indigenous women who have developed a shared critique of women's oppression within Indigenous normative systems and within the dominant society and a collective validation and celebration of traditions that affirm them as Indigenous women. Their active participation in the struggle for Indigenous and gendered rights makes it difficult for the government to monopolize gender discourse as a form of social control, or to define the subjectivity of Indigenous peoples by using a gendered logic of racism. As Martha Sánchez Néstor argues:

> I want to tell you that in Mexico in 2001 in order to enact constitutional reform based on Indigenous Culture and Rights, *"usos and costumbres,"* or customary law as others call it or Indigenous law as we call it, the issue of the rights of women was a point strongly taken up by the Right. The PAN and PRI deputies and senators took it up as [their own] discourse and used it to aggressively attack us during the congressional debate.[22] The government broke [with this agreement and] betrayed Indigenous pueblos saying, "We cannot approve a law that gives [Indigenous] pueblos territorial resources and [the right to] free self determination to autonomy because those pueblos violate the rights of Indigenous women ... Because they hit them, sell them, mistreat them [and] because they are

not asked for their consent to have children." It is true that all this happens but not only in Indigenous communities. In the cities, in many non-Indigenous communities, mothers are forced without consent, and are raped, or beaten to this day. With all respect, *compañeras*, I am telling you that many of us here have been harassed by men ... this means we cannot say, it's "only them" [Indigenous people].[23]

Critically, Martha made these arguments at the Latin American Feminist Encuentro in Brazil, which I discuss in the next chapter, while confronting feminist NGOs' racism that posited Indigenous cultures as noble in their precontact grandeur but as savage and backward in their description of their work in the area of Indigenous women's human rights.

In the days just before Comandanta Esther's famous speech on the floor of the Mexican Congress in 2001, CONAMI held a forum on Indigenous women's rights just down the street from the legislative chambers to advocate for the passage of the COCOPA initiative and to strategize other legislation (see figure 1.8). With only two specific paragraphs addressing gender in the proposed COCOPA law, some Indigenous women's organizations and feminist allies, supported by legislators of the PRD, worked on secondary laws to amplify the guarantees of Indigenous women's rights. Martha Sánchez was at the forum and reminded participants that "the COCOPA initiative is not the problem. The very

Figure 1.8. Nellys Palomo (*left*), Tomasa Sandoval (*second from right*), and Martha Sánchez (*far right*), of CONAMI, debating how women's rights can be part of multicultural constitutional reform, Club de Periodistas, Mexico City, 2001. Photo by author.

Revolutionary Woman's Law was not a gift from anybody. It was a product of a struggle Indigenous women mounted that we have made our own."

Around the same time, Indigenous women community organizers and the Zapatista Caravan celebrated International Women's Day in Milpa Alta, on the outskirts of Mexico City, where I joined the swelling crowds. During the lively celebration, representatives from CONAMI read a speech and women delegates of the Zapatista Caravan, including Comandanta Esther, Susana, and Yolanda, shared stories of encouragement and struggle. Comandanta Esther greeted the crowd and reinforced the idea that Indigenous women's organized presence and gains have not been a gift of concessions by others, but the result of long struggle:

> In the beginning, I had to pay the price for truth. The men didn't like the idea [of women joining the struggle]. According to them, women were only good for having children and they should take care of them. And there are some women who have that idea in their heads. Some men said it wasn't good, that women didn't have the right to participate, that women are stupid.... Little by little the men began to understand and the women also. That's why women are fighting now.... We see women can be strong.

Although much of the Indigenous movement's momentum was strategically outside of the state (after the state's use of violence and the lack of forward movement after the 1996 negotiation of the San Andrés Accords), the debate on what would become the 2001 counterreform for Indigenous rights illustrated that state-defined notions of gender equity would be used as a form of governance to deny Indigenous autonomy. That does not mean that gender struggles and inequities do not occur in Indigenous communities, but that Indigenous women, men, children, and elders are the ones who will lead the movements and the social, political, economic, and cultural processes of change, not the state. Some of the patriarchal order of communal life, as I explore in chapter 3, was a direct result of Mexican state—and before that, Spanish colonial—imposition. The 2001 moment revealed the state's gendered governmentality based on a gendered logic of racism and the importance of Indigenous women's multi-scalar strategies for change. While the state co-opted the discourse of gender as a way to govern cultural difference, to regulate Indigenous subjectivity, and to refuse Indigenous autonomy, Indigenous women organizers multiplied the scales of autonomy and the terrains of struggle in which the meaning of autonomy is waged.

The blockages in the national terrain created by the Mexican government's failure to implement the San Andrés Accords, along with the stance CONAMI took to gain organizational autonomy in relation to K'inal Antestik DF, reduced their capacity to organize national workshops and bring regional organizers into the capital for training. CONAMI'S leadership continued to mobilize at the continental scale (see chapter 2) and at the local and state levels (explored in chapter 3) until there was a national resurgence after almost twenty years of organizing occured.

Looking Forward, Looking Back: Using Social Media to Make Visible Violence Against Indigenous Women

I accompanied CONAMI activists until 2005, when I turned my attention to accompanying Indigenous women migrant organizing. I returned to Mexico in 2014 to conduct interviews with numerous new leaders and with those I had interviewed during the first seven years of CONAMI's history. I have had the privilege to work with the historic and recent leaders as well as those who bridge those two generations. When CONAMI became autonomous from K'inal Antsetik it was left without an office, resources, equipment, and only one directory of members. Fabiola Jurado, who joined CONAMI in 2003 when she was twenty-four, served in the leadership during these difficult years of transition and rebuilding. Raised in Tepoztlán, Morelos, Fabiola learned her sense of community from her grandmother Amada who was a curandera and land defender. Inspired by attending the IV Continental Encuentro of ECMIA in Lima, Peru, Fabiola returned to the Mexico to start the Mujeres Indígenas Líderes Comunitarias (Communitarian Indigenous Women Leaders).

Fabiola explained one challenge was building convergence between diverse organizational experiences and ideologies including members who came from political parties; from mixed gender movements; and from revolutionary groups and armed organizations (Jurado, interview, June 30, 2015). In the process of rebuilding, they realized "we cannot continue be centralized in the capital so we traveled to Michoacán, Quintana Roo, Yucatan, Campeche, Veracruz, Chiapas, Morelos, and Baja California" (Jurado, interview, June 30, 2015) to forge the regional strength of the network. In 2016, CONAMI revised its leadership structure to include an elders council comprising historic members and to have regional representatives in a horizontal structure of collaboration, versus having one general coordinator and standing committees. In 2017, I celebrated CONAMI's twentieth anniversary with its members at their national encuentro in Mexico City; this meeting brought historic members back into the organization to connect with younger generations to begin to bridge their experiences and share knowledge. This decentralized structure featured the strength of regional leaders within CONAMI, many of whom I witnessed in full effect the next year at the encuentro in Felipe Carillo Puerto and Bacalar, Quintana Roo, Mexico hosted by powerful, young Maya women organizers and in the multigenerational leadership that organized the twenty-fifth anniversary encuentro in Chiapas in 2022. Hosting the national encuentro interweaves the interscalar links between the regional and the national, strengthening and fortifying organizing on both scales. This interscalar weaving is taken to a whole new level with the community built by the organization's robust social media, through which they share activities, workshops, declarations, news of personal achievements (like graduations) or losses (like the passing of a member's beloved mother). What is happening in the group's organizing processes can be shared more broadly and thereby impact multiple scales of activism—at the local, regional, and continental levels—as members share what happens in meetings and presentations and document their own organizing process, as with a selfie snapped after one meeting (see figure 1.9). This has been critical to CONAMI's ability to survive and thrive when crises like

Figure 1.9. Selfie of participants from the CONAMI Workshop on Documenting the Violence Against Indigenous Women, Mexico City, 2018. *Front to back, left to right:* Vivían Jiménez Estrada, Fabiola del Jurado Mendoza, Maritza del Carmen Yeh Chan, Laura Hernández Pérez, Patricia Torres Sandoval, Norma Don Juan, Teresa Rios Cruz, and Dolores Figueroa. Photo courtesy of CONAMI.

the COVID-19 pandemic hit, differentially impacting Indigenous communities in Mexico and its diaspora. Yet in the middle of the pandemic, CONAMI held its national encuentros virtually, via Facebook live, in early August 2020 and 2021 with multigenerational panels that both honored the history of the organization and tackled the critical issues presently facing Indigenous women.

Neoliberalism has led to deregulation, privatization of land, gutting of the social welfare state, and growth of the informal economy (including the drug economy); these, coupled with the militarization of the drug war and collusion between law enforcement and the military, have led many social analysts to talk of a narcostate (Fregoso 2003, 2006). Economic desperation along with weakened juridical institutions and resulting wide-scale impunity created a context of mass violence. Violence dramatically increased throughout Mexico during the 2006–12 sexenio of Felipe Calderón, who heightened the war on drugs and implemented a crackdown on social protest.

Although Indigenous communities in rebellion had been militarized in Chiapas and Guerrero, among other places, during the 1990s and early 2000s the context of Mexico—specifically, the context of activism—grew increasingly dangerous in terms of increased repression of Indigenous and environmental activists, narco/state violence, and mining and resource extraction. Victoria Tauli Corpuz, the UN Special Rapporteur on the Rights of Indigenous Peoples, documented this increase in violence when she visited Mexico City, Chihuahua, Guerrero, and Chiapas in 2017, meeting with more than two hundred people, half of them women, from twenty-three Indigenous groups. Her findings highlight the historical and structural discrimination afflicting Indigenous peoples, as evidenced by an increase in poverty, marginalization, violence, and impunity. Her report calls attention to an alarming 99 percent impunity rate in cases of human rights violations, particularly those that affect Indigenous peoples (feminicides, massacres, murders, human trafficking, and land seizures). Tauli Corpuz notes that Indigenous peoples are not being adequately consulted in accordance with international standards in relation to "megadevelopment" and extractivist projects in Indigenous territories, resulting in an increased loss of the right to territory (Report of the Special Rapporteur 2018). According to the Front Line Defenders report for 2017, there were thirty-one murders of activists involved in Indigenous and environmental movements, and Mexico ranked fourth among the world's most dangerous countries for defenders of human rights. This fact is directly linked to the twenty-nine thousand mining, hydroelectric, and wind power concessions currently active in the country, collectively accounting for more than 35 percent of its national territory. Half of the operations in this area are on Indigenous territories.

In a disturbing correlation, some analysts have made a connection between organized crime and extractivist industries, both national and transnational, and violence in organized Indigenous communities. Zósimo Camacho points out that hundreds of communities live in states of violence as drug cartels occupy their mountains, waters, and territories to facilitate the arrival of governmental and corporate megaprojects. "Drug trafficking cartels have sparked a direct war against original [Indigenous] communities, especially those in which they find organized resistance such as the National Indigenous Congress (CNI)" (Camacho 2019, n.p.). Other analysts comment on how these developments benefit not only the owning class in Mexico but also transnational corporations, leading anthropologist Gilberto López y Rivas to argue that the Mexican state has not fought the drug war but has merged with organized crime, becoming a narcostate to implement a type of capitalism he calls "necrocapitalism, based on death, destruction and war" (quoted in Camacho 2019, n.p.). Cristian Chávez González, a member of the CIG of the National Indigenous Congress (discussed in the coda) makes a connection between these forces, arguing that "organized crime defends private property against collective property; and it sells the products that big capital is demanding, whether they are avocados, gold, iron, silver, wood, water, oil. It seems that at the moment the objective of armed groups, whether they are State or non-State, is the appropriation of the territory and the appropriation and concentration of power for the service of the great capital" (quoted in Camacho 2019, n.p.).

These conjunctures of violence may seem new, but in their 2017 collaborative piece, "Gender Community Emergency: Indigenous Women's Response to the Multiple Violences and the Dispossession of Land," former CONAMI coordinator Fabiola Del Jurado Mendoza and the director of communications (at the time of writing) Norma Don Juan Perez argue that the context of violence against women goes back to the era of invasion and colonization, and they call for building a collective memory. Part of CONAMI's anti-violence work has been to engage with the broader movement across Abiayala, specifically the movement against missing and murdered Indigenous women in Canada. For example, Norma Don Juan Pérez participated in the Virtual Forum on Violence Against Indigenous Women of the Americas. She linked colonial violence to the patriarchal hierarchy of power and continued violence against Indigenous women's bodies, minds, spirits, and collective lives: "This colonization involved the invasion of our territories, and when I say territories I include our own bodies, our spirituality, mentality, and every aspect of our individual and collective life. The conception of feminine-masculine duality was replaced with the hierarchy of the sexes[,] with men being dominant. In his role of protector, man adopted the role of guardian of the woman, we became the property of men and society and in this way we are violated in public and private spaces" (Don Juan Pérez, quoted in Figueroa Romero et al. 2017).

Although there are huge gaps in reporting feminicides, what data exist demonstrate an increase in feminicide in Chiapas, Guanajuato, Jalisco, Nuevo León, Oaxaca, Puebla, Estado de México, Veracruz, Quintana Roo, Mexico City, and Juárez. It was because of this crisis of violence that feminists created the Alerta de Violencia de Género (Gender Violence Alarm), to call attention to the gendered based murder of women taking place in the states of Chihuahua, Morelos, Guerrero, Michoacán, and Oaxaca. Longtime ally of CONAMI, feminist sociologist Dolores Figueroa argues (2019) that the way feminicide is conceptualized in Mexico has erased Indigenous women. She says "the one-dimensional, mono-causal feminist analytical gaze has certainly neglected forms/places of victimization and historical dehumanization of indigenous women and the colonial violence to which they are subjected" (66). CONAMI called attention to the way Indigenous women were invisible in the figures on feminicide and gender violence, despite being a disproportionately high number of victims. They created the Emergencia Comunitaria de Género (Gender Community Emergency, or ECG) to respond to the failure of the Mexican government and federal entities to recognize these high indices of violence and to provide protection and justice to women, especially Indigenous women. At the twentieth anniversary event gathering of CONAMI in Mexico City in 2017, I sat in the audience as Paty Torres described the Gender Community Emergency project as a call to action:

> Because of being Indigenous, women, rural and poor, we are hurt, we are beaten, we are marginalized, and when we speak out we are isolated and stigmatized further by those who would say that violence against women is an exaggeration. We have been deceived so much that we have lost our fear. In Cuernavaca, Morelos, we decided as the National Coordinator of Indigenous Women [CONAMI] to launch the Gender Community Emergency as our plan [to amplify] the voices of Indigenous women in this country to say: Enough!
>
> This is our plan [of action] for the emergency we are living under—this phenomenon that women live a situation of extreme violence, specifically for Indigenous women. The name is a call to action because [the violence] comes from our communities, what we are living day in and day out in our organizations, in our community work, in our communities. We realize that these women who are being raped do not appear in the

official numbers. If you take into account how many of us Indigenous women are being assassinated, we are being raped, then you can see why the Community Gender Emergency is a tool to make visible what society that has historically [erased because it has] been machista. We live in discriminatory situations that include emotional violence, domestic violence, sexual assault as well as feminicide, the most extreme expression of violence against women. Gender Community Emergency is gender communitarian defense based on this broad public denunciation: to complain and to document Indigenous women's cases and demand that the state be responsible to us for these human rights violations.

Fabiola Jurado went on to explain, "the issue of feminicide is even more challenging due to the invisibilization of the allegations of Indigenous women. We want the murders of Indigenous women to appear in the statistics and until then, we will continue to use all the means we can access. Now, we use the Facebook page we created, Gender Community Emergency, that many follow to share the accusations and that has helped at various moments to get information out through that means."

The ECG's first action took place November 25, 2013, with a march and press coverage to make visible the violence against Indigenous women (see figure 1.10).

Figure 1.10. Fabiola del Jurado Mendoza and her daughter marching with CONAMI to call attention to the "Gender Community Emergency" of the invisible feminicide of Indigenous women, 2013. Photo courtesy of CONAMI.

CONAMI's objectives with the ECG are to "1) visibilize the violence against Indigenous women and understand the specificities of this violence for them and their pueblos; 2) recognize that violence against Indigenous women is the result of a concentration of historical conditions and acts, and that violence against women and Indigenous pueblos are interconnected and cannot be treated as separate; and 3) to generate policies that are culturally pertinent to eradicate violence, incorporating legal pluralism, and the principles, values, and practices of original pueblos for prevention, protection, and access to justice and damage reparations" (Del Jurado Mendoza, Don Juan Pérez, and CONAMI 2019). Of the three objectives, the one that is most visible is a "virtual space," which consists of a Facebook page on which everyone affiliated with CONAMI can post news articles and public denouncements that circulate online to document violence against Indigenous women. ECG keeps an updated spreadsheet of all the information from the Facebook posts, which they compile as an annual report and release every November 25, the day that activists at the first Latin American Feminist Encuentro in 1981 identified to create visibility around all forms of violence against women in honor of the Mirabal sisters, who were assassinated in 1960 in their fight against the Trujillo dictatorship in the Dominican Republic. In 1999 the UN General Assembly adopted November 25 as the International Day for the Elimination of Violence Against Women.

    This digital activism and data collected from journalistic reports from 2013 to 2019 have been compiled, systematized, analyzed, and interpreted by a group of Indigenous activists from CONAMI in collaboration with academics. Fabiola Del Jurado Mendoza and Norma Don Juan Pérez also identify the need to expand the work of the ECG to "urban environments, where more and more youth are migrating to find work or education; youth who are separated from their families and communities are susceptible to violence, and often bring that violence back to their communities" (Del Jurado Mendoza and Don Juan Pérez, 2019). Beyond collecting and analyzing data, CONAMI activists have also sought to frame the violence of feminicide through a framework that views the continuity and interrelationships of multiple forms of violence and that defines human rights in a broad sense—a definition that encompasses the collective rights of Indigenous peoples who have been left out of the feminist movement. They reflect: "for us the violence has to do with the violation of human rights; that is, we begin with a broad definition that includes situations such as displacement, territorial dispossession, and dispossession of natural resources, among others, which are not a priority in feminist agendas. For us, Indigenous women are the priority, like femicide, physical and psychological violence, et cetera. Because we cannot separate our specific rights from the collective rights of Indigenous pueblos" (Del Jurado Mendoza and Don Juan Pérez 2019, n.p.). This critical reframing of multiple forms of violence and the historic, interlinking nature of colonial and state violence with gender, intimate partner and sexual violence, along with the impact of intergenerational trauma has been theorized by native feminists and women of color (Deer 2015; INCITE! 2006; Million 2013; Robertson 2012; A. Smith 2005; Speed 2019; Velásquez 2003). Maureen White Eagle and I (2007) discussed the ways colonial violence was articulated through state and narco violence and intersected with intimate partner violence and sexual assault—and most importantly, how we decolonize our bodies—when we spoke in solidarity as native women with Indigenous women's struggle against violence in Mexico. Feminist anthropologists such as Aida Hernández Castillo (2016), Lynn Stephen (2021), and Mariana Mora (2015, 2017c) have recently documented the many forms of violence against Indigenous women as a continuation of colonial violence. For example, Mora (2017b) points to how Indigenous women activists are theorizing feminicide in southern Mexico as an extension of the racialized sexual violence Indigenous women confronted in the finca system. Focusing on the speeches Indigenous women leaders and members of the Indigenous Governing Council delivered at the 2019 Zapatista Encuentro for Women Who Struggle, Mora (2021) shows how these forms of gendered violence against women are understood as extensions of the neocolonial order in the context of narco/state violence. The sexual exploitation of Indigenous women is linked to the gendered violence of colonial labor extraction in the finca system, in which the ruling racial and economic class of landowners, or hacendados, extracted labor in a feudal system that was enforced through racial violence and, for Indigenous women, through racialized sexual violence (Mora 2017b). She analyzes the way the women frame these multiple forms of violence as a "war against life" that connects "land dispossession and environmental destruction, primarily propelled by extractivist and narco-economies, with struggles against violence directed at women" (Mora 2021). Her analysis converges with that offered by Norma from CONAMI, illustrating a growing shared understanding of an interconnection between the legacy of colonial violence within economic hierarches and current economies of extraction and narcoviolence.

Conclusion

The practice of Indigenous autonomy that women activists have elaborated contests the gendered terrain on which the struggle for racism is waged. They have expanded purely legal understandings of autonomy by creating a lived practice of autonomy that forms new relations of sociality, politics, and historicity. Although these new practices of autonomy are constructed from older traditions, they have led to transformations of Indigenous governance structures and ways of belonging and have the potential to shift relations of rule in Mexico.

Women have played a vital role in constructing and mobilizing a national Indigenous movement in Mexico. Indigenous women have not only become important actors in the Indigenous movement; they have effectively expanded Indigenous political demands for autonomy by adding their own analyses of how Mexican politics and culture have been organized by gender, indigeneity, and class as vectors of power. They have articulated their demands in relation to the recovery of social, political, and cultural forms of Indigenous autonomy. This practice of construction and consultation has sustained the movement beyond claim for rights in the face of military repression and governmental recalcitrance, represented by the Indian Rights Bill, a counterreform that many critics say fails to meet the basic agreements of the San Andrés Peace Accords, which were signed by the government in 1996. The strategy of Indigenous women organizers in scaling Indigenous autonomy down to the body and the community was an important one that kept the movement's goals alive in daily lived practices across the country. While the Indigenous women's movement supported juridical, territorial, and cultural claims to autonomy, it also expanded the meaning of these claims to include women's bodily, political, and economic autonomy. Expanding the terrain of struggle for Indigenous autonomy beyond rights discourse, Indigenous women activists have located their own demands in a *practice* of autonomy, and they work toward transforming the Indigenous cultural practices embedded within their daily lives, within the social worlds of their communities, and within structures of governance and jurisprudence.

2. Abiayala as Scale

The complex, transnational, and transindigenous dialogues among Indigenous women activists in the Americas are reshaping local ideals of gender, justice, and indigeneity. Organized Indigenous women have forged new scales to build collective political subjectivity, cross-border solidarity, capacity, and organizational power by weaving in and between local, national, regional, transnational, and even international scales of power across Abiayala, or what is known colonially as the Americas (Blackwell 2006). Effectively utilizing these multiscalar experiences, they have created new sites (and modes) for participation and new discursive strategies within local, national, transborder, and transnational politics. Continuing the focus on the organizing of women in the Coordinadora Nacional de Mujeres Indígenas (National Coordinator of Indigenous Women; CONAMI) of Mexico, this chapter explores how CONAMI members joined with other activists to scale up to the transnational level by helping to found the hemispheric network Enlace Continental de Mujeres Indígenas de Abya Yala (Continental Network of Indigenous Women of Abya Yala; ECMIA) in 1995. Examining the development of this dense regional network of Indigenous women activists hailing from twenty-six organizations and twenty-two countries, this chapter analyzes new forms of transnational consciousness and political organizing across *Abiayala*, a term meaning "Continent of Life" in the language of the Guna peoples of Panama and Colombia.[1] Over time, ECMIA has become a political force on the global political stage that advocates for Indigenous rights, women's rights, climate change activism, and a realm of other issues from the point of view of Indigenous women across the continent (see figure 2.1).

I draw on oral histories with founders and leaders of the network, my observations at the twentieth-anniversary celebration of ECMIA during the Seventh Continental Gathering in Guatemala City in 2015, and my participation in continental encuentros in 2011 and the Global Indigenous Women's Meeting in Lima, Peru, in 2013. My insights are also informed by my participation in nu-

Figure 2.1. Indigenous women from different Indigenous territories across the continent marching together at the Fifth Continental Encuentro, organized by ECMIA and Femmes Autochtones du Québec (Quebec Native Women), Quebec, Canada, July 2007. Photo courtesy of Sonia Henriquez.

merous transnational regional women's meetings, such as the Latin American and Caribbean Feminist Encuentro, a biannual gathering started in 1981 that regularly brings together 1,200 to 1,500 activists (though more than 3,200 attended at its highest point) from the region's multiple currents of the feminist movement. I pay particular attention to how questions of racial/ethnic diversity were debated in Brazil in 2005 and in Mexico in 2009, how Indigenous women were marginalized within those encuentros, and how they organized to fight against it. Attention to shifting geographies of difference will enable us to see how Indigenous women activists navigate power differentials between themselves and their non-Indigenous counterparts across multiple scales; how strategies and discourses travel over unequal terrains of meaning, access, and power; and how effective movements traffic and translate tactics, knowledge, and identities from one scale to another. Further, it allows us to understand how activists create scales to avert blockages at one level through new forms of organizing so they can articulate themselves at scales where they want to build organizational strength and build parallel formations when they want to leverage accountability.

Specifically, I examine how Indigenous women navigated power differentials between themselves and the Latin American feminist movement in terms of racial and class power, differing political priorities, and unequal access to resources. In the preparatory process for the Fourth UN World Conference of Women and the Latin American and Caribbean Feminist Encuentros, Indigenous women refused the exclusionary politics of hegemonic feminism; instead, they asserted their presence, knowledges, and agendas. The women who formed CONAMI used their growing organizational experience not only to call out the exclusion and discrimination they encountered as they scaled up to regional, international, and transnational levels but also to create new scales where their solidarities, identities, and shared histories could be centered. ECMIA's very emergence as a continental network was thus born partially out of the need to build an autonomous space for Indigenous women in relation to Latin American feminist NGOs at the regional, international, and transnational levels. The formation of ECMIA was, in many ways, an act of refusal by Indigenous women that challenged the patronizing attempt of mestiza feminists to shape their political destinies or make decisions for them. It also illustrates how the roots of Indigenous women's gendered politics emerge from an alternative feminist wellspring based within struggles for their communal survival and practices of community well-being that has the potential to reinvigorate feminist movements in the region.[2]

Furthermore, activists drew on the Guna concept of Abiayala to develop a specifically Indigenous transnational imaginary and scale of solidarity and action. This chapter helps us think about how scale is made not just by states, capital, and the international system, but also by social movements and Indigenous peoples themselves. As Anna Tsing (2005) so effectively reminds us, "Scale must be brought into being: proposed, practiced, and evaded, as well as taken for granted. Scales are claimed and contested in cultural and political projects" (58–59). In this way, scale and scale-making are not just imposed from on high; they can also be coproduced, whether through collaboration or acts of resistance. By denaturalizing colonial and settler state political landscapes, Indigenous political imaginaries locate activists on a shared terrain of connection, relation, and responsibility through spatial epistemologies like Turtle Island or Abiayala. Indigenous activists and thinkers, for example, rejected Cold War geopolitics and cartographies of First, Second, and Third Worlds by announcing that Indigenous peoples formed a Fourth World—a move that created gestures of solidarity with other Indigenous people across the globe and called attention to global geopolitics that have led to the erasure of Indigenous peoples and, in some cases, to genocide, for example, against Mayans who were targeted for mass killing and extermination when they were labeled subversives by US-backed paramilitaries in the Guatemalan civil war.

Such alternative positioning is critical because the international system is a contradictory space for Indigenous peoples. On the one hand, the United Nations, for example, is a member organization formed by nation-states, many of which were created through conquest, colonialism, and settler projects of extermination of Indigenous peoples. On the other hand, building on a long history of Indigenous diplomacy that stems back to the League of Nations, the global Indigenous movement has sought to build a framework and a set of mechanisms that recognize international Indigenous laws and norms through, for example, ILO Convention 169, the struggle for Indigenous peoples to be seen as collective subjects of self-determination, the struggle to put the *s* at the end of *Indigenous peoples* at the UN World Conference against Racism in 2001 (see figure 2.2), and, most recently, the UN Declaration on the Rights of Indigenous People (UNDRIP).

Indigenous movements are said to be "born transnational" (Brysk 2000), in large part because the existing structures of governance/justice are colonial, yet, activists weave not only in and between scales but also between epistemological registers—between the "Americas" and Abiayala, between colonial and Indigenous notions of space, between Western political philosophical traditions

Figure 2.2. Jennie Luna, Margarita Gutiérrez, and Cándida Jimenez at the UN World Conference against Racism in Durban, South Africa, 2001. Photo courtesy of Jennie Luna.

and Indigenous knowledges. By interweaving across geographies of difference and by traversing both settler/colonial and overlapping, preexisting Indigenous borders, Indigenous women activists unsettle and help us to rethink notions that are seemingly fixed by settler/colonial impositions. Internationalism, whether it focuses on state actors or nonstate actors, uses the colonial form/scale of the nation, which has often been built on setter projects of elimination and disappearance of Indigenous peoples, knowledges, and social/spiritual worlds (pluriverse). A historical and ethnographic grounding helps us to go beyond the forked tongue of globalization, combatting the doublespeak of neoliberal globalization and the lack of shared vocabulary or conceptual clarity between various fields.

For the women of ECMIA, creating an alternative scale to the Americas was a strategic move made necessary by the specific power relations they encountered at the regional, international, and transnational levels, vis-à-vis not only the governing entities and actors they had to engage with there but also other, mestiza feminists within Latin American and Caribbean organizing. I argue that Indigenous women activists, faced with this need to navigate geographies of difference on both fronts, not only weave in and between various scales but also interweave multiple epistemologies, spatial knowledges, cosmologies, and strategies—feminist and Indigenous, Western and Indigenous, for example—creating what Indigenous (Amuzgo) feminist activist Martha Sánchez Néstor (2005) refers to as the *"doble mirada."* In the introduction to *La doble mirada: Voces e historias de mujeres indígenas latinoamericanas*, Sánchez Néstor asserts that the contributions by Indigenous women activists to the collection help make visible a set of doble miradas between the Indigenous struggle and the specific demands of Indigenous women. Whereas *doble mirada* can be translated as double looks or double gaze, I argue that it is more suggestive of a double or even differential consciousness that results from being located between at least two points of view (cosmologies)/fronts of struggle—in this case, between Indigenous and women's movements. Less a state of being than a way of doing politics, doble mirada accounts for how Indigenous women have constructed multifaceted social movement networks that center Indigenous epistemologies, women's visions of communal justice, and transborder political projects that bridge multiple communities. The double mirada echoes the Mesoamerican pre-Columbian concept of Kab'awil, or double gaze, that Indigenous (Chorti) cultural studies scholar Gloria Chacón (2018) theorizes as a powerful analytic that can see both night and day, past and present, as Kab'awil is based on a cosmoletic understanding of the direct and retrograde movements of planets such as Jupiter. Kab'awil surfaces in preclassic Maya glyphs as a smoking mirror glyph, which can stand for obsidian or lightning, and in later representations appears as a serpent foot with versions of bird wings, beaks, and claws. Chacón calls attention to how Kab'awil opens, moves beyond, and provincializes Western conceptions of the dialectic with her concept of Indigenous cosmolectics, which encompasses "the role of cosmos and history, sacred writing and poetry, nature and spirituality as well as glyphs and memory play in articulating Maya and Zapotec ontologies" (12). Kab'awil—the double gaze—is a philosophy and logic that embodies past and present temporal modes in ways that dissolve contradictions (2018, 4) and move beyond dualities that Indigenous women cultural producers use to "assume an autonomy outside of usos y costumbres or customary law" (17). Chacón argues that "Kab'awil becomes productive in thinking about gender and genre across Mesoamerican geography because through it women maintain a critical gaze to sexist practices in the guise of tradition" (17). The doble mirada/double gaze that Sánchez and Chacón theorize describes what happens when Indigenous women activists interweave scales and epistemologies. As I discussed in the introduction, weaving in and between scales, Western and Indigenous spatial epistemologies not only produce the doble mirada or Kab'awil; they are a form of doubleweaving that Qwo-Li Driskill (2010) theorized between queer and Indigenous worlds. Thus, looking at two fronts of struggle and interweaving scales can produce a third space of consciousness.

Finally, it is important to note that such negotiations are not without contingencies, limits, and unexpected outcomes—what Anna Tsing (2005) aptly terms "friction"—particularly in the international political arena, which is often created and maintained by nation-states many of whose national projects are based on the extermination and erasure of Indigenous peoples. Abiayala, as an Indigenous political project and articulation of scale, works precisely to disrupt and shift scale (spatial projects of solidarity, in this instance) rather than fit neatly into a global order not of their making or worse, based on their/our destruction. I thus trace ECMIA's eventual decision to change its name from the Continental Network of Indigenous Women of Abya Yala to the Continental Network of Indigenous Women of the Americas, for it reminds us to pay attention to not only what successfully translates from one scale to another, but also that which resists scalability and requires new strategies.

Attending to the articulation of Indigenous scales alongside what is nonscalable is a critical index of incommensurability. As much as Tsing reminds us of scale and friction, she also calls attention to nonscalability as an important critique of ways that scale functions in global economic frameworks. Tsing asserts that "scalability is possible only if project elements do not form transformative relationships that might change the project as elements are added" (2012, 507). Rather than neatly nested notions of scale, my project in this chapter is to take up Tsing's call for a *"critical description* of relational encounters across difference"* (523) in order to map how non/scalability is negotiated when interweaving dominant/colonial geopolitical formations, between the conceptualization of the Americas/Abiayala, that produce a genealogy of the doble mirada. The "encounters across difference" in which members of the Continental Network of Indigenous Women negotiate nonnested, nonuniform projects through their strategies of interweaving dominant and nondominant forms and knowledges that produce doble miradas—a way of seeing two worlds, two perspectives, that has the possibility of transforming both. The concept of Abiayala indexes important ways in which Indigenous women activists used their own epistemological registers to craft a politics of interconnection and solidarity in building a hemispheric political project that centered their own cosmovisions on articulating their collective responsibility to their relations to land, water, weaving, rights, and much more. It was an early attempt of the activists of ECMIA to invoke the Earth and her relationships and responsibilities and shift the geopolitical scale of the hemispheric colonially known as the Américas. In doing so they were working to "abandon the scaffold imaginary, to imagine relations that don't rely on narrative scaffolds or borders for their definition, their articulation" (Brady 2021, 27). This move is one answer to Pat Brady's (2021) call to action to think beyond the monoworld that scale has conjured and her questions of how to "think the textures of connections without relapsing into possession, into emplacement and orientation, into an architecture of explanation that enfolds all form, all narration, all being, into a nested scalar hierarchy? Put differently, how does one read and write knowing the world is many? Undoing the strictures of monoworlding, some would say decolonizing, entails a turn to writers who know the pluriverse, who scrutinize the coloniality of perspective" (27).

The Spark That Ignites: Indigenous Women's Organizing, the International System, and the Formation of ECMIA

In 1994, when Indigenous women activists arrived at the Mar de Plata NGO preparatory meeting for the Fourth World Conference on Women, to be held in Beijing in 1995, they were unsettled by their lack of representation. They questioned why an advisor on Indigenous women's issues—a person they should have selected—had already been assigned to them (Robles, interview, August 31, 1999). The preparatory process leading to Beijing facilitated, in both positive and negative ways, a space for Indigenous women in Latin America to articulate a transnational, transindigenous regional identity and strategize their participation at the Fourth World Conference on Women and vis-à-vis other international Indigenous peoples movements, specifically at the United Nations. The marginalization that Indigenous women encountered in the Beijing process led them to build ECMIA. This move aligned with the emergence and growth of Indigenous mass mobilizations and social movements across Latin America in the 1990s, and with the development of specifically gendered demands for Indigenous autonomy (Rousseau and Rosales Hudson 2016).

ECMIA is one of many regional networks worldwide, including those in Asia, Africa, and the Pacific, that comprise the global Indigenous women's movement. These transnational regional networks have played a crucial role in developing policy advocacy strategies and training activists to engage with various UN processes and protocols, such as those of the UN Permanent Forum on Indigenous Issues and UNDRIP, the Convention on the Elimination of All Forms of Discrimination against Women (CEDAW), and the international Convention on the Elimination of All Forms of Racial Discrimination (CERD). Since its original platform for Indigenous women at the Fourth World Conference on Women in Beijing, ECMIA has been a space for articulation and each iteration allows the network to update and advocate for its goals, for example, Bejing+20. Critically, ECMIA not only orients activists toward the international arena; it also provides a vital space of exchange in which Indigenous women forge solidarity and figure out how to take back to their communities the issues and strategies discussed at the international level—strategies to combat violence against Indigenous women; to organize against militarization, mining, and other forms of resource extraction; to defend intellectual property rights; and to protect women's human rights within their communities.

Mexico's Indigenous women's movement has a rich history with ECMIA. The national network, CONAMI, was not merely the result of women's participation in nationwide mobilization following the Zapatista uprising but also the product of a transnational formation. The genesis of the 1997 founding meeting of CONAMI was rooted in the First Continental Encuentro of Indigenous Women of the First Nations of Abya Yala in Quito, Ecuador, in 1995. The delegation from Mexico included Sofía Robles from Services of the Mixe Pueblo, Margarita Gutiérrez from the Frente Independiente de Pueblos Indígenas, Martha Sánchez Néstor from the Consejo Guerrerense 500 Años de Resistencia Indígena y Popular, and Beatriz Gutiérrez from the Red Nacional de Mujeres Indígenas. Indigenous women leaders from Mexico who had attended the encuentro in Quito, including Margarita Gutiérrez (Hñähñú), Sofía Robles (Zapotec/Mixe), and Martha Sánchez Néstor (Amuzgo), helped to found ECMIA and agreed to organize the second continental encuentro two years later in Mexico. Mexico was selected to bring solidarity, support, and critical attention to the Chiapas uprising. The 1997 National Encuentro in Oaxaca, the founding convention of CONAMI, was organized as a national preparatory meeting for the Second Continental Encuentro of Indigenous Women held later that year in Mexico City. The existence of a transnational network of Indigenous women helped formalize the formation of an autonomous national Indigenous women's network in Mexico, which linked the struggles of Indigenous women in different regions of Mexico and outside of the country transnationally throughout the continent.

Although Indigenous women had already been using UN meetings as a springboard for their organizing in international arenas, the Beijing process—like many other forms of women's organizing around the world—provided them an opportunity to build an alternative transnational, transindigenous network. The Latin American and Caribbean Preparatory Conference for Beijing was held in Mar de Plata, Argentina, September 20-24, 1994. Twelve hundred participants from forty-one countries convened to develop a regional plan around structural adjustment, democracy, citizenship, and violence against women.[3] The Latin American regional coordinator, Virginia Vargas, referred to the Beijing meetings as a pretext for continuing the organizing of the already vibrant regional feminist movement (Virginia Vargas, interview with Maylei Blackwell, December 8, 1999). Yet Sofía Robles of CONAMI, who served as the state of Oaxaca's representative to the Mexican delegation in Mar de Plata and later would be the Latin American regional Indigenous women's representative in Beijing, described the preparatory meeting as deeply exclusionary. The discussions that led to forming ECMIA began, quite literally, in direct response to this sense of exclusion, as Robles explained to me: "There in Mar de Plata we created an Indigenous women's session, but from the beginning, we had many demands because they gave us the worst space that could possibly be shared with us, and it began from there.... We began to talk with the NGOs about having to respect us, support us, and share financing with us" (Robles, interview, August 31, 1999). To combat their marginalization within the Beijing preparatory process specifically and the international system generally, Indigenous women organizers developed a transnational space in which to organize themselves, formulate their strategies, and coordinate their actions on a continental level. After Indigenous women met at the Mar de Plata meeting, they decided that they needed their own space to strategize their participation at the Fourth World Conference in Beijing and the regional processes leading up to it. They organized the First Continental

Encuentro of Indigenous Women of the First Nations of Abya Yala convened by the Confederación Nacional de Mujeres Indígenas del Ecuador. A total of 170 Indigenous women from 20 countries across the continent attended the Ecuador meeting with two primary goals: "To analyze [their] proposals in the face of the IV World Conference of Women and to initiate projects and strategies of action for the long term under the framework of the International Decade of Indigenous Peoples."[4] While their proposals were accepted too late to affect the preparatory discussion of the Platform for Action, Indigenous women organizers felt they had made important strides.[5] Robles recalls:

> For us, it was important to meet because we firmly believe that we deserve our own space to discuss our problems and points of view without closing ourselves off to alliances with other sectors. Since Mar de Plata, we felt the necessity to seek a preparatory space before arriving at Beijing, [although] we recognize ... the document of the Platform for Action had already been discussed in the Prepcom [preparatory meeting]. Nevertheless, there were some points that we were able to push for such as the ratification and application of Convention 169 of the ILO. In all the points that refer to research carried out in Indigenous communities, we demanded that we no longer continue to be objects of study unless such study brings programs for real [community] development. (Robles, interview, August 31, 1999)

The documents from the continental meeting show critical discussions and strategy-building around Indigenous women's lack of representation and their experience from the NGO forum at Mar de Plata that reveal their concern that if they did not organize and represent with their own voice, somebody else would speak for them. They resolved to work on a document representing the women of the "First Nations of Abya Yala," produced in their final declaration, *Declaración del Sol*.[6] This regional meeting helped women to prepare for the Fourth World Conference on Women, where the "Beijing Declaration of Indigenous Women" was drafted with a fifty-point platform including a diverse range of issues that Indigenous women confront.[7]

ECMIA was formed to allow Indigenous women to protest the ways their autonomy was undermined in the Latin American NGO forum that had been held in preparation for the UN Fourth World Conference on Women. Yet it would be a mistake to identify the emergence of a continental Indigenous women's network with struggles for inclusion only within the region's feminist movement. Indigenous mass mobilizations throughout the region—including those in Panama, Ecuador, Colombia, and Mexico—in the 1990s also inspired the power and energy of this articulation, building on and reinvigorating the hemispheric connections built in 1992 in opposition to the celebration of the five-hundredth anniversary of Columbus's arrival. International Indigenous organizing in what is now known as the Americas—or as Abiayala, as I propose below—has a long history in which Indigenous nations have used the international sphere to lobby for their land and treaty rights and to petition against land seizures. Indigenous activism complicates narrow conceptions of the meaning of *transnational* because of the long pre- and post-colonial, and I would argue decolonial, histories of Indigenous nation-to-nation relationships and diplomacy that are already transnational but often unrecognized. Indigenous transborder activism challenges the borders of colonial settler nation-states and creates alternative relationalities grounded in Indigenous epistemologies (see Blackwell, Briggs, and Chiu 2015). Such activism also has a long history, from Deskaheh of the Haudenosaunee Confederacy presenting "The Red Man's Appeal to Justice" to the League of Nations in 1923 to Indigenous activists using the notion of the Fourth World to describe how Cold War geopolitics erased Indigenous peoples (Dunbar-Ortiz 1984).

Indigenous movements had grown in number and strength in the Americas since the 1970s. Still, by the time of the Beijing World Conference on Women, the density of cross-border contacts had also increased, particularly through the numerous events organized to protest the 1992 quincentenary celebration of Columbus's stumbling onto the New World. The United Nations declared 1992 the "Year of Indigenous People," and Rigoberta Menchú was awarded the Nobel Peace Prize. In 1993, the UN announced that the Decade of Indigenous People would take place between 1995 and 2004, and Menchú was named its goodwill ambassador. While the 1990s thus saw extensive mobilization by Indigenous peoples in Latin America, it also witnessed the simultaneous implementation of neoliberal regimes in the region that applied neoliberal multiculturalist strategies that did little to redistribute power, recognize territorial rights, or grant political autonomy. Critics began to see these processes as being intertwined to form a type of governmentality called neoliberal multiculturalism (Hale 2002; Postero 2007; Povinelli 2002; Speed 2008). Zapotec scholar Isabel Altamirano-Jiménez (2013) argues that "the recognition of cultural difference and the 'compensatory measure' of granting collective rights to 'disadvantaged' social groups are integral to neoliberalism. These cultural rights, along with the socio-economic components, distinguish neoliberalism as a specific form of governance that shapes, delimits, and produces difference (Hale 2005, 12–13)" (5).

In international politics, the UN had two goals for the decade: to establish a permanent forum for Indigenous peoples in the UN and to get the UN General

Assembly to pass a draft Declaration on the Rights of Indigenous Peoples. Although Indigenous peoples have historically taken their grievances with governments to the UN and other international bodies, at the time, they had no formal mechanism to represent their interests within the UN. Compromises were made to form the Permanent Forum on Indigenous Issues. Still, it was formally established on July 28, 2000, by the Economic and Social Council on the recommendation of the Commission on Human Rights. After years of negotiation, the UNDRIP was also passed in 2007.

While the continental scale has specific power arrangements, regional histories, and actors, it provided a new terrain for coalition and blockage. Beyond regional, national, continental, transnational, and other geographic concepts of scale, equally important are different political and epistemological ways of thinking about scale. The articulation of an Indigenous scale, grounded literally in the earth beneath our feet, connects activists to different epistemologies, different sets of urgencies, priorities, and commitments.

The Scale of Abiayala

The idea of Abiayala is not only a specifically Indigenous articulation of scale but also an Indigenous political project. Its work is precisely to disrupt and shift hegemonic notions of scale rather than fitting neatly into a global order, not of Indigenous people's making. Abiayala is based on a Guna epistemology of land that creates a broader political imaginary of connection through territory and solidarity. *Abiayala* is defined as "territorio salvado, tierra de sangre, tierra madura, continente americano" ("saved territory," "land of blood," "mature land," "American continent") (Orán and Wagua 2010, 20).[8] "Abya Yala in the Guna language means 'land in its full maturity.' The Guna believe that there are four cycles of life that have developed the planet earth: Kualagun Yala, Tagargun Yala, Tingua Yala, and Abia or Abya Yala," according to Maya K'iche scholar Emil Keme (Del Valle Escalante 2014, 2018).[9] Following a Guna victory against land developers in Dulenega (San Blas, Panama), Takir Mamani, part of the Tupaj Katari Indigenous rights movement in Bolivia, met with Guna elders, or saylas, who requested that Indigenous movements use *Abya Yala* to refer to the continent, instead of *the Americas* or *Latin Americas*.[10] Calling on all Indigenous organizations to use the concept of Abiayala in their documents and declarations, Mamani argued that "placing foreign names on our cities, towns, and continents, is equal to subjecting our identity to the will of our invaders and to that of their heirs."[11] The colonial compulsion to name is a form of "political cartography that fixes" the colonial as dominant while eradicating or subordinating

Indigenous knowledges (Zavala cited in Muyolema 2001, 2). Indigenous intellectuals and activists have called for the use of *Abiayala* as a "way to refer not only to the continent but also to a differentiated Indigenous locus of cultural and political enunciation" (Muyolema cited in Keme 2018, 43).

Armando Muyolema (2001) has argued that "Latin America is more than an idea; [it] represents a set of ideals, actions and representations of the world that, interrelated, embody a long-term cultural project that is formulated in terms of a struggle that is waged on two fronts: in confrontation with Anglo-Saxon cultural expansion and, inside, as a continuity of the "civilizing" project inherited from the colony against the original peoples" (3).[12] In the face of these two fronts of struggle, he recovers the use of Abiayala as a political and intellectual position that is not geographic but based on historical experiences and sensibilities from which Indigenous people in the Americas think and act. Muyolema illustrates how the *Latin* of Latin America represents not merely an exertion of power among competing colonial forces (Spanish, Portuguese, and French against English domination) but also a settler project to supplant the Indigenous in terms of population and through, among other things, the repression and eradication of Indigenous languages (and epistemologies and ways of understanding the world). For Muyolema, "From the recuperation of this other place [Abiayala], as our political and intellectual position, we realize a first critical approximation toward the process of emergence and constitution of Latin America as a cultural project of westernization and its ideological articulation with certain lines of indigenismo and mestizaje" (2001, 4).

Keme argues that "for us to recognize and endorse categories like America or Latin America will contribute to affirming a colonialist logic that overlooks our needs as Indigenous Nations. In particular, our continued efforts to recover and defend our territories, and restitute our linguistic, cultural and religious specificities, efforts that Latinamericanism and Americanism in general, in all of its forms, have failed to deeply address and understand" (2018, 58). In relation to thinking about ECMIA, his argument points to the importance of this concept in relation to political mobilizations: "Since the 1980s, many Indigenous activists, writers, and organizations have embraced the Guna people's and Mamani's suggestion, and Abiayala has become a way to refer not only to the continent but also to a differentiated Indigenous locus of cultural and political enunciation (Muyolema, 329)" (Keme 2018, 43). Building on this locus of enunciation, Abiayala creates a logic of connection and solidarity while disrupting the colonial underpinnings of other "Americanisms" for Indigenous activists and intellectuals. This logic of solidarity, identity, and connection are echoed in other projects of Indigenous hemispheric analysis (Castellano, Gutiérrez, and Aldama 2012; Hernández Ávila, forthcoming).

In my 2014 oral history with Sonia Henriquez, a Guna Yala leader from Panama and former coordinator of ECMIA, she shared that "Abiayala means territory. In the Guna language it is territory; it is land." Yet she also linked the relationship to land, and the loss of it, to the daily, lived experience of what displacement means: "Within Indigenous pueblos, what is very strong for us is territory, so we continue to struggle for territory and against land evictions because the worst comes when problems arise with the territories—poverty comes, family disintegration comes, economic problems come, and problems of identity come as families . . . leave because they no longer have land. For this reason, when they say Abiayala, meaning what has been called the Américas, Abiayala, is to speak of territory" (Henriquez 2014). Henriquez's holistic, expansive view of Abiayala as territory scales the implication of the loss of land down to the family in terms of poverty and displacement and the collective loss of identity at the familial level. This echoes the way Indigenous women activists in chapter 1 understand Indigenous political claims in a multiscalar way from the national arena to the family, the body, and the community.

Abiayala forges an alternate transindigenous political scale that names an alternative sense of relations and responsibility to one another and a way in which Indigenous actors at multiple scales root their own nations' and communities' struggles to broader international Indigenous rights frameworks and practices of solidarity. Abiayala is a spatial project of Indigenous solidarity and commitment to land, peoplehood, and the relationship and responsibilities between the two. Altamirano-Jiménez (2013) argues that "spatial representations are important for political purposes because they anchor historic claims to land/territory and validate identities. Since places are loci of collective memory and political identities, Indigenous peoples' ability to mobilize identity into forces of solidarity depends largely upon the specificities that determine the construction and maintenance of their identities" (7). Abiayala anticipates what Chadwick Allen has theorized as a transindigenous methodology for understanding Indigenous literary production. Transindigeneity troubles the ways in which transnationalism can reaffirm nation-states and reinscribe Indigenous people's fraught (settler) colonial relationships to them (Allen 2012; Huhndorf 2009). Abiayala, as a transborder imaginary, calls forth Indigenous notions of connection and belonging and, while working under the international system of the United Nations and other international policy bodies, complicates the terms by which these geopolitical categories are imposed and exposes their colonial nature.

Nonetheless, by ECMIA's second Continental Encuentro, held in Mexico City in 1997, the organization decided to take Abya Yala out of its name and became instead the Continental Network of Indigenous Women of the Americas (the acronym remained the same). Margarita Gutiérrez, a CONAMI founder who served as one of the bridges between ECMIA and work at the UN, shared with me that this change was pragmatic, aligning the continental network to the global regions of the UN and the global Indigenous movement. Activists also recognized that Abiayala, as a specifically Guna framework for land, did not resonate with all Indigenous peoples in the same way.

I argue, however, that this moment reveals an important dimension of scale that is too rarely discussed, specifically "unscalability." Anna Tsing (2012) calls for a theory of nonscalability that "makes it possible to see how scalability uses articulations with nonscalable forms even as it denies or erases them" (506). Tsing argues, "We need nonscalability theory to tell a different story, a story alert to the awkward, fuzzy translations and disjunctures inherent in global supply chains. There are many scale-making projects here, and they do not nest neatly" (523). "Nonscalability theory shows us the architecture of non-nesting, which is key to the (re)making of cultural diversity, capitalist and otherwise" (522). Tsing's thinking "allows scales to arise from the relationships that inform particular projects, scenes, or events" (509), and thus helps us understand Abiayala as a scale-making project, one that articulates an Indigenous politics of relationality to other living beings (land, water, plant nations, for example) and responsibility to those relations and each other. But precisely because Abiayala is constructed through a "diversity of social relations," it can resonate or, conversely, *lose resonance* as projects shift, change, or move in and between policy arenas and fields of action. Whereas Abiayala is a place of enunciation, as articulated in Emil Keme's call to action, it is not one that nests neatly across scale, nor can it always and effectively function as an alternative scale, as ECMIA eventually discovered when it tried to use Abiayala as a new scale through which to intervene in the international system.

ECMIA's decision to change its name does not necessarily represent an absolute break from or rejection of the politics and commitments embodied in the notion of Abiayala. I argue, rather, that it reveals the existence of two logics, as theorized by Sonia Alvarez (2000) in her work on the NGO boom among Latin American feminists in the lead-up to the Beijing conference. Alvarez differentiated between two logics—identity solidarity and policy advocacy—that exist simultaneously with the region's feminist organizing. It may be that the decision to rename ECMIA reflected the increased need for, and the prominence of a more outward-facing policy advocacy logic for the organization, given its need to operate within the international arena—hence the shift to "Americas" in the title. Abiayala meanwhile, could still serve as the logic of solidarity and identity that informs internal organizing. This strategic use of two different logics represents yet another instance of Indigenous women drawing on their doble mirada, their double consciousness, but also strategically using the forms of differential consciousness to doubleweave or interweave, making themselves legible to the world of global policy advocacy as needed, but also moving in and between their own epistemologies, knowledges, and scales. Such interweaving may be an important strategy when international policy creates hegemonic understandings of indigeneity and even nature itself (Altamirano-Jiménez 2013) and when states position themselves as the only arbiters of power by identifying who is worthy of rights through their own construction of the good/bad Indian dichotomy (Hale 2004). Altamirano-Jiménez cautions that "[i]n their demands for recognition, territory, and self-determination, Indigenous peoples have articulated meanings of indigeneity and cultural difference that are intelligible to the state and other transnational actors and institutions. In doing so, these peoples have reproduced the problematic distinction between "authentic" or "intelligible" and "inauthentic" indigeneity, a distinction that perpetuates structural inequalities (Hale 2005; Povinelli 2002). In challenging these inequalities, Indigenous peoples have also attempted "to expand the grid of intelligibility that neoliberalism has imposed on indigeneity and have also articulated non-state-centered understandings of identity" (Altamirano-Jiménez 2013, 2–3). Thus, the use of Abiayala as a scale of resistance to neocolonial, extractivist, and neoliberal projects is part of understanding the complexity of Indigenous women's organizing and breaking apart the ways activists fix and essentialize those identities and projects, if even strategically (Spivak 1993).

The point is not to identify moments when projects, strategies, or ideas did or did not "successfully" scale. Rather I want to take up Anna Tsing's useful call to provide "critical description[s] of relational encounters across difference" (2012, 523), precisely the forms of power negotiated by scaling within geographies of difference. It is with this in mind that I turn next to Indigenous activist's experiences with interweaving their two logics of policy advocacy and identity solidarity to build ECMIA and protect their knowledge and production through Western intellectual property rights regimes and how Indigenous women forge their own forms of feminism in the face of exclusion and discrimination among the region's feminist network.

Interweaving: Continental Indigenous Women's Activism

I have described the formation of ECMIA, how the founding members conjured Abiayala as an Indigenous scale of relation to land and each other, and how Abiayala became untenable as a scale or, to use Tsing's word, *unscalable*, within ECMIA. I move now to describe how they built this continental network and interwove their own epistemologies, knowledges, and views of the pluriverse with dominant forms of knowledge using various strategies, from protecting their weaving technologies with international intellectual property law to integrating their own notions of gender justice with and against Latin American and Caribbean feminisms. The First Continental Encuentro of Indigenous Women in Quito, Ecuador, in August 1995 helped create a collective agenda for Indigenous women in relation to the Fourth World Conference on Women in Beijing, but it also facilitated the formation of ECMIA. The hemispheric organization emerged from earlier cross-border Indigenous women's organizing, an initiative of First Nations women of Canada in 1993 that included three regional workshops held in Panama, Colombia, and Canada between 1995 and 1996. At those workshops, Indigenous women leaders from northern, central, and southern countries in the hemisphere created a continental strategy and vision to create a space where "Indigenous women promote linkages, solidarity, and exchange of experiences in order to find collective alternatives."[13] Designed to enrich women's political capacity through regional meetings and working commissions, ECMIA supports and forges Indigenous women's organizing at the community, national, and international scales. At the Second Continental Encuentro of Indigenous Women, held in Mexico City in December 1997, Indigenous women from twenty-two countries came together to create an organizational structure that designated three regions and four working commissions.[14] The third encuentro was held in Panama in March 2000, and the fourth was held in Lima, Peru, April 4–7, 2004.

The Northern Network and Quebec Native Women hosted the fifth encuentro in Kahnawake, Québec, Canada, in July 2007. The sixth encuentro returned to Mexico in 2011 and was hosted by CONAMI Mexico and the Indigenous communities in the state of Morelos. In 2013, the seventh encuentro was held in November 2015 in Guatemala City, where ECMIA celebrated its twentieth anniversary. Ironically, the encuentro was held at the Conquistador Hotel and Conference Center. Reflecting their mode of interweaving between dominant colonial and Indigenous knowledges, conference organizers, hosting more than 350 participants and 100 observers, occupied the space of the conference center by renaming meeting rooms. Those named for infamous conquistadores were reinaugurated with defiant handmade signs. A piece of yellow legal paper posted on the community board listed Wi-Fi codes for all the newly named rooms:

Ixmucané (Ex Hernán Cortes room)
Itzá (Ex Francisco Pizarro room)
Quetzalí (Ex Juan Ponce de León room)
Colibrí (Ex La Pergola)
Ixkik (Ex Espaldas room)
Gran Jaguar (Ex Gran Gobernador)
Tijax (Ex Martín de Usuou Room)

Indigenous women activists from across the hemisphere, as well as UN functionaries, NGO staffers, and other observers, gathered for keynote presentations in the Gran Jaguar meeting hall. Delegates discussed, debated, and made agreements about ancestral justice, healing, food sovereignty, land rights and the environment, Indigenous women political leaders, and the violence of extractive industries; they also created an intergenerational dialogue. As I sat in the audience of the opening plenary, I could see both the policy advocacy logic and the identity solidarity logic at play, sometimes being interwoven skillfully and other times causing friction. For example, some leaders welcomed various governmental functionaries and the director of the Ford Foundation, who addressed the convention by video conference, as signs that ECMIA was becoming a recognized political force with policy advocacy circles. Whereas others, specifically the CONAMI leadership, stood up to challenge those state actors in the room about the lack of justice for murdered Indigenous women and about their neoliberal policies that support extractivism in Indigenous territories, aligning with the ways those activists build their identity solidarity logic autonomous from the state.

Other topics debated and discussed at the encuentro included intellectual property, treaty rights, and gendered meanings of Indigenous autonomy. Their dialogues created bridges from remote pueblos to the United Nations and back. ECMIA has been a training ground for new leadership and the space to discuss Indigenous women's political subjectivity, discursive strategies, and representation struggles. It is historically important because it spans North, Central, and South America and facilitates critical linkages between regional and national movements, which are especially needed given the regional economic integration and new conditions engendered by neoliberal economic policies under

Figure 2.3. Activists from across Abiayala (North, Central, and South America) at the Seventh Continental Network of Indigenous Women, Guatemala, 2015. Pictured here (*left to right*) are Guidai Vargas Michelena, a Charrua youth from Uruguay; Rosalee Gonzalez of la Red Xicana Indígena; Tania Pariona of Chriapaq and ECMIA; Chief Caleen Sisk of the Winnemem Wintu Tribe; Rigoberta Menchú; Corrina Gould, the Tribal Chair of Confederated Villages of Lisjan/Ohlone and cofounder of Sogorea Te' Land Trust; and Alicia Niria, a youth representative for ECMIA North. Photo by the author.

the guise of free trade in addition to a global ecological crisis (see figure 2.3). ECMIA has also helped Indigenous women to become more effective actors within international spaces because it has functioned as a parallel Indigenous scale and transborder network in which Indigenous women come together to discuss shared issues, formulate strategies, and share political knowledge. This parallel structure serves as a space where Indigenous women activists launch their collective interventions and helps them to access and engage the formal mechanisms of the international system and UN bodies. More than just a parallel arena, ECMIA has also served as a mediating space in which Indigenous epistemologies can guide the activist, policy advocacy, and culture shift work enacted by Indigenous women at local, national, and international scales of power.

The member organizations of ECMIA recommitted to forging capacity, research, new proposals, and advocacy in the following areas:

- Ending violence and ancestral justice;
- Territory, environment, climate change, and food sovereignty;
- Intellectual property and biodiversity;
- Health and spirituality: sexual and reproductive health, teen pregnancy prevention, maternal mortality, and intercultural health advocacy;
- Political participation; children, indigenous youth, and intercultural education;
- Racism and discrimination.[15]

In addition to the regional networks that member organizations comprise, there are thematic commissions that move ECMIA's agenda forward by generating proposals, strategies, and coordinated campaigns for "the defense, respect and inclusion of their individual and collective rights, as women, youth, and Indigenous peoples in state policies, international and regional organizations."[16]

Moving in and between local, national, transnational, and international, as well as transindigenous and transborder scales of organization has produced new identities, new forms of consciousness, new strategies, and new frames through which to understand the issues organized Indigenous women share, especially in these times of increased globalization. For example, organizers and weavers from Mexico have entered into a transborder, transindigenous conversation with other Indigenous women on cultural production and weaving that was formerly understood as a local issue. Because of the global forces of tourism, commercialization, and corporate co-optation of a range of Indigenous knowledges, including art and textile, medicinal, herbal, and agricultural sciences, a new conversation about intellectual property law has begun. The ECMIA Commission on Craft Commercialization sponsored research by a Canadian member organization on native women's arts production and commercialization and the protection of intellectual property rights. Other member organizations carried out similar research in Guatemala. They all came together in April 1999 for the Inter-American Training Workshop on Intellectual Property Rights as it applied to Indigenous women's art designs.

Working groups on Indigenous knowledge, globalization, and Western and Indigenous concepts of intellectual property found that their designs are an intergenerational cultural inheritance. From this, they understood the need to protect the autonomy of their cultural traditions from the forces of commercialization and globalization. Whereas intellectual property law refers to individuals and applies only to marketed goods, their designs collectively belong to the community, and internal rules, protocols, and codes of ethics guide their protection and reproduction and thus require an interweaving between Western juridical traditions that inform international law and Indigenous knowledges and practices. Further, the workshop generated a proposal for action and supported drafting a common code of ethics. In the previous chapter, Lorena described the local empowerment of women's leadership in her weaver's cooperative. She also discussed the importance of participating with women from pueblos throughout Mexico and with Indigenous women throughout the hemisphere. These experiences help women to link local, transnational, transborder, and international scales of resistance and empowerment to local and even dream scales, as Indigenous weavings of Abiayala are often woven symbols of place that incorporate sacred and territorial geographies that mark one's belonging in the cosmos transmitted by dreams and through ancestral knowledge. Weaving is often an intergenerational and collective process of social reproduction, argues Maya K'iche scholar Floridalma Boj Lopez (2017b), as one blouse can represent an entire system of meaning and relating. Further, she argues that Maya clothing is a form of Indigenous geography that links Indigenous people, specifically migrants, "to particular histories and landscapes of the regions they are from. It is through this specificity that Mayas connect to their ancestral places of origin" (199). Because many weavings are worn at the scale of the body, they have been identified by Indigenous women activists as part of their bodily autonomy, often marking important times in a girl's or woman's life. The rebozo, for example, is worn in Mexico and Guatemala for warmth and utility, but it also is used as a woven cradle for children not limited only to mothers, but worn by their mothers, sisters, aunts, friends, neighbors, and grandmothers.

Yaqui legal scholar Rebecca Tsosie discusses the ways Indigenous cultures are viewed through the lens of colonialism and seen as part of the "'common goods' that belong to society as a whole, rather than as a source of legal entitlements for native peoples" (1997, 6). Others argue that the Indigenous notion of stewardship of territories and relatives (or of natural resources, in the Western view) originates in Indigenous normative systems that define the relationship between people and the world around them and that date back to the origin stories of many First Nations, which predate Anglo-American legal principals and, as such, are not dependent on them (Carpenter, Katyal, and Riley 2010, 587). Finally, other legal scholars focusing on Indigenous intellectual property rights have recognized the unique nature of Indigenous knowledges. They view it as unlike any other intellectual property because it not only touches on copyright, patents, trademarks, design, and restricted or confidential information but also raises ethical, cultural, historical, political, religious/spiritual, and moral issues (Anderson 2010).

The interweave of Indigenous knowledges and protocols and Western legal traditions produce new strategies that allow traditional knowledge to blend with women's rights, human rights, and Indigenous rights discourses. The book *Our Weavings Are Books the Colonizer Could Not Burn* (2020) tells the story of how the National Movement of Maya Weavers of Guatemala fought against the corporate takeover of their territories, bodies, weavings, and knowledges that have been, for millennia, protected in a communitarian and collective manner. Their scalar analysis calls attention to the multiple plundering of their bodies being folklorized for state and private tourism, and of their collective creations by those wanting to patent them. They fight against the colonial perspective that Indigenous cultural knowledge "belongs to nobody" by insisting the collective knowledge and consciousness is woven together and belong to all Indigenous people. Hence, they argue, any individual business appropriation represents a form of dispossession, expropriation, and theft against the pueblo. Next, I show how these forms of doble mirada create differential consciousnesses that allow Indigenous women activists to engage, incorporate, and challenge social movement discourses and actors at each scale of their organizing while remaining rooted in their struggle for Indigenous autonomy. Differential consciousness is produced by interweaving and has become an important strategy for navigating geographies of difference and the different organization of power at each scale.

Feminism's Others: Indigenous Women's (Mis)Encounters with Latin American and Caribbean Feminism

With an eye toward understanding transnational politics of difference, I have attended four Latin American and Caribbean feminist encuentros (the ninth through twelfth gatherings in the Dominican Republic, Costa Rica, Brazil, and Mexico), as well as numerous other women's movement, lesbian feminist, and Indigenous gatherings in the region. As Sonia Alvarez (1998), a leading scholar of women's movements in Latin America and the Caribbean, noted, the 1995 World Conference of Women in Beijing, China, was an important moment in the growth and expansion of feminist networks in the region. Yet this expansion of the multiple, new ways feminism and feminists were being engaged did not come without negotiation and conflict between certain diverse forms of feminism and what some called "hegemonic feminism" (Hernández Castillo 2008) in the region; one that foregrounded a single lens of analysis based on gender, ignoring other structures of power and exclusion. The political project of feminism in Latin America and the Caribbean has long grappled with the challenge of "inclusion" and, conversely, its practices of exclusion based on class, sexuality, and race. Demands by lesbian feminists, popular feminists, Black feminists, and others throughout the region caused many históricas (historic feminists) consternation and concern as they asked themselves whether feminism would be watered down (Lamas 1991). Would each meeting be a school for new activists to learn about feminism instead of a meeting of activists with a shared agenda to forge ahead? Although some of these concerns were legitimate, others exposed subtle and not so subtle class and racial/ethnic prejudices and a failure to recognize that gender oppression is lived through forms of class, racial/ethnic, and Indigenous oppression. The understanding of the double or triple burden of multiply marginalized women had sometimes been articulated in earlier Latin American and Caribbean feminist encounters, but usually only when a critical mass had been reached, or multiple movements provided momentum (Alvarez et al. 2002). Over the past forty years, these allied political formations have challenged narrow notions of feminism and expanded both the political philosophy and the political subjectivity of feminism—what some have called decentering feminism (Hernández Castillo 2008).

This contentious process of expanding Latin American and Caribbean feminism has been uneven and, as with any contentious process, not without political battles over the inclusion of working-class and popular feminisms, lesbian women, Afro-descendant women, Indigenous women, and transwomen. Some currents that became separate movements in their own right emerged within the region's feminist movement. The lesbian movement in the region, for example, was arguably born within the feminist movement, but it branched off when activists decided they needed to focus on their own alternative cultures rather than leading the women's movement, the labor movement, political parties, and so on (Mogrovejo 2000). To various degrees, many other forms of feminisms emerged as a set of tensions and preoccupations between two different movements. For example, women in the Latin American and Caribbean Afro-descendants movement formed their political subjectivities, demands, and specific mode of hacer política (doing politics) within one movement while confronting blockages and limited analysis there. Many early Black feminists participated in the feminist encuentros and found solidarity there, but also racism, exclusion, and a narrow vision of liberation based solely on gender (Carneiro 2000, Carneiro 2016; Perry 2016; Pons Cardoso 2016). This was also true of the Indigenous women's movement, whose regional articulation first occurred within the Beijing NGO process and its discontents, but its appearance was a reflection of the growing strength of Indigenous mass mobilizations that exploded onto the scene in the 1990s.

Whereas the concept of autonomy (explored in chapter 1) has been key to defining the political agenda of the Indigenous movement in Mexico, the feminist movement has generated at least two other concepts of autonomy. Latin American feminist forms of autonomy were formed by two different fierce ideological battles. With roots firmly in the Left, the first debates about autonomy within Latin American feminism developed the notion of feminist autonomy vis-à-vis political parties and revolutionary movements. Leftists and revolutionary activists who conceptualized their feminism as a form of doble militancia (double activism) learned a form of organizational autonomy that kept their feminist activism distinct from their roles in leftist parties. The second struggle emerged from the Beijing process itself and the intense debates therein between autonomous feminists (autónomas), who critiqued the "NGOization" of feminism under neoliberalism and called for autonomy from institutionalized control by foundations, funding agencies, universities, NGOs, and the state, and feminists who worked in them, whom the autónomas referred to derisively as institucionalizadas (Alvarez 1998; Alvarez et al. 2002).

When I attended earlier encuentros, Indigenous women had no organized presence, although a few Indigenous women were there. The painful lack of space for and the huge chasm between movements for gender and sexual liberation and the Indigenous resurgence was painfully illustrated by a comment from a powerful young activist in the lesbian caucus at the ninth encuentro in Costa Rica in 2002. As an activist formed in multi-issue organizing and women of color feminist space, I had asked about the spaces for Indigenous and lesbian of color organizing. A young, powerful lesbian activist from Guatemala looked at me and said, "Because I am lesbian, I am no longer Maya." Her comment represents the incommensurability between her two life experiences/life worlds at that time but also the notion that in order to participate in lesbian and feminist spaces, one has the impossible task of checking one's class, racial, or Indigenous identity at the door and the crushing reality that many lesbians could not live in their families and communities without tremendous violence and discrimination.

For this reason, the Tenth Latin American and Caribbean Feminist Encuentro in São Paulo, Brazil, in 2005 was much anticipated. It was the first to deal with questions of racial, ethnic, sexual, and generational differences in a structured and direct manner by including breakout sessions called "Complex Dialogues" for all fifteen hundred participants. These small sessions, facilitated by movement leaders, were designed to facilitate discussion and debate around questions of diversity in relation to processes of democratization.[17] In addition to the "Complex Dialogues," workshops and presentations, led by women from a wide range of feminist organizations in the region, created a space to share projects, strategies, and histories. One of the most prominent feminist

NGOs in the region organized a session on "Amazonian Indigenous Women, Organization, and Resistance." But, it soon became a flashpoint of debate regarding race, indigeneity, and representation. This unprogrammed "complex dialogue" inadvertently threw into sharp relief the problematic way in which Indigenous women's struggles for rights are framed within feminist activist and human rights circles, raising a thorny question: Are Indigenous women merely clients of feminist NGOs, or equal partners who articulate and enact their gendered critiques and at times Indigenous feminist analyses? The debate revolved around power, feminist racism, issues of representation between subjects and objects of research, mestiza and Indigenous visions of feminism and human rights, and the place of feminism's Others.

The workshop initially seemed to proceed as planned until a lawyer for a prominent NGO began her portion of the presentation on Indigenous women's human rights in the Peruvian Amazon. Using the logic deployed by mestizo nationalism, she prefaced her talk with comments about the grandeur of ancient Indigenous cultures and the former power of their science, arts, and architecture. Upon returning to current times, the NGO lawyer's report couched human rights violations in highly sensationalized terms, portraying Indigenous women as passive victims and Indigenous men as ignorant savages. In describing the human rights violations that men perpetrated on women, the lawyer represented Indigenous cultures through the tropes of disgust and fascination common in colonial modes of narration and representation. This did not sit well with the numerous Indigenous women from throughout the region who attended the workshop, particularly because this event was one of the only sessions dedicated to Indigenous women's issues at the tenth feminist encuentro, which in itself is telling.

Without having met each other before the workshop, one by one, all the Indigenous women in the room condemned the human rights violations while applauding the goals of the NGO's work. Still, each one interrogated the way in which the mestiza lawyer chose to represent Indigenous peoples and cultures. We demanded critical reflection on relations of power and the need to conduct human rights work that allows victims to speak, narrate, and make meaning for themselves by engaging in a politics of empowerment rather than a missionizing savior narrative. The first to speak up was Ana, a seasoned Garífuna and international human rights activist who was so indignant she had tears in her eyes as she asked why this mestiza feminist would portray Indigenous communities as savage and uncivilized. Mobilizing all the authority of social science objectivity, the feminist NGO lawyer pointed out that she had begun her talk by saying that Indigenous people of the Amazon were once part of a great and mighty civilization. Rejecting this alibi of a romantic past, I introduced myself and asked why the women themselves were not present to share their own participation in the project and devise their own strategies for confronting these human rights violations if indeed the goal of the project was to build their capacity to document, present, and analyze human rights violations. The NGO worker responded: "Because they are not feminists and this is a feminist gathering."

Next, a powerful young leader of the regional network of Brazilian Amazonian Indigenous women claimed the word *feminist* as her own and, after congratulating the NGO on the project and the work being done, called into question the kinds of unequal relationships mestiza feminists were building with Indigenous women. In a passionate speech, she called for a kind of feminist politics in which Indigenous women represented themselves, their stories, their own struggles, and their own political interests. As each Indigenous women leader spoke in turn, it became clear that a shared agenda and vision of Indigenous women's feminism was in the making—one that challenged those who would claim to speak for them. After the workshop, the Indigenous women in the room decided to form an Indigenous caucus within the feminist encuentro. They called activists to attend a meeting in which they discussed their own visions, strategized about how to network better, and wrote a declaration that was presented to all the attendees of the encuentro at the final session.

The stakes over who controls the discourse about Indigenous women and how they seek and safeguard their own human rights went far beyond the immediate debate in that room in São Paulo. The inverse of a cultural alibi, human rights discourses that use the supposed brutality and inherent inequality of Indigenous cultures—what I term the gendered logic of racism (see chapter 1)—perpetuate a logic whereby states can deny Indigenous peoples their rights because of their purported backwardness. Martha Sánchez Néstor, CONAMI leader and then General Coordinator of the National Indigenous Plural Assembly for Autonomy (ANIPA) spoke powerfully about how cultural racism within feminist discourse especially within the NGO sector, colludes with state power that has attempted to define Indigenous cultures. Yet as the comments and the opposition within the NGO workshop illustrate, organized Indigenous women contest the power of other civil society actors—namely, NGOs—to define, represent, and regulate their identities and cultures. More than a struggle over racism and representation, this was a process of constructing Indigenous subjectivity and a mode of contesting the uneven terrain of power where NGOs and civil society have been given a larger role in neoliberal governance and in the regulation of identities that were once only the purview of the state. The activists at the workshop organized as Indigenous women for the first time in the history of the encuentros. While other participants were attending the final dance party of the encuentro, activists from Argentina, Guatemala, Mexico, Brazil, and the United States stayed in the computer room to draft and revise our final statement (see figure 2.4 for a photo taken after that work). Activists from Guatemala and the Amazonian Indigenous Women's Network were selected to read the statement. They prepared themselves as the 1,500 feminists from across the region gathered, and they read the Indigenous Women's Caucus statement at the final plenary (see figures 2.5, 2.6, and 2.7). The pain and anger that Indigenous women confronted at the tenth encuentro generated a response that provided a new opening through which to articulate their visions of feminisms at the continental level.

Nonetheless, the path toward conversation and coalition has been full of challenges. Indigenous women activists attended the Eleventh Latin American and Feminist Encuentro in Mexico City in March 2009 in record numbers. Organizers put together a forum to discuss racism within the feminist movement and the advancement of women's rights by Indigenous rights activists. The organized presence of more than one hundred Indigenous women was a

Figure 2.4. After the organizing meeting of the First Indigenous Women's Caucus, Tenth Latin American and Caribbean Encuentro, 2005. Photo courtesy of the author.

Figure 2.5. Members of the Amazonian Indigenous Women's Network at the Tenth Latin American and Caribbean Encuentro, 2005. Photo by the author.

Figure 2.6. Preparing to read the statement from the Indigenous Women's Caucus at the Tenth Latin American and Caribbean Encuentro, 2005. Photo courtesy of the author.

Figure 2.7. Reading the Indigenous Women's Caucus Statement at the Tenth Latin American and Caribbean Encuentro, 2005. Photo by the author.

first in the gathering's twenty-five-year history. Nonetheless, the Mexico City meetings were marred by charges of racism and exclusion. Despite being some of the largest concurrent meetings, the Indigenous women's sessions were held in the smallest rooms, with inadequate space and lighting and no sound system (see figures 2.8 and 2.9). Held in a former convent in the colonial center of historic Mexico City, the event space was under construction, and attendees had to pass through huge hanging sheets of plastic to move from space to space. The Indigenous women's sessions were held in small, dark cement rooms with no lighting, whereas the main gathering space looked like a set for a talk show, complete with a stage, modern pink leather couches, and a large screen (partially visible in the photo of Indigenous women reading their statement denouncing racism and calling for solidarity with the Indigenous movement see figure 2.10). As a result, those activists from the Indigenous rights movement throughout the continent who had entertained the feminist label to describe their activities left the conference reasserting their difference and distancing themselves from feminists. Conference organizers gave no official response. When I spoke to an organizer at the eleventh encuentro, she was dismissive and did not seem to care. It became clear that within the feminist

Figure 2.8. Martha Sánchez Nestor addressing one of the largest breakout sessions, focused on Indigenous women, at the Eleventh Latin American and the Caribbean Feminist Encuentro, Mexico City, 2009. Photo by the author.

Figure 2.9. No light or microphone was available during the session on Indigenous women's activism at the Eleventh Latin American and the Caribbean Feminist Encuentro, Mexico City, 2009. Photo by the author.

movement, at least as articulated within the organized space of the region's encuentros, Indigenous women were unintelligible and inaudible as feminist subjects who speak for themselves.

Over the years, the Latin American feminist movement has sought to embrace diversity, and yet the chasm and disconnect between Indigenous activists and a largely middle-class, urban, and mestiza feminism have proven a stubbornly difficult gap to bridge (Alverez et al. 2002; Alvarez et al. 2014). To be sure, some feminist activists and scholars have informed and engaged with Indigenous activists and helped lead workshops and facilitate dialogue, but some Indigenous activists remained so alienated that they did not even go to the Mexico City meeting and dismissed it as "the hegemonic feminist conference." Although feminism in the region was initially an oppositional force of social transformation that challenged the patriarchal organization of power, it has not always been attentive to the ways patriarchal power is organized around indigeneity, class, race, gender normativity, and disability, among other vectors of power. Despite many young feminists in Mexico growing up and coming of age during the Zapatista era, few at the eleventh encuentro seemed to understand or express solidarity with Indigenous women's struggles. They did not seem to be invested in a politics of difference or solidarity. Following tradition, at the final plenary, Indigenous, Black, youth, transgender, and lesbian groups read their statements, but the atmosphere, instead of promoting debate and discussion, seemed like a parade of the excluded (see figure 2.10). The audience was silent and somewhat mystified. For a growing number of Indigenous feminists and other gender-based activists, the fight for women's rights is something undertaken within their communities and the Indigenous movement. The push to emphasize gender separately from the struggle for Indigenous rights has been externally imposed and impedes productive intercultural dialogue and alliance building.[18] Increasingly, as I show in the coda of this book, Indigenous women movement leaders challenge what they call capitalist heteropatriarchy as part of their challenge against racism, violence, colonialism, and extractivism in Mexico and are thus forging their own forms of Indigenous feminist praxis.

Other Paths of Feminism: Indigenous Women's Gendered Insurgencies across Abiayala

After a morning ceremony and an event at the historic center, I was still recovering from twenty hours of travel. I arrived late at the large auditorium where more than a hundred Indigenous women gathered for the national gathering of CONAMI. In honor of its twenty-first anniversary, CONAMI members

Figure 2.10. Indigenous women reading their declaration denouncing racism at the Eleventh Latin American and the Caribbean Feminist Encuentro, Mexico City, 2009. Photo by the author.

gathered in 2018 at ceremonial and meeting spaces scattered throughout Maya Territory, between Felipe Carillo Puerto and Bacalar, Quintana Roo, Mexico. As I walked in, I heard Tomasa Sandoval, a P'urépecha activist I have known almost twenty years, passionately declaring, "I am not a feminist. I am a defender of Indigenous peoples." The first plenary session format moved between one mayora (elder) and one youth member. In response to Sandoval's comment, a young Hñähñú activist, Liz Hernández Cruz, shared: "I get frustrated when we are always asked to serve. Men have hands and arms." After more reflection, she added, "we have the right to decide [about our bodies]." Margarita Gutiérrez, a Hñähñú activist whose story of coming to consciousness around Indigenous women's rights during the San Andrés Accords I discussed in chapter 1, stated: "Feminisms, yes, we believe in equality and human rights [for Indigenous women]. I learned in the San Andrés Accords that Indigenous women's rights exist. We don't share many feminist practices. For us, it is not a struggle of individuals, it is a struggle against a system. In Geneva, we created a document about equality and duality. Feminism from our cosmovision."[19] Margarita concluded by turning to her left and greeting the young Hñähñú activist who had spoken just before her in their language; she told the younger woman that she was happy to see her there and hugged her. Adriana Boj, a Maya leader from Felipe Carrillo Puerto and one of the organizers of the encuentro, contributed to this line of discussion, stating, "Feminism is an individual way of living, but it is also a collective struggle. For Indigenous women, it is a process of construction. . . . It is not a struggle of genders one against the other, but it is a collective struggle." Adriana puts her finger on a crucial tenet of Indigenous women's political thought and how it disrupts the either/or binary thinking that would posit Indigenous rights as collective rights in tension with women's rights as individual rights—as though women are not a group themselves or as though Indigenous women could stop being Indigenous to become individuals and therefore bearers of (women's) rights. I first learned how activists view Indigenous rights and women's rights as inextricably bound from the theoretical insights that Tomasa Sandoval had elaborated almost twenty years earlier, in 2001, at the second national encuentro organized by CONAMI in Chilpancingo, Guerrero.

Triqui organizer Esther Gonzalez, who has lived in the large Oaxacan Indigenous migrant community of agricultural workers in San Quintin, Baja California, since she was a child, continued the discussion by speaking of alliances and allied histories of struggle and how the organizational roots of Indigenous feminism grow out of their own organizational experiences: "Feminism was a collective struggle of economic but more [of] political equality. I don't call myself a feminist but thanks to them, we are where we are here. I didn't learn about the struggle for women's rights in the community or even the university but in the organization of Indigenous women in San Quintin. . . . There I learned the struggle for Indigenous women." Teresa Emeterio, a Mixe organizer who was active during the very first years of CONAMI and returned to attend the encuentro after almost twenty years, stated, "I'm with the Consorcio [para el Diálogo Paralamentario y la Equidad Oaxaca (Consortium for Parliamentary Dialogue and Equality Oaxaca)] a feminist organization . . . some people think feminism is the opposite from machismo . . . but we have a communitarian feminism." Paty Sandoval, a P'urépecha activist who grew up in the Indigenous movement (both her parents are activists; her mother is Tomasa, who opened this conversation), emphatically stated, "There is not just one feminism, but many feminisms. We have to rethink feminisms to place ourselves in the individual identity and the collective struggle. I identify individually as a feminist. In the collective, we have to think through what we want in terms of our own realities. Allies made this possible." From there the conversation went on to focus on the body, moving from how the debate for voluntary motherhood has erased Indigenous women and the right to bodily integrity and autonomy until the room erupted in laughter and cheers when someone asked, "What about pleasure?"

I share this discussion at length because it illustrates the diversity of perspectives within Indigenous conversations about feminism in Mexico. Further, it illustrates many rich threads of Indigenous feminist and women's activism and thinking. The dialogue reveals important intergenerational dialogues, differences, and history sharing, the alternative sources of Indigenous women's gender activism, which some call feminism; tensions in Western juridical, political, and feminist thought between individual and collective subjects, and how Indigenous women navigate these tensions; their thinking about allies; and their need to have their own spaces of reflection and articulation. Contrast this conversation with one at the twentieth anniversary of ECMIA in 2015 in Guatemala, three years before the CONAMI meeting in Quintana Roo, when a mestiza in attendance asked, "What about feminism?," shifting the discussion away from what was being discussed at the time. This intrusion flattened the dialogue as frustration roiled around the room; feminism became some kind of political litmus test rather than an understanding of the nuanced and complex ways Indigenous feminism and gender-based activism are rooted in other concerns central to Indigenous communities and organizations. At the same time they have points of connection to mainstream feminist movements. While there are clear alliances with some feminists, other sectors of the feminist movement have been critiqued for their ethnocentrism, racism, class-bias, and exclusionary practices leading some activists and thinkers to refer to them as hegemonic or colonial feminisms (Cumes 2018). In what felt like a forced debate, Indigenous women from around the continent identified as feminists, whereas many others roundly rejected the term because of the racism many had experienced in the women's movement in their own countries and perhaps because of the frustration they felt when their agendas were waylaid to check this box. The ways hegemonic feminists have repeatedly asked Indigenous women to split their gender justice struggle from their land defense or work fighting for Indigenous rights is part of why many Indigenous women distance themselves from feminism. For example Maya Kaqchikel writer, activist, and thinker Aura Cumes (2018) states, "I do not define myself as a feminist because I fight from indigenous ideologies, from a sense of life that has to do with a more plural reach" (2). She argues that colonial feminism is characterized by the assumption that it already encompasses all women's struggles without understanding the intersectional struggle of Black and Indigenous women. While feminism has not been the source of Indigenous women's political consciousness, for the most part, Cumes reflects, "When indigenous women name ourselves feminists, it is [treated] almost as if feminism had given us the only possible political existence, and that is not so, I do not want to subordinate myself at any time under feminist epistemology as the only form of existence ensures" (2–3).

Organized Indigenous women have created a parallel and independent movement for Indigenous rights that engages in intersectional gender justice and antiviolence work in which their own national contexts are interwoven with transborder spaces of action and solidarity. Martha Sánchez Néstor (2005) theorizes the "doble mirada" of Indigenous women organizers who work for women's rights within an Indigenous or collective rights framework by calling for gender balance, equity, and an end to gendered and sexual violence, and by honoring the interconnection of cosmovision with political economy. The concept of the doble mirada names not just a political positionality but a way of *doing politics* that centers Indigenous women, their epistemologies, visions, and political projects while visibilizing their commitment to relationality—constructing their own liberation connected to the web of relations that situate them, thereby bridging and transforming themselves and their relations. The doble mirada or considering the knowledges, feelings, ontologies, desires, and politics articulated between two positionalities that in Western thought have been conceptualized as separate offers ways to bridges the dualities imposed by these rationalities. The doble mirada looks between the Indigenous and the women's movements; the collective and the individual, the local and the global; to name a few. Sánchez Néstor (2005) describes how the doble mirada between "our compelling heart in the struggle of our indigenous peoples [and] the struggle for our rights as women, [is where] we build an identity as indigenous feminists so that we know how, when and where to act in our community, collective and personal field" (98).

Activist Indigenous women have generated their own critique of racism and patriarchal violence, and at times they interface with hegemonic feminism but are not indebted to it philosophically or organizationally (Hernández Castillo 2010a). Although scholars have called attention to the development of what they call the "sidestreaming" of feminism into new and unexpected places (Alvarez et al. 2017), the different roots of Indigenous women's gendered analysis and politics have created an alternative feminist wellspring that emerges from gendered struggles within their communities and movements, leading to different feminisms—ones whose constellation of practices is informing Indigenous struggles in Latin America but also has the potential, along with the work of Black feminisms, the gendered political activism within Afro-descendants movements, trans and other feminisms from the margins, to reinvigorate feminist movements in the region. Indigenous women's gendered activism, consciousness, and cultural and contextual differences are diverse, making it impossible to define Indigenous feminism or gender consciousness as a homogenous or unified field, yet they do share political currents, visions, discourses, and other common threads. Some Indigenous women activist leaders have elaborated an Indigenous feminist posture, whereas others reject it, sometimes strategically, to protest the way the term has been associated with Western individualism and limited by Eurocentric, elitist assumptions based on cultural and political hegemonies. At the same time, however, they often do what many would call feminist or underground feminist work. Ultimately, multiple Indigenous feminisms exist. Many of these rich traditions of gendered analysis and resistance are obscured by hegemonic feminisms in the United States and Latin America. Indigenous women activists have challenged the idea that gender could be isolated from colonialism, race, class, sexuality, and other axes of power. Their politics challenge gender and sexual hierarchies from theories, philosophies, and paradigms that are deeply embedded in their cosmovisions. Hernández Castillo (2001) has called attention to how Indigenous women's organizing and forms of feminism decenter feminist ethnocentrism and Indigenous nationalism.

While a diverse array of Indigenous women's politics and philosophies can be called feminist, one thread many share is that Indigenous feminist consciousness and gender-based activism emerges within and along with Indigenous struggles. Indigenous women locate the struggle for and possibility of gender justice and dignity within their communities and society at large. For example, Myrna Cunningham, Nicaraguan Miskita feminist, Indigenous rights activist, surgeon, and former United Nations Permanent Forum on Indigenous Issues, reflects on "Indigenous Women's Vision of Inclusive Feminism" (2006), arguing, "Our cultures, then, offer a model of gender justice that Indigenous women can draw from. This egalitarian ethic has been eroded over centuries of colonization. Yet it remains at the core of our cultures. We believe that Indigenous women's struggles should be against the patriarchal systems, which grew out of colonialism, and not against Indigenous men" (57). Indigenous feminist and women's rights activists by and large reject the false duality that frames how women's rights are articulated in Western juridical traditions—as an individual right, whereas Indigenous rights are seen as a collective right—and specifically how these are considered to contradict each other (Blackwell 2012; Espinosa Damián 2009). Repeatedly, Indigenous women leaders offer clarity surrounding this seeming contradiction by stating that full Indigenous/collective rights cannot exist without women's rights within the collective. In turn, full women's rights cannot be enjoyed without Indigenous rights, as Indigenous women cannot, and should not be made to, separate their gender from their indigeneity. Also, activists remind us that if Indigenous and Afro-descendent women are not free, then women are not free. The intersectional understanding of their struggles—that they must fight capitalist, racial, and gendered oppression—allows many of them to see their own struggles as interconnected with others'. Activists of ECMIA (2010) described it as a set of interrelated scales in this way: "Identity for indigenous women is constructed in an equilibrium of belongings: a collectivity, a pueblo, and as an individual as a woman" (58).

Indigenous women's forms of feminist consciousness are rooted in what Lenape scholar Joanne Barker (2015) calls the *polity of Indigenous people* which she defines as "the unique governance, territory, and culture of an Indigenous people in a system of (non)human relationships and responsibilities to one another" (1). Indigenous gender consciousness and feminism emerges from the web of sociospiritual relationships in Indigenous cosmovisions, which often foreground interbeing and interconnection (Cabrera Pérez-Armiñan and Macleod 2000). For example, numerous Indigenous thinkers and strategists conceptualize women's bodies as being linked to land as a way to express embodied knowleges and interconnections. They view Mother Earth's well-being as inextricably interlinked to the well-being of Indigenous women's bodies and of people more generally. Once dismissed as essentialist, scientific, environmental, spiritual, healing, and many other knowledge holders now embrace the idea that what happens to the earth happens to all of us and is manifest in our bodies (as evidenced by pesticides and heavy metals being found in human tissue and breast milk). Indigenous feminists, in general, insist that struggles for Sumak Kawsay (buenvivir, or good living), for land and water defense, and for the health and well-being of Mother Earth are women's issues, indeed feminist issues. While some Indigenous feminists conceptualize gender roles through Indigenous cosmovisioins, others, such as Xinca communitarian feminist Lorena Cabnal (2010), call attention to ancestral patriarchy that shapes Indigenous cosmology and ideas of reciprocity. In doing so Cabnal questions the ways the Earth is gendered female, receptive, reproductive, and life generating while the sun is gendered male with superiority and power over the Earth (19). Uprooting the heteronormative and patriarchal roots of Indigenous cosmologies allows her to question compulsory motherhood, heteronormativity, and to radicalize the body-territory couplet. She says, "I do not defend my land territory just because I need the natural goods to live and [want to] leave dignified life for other generations. In the approach of recovery and historical defense of my land body territory, I recover my expropriated body, to generate life, joy vitality, pleasures and [to] build liberating knowledge for decision-making" and defend land territory to have "a space on earth that dignifies my existence, and promotes my life in fullness" (23). Despite differences in approach, Cunningham (2009) points to the folly of ignoring the urgency of Indigenous women's issues: "we have seen ongoing violations of our human rights and fundamental freedoms as armed conflicts rage on our lands and as our seeds are pirated by industries that contaminate our bodies and ecosystems with genetically modified organisms. These are not only 'Indigenous problems.' These are the crises that threaten to undermine development and human rights around the world. Therefore, these issues should be at the top of the agenda of the women's movement, for we are all seriously affected by the processes of economic 'expansion' that are taking place within our territories" (57). Many Indigenous women's rights activists have worked to ground themselves in Indigenous epistemologies and break the legacies of colonialism or in their words racism, patriarchy, and capitalism. While initially attention to women's rights was called divisive, Zapotec feminist and migrant rights activist Odilia Romero Hernández, has flipped the script by framing the work of dismantling patriarchal structures as central to the work of decolonization. For example, in chapter 4, I discuss a binational workshop we led where she presented a history of the colonial origins of the contemporary binary sex/gender system imposed through domination and gendercide (Miranda 2010). Using that analysis as part of her popular political education training, she worked to convince the male comrades in her mixed-gender organization to take action is to uproot patriarchal systems of power in their organization and society at large. Precolonial notions of duality, complimentarity and balance have been central to Indigenous conversations about gender throughout Abiayala in ways that empower and silence Indigenous feminisms and women's rights work.

Margarita Gutiérrez edited *Dualidad y Complementariedad* (2010), working with women activists gathered for a meeting the of ECMIA. They wanted to systematize and foreground the concepts of duality and complementarity in relation to gender in their Indigenous communities that included the Quechua of Ecuador, Muisca of Colombia, Mapuche of Chile, and Hñahñú and Triqui from México. Drawing from the collective knowledge of the activists, they distinguished their own understanding of gender-based activism foregrounding the principles of balance, harmony, and equilibrium in their social and spiritual relations in contrast to the way they viewed European and Latin American feminisms based on individualism and "self-efficiency." They asserted that Indigenous women do not fight against men; they fight against the system that exploits and dominates everyone (22). They drew the analysis of their lived conditions based on the long history of understanding how Indigenous women are situated by intersecting colonial systems of oppression based on race/ethnicity, class, and gender hierarchies. This is a shared perspective with women of color feminist activists in the United States, who in the 1960s and 1970s developed from their social movement praxis naming simultaneous, co-constitutive, and intersecting oppressions, or what was later called intersectionality (Crenshaw 1991). Their work together centered on describing key characteristics important to understanding Indigenous women's consciousness like duality, complementarity, reciprocity, equilibrium, equity, and parity. For example, they defined duality as an important principle that is made up of women and men in a complementary manner (26). Indigenous two-spirit and feminist activists in the north have also identified that more than having a balance of men and women, duality means acknowledging the masculine and feminine energies present in each person. The activists identified complementarity in relation to a partner, to others in society, and nature and its elements since we are all part of the material and immaterial worlds (26). They discussed each of these concepts collectively and highlighted what they meant within their own Indigenous cultures. For example, for the Muisca (Chibcha) of Colombia shared that complementarity is understood as mutual aid, equality, and respect that all rise and no one is left behind, not even opposites (47). Ideas of parity, equity, and equilibrium were described this way: "as indigenous women we struggle for relationships based on equity, fair treatment and social equality in community life, in political life, in representation and in remuneration to maintain equilibrium in balance and in good relation with men and women that walk equally in the struggle for our rights [as a people]. It is fair treatment and equality that we call parity" (27). Cumes (2014) describes three postures among Maya women activists: those who reject Western feminism to embrace ideas of *complementariedad, dualidad, equilibrio,* and *reciprocidad* within Maya Cosmovision; another group that departs from the first to explain the current struggles of women and by complicating notions of *cultura, cosmovisión, complementariedad,* and *dualidad* (243); and the last group, Maya women who have adopted feminism and identify as feminists by incorporating the movement's vocabulary, proposals, and principles. However, they still maintain a strong identity as Maya women. She calls attention to how gender can become a colonizing discourse and challenges the false dichotomy that colonial feminists see Indigenous patriarchy as the source of all oppression of Indigenous women while Indigenous essentialism justifies patriarchy and sexism. Cumes asserts that notions of *complementariedad, dualidad, reciprocidad,* and *equilibrio* are important to understanding the relations between women and men and are important to Maya societies, but not at the expense of Maya women.

Over a decade later, representing multiple generations of CONAMI members, Fabiola Del Jurado Mendoza, Norma Don Juan Pérez, Lizbeth Hernández Cruz, and Laura Hernández Peréz collaborated with feminist academics Patricia Castañeda and Beatriz Gómez Barrenechea on a chapter (2022) to name their relations of gender from Indigenous communitarian practice and theorize their own political experience by using "feel-thinking, a process that dismantles and resignifies ethnocentric and academic notions of information and knowledge" (16). Based on reflections by CONAMI members, they identified the sources of their political thought rooted in ancestral ways of thinking, spirituality, *la lucha de las abuelas* (the struggle of the grandmothers/ancestors), *trabajo, tejido*, and *palabra* (work, weave, and word). Members highlighted key terminology that they use for their activism. While they do not view what they do as part of the mainstream definition of politics, rather they label what they do as service. They write, "to serve means to work without receiving a wage, to realize voluntary communitarian work for and through struggle"(31), which are ideas closely linked to Indigenous notions of comunalidad (communalism) and the gendered labor of comunalidad I discuss in chapter 3. The CONAMI activists/knowledge holders identified this form of service and political philosophy as being informed by what they call ancestral thought—a form of "thought that comes from the earth and the four elements (air, water, fire, and earth), which is where the force to fight comes from, as those who preceded us did, and that, at the same time" as Lourdes Ramires Martinez reflected, they act for future generations or as "'a precedent for the other generations that come behind us'" (29). Acting for past and future generations, CONAMI members reflected on their "Work, Weave, and Word": "A primary source is also the work that is done in communities, linked to the weave of networks, but, above all, the word with which political work is created. The word synthesizes 'the learning and is expressed through traditions' (Esther Ramirez Gonzalez), and 'of our own knowledge and thoughts' (Teresa Rios Cruz) (29). Finally, they reiterated the principals the members of ECMIA had explored more than a decade before, placing the wellspring of Indigenous women's activism within the ideals of "balance, complementarity, collectivity" (35). In fact, Norma Don Juan Pérez reflected, "Complementarity starts from recognizing that we all have something to contribute to the collective good and that it is not about competing" (35).

Indigenous women activists use these ideals to engage in their organizations and spaces through their collective notion of equilibrium between genders and a commitment to carry out their work in mixed organizations, in their families, and their communities at large. The notion of balance between genders functions alongside the often touted concept of complementarity, which some Indigenous feminists point out is often used as a way to silence their fight for inclusion and gender justice. Other Indigenous feminists embrace this pre-Columbian notion of gendered parity or even see it as aspirational. For example, Chancoso discusses complementarity: "Complementarity is to treat each other on equal footing, to wash the face with both hands, to be [of] mutual help. It is also breaking the imposition, selfishness, [and] individuality. It is the contribution of what the other lacks, not a cane, nor a crutch [to carry the weight] of the other and even less, or to do labor of the other. It is to support each other to address, develop and foster joint dreams" (Chancoso 2010, 7, cited in Caudillo Félix 2012, 193).

Alma López, a K'iche' feminist and former council member of the City of Quetzaltenango, states:

> The philosophical principles that I recover from my culture are equality, complementarity between men and women, and between men and men and women and women. That part of the Mayan culture currently doesn't exist, and to state the contrary is to turn a blind eye to the oppression that indigenous women suffer. Complementarity is now the only part of history; today there is only inequality, but complementarity and equality can be constructed. I would also recover the double vision, or the idea of the *cabawil*, the one who can look forward and back, to one side and the other, and see the black and white, all at the same time. To recover this referent, as applied to women, implies knowing one's self with all the sad and terrible things that are part of my reality as a woman and to reconstruct myself with all the good things I have. (Duarte Bastian 2002, 18)

This doble mirada or Kab'awil strategy, as Chacón (2018) calls it, and a growing antiracist critique within Latin American and Caribbean feminisms, has also meant that Indigenous women's feminist and gendered politics and activism are a provocation that has pushed mestiza feminists and theorists to begin to rethink what María Lugones (2008, 2010) has called the coloniality of gender and the Western assumptions of Latin American feminism (see also Espinosa Miñoso, Gómez Correal, and Ochoa Muñoz, 2014; Gargallo Celetani 2014; Hernández Castillo and Suárez Navaz 2008; Millán 2014).

In case it is not already apparent, I must emphasize that the various forms of Indigenous feminism emerged from histories of women's participation in the Indigenous movement, and as such, they are deeply embedded in collective, communal, and communitarian struggles (Espinosa Damián 2009). For example, Tarcila Rivera Zea, a founder and president of ECMIA, the Indigenous Women's Forum, and president of Chirapaq, the national Peruvian Indigenous organization, has argued in an interview with Grau Villa and Mangas Urkizu (2018) that "it has cost Indigenous women to understand feminism from others and to understand whether or not we are feminists. So we came to the conclusion that we need to build our own concept of feminism, from our own references" (para. 8) (see figure 2.11). As a Quechua activist whose activism spans more than thirty years, Rivera Zea, from Ayacuchoes, Peru, is herself seen as a "referent in the struggles for Indigenous feminism." In her early days of activism, when she started working in the Indigenous rights movement, she met with many challenges, such as men who wanted to force her to quit, whereas others denied any gender problems in the movement and "that all that was western. I, as a woman, was always in one space. As an Indigenous person, in another" (para. 7). This statement echoes the experience I shared earlier from the encuentros.

Another thread of Indigenous feminist thinking is the need to break histories and relationships of servitude vis-à-vis dominant society, mestiza feminists, and even Indigenous communities and organizations. Tarcila Rivera Zea observes that Andina, Aymara, Quechua, and Amazonian women are often reduced to being seen as no more than servants, as many grow up in domestic service. "As Indigenous women, we are considered less, we are seen as backward;

Figure 2.11. Tarcila Rivera Zea speaking into the microphone while leading an ECMIA event. Photo courtesy of ECMIA.

our culture has no value. This has totally damaged our self-esteem" (para. 5). For this reason, she reflects that Indigenous women in Peru initially defined the worst form of violence as racism. In the long path to bring these two struggles together at the center of her life, she says, "I was joining my role as an Indigenous person and a woman, until it developed, now I can say, a broader vision of being a woman that struggles for human rights, without leaving out the imbalance that exists in relations in the Indigenous world between men and woman, boys and girls" (para. 8). She grounds the issue of gender equality within Indigenous cosmovisions by stating,

> I learned from an elder from Ollantaytambo that for our people and in our lifeways, things are valued when they are at their point of equilibrium. Imbalance is the equivalent of gender problems in our world. Our priority is collective rights, the rights of territory as a people and then individual rights. Recently a feminist who was a member of CEDAW [Convention on the Elimination of All Forms of Discrimination against Women] said to me: "you speak of collective rights, but that is not for everyone." And I said: "Of course, it is because with collective rights you can have a healthy environment to breathe in your collectivity. That is a collective right." She was silent. (para. 8)

Thus Indigenous women's activism and feminism have largely emerged from their own hard-earned lessons and histories of collective self-determination as Indigenous peoples rather than through engagements with feminism or through universities. Another central characteristic is the way in which Indigenous women ground their struggle for gender equality and balance within their communities and families, often with men, women, elders, and children. This Indigenous women's activist practice provided an important lesson for Afro-Colombian socialist feminist and therapist Nellys Palomo, director of K'inal Antzetik of Mexico City and early advisor to CONAMI. Palomo, one of the first people I interviewed in 1999 when I began accompanying the Indigenous women's movement in Mexico, shared what she learned from Indigenous women's organizing after twenty years of being in the feminist movement:

> I believe that one thing that, from my experience in the feminist movement, we are seeing [in] the Indigenous women's movement is how to do things in a different manner. Because they have achieved [so much] by integrating [in]to the family, the community, that which we have not in the feminist movement. In other words, we [in the feminist movement] have tried to make changes with women and to participate with women but our

> everyday lives stayed intact. So it was as if women took a step toward the public world, but men did not give way in the private sphere. So then, this is the situation that we have twenty years after in the feminist movement, where we find that we have achieved and gained things, but the change of consciousness in men [in general] has not been profound. I believe one of the challenges it has raised in the women's movement is that if the community does not advance, there will be no change. This is important because how can half the community advance when the other half does not? It is not possible to move forward on one's own while the other says behind. This is why we say we need parity or to walk in partnership. It is not possible [for social change] that one walks forward and then the rest of us stay behind so this has been a reconceptualization or reworking [of] feminism from the community. (Nellys Palomo, interview with Maylei Blackwell, August 24, 1999)

I have witnessed the practices and strategies Palomo describes with Indigenous women activists in Mexico and its diaspora in the United States. This sentiment is echoed in the slogan woven into Zapatista culture, "Cuando una mujer avanza, ningún hombre retrocede" (when a woman advances, no man moves back). Examples of such practices are woven into chapter 3, with Nahua community leaders in Jalisco who discuss and negotiate women's rights during an assembly with male community authorities to solve the root of violence against women, and in chapter 4, when migrant Indigenous women organizers encourage male partners and kids to attend women's leadership workshops to learn together as a family.

But if one root of Indigenous women's gendered/feminist consciousness emerged from within mixed-gender organizations, it is also important to note that another root is grounded in the formation of Indigenous women's organizations at critical junctures, such as the formation of ECMIA. Also, at the national level, the founding of CONAMI was related to transnational, transindigenous, and transborder processes; it gave activists a way to coordinate themselves to engage both national Indigenous rights organizations, the CNI and ANIPA described in chapter 1. It gave support to women who did participate, and even led, the national Indigenous rights organizations in Mexico by providing a national space of support and reflection for women, one that connected them to other scales of Indigenous women's resistance linking them to local and continental networks. Such was the case in the autumn of 2015, when I spent time with Amuzgo activist Martha Sánchez, who was just finishing her term as the general coordinator of ANIPA. As one of the national leaders who emerged from

Figure 2.12. Martha Sánchez Nestor and Margarita Gutiérrez of CONAMI at the VII Continental Network of Indigenous Women, Guatemala, 2015.

CONAMI, Martha was at the founding meeting of ECMIA. She and I had first met nearly twenty years earlier, and I had interviewed her several times during the intervening years. When I asked Martha, who considers herself a feminist, whether feminism is an important front of the struggle for Indigenous women, she responded:

> It is a front of struggle for influence, I believe. We have defined some declarations [movement statements] of Indigenous women around that of feminist women so that they also understand that this struggle of Indigenous peoples is not an isolated struggle. For example, many feminists work around the environment, but Indigenous people carry the debate more toward buen vivir or of Mother Earth, of territory, of the extraction of resources. That is, we put other themes [on the table] and demand that feminists see that the conception of that which many would say is rhetoric from another world is possible to be linked to the inalienable struggle for collective rights, and that must, therefore, take importance in their programs and speeches, and their political positions. So, it is an effort to sensitize them, include them, and discuss their point of view. (Martha Sánchez Nestor, interview with Maylei Blackwell, November 18, 2015)

Martha Sánchez's reflections point to a more profound wellspring of Indigenous feminism, its rootedness in a different historic imaginary; a unique epistemology. Although Indigenous feminism does have points of connection with hegemonic feminism in the region, it articulates a different vision of relationality, cosmovision, and bien vivir, the Spanish translation of the Ecuadorian Indigenous concept Sumak Kawsay (Chancoso 2014). It is born out of the experiences of women in the Indigenous rights movement and their powerful analysis of gender, and it is firmly grounded in their own cosmovisions and lifeways.

I asked Martha what the impact of Indigenous women's organizing has been in Mexico, and she pointed out that Indigenous women have a greater presence and there is now more awareness within the Mexican women's movement of Indigenous women's political demands. Speaking about the national women's movement, Martha explained: "It has diversified. It has tried to be more inclusive of Indigenous movements. That is to say that I cannot imagine a feminist encuentro (gathering) or feminist process ever not contemplating Indigenous women now." Recalling the numerous feminist encuentros we had participated in that were clearly racist and exclusionary, I followed up by asking her about the difficult conversations surrounding feminism among Indigenous women—even referencing one we both participated in the day before at an ECMIA gathering, which I mentioned above. Martha responded:

> Yes, yes, yes. I believe now that we are here at the Encuentro de Enlace Continental, it is important to remember that inside of the network, all those [diverse] views are shared, the view that Indigenous women have been undergoing a feminist process, not to invisiblize us, but to [have the space] to propose, debate, question the perspectives, and for us to join along the points where we agree. Not all subjects bring dissent. There are many very important topics where we find consensus.
>
> The feminist encuentros have always been difficult for Indigenous women to speak for themselves, for Indigenous women to have a high presence, to have a voice on the central panels. Little by little [our voice and presence] have been woven. One, ... because there are more Indigenous who dare to go to those spaces. Two, because there are more Indigenous women who write now about those ... well, those ideologies, all that philosophy. Others question it. But some weave alliances to reach a political stance [and we are gaining recognition], not only to be invited as guests to an event. So, it was these gestures of [alliance that] many compañeras who achieved the attendance of over one hundred Indigenous women at encuentros, in the case of [the Encuentro Feminista] in

Mexico and the recent one ... in the events that have taken place, there has been growth, I think, in the arrival of informed Indigenous women that speak, propose, that generate [ideas] including their own panels. (Sánchez Nestor, interview, November 18, 2015)

Interweaving scales, epistemologies, and (policy advocacy or solidarity) logics produces what Chela Sandoval has called "differential consciousness" to describe how US Third World women shift between modes of consciousness to respond to how they read various configurations of power in any given political situation. Responding to their marginalization and discrimination in the Latin American and Caribbean regional preparatory processes for the Fourth World Conference on Women, organized Indigenous women took their experience of weaving in and between local, national, and international movements for Indigenous rights to conjure their scale of Abiayala. The invocation of Abiayala, as a specifically Indigenous scale, was a way of responding to the geography of difference—namely, an exclusionary configuration of feminism that Indigenous women encountered at the regional and international levels of the women's movement. Yet invoking the idea of Abiayala is in itself a *feminist* response that weaves in interconnection to the land and other (nonhuman) relations to create a sense of embodied solidarity—material and spiritual consciousness that recognizes that anywhere we touch the earth, we are connected and that the well-being of all women is interrelated to each other and tied to the well-being of Earth. These threads were part of Indigenous feminisms and cosmovisions that were articulated because of friction and ultimately proved to be unscalable in that initial form. Whereas chapter 1 focused on the successful scaling strategies of Indigenous activists, this chapter has revealed some of the frictions that arise between hegemonic and Indigenous feminisms, between a policy advocacy logic and a form of the identity solidarity logic grounded in our shared relationship to land. The choice of ECMIA leaders to replace *Abya Yala* with *the Americas* does not necessarily signal the complete triumph of one logic over another. These frictions are not necessarily negative or something to be avoided altogether. Rather, these frictions and moments of unscalability are precise reminders that within geographies of difference there is a need to reconfigure and restrategize at each scale because things that work at one level will not work at another. Yet a more profound reminder is that not all political projects—even one as powerful as Abiayala as a vision of connection and solidarity—will be scalable. Speaking and acting from those realities are part of the interweaving of epistemologies, knowledges, and scales of continental Indigenous women's organizing that provide alternative visions of feminism and gender justice.

3. Rebellion at the Roots

The formation of Indigenous women activists, their analysis, and their outlook is often deeply grounded in long histories of Indigenous community organizing—forms of place-based activism that interweave multiple localities with other scales of resistance. The Zapatista rebellion is often held up as the vanguard of a movement against neoliberal globalization, but that rebellion, and those that led to the formation of the national network of Indigenous women, were born from local roots. Oral histories with Indigenous women activists reveal that struggles for women's rights and participation emerged within and alongside Indigenous community struggles. The very strategy that Indigenous women activists have adopted—of weaving in and between scales of organizing—is one that emerged from the process of working within community-based or local struggles, getting blocked, and then moving forward at other scales. Yet local roots are often overlooked or dismissed because activists operating at this scale do not articulate a "women's rights" agenda in ways that are legible to Western feminism. Nonetheless, Indigenous women do engage in their own forms of gender-based advocacy, some call it feminism, while participating within their own community and cultural contexts. Organized Indigenous women locate their struggle within their own communities and in the face of economic, racial, and colonial domination, despite the ways they are posited as victims of their own cultures (Newdick 2005). This is significant because it challenges the ways Indigenous communities are portrayed as more sexist (backward, nonmodern) because of gendered power arrangements that are themselves often impositions of colonial rule and state regulation. I do not mean to idealize Indigenous communities as somehow immune to patriarchal power structures. Rather, I want to illustrate how Indigenous women's community organizing and advocacy on behalf of Indigenous pueblos and of themselves as women refuse the ways gender has been used as a form of governmentality to regulate who is a "good" or "bad" Indigenous subject (Blackwell 2012).

Although the local is a vibrant site of resistance, it can also be a vexed and complex site of struggle for Indigenous women. I start this chapter about the local expressions of multiscalar activism by calling attention to the ways in which constructions of the local in Mexico are often deeply gendered, racialized, and classed. The local is signified through colonial representations that portray indigeneity in terms of poverty and lack or, in its positive inverse, as quaint and folkloric. Indigenous women are represented as the ultimate symbols of the local and as embodiments of the authentic. Often portrayed in static or even backward temporal frames, Indigenous women stand for the romantic Other to modernity or as stubborn roadblocks to its progress. Such meanings of the local, which represent Indigenous communities as rural, closed, bounded, and fixed are produced and reproduced through tourist and media representations in urban metropoles and academic centers of knowledge. That is, knowledge and theory about Indigenous women are often produced without their awareness, collaboration, or input and do not without taking their visions, desires, and analysis into account. These bounded views of the local do not consider how Indigenous women activists are part of communities that are often part of networked and multiscalar webs of power, mobility, economic, cultural, and political flows that are shaped by neoliberal economic and neocolonial states nor how those communities have forged a resilient response to these conditions, fighting and organizing for their own visions and desires as well as their own political, social, cultural, and economic projects.

Dominant cultural representations of Indigenous women and their communities are being challenged as organized Indigenous women have multiplied the locales of their political work by traveling to meetings in other Indigenous municipalities, states, and national centers, to continental and transnational gatherings, or to the United Nations in Geneva and New York. Other Indigenous women activists have become organizers in their original communities and in the receiving communities where they live and work along the migrant stream. For example, migrant Indigenous women from Oaxaca organize in Mexico City, Baja California, and Oregon, and throughout California. Indigenous women leaders are increasingly being recognized as experts and knowledge-holders in their communities, and some of those of the younger generation in particular are receiving professional and university training. Indigenous women's activism has been significantly shaped by these networks of travel, activism, and migration, transforming even those women who stay in their communities, and it is increasingly difficult for others to speak for them without their input and collaboration. As many Indigenous women's organizations have emphatically stated: "Nothing about us without us."[1] Moreover, Indigenous women activists operate within, and activate a much different understanding of the "local"—one that is not isolated, but rather linked, networked, and scaled to regional, municipal, national, global/transnational, transborder, and transindigenous processes.

With this in mind, through the life stories of several key members of the Coordinadora Nacional de Mujeres Indígenas de México (CONAMI), I focus here on the ways Indigenous women activists have narrated their own politics at the local level in the states of Jalisco, Oaxaca, and Guerrero. Through the lens of activist Indigenous women's narratives and experiences, we can understand how the local scale—conceptualized, for the purposes of this chapter, as largely within Indigenous pueblos, municipalities, and (trans)regions—have shaped these women's gendered consciousness and activism and has become an intersection through which they can bring Indigenous and gender rights together. Some women involved in CONAMI became activists through local organizing processes, whereas others learned to build capacity at the national scale and then came back to their communities to provide leadership at the local level. Whatever their particular route to activism, most Indigenous women activists are motivated to take action by the conditions they see in their everyday lives and by their desire to localize in their communities what they have learned from transnational, transborder, and national scales.

Chapter 1 explored the ways in which Indigenous women activists scale the discourse of rights down to the intimate scales of the body, the home, the organization, and the community. This scaling down helps forge a practice of autonomy that reconceives Indigenous rights as embedded in daily life rather than as contingent on government permission or recognition. This chapter complements chapter 1 by exploring Indigenous activists' rootedness in the local and the importance of weaving in and between scales, revealing alternative genealogies of Indigenous resistance and highlighting how building at local and translocal scales has been a movement response to blockages at the national level. These shifts between scales have helped the Indigenous women's movement survive selective neoliberal state co-optation that resulted in years of demobilization at the national level and an intense period of increased state and narco violence that targeted Indigenous communities in devastating ways.

I use the framework of *meshworks* to illustrate the ways in which Indigenous women's activism and organizing in Mexico use scales in ways that are tied to politics of the local. I build on Harcourt and Escobar's (2002, 2005) notion of meshworks to track Indigenous women's more "horizontal," translocal organizing within one scale, which operates in tandem with the largely "vertical" shifts between different scales. Harcourt and Escobar argue that meshworks are "nonhierarchal and self-organizing networks [that] often grow in unplanned directions" (2002, 12); in the case of Indigenous women's local organizing, such meshworks function as "rooted networks" of vertical and horizontal connections (Rocheleau and Roth 2007). In his study of the 2006 popular uprising in Oaxaca, anthropologist Maurice Magaña argues, "the concept of meshwork are 'multilayered entanglements' (Escobar 2008) where various interlinked networks bridge scale and difference" (Magaña 2010, 74). Magaña also explains why meshworks are critical to multiscalar organizing in local contexts: "Meshworking is an increasingly practical and necessary form of engagement between various sectors of civil society; regional, national, and international institutions; activists; and discourses in an era where the hegemony of neoliberalism is increasingly shattering the illusion that social and political change can be achieved by local actors via traditional forms of political engagement with the state, such as formal electoral politics" (73). Further, Harcourt and Escobar (2002) recenter place in studies of globalization through, for example, a focus on the body, the home, the environment, or the economy. The politics of place, they argue, largely comprise contests over meaning and the interplay of culture and power. Meshworks "are created out of the interlocking of heterogeneous and diverse elements brought together because of complementarity or common experiences" (Harcourt and Escobar 2002, 12). Musician and scholar Martha Gonzalez uses meshworks to "emphasize fluid forms and ever-changing strategies of survival" (2020, 85). In her study and practice of transborder Chican@ artivist musical community building through son jaracho or fandangos sin fronteras, she theorizes how meshworks "disrupt the social science focus on binaries (global/national, local/transnational) and instead make visible the material survival strategies within the various communities" (85).

Meshworks often weave dominant and subaltern knowledges and forms of being, as illustrated by how the Continental Network of Indigenous Women of Abya Yala (ECMIA) engaged dominant institutions and NGOs emerging from the United Nations or Latin American and Caribbean feminist networks (see chapter 2). Here I use meshworks to describe how activists localize and interweave discourses, identities, knowledges, epistemologies, and practices across scales. Harcourt and Escobar call "glocalities" "the places and spaces produced by the linking together of various social movements in networks and meshworks of opposition, or by the connection of places to global processes," and because of this they are "both strategic and descriptive, potentially oppressive and potentially transformative" (2002, 13). Here, nodes can be understood when scales or locales are linked by Indigenous knowledges, strategies, or epistemologies, and in this chapter they can be seen as rooted networks (Rocheleau and Roth 2007;

Roth 2011) grounded in the local. These concepts help highlight ways Indigenous women enact multiscalar strategies by moving in and between, localizing, and interweaving scales of both vertical and horizontal connections.

CONAMI built statewide networks by not only localizing from the national to the local but also interweaving the work of Indigenous women activists and organizations horizontally across diverse regions and pueblos within states (within and across what are called "ethnicities" in Mexico). The work at the national scale informed the local Indigenous rights organizing of Me'phaa community leader Felicitas Martinez Solano. Felicitas, who received training from and experience with national workshops organized by CONAMI and took them back to the mountains of Guerrero, where she assumed a leadership role in the Indigenous community police. Yet, local Indigenous movements also shaped national Indigenous organizing in untold ways. The oral history, spanning three interviews and two decades, with early CONAMI leader Sofía Robles, a Zapotec/Ayuujk (Mixe) community organizer reveals the rich genealogies of Indigenous women's organizing, specifically their rootedness in largely unexplored Indigenous autonomy struggles at the local level that predate the 1993 Zapatista Women's Revolutionary Law.[2] Along with other Indigenous women, Sofía played a central role in such early struggles in Oaxaca—yet the Zapatista Army of National Liberation (EZLN) rebellion is still most often cited as the beginning of Indigenous organizing in Mexico, when in fact local Indigenous knowledges, organizing histories, discourses, and subjectivities shaped how the Zapatista rebellion moved from a more Marxist Lenist praxis toward an Indigenous rights framework. Ideas about Indigenous autonomy scaled up to national organizing through Indigenous civil society organizing and Zapatista communiques, and then were globally networked into broader international and transnational scales. The horizontal interweaving of approaches, histories, and practices of Indigenous autonomy is how activists from Oaxaca influenced not only Zapatista philosophy, but ultimately helped build several different national networks of activists (Stephen 2002). These rooted networks of CONAMI show how Indigenous women have been active in many Indigenous rights struggles since before the EZLN uprising, and how they both were blocked from full participation and yet still created organizing projects before the EZLN's Women's Revolutionary Law ever drew attention. Maurice Magaña (2020) calls this a form of social movement spillover, whereby one social movement informs another; one political project of Indigenous autonomy informs others at different scales, from local to national in this instance.

Sofías long history of organizing calls into relief another local scale of Indigenous women's community participation and organizing: the municipality.

As the result of decades of community organizing and participation, Sofía became municipal president of the Ayuujk (Mixe) municipality in Tlahuitoltepec, Oaxaca in 2012. Among the 570 Oaxacan municipalities, 417 are governed by Indigenous normative systems, which are forms of governmentality that have resulted from precolonial and postcolonial formations mixed with state impositions and Indigenous negotiations. Before changes in national and state law, critics pointed out that women served in leadership positions in only 11.5 percent of the municipalities governed by Indigenous normative systems in Oaxaca, compared with 51 percent of municipalities run by the political party system (Barrera-Bassols 2006). Others were alarmed that in nearly a quarter of municipalities ruled via internal normative systems, women could not vote (Hernández Díaz 2014). Below I discuss how some of the rules shaping who could be included in a community assembly, and thus vote, are tied historically to state-imposed patriarchal norms that are now naturalized within Indigenous communities as "tradition," and given as evidence of the "backwardness" of Indigenous communities. Holly Worthen (2015) explores "different conceptions of women's political participation in nonliberal contexts of Indigenous communities in Latin America, raising questions about the misinterpretation of gender relations based on Western frameworks of political rights" (916). Although Indigenous women in her study agreed that women should participate and have leadership positions, they rejected a state mandate that they do so, because it failed to recognize the multiple forms of labor, service, and care women already perform. Western feminism has classically centered individual political rights to the exclusion of collective, cultural, and economic rights, which produces the seeming contradiction of Indigenous women's activism within autonomous Indigenous municipalities. In this chapter, I center Sofía's conceptualization of the logros (achievements, successes, or wins) of Indigenous women's participation and activism that expand limited Western frameworks of women's rights in order to ground Indigenous women's long history of struggle for inclusion and the right to shape community decisions from the bottom up. This bottom up perspective is important in the face of top down, state-imposed gender equity strategies, and contributes to the literature on women in Indigenous normative systems in Oaxaca by centering how Indigenous women activists frame their own participation. At the national level, Mexico adopted gender parity for elected positions in 2014 and a year later, in 2015, there was a constitutional reform of Article 2 to ensure the participation of women in conditions of equality within elections governed by Indigenous normative systems (Secretaria de Gobernacion Estados Unidos Mexicanos, 2015). In 2016, the State Constitution of Oaxaca was reformed to require a greater number of women on the community councils and as municipal presidents with the goal of full gender parity by 2023. These legal reforms have changed the landscape significantly. "Between 2005 and 2020 the number of female municipal presidents has gone from 8 (1.4%) to 71 (12.5%)" (Cárdenas Acosta and Lopez Vences 2021, 59).

Years of participating in political spaces and drawing on the knowledge Indigenous women have shared with me has shown me that what people refer to as gendered struggles, and others call Indigenous feminisms, emerge within, through, and alongside community struggles for Indigenous autonomy. These struggles for Indigenous women's dignity are therefore embedded in community struggles. Western feminism has classically located the struggle for gender equality, rights, and liberation within legal and political realms that are largely outside of the family and disconnected from questions of community. Western individualism has shaped the understanding of feminism in a way that normalizes the assumption that a rights-bearing subject gains freedoms outside of the collective rather than within it. Indigenous women's struggles emerge from the root of Indigenous communal struggles because, as many activists including Tomasa Sandoval have argued, they cannot be free as Indigenous women without being free as Indigenous people (see chapter 1). Activists argue that they are not rights-bearing subjects who can split their gender or individual rights from how they are structurally, culturally, socially, economically, and spiritually located as Indigenous people. Centering the formation of the Mixe Women's Network, the chapter concludes by considering women's organizing on the scale of Indigenous territory/municipality. Expanding feminist, rights-based strategy beyond the question of legal reforms or rights, Sofía identifies the logros Indigenous women have won including increasing Indigenous women's participation, creating new spaces where they can share learning and express their visions of the world, and forming vínculos (connections, links) as they weave their visions of community and social change with those of other activists, organizations, and scales.

Given how organized Indigenous women's meshwork of multiscalar activism insists on grounding their project of gender justice within their communities, I explore the way their modes of organizing and creating community illustrate how comunalidad is gendered. *Comunalidad* (communality) is a term associated with Mixe thinker Floriberto Díaz and Zapotec teacher, musician, and researcher Jaime Martínez Luna. The latter speaks of the centrality of community in maintaining Indigenous knowledges, practices and epistemologies in the face of colonial oblivion. Martínez Luna (1993) argues, "By necessity perhaps, our pueblos have taught us to fulfill community responsibilities [cargos], tequio [communal work], and participation in communal assembly.

Our elders have transmitted, from generation to generation, the limits of our territory, histories about land, the mountains, hills and the caves" (159, cited in Mattiace 2003, 106). Indigenous identity as a communal project is linked to the scale of community. Martínez Luna asserts the persistence of community Indigenous identity is the result "of the dynamic between our ancestral and present organization, which rests on communal work: work to make decisions (assembly), work for coordination (cargo), work for construction (tequio), and work to enjoy (fiesta)" (Martínez Luna 1993, 160, cited in Mattiace 2003, 106). Floriberto Díaz (2004) goes deeper into the cosmological or pluriversal nature of comunalidad. He states, "[A]n indigenous community is not only understood as a group of houses with people, but people with history, past, present and future, which can not only be defined concretely, physically, but also spiritually in relation to the whole of nature" (367). He defines the interrelationship and interdependence of nature and generations of Indigenous people as the primary elements of what he calls the immanence of community. Díaz explains, "We refer to its dynamics, the underlying and acting energy between human beings and of these with each and every element of nature. It means that when we talk about organization, rules, community principles, we are not just talking about the physical space and material existence of human beings, but about their spiritual existence, their ethical and ideological code and, consequently, their political and social, legal, cultural, economic and civil conduct" (367). Emphasizing the communal, the collective, and ideas of complementarity and integrality, he defines the elements of communality as:

> Earth as Mother and Territory.
> The consensus in the assembly for decision-making.
> Freely given service as an exercise of authority.
> Collective work as an act of recreation.
> Rites and ceremonies as an expression of the communal gift. (368)

Indigenous women play a central, if sometimes obscured role, in comunalidad. Ayuujk (Mixe) writer, linguist, and activist Yásnaya Elena Aguilar Gil (2019) documents the forms of women's communal labor leading to Ayutla becoming, in 2007, the first pueblo in the Sierra and in the Ayuujk (Mixe) region to elect a woman municipal president through the normative system. Her analysis, along with the work of Holly Worthen (2015), points to how gender equity strategies imposed from the state from the top-down may ironically invisibilize women's labor and add to their burdens. She challenges the Western liberal rationalities underpinning hegemonic feminism. Zapotec social worker, advisor to the EZLN during the San Andrés Peace Accords, and translator of Zapotec codices, Juana Vásquez Vásquez, analyzed the role of women's labor in constructing comunalidad in her community of Yalalag, Oaxaca where women do participate in community assembly. She says "when a women assumes a cargo it effectively means more work for her, but in fact when the husband has a cargo, it also means the woman will assume almost 60% or more of the work that her partner leaves behind in order to complete his [community] service so I think this too is a thing we have to see and deal with in the Assembly" (101). Based on these insights and those generated by Sofía Robles's long history of community service, I posit the notion of gendered comunalidad as a way to name the unrecognized forms of gendered labor and women's work that make comunalidad possible—supporting men who have official cargos; running the cultural, emotional, economic, spiritual processes and the foodways that support communal gatherings, fiestas, celebrations, rituals; and fundraising.

If we think of comunalidad as a local autonomy project that is practiced first and foremost at the scale of community (Mattiace 2003) then we also can understand the centrality of women's labor to comunalidad. I foreground comunalidad as a form of social thought and a set of communitarian practices of the Mixes, Zapotecs, and Mixtecs from northern and central Oaxaca that honor the centrality of community in maintaining Indigenous knowledges, practices and epistemologies in the face of colonial oblivion. Indigenous identity as a communal project is linked to the scale of community. Yet, Maya K'iche sociologist Gladys Tzul Tzul (2015) theorizes Indigenous communal governance as embedded within practices that occur at the scale or unit where daily life is reproduced. First Tzul Tzul defines "indigenous communal government systems as the plural schemes/plots/weaves of men and women who create historical-social relationships that have body, force and content in a concrete space: communal territories that produce structures of government to share, defend and recover material means for the reproduction of human life and domestic and non-domestic animals" (128). She then goes deeper, defining how she thinks of the scale of social reproduction: "In this sense the units of reproduction, namely: The houses inhabited by nuclear families and extended families (grandmothers, uncles, cousins, godchildren) is where the organization of life is organized and embedded" (135). Tzul Tzul identifies the scales of Indigenous governance, as resistance to colonial and capitalist oppression, as Indigenous land/territory and the household, which helps us see the multiple local Indigenous scales of resistance and the importance of women's labor within them.

Interweaving Locales, Rooting the Inter/national: Statewide Networks in Jalisco, Guerrero, and Oaxaca

CONAMI strategically encouraged the organization of statewide networks to amplify the work its members were doing and have activists interweave their work horizontally, or translocally across the same scale, into other areas specifically to reach more Indigenous women, many of whom live in rural areas. Several of the organizations that initially formed CONAMI in the state of Oaxaca continued to organize statewide workshops and build a network that would bridge the different scales of organizing at the international and national scales (Artía Rodriguez 2001). As I explored in chapter 1, the National Gathering of Indigenous Women (Encuentro Nacional de Mujeres Indígenas) on August 30, 1997, in Oaxaca brought together seven hundred Indigenous women activists who used the meeting to formally constitute CONAMI. After the 1997 encuentro, that same year Sonia from Unión de Comunidades Indígenas de la Zona Norte del Istmo (Union of Indigenous Communities of the Northern Zone of the Isthmus), an Indigenous rights organization founded in 1985 and known for its human rights and grassroots democracy work from the isthmus of Oaxaca, coordinated a workshop for the state of Oaxaca. During the workshop, she explained to new compañeras CONAMI's origins and objectives and how the network functions through commissions that (1) create linkages, facilitate organizing, provide capacity building and finances, form activists; (2) create a collective space to learn about Indigenous law, constitutional reform, and international law; and (3) provide mechanisms to recover and strengthen Indigenous culture (Artía Rodriguez 2001, 58). Sonia's work illustrates how Indigenous women's local organizing interweaves between scales: local organizations in Oaxaca and the international Indigenous movement. In her own analysis, for example, she argues that CONAMI's roots did not originate at the national encuentro in 1997 but in 1989 during the first International Forum for the Rights of Indigenous Pueblos. From there, she draws an arc of transindigenous, transnational, transborder, and international work that calls attention to the power of the continental movement organized in 1992 to protest celebration of the five-hundred-year anniversary of the so-called discovery of the Americas. That mobilization was hemispheric in scale and led to the founding not only of organizations in Mexico, such as 500 Years of Indigenous and Black Popular Resistance in Guerrero, but also of the Frente Indígena Oaxaqueña Binacional (FIOB) in Los Angeles, California (an organization I examine in depth in chapters 4 and 5). This work, Sonia argues, strengthened existing links with Indigenous peoples in the United States and Canada and increased the visibility of an Indigenous movement across the continent. Indigenous women in Mexico, whose Indigenous pueblos are often defined as "ethnicities" by the Mexican nation-state, have increasingly begun to see beyond the rights of the nation-state to an entire regime of rights and international legal norms established through the United Nations and the International Labor Organization. In learning of these rights and norms at different scales, Indigenous women do not merely reproduce what they learn from "outside"; they bring it into conversation and interweave it with the knowledges, epistemologies, discourses, and identities of their own communities. Then, through processes of interweaving, translation, and localization, they leverage new spaces of participation, relationalities, and relationships that serve their broader project of communal and individual (articulated as separate things in Western legal traditions) well-being and dignity. Activists use these processes—what Hernández Castillo (2016) and Engle Merry (2006) have described as vernacularization—to interweave knowledges, discourses, and practices from different scales.

At the national scale, Sonia points to national developments such as the 1994 emergence of the EZLN into public view; the formation of the Congreso Nacional Indígena (National Indigenous Congress) and its women's commission; the National Democratic Convention; the first National Meeting of Indigenous Women in 1995 in San Cristobal, Chiapas; and all of the meetings of Indigenous women that culminated in the first National Gathering of Indigenous Women in Oaxaca and the formal constitution of CONAMI. CONAMI members, one representative from each state, initially met monthly in Mexico City throughout the year. In addition, they attended national and statewide workshops, talks, and forums organized in different places. Many Indigenous women activists built the national network from the local ground on which their activism started. When CONAMI was first established in 1997, part of its founders' vision was to connect local communities and Indigenous regions by creating statewide networks. Thus, CONAMI helped to support statewide networks in several states as a point of articulation between local communities and regions.

Local movements used these networks to articulate collectively their political subjectivities as Indigenous women and devised their own political agendas. Many women were already active in mixed-gender Indigenous organizations, and the networks facilitated by CONAMI allowed them to remain active in the Indigenous movement yet also build connections and alliances for Indigenous women's organizing. Furthermore, these statewide and local organizing efforts were one site where ideas of women's rights in Indigenous autonomy and governance were localized into community practices. In 2000, when I first met María de Jesús Patricio, known by her nickname Marichuey, she recounted the importance of the first Indigenous Women's Gathering of Jalisco in March 1998. At that event, activists linked gains made in the national movement back to local communities through statewide Indigenous women's networks that formed in Jalisco, Guerrero, and Oaxaca (Blackwell 2006). Challenging the hegemonic vision of feminism that has historically excluded men from meetings discussing gender and "women's issues," Marichuey explained why it was so important that men were present at the first historic gathering of Indigenous women in the state of Jalisco:

> The women told the men that it was important to have men there at a gathering of women ... so they can listen to what the women like and what they do not like. Apart from the Indigenous women in attendance at the first gathering in Jalisco [about 250 delegates], there was the same number of men present. To me, it was really important, most of all in Jalisco, because women should be stating directly to their husbands, or their brothers, or their fathers the things that they did not like of the customs. And so they told them. They spoke of quitting negative customs that were affecting the development of the Indigenous peoples. I liked it very much because the traditional authorities publicly committed themselves to creating new statutes on the participation of women. (Patricio, interview, April 1, 2000)

Community meetings deliberating usos y costumbres, or Indigenous normative systems, proliferated throughout Mexico in the 1990s. Such meetings show how women have, through historic, community-based dialogues, increased their participation in Indigenous communities' decision-making processes and how these vibrant practices have the potential to allow women a greater role in the collective self-determination of Indigenous peoples in Mexico. After numerous decades of struggle, some of the tangible results of the pedagogies of autonomy used within these meetings and consultas (community consultations) have shifted perspectives about gender (these are explored in chapter 1).

Changes in cultural practice are often slow processes, and so Marichuey reflected on more concrete results:

> In fact, the women asked for a few things, for example, the suspension of alcoholic beverages in community events and meetings [because it leads to an increase in violence against women].... Now they [the authorities] are now valuing women and the women are learning they can make these types of decisions. The sale of alcoholic beverages [has] been sus-

pended on days the community assembly meets. So these are little, slow steps, but they move us toward something, right? And it is necessary to say this to the men. This is why it is important that they hear that we women want our own space as women or meetings specifically of women. It is not to be exclusive and outside of the men but to talk about how we are feeling as women, how things are affecting us, how we have to continue to work toward equity ... in this shared path [where] women's participation is also respected, and ... women can decide, and be in charge ... together.... This is why we say that we have to have men listen. It is necessary that they respect us women, support that we have the same rights as [they do], that we can also assume positions in the community and anywhere. That we have the ability if we are given the opportunity. (Patricio, interview, April 1, 2000)

These kinds of consultations are vital to the process of consensus-building and change that Indigenous women activists have engaged in in order to understand and promote their own rights within Indigenous communities. Indeed, the meetings themselves enact the practice of autonomy. These local practices of autonomy and the effort to (re)root their activism in the local scale became even more important in the context of the 2001 Law on Indigenous Rights and Culture, which many interpreted as the Mexican government backtracking on the right to Indigenous autonomy it had committed to when it signed the San Andrés Peace Accords. As a result of this new national reality, CONAMI became less active at the national level for a time, and organizers from the national network scaled down as a strategy to sustain and root their work; some turned toward building state networks specifically, whereas others built municipal and local organizations.

After the founding of CONAMI, its strength and organizational presence continued through statewide Indigenous women's organizing in Guerrero and Oaxaca. In 2004, a confluence of Indigenous rights activists formed the Coordinadora Guerrerense de Mujeres Indígenas (Guerreran Coordinator of Indigenous Women, CGMI); its members were either leaders of CONAMI or being trained in the monthly capacity-building workshops CONAMI ran in collaboration with the Mexico City–based organization K'inal Antsetik, under the leadership of Nellys Palomo. The CGMI was a statewide coordinating effort of Indigenous women in Guerrero and included Mixtec, Me'phaa (Tlapaneco), Amuzgo, and Nahua activists. The roots of that formation stemmed back to 1997, when CONAMI organized a series of workshops in Guerrero and invited women from various organizations to trainings about Indigenous rights.

Training with CONAMI catalyzed processes that had begun years before in Guerrero, as all the promotoras (community educators) of the CGMI emerged from CONAMI. In short, CONAMI was decisive in terms of helping participants imagine a project for women that was different from what they'd known until then in the mixed organizations (Espinosa Damián 2010). For example, practically all the women interviewed for a collaborative project between Gisela Espinosa Damián, a historian of women's organizing in Mexico, and CONAMI members Martha Sánchez Néstor and Libni Iracema Dircio emphasized that before participating in the training processes initiated by CONAMI, they didn't know they had rights as women, and that learning this was a key factor in their organizing (Espinosa Damián 2010). The principal promotoras of the CGMI included Martha Sánchez Néstor (Amuzgo), Libni Iracema Dircio (Nahua), Felicitas Martinez Solano (Me'phaa (Tlapaneco)), and Hermelinda Tiburcio (Mixtec), many of whose testimonios form the basis of earlier chapters. Martha and Libni reflected that the work of building the CGMI was an example of interweaving spaces and scales: "We resist from our own pueblos, in our mountains, in our homes, in the community assemblies, in our social organizations, before those who govern, in all the spaces we try to liberate our voices and breath, to own our own bodies. It has not been easy" (Sánchez Néstor and Dircio Chautla 2010, 10).

From the workshops in Guerrero and the First National Gathering of Indigenous Women in Oaxaca that formed CONAMI in 1997, CGMI's activists began to form "a conceptual, critical, and political scaffolding about gender inequality, affirming their gender identities, and constructing a perspective of gender equality" (Espinosa Damián 2010, 63). Gisela Espinosa Damián points to the interweaving of knowledges and epistemologies, which I have argued are part of organizing along meshworks, when she explains that Indigenous women organizers "took axes of reflection and mobilization from the feminist movement, but with their own content, amalgamated—not without difficulty—by the discourses of the Indigenous movement, reelaborated within the cultural and socioeconomic contexts of pueblos and of Indigenous women. For the first time, collectively the idea of forming a coordination of Indigenous women started to take shape in the state of Guerrero centered Indigenous gender identities and the decision to struggle for gender equality and women's rights in every level and space" (Espinosa Damián 2010, 63). In an essay written by activists Martha and Libni, they reflect that building the "coordinadora has been about making sure Indigenous women know their rights and can demand them, that they don't feel like they're being done a favor, but on the contrary, that they know that irresponsibility and discrimination against the pueblos and Indigenous women is actually a violation of their rights. We've barely begun to think about legislation and procuring gender justice" (Sánchez Néstor and Dircio Chautla 2010, 416).

In addition to organizing Indigenous women, as a statewide formation the CGMI was also a platform to articulate their interests within their own movements and with allies. In 2007, for example, the CGMI joined with various women's and mixed community and regional organizations to hold the Convención Estatal Indígena Afromexicana (Indigenous and Afromexican State Convention) of Guerrero. More than eight hundred delegates gathered, and CGMI women were practically the only women in a world of male leaders from other areas. Martha and Libni point out that, "for the first time in the long history of the mixed movement, women were not in the eternally silent role of logistical support, they had active participation, presence, their own voice, [and] leadership recognized not only by other women. This experience indicates that we are slowly constructing our right to make decisions in public space" (Sánchez Néstor and Dircio Chautla 2010, 419). Still, the gathering was not without challenges. Martha was the only woman put forward among a slate of all men to assume a statewide leadership position, but she was ultimately denied because of political motives and pressure from multiple sources that a man should occupy the cargo, whether or not he was well qualified (417).[3] Ultimately, the CGMI continued to organize for ten years and was the only statewide network of Indigenous women in the country that lasted into the 2000s. Yet, as Martha and Libni reflect, "Our road is very long, we are still far from our pueblos and Indigenous women of Guerrero being able to live the way we want to" (413).

From the National to the Regional: Localizing Knowledges and Practices of Indigenous Women's Justice

Other activists took what they had gained through their organizing and CONAMI workshops to build women's leadership in mixed-gender organizations within Indigenous regions throughout Mexico. Me'phaa community leader Felicitas Martinez Solano joined CONAMI with the encouragement of Martha Sánchez Néstor, and she began training as a reproductive health specialist while living and working in Chilpancingo. Building on the harrowing story of sacrifice and labor exploitation in her struggle to gain an education shared in chapter 1, Felicitas recalled that her father had originally wanted her to become a bilingual teacher, but Felicitas was worried about being sent far away to work in a distant rural Indigenous community, so she decided to attend the university, where she chose to do her one year of service with the organization 500 Years of Indigenous, Black, and Popular Resistance.[4] It was there that she met Martha. Felicitas recalled,

> I was not motivated to return to the region [of her pueblo] or none of that. [Then] I participated in the first regional assembly that the commissioners [of the community police] did back in '98 before my service [with 500 Años]. I participated as a listener because I didn't know they were already organizing the community police, that they began in '95. I almost never went to my pueblo because I did not have money [to travel] and one day I went, when I was doing my service, I returned to my pueblo.... A brother of mine was in the [community] police, and another brother was a commander. When I asked where they were going, they said, "Let's go to a meeting." (Martinez Solano, interview, November 19, 2015)

Felicitas applied the knowledge and skills she acquired through CONAMI when she was nominated as an authority of the Coordinadora Regional de Autoridades Comunitarias—Policía Comunitaria (the Regional Coordinator of Communitarian Police, CRAC-PC), popularly known as the "Comunitaria." The Comunitaria includes at least 2,000 community-based police from 152 communities in 22 municipalities and a regional Indigenous justice system (Chavez 2016).

Guerrero has a long history of political struggle, mobilization, and state repression, going back to the emergence of armed guerillas in the late 1960s and 1970s, and more recently the Ejército Popular Revolucionario (Popular Revolutionary Army). The 1980s witnessed the creation of producer organizations like La Luz de la Montaña, Solidaridad Social de Café y del Maíz, and la Unión Regional Campesina, as well as human rights organizations. The organization 500 Years of Indigenous, Black, and Popular Resistance that Felicitas had joined formed in 1992 to protest the quincentenary celebration of Columbus's "arrival." Unfortunately, according to juridical anthropologist Teresa Sierra, "Guerrero's popular political mobilizing unleashed a dirty war against social organizations, with military and paramilitary incursions and continual violations of the human rights of Indigenous people and social activists" (2010, 34). Nonetheless, Sierra argues that in the context of a national security crisis in Mexico, Indigenous-based justice systems have become an important example of the creative and innovative potential of the Indigenous peoples of Mexico: "Today, within the context of the country's national security crisis—28,000 killed in the last four years as a result of narco-violence—the community police of Guererro stand out for demonstrating the possibility of addressing crime, confronting insecurity, and working for peace when the force of a community and its cultural identities are mobilized to weave the social fabric" (34).

The CRAC-PC is also an example of a multiscalar Indigenous juridical system that is based on traditional Indigenous governance in the region that functions in conversation with other scales of justice. Guerrero's communitarian justice is not based solely on Indigenous legal frameworks; it is an interlegal product in that it combines Indigenous judicial traditions with common features of statutory law, as well as new regulations generated in the confluence of international and national law on Indigenous rights. This reflects the globalization of Indigenous rights and the ways in which these processes are localized, and how local Indigenous justice systems are networked at national and transnational arenas. In addition, it resonates with other Indigenous autonomy projects in the hemisphere that operate with or without state forms of recognition. Sierra observes that "the Communitarians are not willing to submit themselves to a legal framework that will fragment them, which is why they often say, 'We don't want recognition, only respect'" (2010, 38). So, though they may have a multiscalar approach to Indigenous justice, their broader strategy refuses state recognition as a form of neoliberal incorporation and instead mounts their own autonomous practices of governance.

Felicitas's process of formally joining the CRAC-PC illustrates the importance of networked scales between regional scales and the national articulation of the Indigenous women's movement. When she was asked to join the leadership of the CRAC-PC, she was also serving as the coordinator of CONAMI:

> I began to participate [in the CRAC-PC] but I did not stop participating in the Coordinadora Nacional. At that time, we were receiving all the training courses. They told us that everything they were teaching us in la Coordinadora, we would have to return to our communities. We had the commitment to multiply the information. All that we were receiving was based on a commitment that we had to meet so I finished my training on reproductive health and returned to hold a meeting in the communities, in the regions. We had to share with a community source, an organization, to reinforce the participation of women. Many times, we went to meetings in Pueblo Hidalgo [in Guerrero] with Martha [Sánchez] and Cándida [a Ayuujk (Mixe) organizer from Oaxaca], I'm not sure you remember? [I nodded yes.] From there, Cándida accompanied me walking all the way to my pueblo. After a while, I returned to my

pueblo and began participating in the comunitaria [community police, CRAC-PC]. To participate, it was very difficult because I was young, and the people thought, "What does she have to say to me?" So, the early days, I didn't talk, I didn't talk, I didn't talk. About three or four years went by without talking, without giving an opinion, only listening. Until then, I remained in the Coordinadora participating in meetings, workshops, events, forums.

They had named me as the coordinador of CONAMI in Mexico [City]. I served as the coordinator about six or seven months. Then, in an event in 2006, I was elected to be the regional coordinator for community activities of the CRAC-PC, for me to be an authority. But, at that time I had the coordination of CONAMI. That was when we had a trip to Spain in March, and they named me [to the CRAC-PC] in February. Martha, Hermalinda [Tiburcio], and I were funded to go on the trip by the casa de salud, Manos Unidas Ometepec, because we are from the Costa Chica region [of Guererro]. So, I went with them to discuss the issue. I asked them, "What am I going to do? I have two positions. One in Mexico [City] that is a great distance, like eight or nine hours by car [from Guerrero]. I'm not going to be able to carry out my responsibilities here or there. But if I don't complete my role there in the Coordinadora, they will have to sanction me [and I will] be suspended from the CRAC-PC." (Martinez Solano, interview, November 19, 2015)

After much discussion and deliberation, Felicitas decided:

I am going to return to the Comunitaria [CRAC-PC] to assume my role. All the courses, the formation that I had had in the Coordinadora ... like going to Geneva for the United Nations courses, and when [UN Human Rights Commissioner] Rodolfo Stavenhagen came to the communities [in Guerrero] to address the issue of security and we met with other [Indigenous] organizations in Mexico about maternal health.[5] We had the forum in Chilpancingo with the secretary of Indigenous affairs of the state and to see if the Law 701 could be enacted in the Comunitaria.[6] So, in this way, I returned to the Comunitaria [CRAC-PC] with all the information and the training I had gathered. They [the CRAC-PC] never gave me a training course, or said, come be trained. Nothing. So, I had to resolve each problem on my own and rely on the learning [I gained] from the Coordinadora [CONAMI]. At the end of the day, it was the Coordinaora that formed me but I applied what I learned in my local organization, the community police. (Martinez Solano, interview, November 19, 2015)

While Felicitas did not return to the leadership of CONAMI, she took what she had learned back to the Indigenous communities of her region, the Costa Chica of Guerrero, through a leadership role in the CRAC-PC.

Still, as she explains, things were far from easy for her, and working on Indigenous women's issues at that local/regional scale was still a challenge (Mora 2017a). When I asked Felicitas about the issue of women in the CRAC-PC, she replied, "It is very complicated, I'll tell you, very complicated the issue of women there [in the CRAC-PC]. It was very difficult. I was the first women that assumed a position of authority, but the assembly had to approve. If the regional authority does not approve, then you cannot assume your position" (Martinez Solano, interview, November 19, 2015). Still, she was able to do important work establishing norms for handling rape cases, mandating that rape not be adjudicated between the two parties but in a trial. Felicitas was the first women to hold the office of Coordinator, a position that she has held on several occasions, and now serves as a counselor, which is the most prestigious position in the organization. She has used her positions to focus on women's claims of gender violence, including rape and domestic violence. Although women in Indigenous regions where the CRAC-PC operates have greatly benefited from the 95 percent reduction in violence that has allowed them to have mobility and to share transportation, the practices of community justice and policing still have yet to include a broad gender justice component (Sierra 2009).

According to Teresa Sierra (2009, 2012), who has collaborated with the CRAC-PC and women in the organization for more than a decade, when the regional juridical structure, the Regional Coordinator of Communitarian Authorities, emerged in 1998, there was an initial women's commission to develop issues of gender and justice, but the commission was soon defunct. At the organization's tenth anniversary in 2005, there was a renewed effort to include a women's commission and elect women as authorities for the following year (2006). In 2007, they also elected more women coordinators who were open to pursuing translating women's rights into their own community's structures and norms. These developments were a response to the need to incorporate the perspective of women in the practice of justice, given the volume of gender issues that come before regional authorities (Sierra 2009). Felicitas and others have lent their experience and knowledge to making the CRAC-PC in Guerrero more inclusive, but the participation of women has not been sustained, nor has it received enough support to incorporate a vision of gender equity within CRAC-PC structures. In fact, researchers have found that women leaders are more severely criticized and surveyed than male leaders. The irony is that the CRAC-PC continues to be a model of community safety and security in light of an increase in narco violence and state repression, so that despite the organization's internal shortcomings when it comes to integrating women, CRAC-PC has nonetheless increased the security of Indigenous women in the region. The CRAC-PC suffered a split from 2013 to 2015 in which women's participation was weakened. This split, Sierra argues, prompted the strengthening of the Casa de la Mujer Indígena (Indigenous Women's House, CAMI) in San Luis Acatlán, a parallel institution that "emerged to deal with women's health issues and later transformed also in a space to attend gender violence" (Sierra 76, 2021).

This long struggle, Sierra argues, points to a gender justice process that recovers Indigenous women's own logics, categories and understandings to name their grievances and to face them (Sierra 2021). More recently, Felicitas's role has become even more important in light of a case where the CRAC-PC's authorities protected a man accused of raping a fourteen-year-old girl. When the accusation was dismissed and the girl was, in turn, accused of lying, the girl's family approached promotoras of CAMI, who took the case and pressured the CRAC-PC to administer justice. Because of this case and other splits, tension between the two institutions increased. As the case progressed, the director and attorney of CAMI received death threats and CRAC-PC failed to protect CAMI's staff despite the fact that they were in their jurisdiction. Sierra reports that "Male voices at different levels of authority—CRAC-PC, the municipal presidency and the local news—came together in order to question women's agency and advocacy. Using authoritarian patriarchal language, they reminded the promotoras/advocates that CAMI's sphere of influence was supposed to be confined to their interpretation of what constituted maternal health" (2021, 91). This tense situation illustrates how some Indigenous women struggle within the community institutions and are confronting intense narco state violence. Others find it necessary to build women's spaces outside of community institutions in order to address the patriarchal practices that continue and are often exacerbated in times of violence, repression, and war.

Histories of Local Women's Organizing and the Formation of Indigenous Autonomy

Some Indigenous women activists localized their experience within CONAMI and ECMIA into their own communities and statewide networks, and others used their experiences at the local scale of organizing to create bridges and networks between the national and continental. Even deeper than building these meshworks, what is little known is that Indigenous organizing in Mexico started locally long before the Zapatista uprising, with women playing an active role planting the seeds that grew the roots of the Indigenous movement's frameworks and organizations regionally and nationally (Speed, Hernández Castillo, and Stephen 2006; Stephen 2011). Some have called attention to how Oaxacan Indigenous movements helped shaped the evolution of the Zapatista call for Indigenous autonomy. For example, Ayuujk (Mixe) intellectual Adelfo Regino Montes framed the Zapatista's call for Indigenous rights at the 1996 National Indigenous Forum by arguing that "the recognition of our collective rights is necessary so that we can truly enjoy our individual rights" (quoted in Eisenstadt 2011, 9).[7]

When I conducted my first oral history interview with Sofía Robles Hernández in 1999, I took the bus to Oaxaca City and then a van up to Tlahuitoltepec to meet with her. She is a founding member of CONAMI, which had formed two years before our meeting. We met in her office at the Ayuujk (Mixe) organization Servicios del Pueblo Mixe (SER), where she headed up the Department of Gender and Women.[8] When I conducted my first return interview with her in 2011 in Oaxaca City, she was still the director of women's affairs at SER but she had also become a leader of the Network for Sexual and Reproductive Rights of Mexico (Red por los derechos sexuales y reproductivos en México) and had worked with others to found the Mixe Women's Network, an organization that spread across the seventeen municipalities of the Sierra Mixe region. Our most recent conversations took place in Los Angeles after she completed a term as the first female municipal president of the Ayuujk (Mixe) region and had just spoken at a 2015 International Women's Day event organized by the FIOB.

Sofía had a long road to her term as municipal president. When we first spoke in 1999, she recounted: "I began my work in the Zapotec region, with the regional authorities in around 1980. Then, for three years, I was a member of the support and relations committee for the Assembly of Zapotec Chinaltec Authorities [AZACHIS]" (Robles, interview, August 31, 1999). In the 1980s, her first job was in the Agricultural Secretariat, and she later worked in support of the campesino (rural peasant) economy, attending meetings with Indigenous authorities in the Zapotec community of Yalalag in order to learn about the issues facing Indigenous communities in Oaxaca, including a lack of communication, health care, and education. She described this process of learning about Indigenous struggles for self-determination: "Here, I learned the demand for respect of self-determination. I asked many times what the meaning of it was as I learned little by little, the experience of struggle in Yalalag. It was my foundation, above all, all the participation of women in this process. Here, I had my first maestros y maestras [teachers]" (Sofía Robles, interview with Maylei Blackwell, March 13, 2015). Her understanding of Indigenous self-determination was intertwined with women's participation, and she continued learning during other organizational experiences. "Reflecting on my own identity as a member of the Zapotec community," Sofía recalled, "the AZACHIS had been meeting for three years, with an incredible intensity, with assemblies almost every fifteen days, in diverse locations of the regions, many of which we had to get to by walking all the way to Villa Alta. After we linked with other organizations, we began to promote the regional organization of [traditional Indigenous] authorities. The regional authorities included Zapotec, Ayuujk [Mixe] y Chinantec authorities and, on some occasions, representatives of teachers' unions" (Sofía Robles, interview with Maylei Blackwell, October 6, 2011). She reflected that

> my participation was passive [at that point], I almost never spoke. My participation was to write, take photos, and to do reporting for the bulletin called *el Topil*. On occasions, I was tapped to provide follow up to agreements or proposals that were made with the government. In this process, women were absent from public spaces. They participated by preparing food and I thought that they should be in the assemblies as well. It was just a desire, but the assemblies continued on the same. I thought I would have to do something in order for there to be new paths [for women to participate]. (Robles, interview, August 31, 1999)

Although she believed that women should and could be more involved, Sofía told me that those early days were also when the Indigenous movement began to make strides within the campesino movement. Sofía's reflections reveal that the emergence of Indigenous women's organizing was and is a rebellion at the roots, interwoven with the emergence of the Indigenous movement more broadly within Mexico: "In 1982, those [of us] who were supporting the regional [Indigenous organizing] processes, we made an intervention at the second national gathering of la Coordinadora Nacional Plan de Ayala [the National Coordination of the Plan of Ayala] in Chilpancingo, Guerrero, where they only spoke of the problem of peasants and not Indigenous people, and even less of women" (Robles, interview, August 31, 1999). Sofía vividly remembers that at these meetings, activists began talking about problems Indigenous people faced. Through their discussions, they started to see how their struggles were interconnected, as community members from the Triqui of Oaxaca and the P'urépecha of the Sirahuen lake and plateau of Michoacán, and activists from the Organización Campesina Emiliano Zapata (Emiliano Zapata Peasant Organization) shared their struggles. Sofía recounts that "from that point on, we began to establish linkages with organizations from other states." She contextualized how she came to be involved in community struggles:

In '83, I was a preschool teacher in Yalalag, living there, and I was tapped to witness meetings to analyze the situation of the community. Being only an observer, listening intently, I felt so much admiration of the bravery and commitment that that community had. In '84, I changed pueblos from Zapotec to Mixe by falling in love.[9] All this period was a struggle for collective rights. From the AZACHIS, to the Comité de Defensa de los Recursos Humanos y Culturales Mixes, CODREMI [Committee in Defense of Mixe Human and Cultural Resources] and, especially, collaborating unofficially with the Equipo de Instrumentación de la Educación Básica Mixe, EIBM [Team for the Instrumentalization of Mixe Basic Education] and the Assembly of Mixe Authorities.

I collaborated with the Mixes, on the organizing team for basic Mixe education. In '86, we created a civil association for both Indigenous and non-Indigenous people that lasted a little over a year. But some of our issues were incompatible, so we decided to separate from that civil association and form our own Indigenous civil association. So, that's how Servicios del Pueblo Mixe [Mixe Pueblo Services, SER] emerged in 1988. (Robles, interview, August 31, 1999)

Sofía Robles continued her reflection by describing how her work with Indigenous women also began in the Mixe region and how it was different from working in her Zapotec hometown of Yalalag in the Northern Sierra of Oaxaca:

In the three years I worked in my Zapotec region, I always asked myself, "Where do women go out? And, where are the women?" And, they were in the kitchen. I always wanted to work with women. I thought something, something has to happen with the women but in the Zapotec region I did not achieve this. When I arrived to the Mixe region, the women were everywhere—in the assembly, in the kitchen, in the fields, in the municipality. And so I said, "Here, here you don't have to do anything." There was already a women's community organization, there were already sisters-in-law and aunts.

What I saw when I arrived to the Mixe region was that conditions are different. There's a high level of women's participation. In the assemblies, in some [cargos]. There was already an organized group that was concerned with children's health and women's health. So, I joined right away and that's how my dreams of working with women started to manifest. Around that time, I started working locally in the community. Basically, as a local group from Lauropetec, we were covering that region, providing services for women from '89, '90, and '91. It was a group of women concerned with the issue of malnutrition, the issue of children's health, and women. From there, different work areas start forming [within SER], and one of them was to work with women, so we coordinated [SER's] activities very closely with their work.... SER's first major goal was that the rights of the pueblos be recognized. That was the foundation from which [SER] was created. Because even before then, including with the committee, with CODREMI it was about that struggle for rights—as individuals, as pueblos—for recognition, for them to no longer see us as little children, but as people with our own visions. (Robles, interview, August 31, 1999)[10]

Sofía thrived in this setting and, along with other women in the Ayuujk (Mixe) region, she began to organize around daily life issues. She talked about how her early work with Ayuujk (Mixe) women reflected a politics of place centering on the scales of the body, ecologies, and economies:

In this period, we were already demanding of the government that there be attention to Indigenous pueblos. And there, I came to learn another reality: I joined the women's group, Xaam Të'ëxy [mujeres tlahuitoltecanas] a small group, that had been organizing motivated by other women who had arrived to Tlahui to collaborate with the communal grade school and also animated by the team of EIBM, in which there was a compañera and a compañero from Indigenous Education and two compañeros de la CMPIO [Coalición de Maestros y Promotores Indígenas de Oaxaca]. There were seven compañeras, and I, recently arrived, was well received. I felt very small at the side of these go-getters but I started to learn. Another important issue is that the participation of women in public spaces was very broad [in the Mixe region], in contrast to my [Zapotec] region, so I could contribute to [the work of] Mixe women. Or better said, I went to receive and to learn.

We began to work on questions of nutrition, and later on maternal and child health, with very practical things like promoting gardening, cooking workshops, and later, by request of the women, we began to have sewing and embroidery. From there, we founded an artisanal organization that maintained a store of artesania for many years. At the same time, this was a space for capacity-building in nutrition and women's health. We linked our work with the clinic because one of the compañeras was a nurse. We thought of the health of the children and of women. There was not explicitly the concept of reproductive rights. Yet, later we began to talk beyond to reproductive health, pregnancy care, birth and puerperium, sexually transmitted diseases, etc. (Robles, interview, August 31, 1999)

Building from the scale of the body, the garden, and the kitchen/home, Sofía and the Ayuujk (Mixe) women community organizers founded an economic collective for small-scale producers of artesania, a nutritional center, and a communal kitchen in 1989. In 1990, they went on to apply what they had developed across the Ayuujk (Mixe) region within five communities. Sofia was already involved with SER, so there was a closer relationship between the women's organization, Xaam Të'ëxy, SER, and the Coordinating Council of Self-promotion and Development Fund (Consejo de Coordinación del Fondo de Autopromoción del Desarrollo). While they organized the intimate and often female-gendered scales of the body, home, garden, and family through health and economic projects, they also organized across the Ayuujk (Mixe) region, creating a specifically Ayuujk (Mixe) meshwork. The scale of the pueblo (the town or village) is the scale of much Indigenous political, spiritual, and cultural organizing, but Shannan Mattiace points out that "since the 1970s sixteen indigenous communities in the Ayuujk (Mixe) area of northern Oaxaca have formed a loosely associated region" (2003, 107). The Ayuujk (Mixe) region is the scale at which communities organize the commercialization of their agricultural and artisanal products, organize transportation, and coordinate political activities, an important trend in the early organizing of authorities, economics, and health in Sofía's testimony that led to the formation of SER and the Mixe Women's Network, discussed below. The focus on the regional scale is in part due to historical land struggles that led to the formation of a Mixe district in the eastern part of the Sierra Juárez in Oaxaca during the Cárdenas administration following the Mexican Revolution. Not all scales of governance align with Indigenous territories, but this specifically Ayuujk (Mixe) district was created in 1938, according to Lynn Stephen (1996), facilitating the conditions in which Ayuujks practice Indigenous autonomy and regional organization from below.

Sofía continued with her local work but attended the Centro de Desarrollo Professional, Emocional, Académico (Center for Academic, Emotional, and Professional Development) school in Mexico and later in Celaya, Guanajuato. From 1993 to 1996, Sofía was a MacArthur Fellow in reproductive health in the Ayuujk (Mixe) region and used this position to begin discussions about women's rights, the environment, and citizenship. As she put it, "I didn't know how to do projects but I responded to the questions, was awarded the grant, and from there began to link with other women's and human rights organizing in the country. In this way, I became organized within other spaces like the coordination of NGOs toward Beijing, Milenio feminista, preparatory state, regional and national meetings" (Robles, interview, March 13, 2015). These steps allowed Sofía to be within the networks of women who were preparing for the regional organizing meeting to draft an agenda for the Fourth World Conference of Women (discussed in chapter 2).

One of the characteristics of meshworks laid out at the beginning of the chapter was the idea of interweaving. As we continued our discussions over the years, Sofía emphasized the importance of organizing at every level/scale, though she points out that, for reasons of proximity, the local and regional levels are particularly powerful for women's mobilization. Organizing at one scale often provides the pretext to organize at others. For example, Sofía spoke of how crucial it was both for Indigenous women to gather in Mexico in advance of the continental meeting in Ecuador, and for representatives to gather in Ecuador for the Indigenous women's continental meeting before traveling to the Fourth World Conference on Women in Beijing. Yet despite these links at other scales, she noted again and again how everything she does is made possible only with support from the community, from her sense of comunalidad (communalism).

In this sense, Sofía's life work illustrates the ways ideas of comunalidad are already gendered. At the center of community wellbeing and the collective good, is labor that is often invisibilized as women's labor yet it is the force behind communal social reproduction as well as collective health and balance, among other things. While these gendered forms of comunalidad may not be legible to outsiders, Sofía, along with many other women in her pueblo and across the Ayuujk (Mixe) region, have also centered women's health, civic and economic well-being in their communal work for their communities, and they enact that form of comunalidad at different scales. The meshwork is also helpful in illustrating not just interweaving and networking across difference and scale, but also how the Indigenous women's movement is building political power cumulatively across those experiences.

Much later, during one of our return interviews, I asked Sofía whether the strategy of weaving in and between multiple scales was important in the face of setbacks the Indigenous movement confronted, like the 2001 Law on Indigenous Rights and Cultures, a piece of national legislation that many saw as betraying the basic agreements of the San Andrés Peace Accords—namely, the right to Indigenous autonomy and self-determination. Although it is clear from her history that the Indigenous rights movement in Mexico, and women's participation and leadership in it, has local roots, Sofía explained that scaling down to work at local, municipal, and regional scales was "very related because when this issue [blockage] of the [implementation of the] San Andrés Accords or the [passage of the] Indigenous Law came up, we said, 'Fine, we're going to be autonomous and we're going to work in the regions. You [the government] barely recognize us or our rights. . . .' So, I believe that in some way, the Indigenous movement continues [at the municipal and regional levels], and I think that the women's movement is . . . it continues to be stronger" (Robles, interview, October 6, 2011). Rather than focus on rights or governmental responses, or the lack of them, Sofía repeatedly reflects on the gains won through the decades of organizing. She talks about the goals of Indigenous women's organizing, such as increasing women's participation; gaining access to social, economic, and political spaces denied to women; and creating vínculos, or connections, between scales and organizations.

Gendering Comunalidad: Women's Leadership within Indigenous Governance Structures at the Scale of the Municipality

On a trip to Oaxaca, I returned to interview Sofía Robles Hernández. We met in the offices of the civil association Services for the Mixe Pueblo (SER AC) in Oaxaca City. We were conducting a return interview some twelve years after I had first interviewed her in Tlahuitoltepec, about two and half hours away up the Sierra Juárez. We began talking about how Ayuujk (Mixe) women have built the Network of Mixe Women to organize themselves across the Ayuujk (Mixe) region/territory. As we talked, she updated me on her activities, reflecting on the logros of Indigenous women's organizing. Then she told me that she had been nominated to serve as one of the first woman presidents of the Ayuujk (Mixe) region. Sofía explained the scales of governance in this way: "There is the president of the republic, the governors [of the states], and then at the level of the regions, there are the municipal presidents of the 570 municipalities of Oaxaca." In the state of Oaxaca, she elaborates, among those 570 municipalities, "418 [now 417] are municipalities that are governed by usos y costumbres."[11] When I asked how this process came to be, she explained further:

> Well, this is another achievement of the Indigenous movement. First and foremost, 570 [municipalities] were on the political rolls of parties, but not lead by [political] parties. Indigenous municipalities are elected in assembly. [Community] authorities are elected by assembly but [before] they had to register in the list of candidates of the PRI [Institutional Revolutionary Party], primarily. The Indigenous movement (that I have been talking with you about) began to reflect and question why, after

we had elected our own authorities—that are not from the political parties because we don't elect them by party—why they [those we elected] have to pass on to the party list? Is it possible to have our right to elect our leaders respected? So, there was a change in the electoral law after a struggle of eight or ten years of petition after petition after petition. In 1995, they approved into law the Code of Electoral Procedures and Institutions that states there will be an election for parties and elections by the regime of usos y costumbres, so Indigenous communities adopted election by customary in 418 [417] municipalities. For this reason, we no longer elect our leaders through the political parties, there is no longer the necessity to get on the list of candidates [of a political party]. Now, it is the assemblies directly who report their elections to the State Electoral Institute for recognition. (Robles, interview, October 6, 2011)

With electoral law reform in 1995, Oaxaca became the first and only state in the Republic of Mexico to formally recognize Indigenous law and traditional community authorities in Indigenous municipalities. This law formally established two electoral systems: a sistemas normativas indígenas (Indigenous normative systems), also known as customary law, at the municipal level and election by competition between political parties at the state and federal levels. The law essentially created a form of plurilegality that legitimized existing Indigenous governance and jurisprudence systems such as election by council or community assembly, which was a common practice in Oaxaca. Later, in 1998, the Law of the Rights of the Indigenous Pueblos and Communities was passed, recognizing the "pluriethnic" nature of the state of Oaxaca and the rights of autonomous regions (Recondo 2001).

Several years later, when I saw Sofía again in Los Angeles and had a chance to interview her at the home of Oaxacan Indigenous immigrant rights activists, I asked her what was it like to be one of the first woman to receive the bastón de mando in the ceremony to transfer power (see figure 3.1).[12] She told me a humorous story that gets at the heart of the debate around the exclusion of women within Indigenous governance systems (usos y costumbres) and already existing forms of gendered labor in Oaxaca:

> Well, I was barely awake when I took possession [of the bastón de mando], because we didn't sleep the night before. Because, well, one of the things is if you're an [Indigenous] authority, you have to be at the forefront of the work. I couldn't say, "Okay, you all stay there making the tamales and prepare for the next day, I'm going to sleep because I have to be at the table in the morning and [if I stay up all night cooking], I'm not

Figure 3.1. Sofía Robles and the council after she had been sworn in as municipal president of Santa María Tlahuitoltepec, Oaxaca, 2012. Photo courtesy of Sofía Robles.

going to sleep." No. Everyone that was going to [the ceremony to] take possession, all the wives, and the helpers of those of us who didn't have partners, we were there working. . . . And in the community, [after you take possession of the staff of rule,] you go back to being another person in the community. Meaning, just because you are [the municipal] president now does not mean you can think of yourself as [higher]. No, you become a citizen again after the assemblies, you go back to everything [in your daily life], no? Of course, people do see you differently, now you belong to the circle of the principals, of the elders, the ones who can give their opinion, like that. (Robles, interview, March 13, 2015)

If Sofía had been a male leader, a wife or female relatives would have taken up this task, but as a female leader, she cooked all night along with the other women and then stood for the ceremony in the morning. Her story reveals that for Indigenous women, leadership means being at the head of collective community labor no matter what time your ceremony is in the morning, even if you have to stay up all night making tamales or doing the collective labor of cooking for the ceremony and community feast. As we joked about how a women's work is never done, I began to understand that, despite all the criticism of women's disenfranchisement and exclusion from municipal governments in Oaxaca ruled by Indigenous normative systems, Sofía's story illustrates the complexity of gendered labor, communal leadership roles, and the ways Indigenous women navigate them—complicating the debate on women's exclusion in some communities based on Indigenous normative systems. While men in the community take on public communal labor to serve the community, women already do that work in their everyday labor of social reproduction. Not only is this work invisibilized historically in conversations about comunalidad, when women do take up formal leadership roles, they are challenged by doing a double, or sometimes triple, form of labor.

In fact, as Aguilar Gil (2019) documents, women's communal labor is what led to Ayutla becoming the first pueblo in the Ayuujk (Mixe) region to elect a woman municipal president through the normative Indigenous system. She points out that since then, two more women have been elected into that role through normative systems without the help of the 2015 constitutional reform on gendered equity, which aimed to guarantee the electoral rights of indigenous women living in municipalities (34). Rejecting the experiences Mixe women have had with mestiza feminists, who have arrogantly dismissed Indigenous women's organizing and their labor, Aguilar Gil discusses the unique history of how her town became a destination when the highway was built through it. Indigenous women's ability to prepare and sell traditional foods to travelers was what gave them the economic independence to step up and become mayordomas, one of the first steps on the ladder of cargos (positions) an elected authority has to hold before being elected as municipal president. Many have identified this schema as a blockage to women's formal political leadership in municipalities governed by Indigenous normative systems. Aguilar Gil outlines the complex system of cargos in which positions, from those with less responsibility to the president of the municipality, are assumed for a period of one year with no pay. She reminds her readers that holding a cargo is not actively sought out because of the enormous economic and energetic wear. In Aguilar Gil's analysis, it was Indigenous women with their own communal work who were opening spaces for other women to participate (one of Sofía's logros) without ever reading a feminist text or having a gender equity scheme imposed from the top down from the outside of the community, which ironically invisibilizes women's labor and adds to their burdens, as Worthen discusses below. Instead, Aquilar Gil says women in her community went to "the school of leña, as women elders call it, those who where conquering more spaces, so that if they could be mayordomas, then they could participate in the assemblies, and if they could go, they had a voice and vote, as I saw the women from my childhood" (38).[13] She reminds us that community fiestas serve as a form of resistance and, according to Floriberto Díaz, are a pillar of comunalidad. Aguilar Gil also notes that the election of a woman president in 2007 did not just happen overnight or by accident but was the result of years, perhaps decades, of the women supporting each other in doing the community's work. Describing this complex process, she says, "The fact that in 2007—before the gender parity policies for municipal heads dictated from the state—the assembly of my community had elected a woman as municipal president by entering a whole community process that meant that previously women could be entitled to be communal land owners, to attend the assemblies, to have a voice in it, to vote and to be voted on [elected]; in other words, to be included in the system of cargos and to have served in the lower positions. It is a process that developed over decades" (34). Although traditionally men have held government positions in her town, Aguilar Gil shows how women have, through their communal work and the economic stability they have gained by preparing and selling food, over decades, used the tools of the comunalidad to empower themselves on behalf of their communities.

Tzul Tzul's scholarship (2015) on Indigenous communal governance asks us to look closely at the pillars that uphold these structures, namely communal work, kinship and assembly as modes that reproduce daily life, and as such, are therefore imminently gendered. She argues, "These forms of indigenous communal government produce and control the concrete means for the reproduction of daily life through at least three political forms, namely: the k'ax k'ol (or communal work) that animates the concrete means for life; the patterns of kinship, a powerful and at the same time contradictory strategy, that is used to defend the communal ownership of the territory and organizes the use of it; and the assembly as a communal form of deliberation to solve everyday problems, issues of state aggression, or to deal with how and in what way what is produced on communal lands is redistributed" (128–29). In her thinking, Tzul Tzul helps us understand how communal labor includes the labor of all of the community in ways that governmental schemes for gender inclusion miss. For example, she says, "That is why indigenous communal government is the political organization to ensure the reproduction of life in the communities, where k'ax k'ol is the fundamental floor where those systems of communal government rest and take place and where the full participation of all (todas y todos) is played. I propose a classification of communal work to give an account of how we all work or can work and that the indigenous communal is not confined to one identity, but to the capacity that we all [men and women] have" (133). The reproduction of communal life is the foundation upon which all else is possible and the reproduction of communal life is gendered. These labors include service that produces decisions, service that produces coordination, work that plans parties (from rituals, to music, to communal joy), the communal labor of healing and burial (133-34). Further Tzul Tzul asks us to think of the notion of k'ax k'ol, that which organizes the world of reproduction, and political society, the one that organizes public life, as not completely separated as they have become in Western capitalist societies that divide the world into a public/private dichotomy, one that is based on a gendered division of labor. While divisions of labor exist, Tzul Tzul is asking us to consider the labor of communality and the ways it is gendered in complex and new ways—ways that require we pay attention to local scales of resistance that include Indigenous territories/lands and households.

Velásquez (2000, 2003), Dalton (2003, 2012), Velásquez and Burgete Cal y Mayor (2013) and Vázquez García (2011) have documented women municipal presidents elected in Indigenous municipalities by usos y costumbres. Velásquez (2000) found that usos y costumbres (Indigenous normative systems) inhibited women in exercising their rights to participate in the political process and to vote in elections of the municipal presidents, which legally legitimized forms of social exclusion. In Oaxaca there are diverse practices regarding women's community political participation in terms of who is enfranchised and who is considered a citizen of the community; both depend on how each municipality conceptualizes citizenship. Many Indigenous communities use communal labor, or tequio, as a means of enfranchisement. For example, Worthen points out that "rights are not simply granted as they are in liberal democracies, but rather earned via the enactment of certain types of labor. The right to participate—opine and vote—in the assembly, the maximum expression of local power and decision making, is earned through *cargos* (town service positions) and *tequios* (collective work parties for public works)" (2015, 915-16). Cargos are unpaid positions, and eligibility for the highest cargos of the pueblo often is based on having worked in many of the lower positions in the past as Aguilar Gil outlined above.

Many point to Oaxaca as a successful example of recognizing and enacting Indigenous autonomy at the municipal level, whereas others argue that Oaxaca has always been something of an anomaly because Indigenous autonomy has been practiced de facto there for centuries (Rubin 1997).[14] Although these municipalities are seen as spaces of "actually existing" Indigenous autonomy, where Indigenous-led governance structures are in place, Zapotec historian Luis Sánchez-López (2018) reminds us that those structures are authorized and regulated by the Mexican settler state. Indigenous autonomy regimes grant limited Indigenous autonomy and decision making ability at the local level, but many would argue that a settler colonial governance structure is still deeply embedded at the scale of the municipal. Sánchez-López states that regional and municipal autonomy was a part of settler colonial state-making during the national period. Shannon Speed (2019) has argued more recently that the settler state in Mexico was established during independence.

Those communities that use Indigenous normative systems are plurilegal in that they use a mix of Western and traditional electoral means. Citizens of these communities elect federal and state authorities according to standard electoral processes of secret ballot and universal suffrage, but they elect municipal authorities by Indigenous normative systems. These systems include a range of practices to make decisions, from communitywide assemblies to a council of elders, suffrage based on community citizenship, often governed by land ownership and tequio (communal labor), some of these structures that have excluded women historically, and a process of voting that is public and takes place after communal debate. Before laws mandating gender equity, analysts decried the ways women could face de facto exclusion from political participation since women have not participated in community assemblies in as many as three-fourths of municipalities (Eisendstadt 2013, 5). What is less understood is how the structures of exclusion are themselves Indigenous community responses to externally imposed patriarchal norms mandated by the state at earlier points in the history.

Feminist ethnographers present a more nuanced picture that challenges how Indigenous structures are portrayed as ahistorical and patriarchal. In a comparative study of Indigenous governance systems and women's participation in Chiapas and Oaxaca, Lynn Stephen (2006) argues that things commonly considered "traditional" are historical systems that have changed over time and are specific to regional variation, largely in relation to state structures rather than internal communal values. She points, for example, to how so-called Indigenous traditions of governance that center on male authority in Chiapas were not shaped by community norms but by rules of land ownership in the ejido (collective land tenure system established during the Mexican Revolution) structure that governs who can speak or vote in assemblies—rules that were imposed by the state. In the Zapotec region of the Tlacolula Valley of Oaxaca, Stephen (2005) similarly gives historical context, explaining how both men and women gained authority and prestige from participating in mayordomías, or sponsorships of religious festivities for town patron saints. From the 1800s to the 1960s, the civil cargo system (volunteer offices and positions within the community governance system) was linked to the religious cargo system. "While offices of the civil cargo system were held by men, the *mayordomía* sponsorships of the religious cargo system were held by pairs of men and women, both of whom received authority and prestige" (see Stephen 2005, 234-43). "The contributions of women to the civil cargo system were and continue to be recognized informally as supporting community through the work they do when their husbands are absent doing cargos" (Stephen 2006, 161). As specified in the 1917 Mexican Constitution, civil cargo positions have been elected, which many point to as replacing the council of elders with the municipal assembly. Stephen also notes that the "decoupling of civil and religious cargo systems in Oaxaca and elsewhere since the 1950s is related to the increasing integration of community political structures with those of state and national governments" (2006, 161).

Stephen points to how the state has shaped, and continues to shape, gendered divisions of communal labor that complicate notions of "tradition," giving critical insights into the ways Indigenous women are represented as oppressed, primarily by local patriarchies within their own communities, or are seen to be victims of their own cultures (Newdick 2005). "One of the consequences of the divorce of religious hierarchies from the civil ones in Zapotec communities was that women lost most of their formal remaining link to institutional community politics." Yet, she argues, "[n]evertheless, women continued to use the authority and prestige they accrued through their roles as *mayordomas* (see Stephen 1991, 160-77) and *madrinas* in the ritual kinship system of *compadrazo* (see Sault 2001) to increase their influence in community politics in other spheres of life" (Stephen 2006, 161). Stephen claims that while community political life became more male dominated, "women had a deep and sustained history through their role as *mayordomas* in accruing prestige, respect, and authority that allowed them to have an impact on community politics" (161). Critically, she emphasizes the "importance of looking at community-specific gender roles for women in what have been called 'traditional' forms of local governance and looking at how women's roles in such institutions interact with other forms of organizing that take place at a local level" (173). These insights underscore the ways some Indigenous women not only engaged in communal labor but received respect and social authority for doing so. It also points to the ways those who take up formal elected leadership positions are navigating "traditions" that may have been a result of the hand of the Mexican state historically. It is a cruel irony, or perhaps the classic colonial conundrum, when the rationale state actors give for voting against laws in favor of Indigenous autonomy are patriarchal power arrangements within Indigenous communities, some of which can be traced back to the state itself.

This ethnographic and historical understanding gives more complexity to the ways I argued earlier that gender has become a discourse of governmentality for the Mexican state used to determine the terrain upon which Indigenous people are seen as deserving of rights.

Sofía's long history of service to her community, even the double days and nights of community service, are linked to gendered forms of comunalidad. Women activists in the popular women's movements and socialist feminists have long called attention to the double day of working women who labor in the public sphere at their jobs and then work another shift in the private sphere doing childcare, homecare, and other reproductive labors. Activist women have described their days as a triple day filled with jobs, organizing work, and caring for families and homes. Often when men engage in tequio, the free communal labor offered as part of their citizenship within a community, they must quit their jobs to do so or pay others to do this work for them, especially in the migrant context. In many Indigenous contexts, in addition to women's reproductive labor of households and families, Indigenous women carry out the communal gendered labor of social, spiritual, and cultural reproduction at community level. When they take up a public leadership role, they may be doing not only the double or triple day of labor activists called attention to but a double day (and night as in Sofía's case) of the labor of comunalidad. Stephen argues that whether Indigenous women are successful in "opening up local political systems to their participation and leadership is predicated on the recognition of specific skills and experience they develop in local, ethnic-linked forms of governance—even if such systems formally exclude women—and other forms of organization that may offer more egalitarian forms of organizing for women" (2011, 173). She also notes that "this capacity is rooted in their ability to articulate local gendered contests over political power and ethnic and cultural rights with regional and national forms of association that offer a different set of gendered political roles and often emphasize a specific ethnic identity or pan-Indigenous form of identity as a basis of organization" (173). Indeed, Sofía's skill set and leadership emerged from the collective organizational labor of women in her community and their work on behalf of the Ayuujk (Mixe), in addition to the experiences at the national and continental level, that were then recognized at the municipal level in her presidency. This aligns with Margarita Dalton's groundbreaking study of women municipal presidents in Oaxaca (2003, 2012).

Other ethnographic research complicates an oversimplified view of women's participation in the cargo system and calls our attention to the critical role of gendered labor. Worthen argues that those who remain "focused [solely] on the liberal model of women as individual rights-bearers . . . fail to understand the complex ways in which gendered labor influences political participation in nonliberal contexts" (2015, 914). She studies the 2009 legal mandate to include women in Indigenous normative systems from the Oaxacan electoral institute in the small municipality of Yatzachi, a town of two hundred Zapotec inhabitants, to which the municipal authority responded with its own official letter that said women in the community willingly reject participation. For Worthen, the letter "represents an internal struggle over the gendered labor practices that define and construct the alternative political and economic system on which the community is built" (915). Worthen points out that the struggles of gendered labor play a large part in shaping the forms of Indigenous women's political participation. In that 2009 case, she observed that "although women do important work in their households and the community, it does not count as 'official labor.' Therefore, women are prohibited from assembly participation because they have not 'worked' for the community. When women *do* perform *cargos* and *tequios*, as in the case of single women household heads, participation implies extra official work in addition to the unofficial labor of social reproduction. Therefore, although most women are theoretically in favor of women's participation, the gendered terms of the communal system deter their participation in the assembly and in formal leadership roles" (916). Worthen's notion that labor is an "important subject-producing category" that functions "as an alternative practice in which notions of rights are created in Indigenous collectivities" (921) is key to understanding how gendered labor informs communal politics and membership.

In addition to the central role of women's labors of social reproduction in the life of the community, some wives argued that they do the work of their husband's cargo alongside him, and they certainly make cargo possible by managing fields and generating alterative income. Yet instead of being valued in the same way as men's labor, women's labors are not categorized as part of the obligations of active citizenship (Worthen 2015, 923), an issue that I take up in chapter 4. Worthen found that "for many women performing *cargos* and *tequios* is often seen as a burden rather than an opportunity to be a leader in the community. This is because of the lack of value given to both women's official and unofficial labor" (925–26). Further, women who signed the letter rejecting their own participation in community assembly reported that they did so because the work they *do* perform as citizens was undervalued and did not lead to equal participation; because holding a cargo presented an extra burden in their already taxing work of social reproduction; and because those women who are active as citizens feel that their participation in the communal system places an unfair burden on them. Negating the state's mandate for women's participation was not about the cargos themselves, but their obligatory nature. The process of debate was important in the community assembly that produced the letter rejecting the electoral institute's mandate that women participate. Worthen points out that "women were able to emphasize the role and value of their work within the communal system, an important first step toward identifying the unequal systems of gendered labor upon which local participation is based and validated" (929).

In other contexts, customary law has been critiqued less in terms of Indigenous structures of self-rule and more as a reflection of the colonial management of gender and power, which then gets ascribed as "local," "primitive" patriarchies (Mani 1998). These "local patriarchies" are in fact the product of national, often colonial, impositions that have been fused with communal forms—what Inderpal Grewal and Caren Kaplan (1994) have called "scattered hegemonies" to call attention to the multiscalar arrangement of power wherein colonialism, imperialism, or capitalism operates hand in glove through a national oligarchy and is articulated through local patriarchies, for example (see also Grewal 1992). Moller Okin (1999) has argued that multiculturalism is bad for women and is part of a trend that portrays women as victims of their cultures. Yet, her lack of intersectional analysis of power presumes that women can stand outside of their racial, ethnic, economic, and cultural groups and the ways those categories are stigmatized and marginalized. This view also ignores the idea that what is called "traditional" is often a response to (neo)colonial forms of governance. Thus, it is important to understand these legal exclusions within a broader context of Indigenous women's organization and struggle for participation and inclusion within municipalities. Critical to this broader view is understanding the multiscalar participation of the Indigenous women's movement, the diversity of its actors, and the emergence of a political analysis of autonomy from the point of view of Indigenous women and gender. Regino Montes, a student of Ayuujk (Mixe) anthropologist and activist Floriberto Díaz, stated, "We are peoples and, therefore, require the recognition of our collective rights in order to enjoy the exercise of our individual rights" (Regino Montes n.d., 134, cited in Mattiace 2003). This framing of collective and individual rights was echoed by Indigenous women activists who have challenged the ways these two sets of rights are seen as divisible. Recall from chapter 1 that P'urépecha activist Tomasa Sandoval has argued that women cannot fully exercise their rights without also having collective Indigenous rights, and that Indigenous people will not have full autonomy as long as women do not have rights to land, to political participation and leadership, to bodily autonomy, for example.

When we spoke in 2011, Sofía explained to me that Indigenous normative systems had been in place since 1995 in Tlahuitoltepec, the municipal head in the Ayuujk (Mixe) region of Oaxaca, which has almost ten thousand inhabitants. She reflected on the process of how she was nominated to be municipal president:

> Territorially, Tlahuitoltepec is a very large municipality, there are six agencies (only one called Santa María Yacochi does not belong in the territory but it is part of the municipality politically). Originally and currently the five agencies that are politically a municipality are the same community so all participate. Although they have their own small assemblies, everyone participates in the general assemblies of the community and that's where the elections are held. For the last thirteen years, I was participating in the elections, but I was not elected. Now, I participated in the elections and I was left with the majority of the votes so now I am going to be president which means a commitment. It is also very challenging, first, because I am a woman and second, because I have two identities. I am Zapotec but I am also Mixe, so then it is a challenge as well with the community. I feel a lot of responsibility. I have my fears but I tell myself, "I must move forward, right?" I feel that there are people who truly say, "Adelante," and they motivate me, they support me and they smile. There are others that say, "Let's see how you do." So, there I am. I have to assume the position the best way I can, right? My only plan is to respond to the needs of the community [to] the best extent possible depending on resources, which seem to be cut more each time, but it is one electoral year and we don't know what it will give us. (Robles, interview, October 6, 2011)

When I asked more about the nomination process, Sofía responded: "The nomination process was through community assembly . . . where there were many candidates, like nine candidates. I came out of nine candidates, who kept dropping out until I remained." Although other women have been elected to be municipal presidents, Sofía stated that it is much easier under the political party system because

> parties tell women, "We're going to endorse you," [and the women say] "Yes, yes, let's launch my campaign, I'll do it." But in this case, because in most traditional usos y costumbres, it's the assembly. In the communities that still conserve [usos y constumbres]. It was a surprise, for me it was unbelievable. I said "How? Why me? Why me? Me, why me? Why? If

there are so many brilliant women, so many women that are . . . so many women, why me exactly?" And finally, well the people, like always, we don't value ourselves enough, right? As women we don't value ourselves enough, or you feel that what you're doing is not important. But in the end, you realize that what you do is important, and that you can also achieve other things. (Robles, interview, October 6, 2011)

Although she was concerned that being a woman (and a Zapotec/Ayuujk in the Ayuujk region) might make things difficult, Sofía explained that she had a lot of support from the community authorities:

So, it was a very beautiful experience, with a lot of backing from the cabildo. Because also before we took possession [of the bastón del mando], I told them, "Look, I'm not interested, if you all consider that it's going to be a problem that I'm a woman, I'll get out of the cargo." I mean, I have no problem, really, I have no investment in becoming president. I don't. So, I want cabildo to go well. I'm in the best position to learn, to share, to work together, but if the fact that I'm a woman is going to cause problems . . . I don't want to be a problem. And they said, "No, you are going, or if someone wants you out, we'll all go." And with that assurance that I was going to have their support, I said, "Ok, let's go, now we're going to get to work." (Robles, interview, March 13, 2015)

Sofía's long history of community work is grounded in the historic relationship of the Oaxacan Indigenous autonomy movement, which won state reforms recognizing Indigenous autonomy at the municipal level. When I asked what it took to be nominated, she said, "I don't know how to explain it to you. Work. Commitment. Service to the community." I asked her how it felt, as a former municipal president, to be an elder and have a respected opinion. She replied:

Good, to give your word [dar la palabra], I feel part of . . . the most beautiful part is feeling part of the community. For me that is the most beautiful, to be part of the community, that the community knows you, the community values what you can contribute. And every time the authorities call the principales with some issue, well, I always try to answer. When, sometimes, it's not possible, I feel sorry, but when I'm expecting it, I take care to say, "I have to go to the assembly, I have to go to this meeting, because I feel part of [the community/communal leadership]." If I stopped doing it, I would feel . . . the city, I really don't like it much. The city is for working. But, always, my days off are for community. I have a day off, and, it's, "Let's go to the community, yes." (Robles, interview, March 13, 2015)

We spent some time reflecting on the changes that have resulted from Indigenous women's organizing. Sofía discussed the importance of organizing beyond the local scale, of doing so at every level, because Indigenous women are not static:

> I think that the work is important at every level, because Indigenous women are not in a single place, no? Right now, for example, Flora is here in Oaxaca City [at the state level], she is there in the pueblos on her days off and maybe on her vacations when she says, "I'm going to my pueblo and I'm doing some work with the women who are working there," right? Or, "I'm here, but I spent the weekend in my community doing local work." Now I'm here [in Oaxaca City], tomorrow I go to a national conference for legal abortion. Local work is very important; if you only do national work that's not going to work because you don't have the grassroots [bases]. Or only doing statewide work doesn't work well, because you don't have the community or grassroots; you have to have links with all the levels of organizing. (Robles, interview, October 6, 2011)

Indigenous women's multiscalar organizing strategies are part of what allows them to challenge the ways the state shapes Indigenous forms of governance, which often privilege men, as Stephen showed. It further challenges how gendered labor and the sphere of the collective has been gendered in ways that conflict with the current state's notions of gender equity, as Worthen illustrated. As discussed in the introduction and chapter 1, I argue that gender is appropriated as a discourse of governmentality to regulate who is a "good"/"bad" Indigenous subject, ignoring the long work of Indigenous women to craft a community-based project of "women's rights." Isabel Altamirano-Jiménez also challenges the dichotomy that she argues exists in representations of Zapotec women either as victims of their own cultures or as romanticized matriarchs, both of which obscure structures of gender inequality (2013, 199). Sofía's reflections on her role as municipal president reveal both the exhaustion and the joy of maintaining one's role in the reproductive labor of the community, usually reserved for women, while simultaneously making a different kind of commitment to the community by assuming a position of power within traditional authorities—roles that are often assigned to men. Her reflections reorient us toward how Indigenous women are building collective spaces of participation and connection from below and then, through those nodes of connection, transforming the configuration of power at multiple scales. Although Sofía agrees that local work is critical for Indigenous women, she also recognizes how they are often linked to and overdetermined by the local, and thus she emphasizes again and again the importance of vínculos, or linkages, between scales of organizing. Her work creating another network of "locales" across Ayuujk (Mixe) territory, for example, does not align perfectly with state-organized municipalities, as she discussed above, but rather spans numerous Ayuujk communities thereby creating an Indigenous scale.

Networking the Local: Building the Region through the Mixe Women's Network

La Red de Mujeres Mixes (Network of Mixe Women, REDMMI) officially formed in 2009, but its roots were laid during eight regional encuentros of Mixe women that began in December 2005 (see figure 3.2). It brought together women from fifteen Ayuujk (Mixe) communities who identified the need to forge connection and get to know each other at the Third Regional Encuentro of Mixe Women in Jaltepec de Candayoc, November 25–26, 2006.[15] At the eighth encuentro in San Isidro Huayapam in March 2009, Ayuujk (Mixe) women decided to organize the first assembly of the Network of Mixe Women. The regional encuentros included women of different ages and professions, including housewives, campesinas, students, and professionals. As REDMMI's founding documents pronounced: "It is our space to forge strength and unity, to communicate, orient, animate, transmit knowledge, build capacity and

Figure 3.2. First assembly of the Network of Mixe Women (REDMMI), Ayutla Mixe, October 2009. Photo courtesy of Sofía Robles.

exchange experiences and products from our communities and organizations. Moreover, it is a space of reflection and the different women's issues."¹⁶ This work grew out of the earlier organizing that Sofía had discussed with the Asamblea de Productores Mixes (Assembly of Mixe Producers), which the women founded in 2001 to create economic opportunities for women artisans. Sofía explained how they expanded their idea to include a broader Ayuujk (Mixe) women's agenda: "And so we continue working with them, with community garden projects, health projects such as cervical health testing campaigns, women's rights workshops. In 2005, together with those organizations, we said, "Let's have a regional women's meeting, but not only workers [producers], not only to talk about work, savings, credit and those things, but to talk about rights and political rights," which we also called community participation, and so this issue started coming up" (Robles, interview, October 6, 2011). REDMMI's objective is to "build a single force for the rights of Mixe women to be respected and taken into account in all arenas of life and community."¹⁷ REDMMI works on women's rights, sexual and reproductive rights, legislation, traditional medicine, gastronomy, women's empowerment, gender equity, gender violence, discrimination (against Indigenous people or toward women), self-esteem, and community participation. Their founding documents state that their goals are to "promote the community participation and leadership of Mixe women, to learn about the rights of women and the rights of pueblos indígenas (land and territory, self-determination, culture, and Indigenous law) in order to promote, defend, and exercise them; and finally, to build confidence and strength to achieve a life free of violence in our family, community, and society in general."¹⁸

The group's work interweaves the activism of Mixe women from different pueblos into a network that spreads across the municipal scale, which roughly encompasses Ayuujk (Mixe) territory. Sofía told me, "Right now we have around sixteen communities, women from sixteen communities, so then maybe seventy more or so are active. But at every meeting the numbers change poco a poco [little by little]." I asked whether the goal was to cultivate more women's participation at local scales from the point of view of gender, and a rich conversation unfolded about how we name processes that emerge from community organization.

> SOFÍA: Well yes, just little by little, no? When, for example, I started working with women, we didn't talk about gender, we talked about the condition of women here. We didn't talk so much about gender . . .
>
> MAYLEI: It was more about inclusion . . .

SOFÍA: Yes, exactly ... we were reflecting on gender; we didn't call it "gender," but we were talking about the situation we were in as women, right?

MAYLEI: Not equity?

SOFÍA: Then later, later the question came up, this theory. That's why the theory of gender, that comes afterward, but we were already working from the perspective of rights. And from the perspective of rights, we saw that there was inequity, no? But we weren't saying "Okay gender, let's see, how is gender constructed?," not like that.

I clarified that I was asking about how Indigenous women saw their process specifically as Indigenous women. Sofia explained that their process was internal to the community process of organizing and that, as she learned about other perspectives and concepts—for example, triple oppression—they made sense to her: "Even the issue of triple discrimination, of gender, class and ethnicity ... it took work for me to understand that, no? After listening and reading and all that, I said, 'Ah, of course.' Many men say, 'It's not true, there's no triple discrimination, Indigenous women are very happy,' right? 'They're doing very well, they're participating,' right? And so we say, 'No, you're wrong, because not all women, not all Indigenous women are happy, maybe some are but others are not.'" It is through these processes of learning and interweaving ideas that we can see meshworks in action. REDMMI emerged from the conditions of the local, and it remains rooted in community processes and continually interweaves with various other political formations, discourses, and ideas across other scales. All too often Indigenous women are understood from a unidirectional deficit model that assumes that other (higher-scale) external processes teach, shape, and influence them, but not the other way around. What Sofía calls attention to, however, is the way in which REDMMI's ideas of women's participation and "rights" emerged from local genealogies of struggle and community processes, weaving ideas and formations from other scales with already existing Indigenous knowledge, or what Driskill calls double-weaving (2016) that creates a third space in between.

Sofía emphasizes, for example, how important it is that women's rights emerge from "bottom up" organizing, not just "top down" state impositions, because the issues that go beyond participation in assemblies or that they be given cargos in the community are intertwined with other issues like literacy or violence against women. When issues emerge from within the communities, they can be taken up at the community level; in this Sofía echoes what

Marichuey shared earlier in this chapter. Sofía notes another logro of their organizing is that violence against women is now discussed in public, and women are demanding the right to a life without violence:

> Let's take the issue of violence, right? Before, the issue of violence was a private issue, no? And so, before that [it] was something that everyone resolved on their own; but at least now women who want to, do make use of their right to a life without violence because they can do it, no? Of course, it has to do with how she can be most effective in the community.
>
> So, their [women's] rights that permeate the issue of political participation that start taking form in the '80s. They're saying, "They [women] also read, and women also have rights." And then women start, they start always here at the bottom, always, always. So, how do I lift her up if I'm always going to be here at the bottom? So, starting to say, "Let's see, there's a cargo system and there's a hierarchy, so women should also hold these cargos, so they can also get to here [higher up]." (Robles, interview, October 6, 2011)

When I check in years later, in 2015, to find out how REDMMI's organizing was going, Sofía reflects that the network that emerged from the regional encuentros is now a smaller space: "And the topics—as always, political participation. Political participation from a community focus . . . from the focus of integrating into the community. Political participation, education, health, violence . . . yes, those are the main issues. Women's rights. Those were the principal issues" (Robles, interview, March 13, 2015).

Sofía explained how one scale will fold and another will open—in this case, the expansion of their regional organizing to a statewide network in Oaxaca. "We thought it was necessary to articulate ourselves, to have our own space and create the Asamblea de Mujeres Indígenas de Oaxaca [Assembly of Indigenous Women of Oaxaca, AMIO]" (Robles, interview, March 13, 2015). AMIO is the latest formation of Indigenous women organizing at multiple scales in addition to the other statewide networks that emerged from the organizing initiated by CONAMI members, including those in Jalisco, Oaxaca, and Guerrero, which I discussed earlier in this chapter. Yet AMIO can also be seen as a response to a critical conjuncture in Oaxaca. In 2006, a teacher's strike in Oaxaca turned into a widespread popular movement. Every year, teachers create an encampment while they negotiate their next contract, but in 2006 the annual event was transformed into one of mass violence when then governor Ulises Ruiz Ortiz called in the Policía Federal Preventiva (Federal Preventive Police) and violently repressed the teachers' organizing. In response, youth, teachers, Indigenous organizations, feminists, human rights defenders, and many people in other sectors rose up into a popular movement, shutting down the capital (Magaña 2010; Stephen 2013). The repression resulted in the emergence of a mass movement organized under the Popular Assembly of Oaxacan People (Asamblea Popular de los Pueblos Oaxaca, APPO). Calling for the governor to resign, significant numbers of women, and Indigenous and non-Indigenous social sectors, mobilized. On August 1, 2006, "la marcha de las carcerolas" (the march of the pots and pans) occurred; it was organized by women who decided to take over the radio and television stations (Martinez 2007; Stephen 2013). Women were organized as the Coordinator of Oaxacan Women (Coordinadora de Mujeres de Oaxaca, COMO), and Indigenous women stayed organized throughout "the rupture of the state of law during the 2006–2010 period of government, [which] accentuated the need of members of the AMIO to construct a space of reflection to find and elaborate affairs that challenge them as women and indigenous people of Oaxaca, with the intention of working for the human rights of indigenous women" (Martínez Cruz 2016, 175).

Since then, AMIO has developed statewide encuentros, diverse seminars about citizenship, racism, and access to justice, to name a few topics. It has been a critical gathering space where all Indigenous women can fit and can contribute their own strengths and talents. AMIO has influenced diverse institutions such as the Institute for the Oaxacan Woman in the state's Secretariat of Indigenous Affairs. In addition to working with women at the national level, AMIO members also accompany work in Oaxacan Indigenous communities to strengthen women's participation through trainings to help them to achieve an awareness of rights that allow a more dignified life. For example, in the proposal for the Law for Indigenous Pueblos and Afromexicans of 2013, AMIO demanded access to land for women, and that women be allowed to obtain the status of land as "comuneras" with full rights in ejidos and collective land tenure systems. Further, as a statewide assembly, AMIO provides Indigenous women a space of civic and political deliberation that they are denied in some communities. In her study of AMIO, Martínez Cruz (2016) argues that the importance of AMIO gathering under the name *Assembly* is to recover one of the principal institutions of pueblos governed by normative systems, wherein an assembly is a space of participation for those considered citizens to make decisions about their own communities. In response to the ways community assemblies function "under patriarchal practices that exclude, limit, and subordinate indigenous women from politico-administrative decision making positions, the women of AMIO are trying to promote an alternative space to which women have access to make their needs and demands more relevant, which questions the reality that they live inside and outside their communities" (175).

The work of AMIO emphasizes how Indigenous women interweave organizational scales to use their alliances and knowledge sharing to exert pressure on the government and shape public policy. For example, AMIO has formed alliances with different collectives that share their demands at the state and regional levels (such as the Department of Gender Equity and Mixe Women of SER and REMMI, which Sofía had described), and on the national scale with CONAMI, the Network for Sexual and Reproductive Rights Mexico; the Network of Indigenous Women; the "Simone de Beauvoir" Leadership Institute; the Interdisciplinary Group about Women, Work, and Poverty; and the Seeds Pro Women's Rights Society (Martínez Cruz 2016, 183). Building this work at each scale, Sofía described how the Asamblea de Productores Mixes did the slow work of also building power at each scale and interweaving them, especially the scale of the local: "Yes, well, it's always very, very difficult, women's work. That's how it is, slow, slow, very slow; you have to find the time with women, [with] all the housework, you have to learn to work with women and with children. Because when you work with women of a reproductive age, you know you're going to have a meeting with yelling, with toys, with crying, because children are there." Throughout Sofía's decades of work building strong local Indigenous women's organizations and communities, she has grounded that work in daily, lived realities and the intimate scales of family, body, garden, home, pueblo, territory. Weaving these experiences into grounded networks, or meshworks, has made all their logros (achievements) possible. Strategically combining and using Indigenous, women's, and human rights frameworks often requires interweaving or doubleweaving (Driskill 2016) Indigenous cosmovisions into colonial forms of governance in order to achieve their goals. Rather than achieving "women's rights" as narrowly defined in universal/liberal rights frameworks, Sofía discusses the struggles of women's rights as gaining logros beyond the legal recognition or rights from the state. Success is measured instead in terms of gaining access to and creating spaces of participation in communities and communal decision-making; in the formation of multiscalar networks ranging from ECMIA in 1995, to CONAMI in 1997, to REDMMI in 2009, to AMIO in 2010; and even more importantly, in the creation of linkages between all of these endeavors.

In this chapter I have examined the multiscalar locales of Indigenous women's organizing, from statewide networks that were initially established by CONAMI members in Jalisco, Guerrero, and Oaxaca, to the scales of the pueblo, the municipality, and the region. I describe how Indigenous women's rights and dignity were negotiated with success at the regional and state scales—for example, by demanding that alcohol not be sold on days of communal celebration or when the assembly meets, resulting in less violence against women, or in activists formed by CONAMI using their training to fight for women's rights within community policing. I looked at how women's rights emerged in tandem with the early Indigenous rights movement, that itself had emerged within regional organizing in Oaxaca before the Zapatista uprising. Grounded in three interviews in which Sofía Robles provided an oral history, the final sections expanded, and offered a more complex understanding of women's rights within Indigenous normative systems, challenging narrow individualist and Western understandings to illustrate unexamined forms of women's empowerment and how Indigenous women organizers negotiate unequal gendered structures that are tied to women's labor and communal labor. Scholars and activists argue that Indigenous autonomy is not attuned to the sovereignty of the state but to the sovereignty of the collective, that rights are not granted from above but are earned in relation to the collective (Worthen 2015). If we base our analysis in this reframing of autonomy and belonging, we can see how Indigenous women are claiming power at multiple scales but remain grounded within collective spaces of belonging, or comunalidad. This work then aligns with a broader call to rethink community membership and participation based on a notion of labor that takes into account women's enormous communal labor, not to mention reproductive labor. I've posited gendered comunalidad as a way to name the unrecognized forms of gendered labor and women's work that make communalidad possible. The notion of gendered comunalidad essentially calls attention to the ways comunalidad is *already* gendered but, for women, in invisible ways that shapes how their labor is linked to community belonging. While state mediated mechanisms have shaped how Indigenous women can gain access to assembly (like access to land), who has the right to voz y voto (voice and vote), or whose labor is formally recognized as communal labor or el tequio, shaping who can assume which cargos that form a prerequisite in many communities to serving as leaders. Ideas of gendered labor and comunalidad also highlight the disjuncture that exists between the Western conception of women's rights as "individual" versus organized Indigenous women's understanding of their gendered right as inextricably bound up with their communal life.

Aquino Moreschi (2013) argues, "there is still a need for deeper reflection on the daily relationships between men and women and the family models which construct the future and their autonomies" (14). In her analysis of the contributions and challenges of comunalidad she argues that the concept of complementarity is central to comunalidad. While "in the ideal, complementarity means symmetry, equality and harmony between men and women, the problem is that nothing is said about the specific content in which it would be expressed." As Julieta Paredes (2008) argues, "it is not mentioned that complementarity can also occur within dynamics of oppression and inequality, nor that this discourse can be used to naturalize a division of unfair labor between men and women, in which one of the parts of the 'complement' is responsible for the lowest value, the heaviest tasks, with less pay and recognition" (15). Thinking with Aymara communitarian feminist activist and theorist Julia Paredes, Aquino Moreschi aims to breaks down the colonial and Indigenous patriarchal underpinnings of complementarity to reveal that while gender complementarity is used to organize the labors of nuclear families, we must break open the male/female dichotomy to recognize the multitude of other complementarities that sustain families such as the grandma-mother, sister-sister, or amiga-amiga pairings and to further break open the heteropatriarchal assumptions of the male/female binary that erase mother-mother, father-father, or parent-parent configurations.

Debates on women's inclusion and equity in Indigenous normative systems have emerged from within Indigenous communities and not only in the state of Oaxaca, but across Mexico. The case of Eufrosina Cruz, a Zapotec women who was said to be barred from running for municipal president in 2007 because she is a woman, became the center of controversy and for many years after her story broke "led some to decry the system of local Indigenous autonomy as *'abusos y costumbres'* [abuses and customs] of women's rights within Indigenous law" (Eisenstadt 2013, 4). According to Holly Worthen (2021), Cruz's case brought her national media attention and she soon appeared on the cover of Mexican *Newsweek* and *Forbes*, spoke on the floor of the UN, and met the Obamas. Then Mexican president Felipe Calderón and his wife, Margarita Zalaya, championed her cause and invited her to join the conservative National Action Party (Partido de Acción Nacional, PAN) and, through proportional representation, she was elected on a platform to serve as state and then federal congresswoman, "where she began modifying multiculutral laws on Indigenous self-determination in order to promote women's electoral participation" (1–2). She went on the become the Secretary of Indigenous Affairs in the state of Oaxaca. Yet, through a discourse analysis of media coverage from 2007 to 2014, Wothen (2021) found a colonial resue narrative that portrayed Indigneous governance systems not only as partriarchal, anti-democratic, and authoritarian but illegal. Tracking the move from neoliberal multiculturalim to state securitization, or how the war on drugs was used to justify securing the state thorugh militarization and state violence, Worthen traces a disturbing trend where the neoliberal multicultural dichotomy of good versus bad Indian was mapped on state security narratives that framed the "good" Indians as those who ally with the state and seek its protection against those "bad" Indigenous communities and social movements advocating for autonomy that were then increasingly represented as criminal or illegal. Similar to how I have illustrated how gender has been used as a discourse of governmentality to define who is a good and bad Indigenous subject worthy of rights, Worthen takes the issue into the new context of the emerging security state established in the Calderón presidency to examine the way these discourses changed state relations with Indigenous pueblos. She shows how "[t]he question of Indigenous women's political participation in Indigenous normative systems increasingly became a site of scrutiny and intervention. Cruz's figure served as a way to materialize this issue. But instead of provoking an examination of how structural forms of sexism and racism affect Indigenous women's political subjectivities in particular ways, it shifted blame for Cruz's and other Indigenous women's exclusion on to Indigenous culture" (8). Worthen concludes that while "Indigenous women do often face forms of violence within their Indigenous polities, atrributing this to the sphere of Indigenous otherness helped promote the colonial idea that 'modern' (i.e., non-Indigenous) Mexican society is thus a place of freedom for women, an irony noted by the high rates of gender-based violence throughout the country (Comisión Nacional de Derechos Humanos, 2019)" (9). Along with other stories of women shared in this chapter, Sofía's long history of struggle and tireless work based on ideas of comunalidad, with women's community wellness at the center, reveals Indigenous women's activism and political subjectivities on their own terms from their own homes, pueblos, and muncipalities providing an important counternarrative to the way some analysts wrap gender equity quotas in colonial rescue narratives that ultimately disempower Indigenous women and criminalize Indigenous communities. The longer history of women's decades-long organizing for equity from below and within Indigneous communities should not be forgotten in the face of electoral and legal reforms also aimed and gender equity. In fact, while accompanying Indigenous women community organizers, researching and writing this chapter not only were new laws put into place, Indigenous women were beginning to be elected in greater numbers, a phenomena for future research that I hope does not erase these earlier grassroots efforts. According to a report by the State Electoral Institute of Oaxaca, 1,100 women were elected to cabildos (community councils) within communities governed by Indigenous normative systems in 2016 compared to the 216 women that were elected in 2013, and in 21 municipalities a woman presides over the cabildo, 13 more than in 2013 (Instituto Estatal Electoral 2017). The Gender Commission of the Oaxaca State Electoral and Citizen Participation Institute (IEEPCO) report "Women in the Cabildos, Elections 2019" focused on the results of the elections of Indigenous normative systems in Oaxaca reporting "1,571 women were elected to positions in 404 Indigenous municipalities" in 2019 (*Diario Marca* 2020). The face of local political power is shifting and it will be important to see how these prior organizing histories and networks interface with newly configured rules governing gender parity in Indigenous normative systems. This is especially important within communities that resist these impositions and more careful analysis from the perspective of Indigenous women in the communities is needed (Cárdenas Acosta and Lopez Vences 2021).

In this chapter, I called attention to the multiple locales that comprise the meshwork of "local" Indigenous women's organizing, including rooted networks that move vertically to organize at the transborder, international, and national levels. But just as importantly they move translocally across states, municipalities, regions, and transregions—those regions created by the movement of Indigenous peoples across multiple borders (Jonas and Rodriguez 2015), which I explore further in the next few chapters. As much as the women in this project move both horizontally and vertically in their organizing, critically they interweave their own epistemologies, knowledges, and cosmovisions with other discourses, rights, and strategies. This doubleweaving and multiscalar organizing bring strategic shifts in consciousness, what Chela Sandoval (1991, 2000) calls "differential consciousness," which in this context describes how organizers read power at various scales across geographies of difference and strategically shift gears between forms of consciousness or interweave them to advance Indigenous women's logros. Rather than rigid organizing structures, the flexibility of meshworks, interweaving scales vertically and horizontally, is that it encourages creativity and diversity in organizing and is suited to different actors with access to different resources, strategies, and tools.

4. Transborder Geographies of Difference

I sit perched with my laptop on the edge of my chair in the front row of a large meeting hall in Oaxaca City at the Binational General Assembly of the Frente Indígena de Organizaciones Binacionales (Indigenous Front of Binational Organizations, FIOB) in October 2011, awaiting the election results. As the assembly waits for the announcement, a visceral feeling of anticipation is in the air. The general assembly only meets every three years, bringing together hundreds of delegates and invited observers from Oaxaca, Baja California, Mexico City, and California to deliberate key organizational issues and to elect a new binational leadership council.[1] The most vocal female leaders of the organization had set the goal of having a woman elected as the general coordinator of the organization by these 2011 elections—twenty years after its founding in 1991. That does not happen this year, but something else quite remarkable does. When the election results are announced and the newly elected members walk to the stage, the entire slate of leaders from California are women, and three new women leaders have been elected to the binational council. Such a result would have seemed improbable, if not impossible, earlier in the organization's history, when it was usually only the binational council's women's affairs coordinator position that was occupied by a woman.[2]

Each new member of the organization's leadership stands in a line on the stage, waiting to step forward and formally assume her new cargo (elected position). The audience feels the weight of this moment in the hushed seconds before each activist speaks, as the meaning of the large number of women standing before us begins to sink in.[3] As my eyes scan the stage and across the room full of Indigenous rights activists, I blink away tears and see that many others around me also have tears in their eyes. These results were a victory for the men and women across Oaxaca, Baja California, California, and beyond who had been working to diversify FIOB's binational leadership to include more women, youth, and other Indigenous groups. One of the newly elected women steps up to the microphone and states in Zapotec: "I accept this cargo on behalf of my community, on behalf of you all, members of the organization, for Indigenous women who struggle to be heard and for the ancestors (abuelos)." Cheers explode, fueled by the shared knowledge that it has taken years of struggle to bring this moment to fruition. Adding to the significance of this moment, each newly elected woman accepts her new cargo by speaking in her ancestral language. The women accepting their new leadership roles in Zapotec and Mixtec not only highlights women's pivotal role in connecting ancestors and younger generations but also embodies the hope within the concept that when a woman steps forward, the whole community advances.[4]

Organized youth in FIOB showed their increased participation and leadership at the 2011 Binational Assembly when the general membership voted to modify the estatutos (statutes) governing the organization and the binational council based on suggestions—mostly from FIOB members in California—to recognize youths' involvement and their unique contributions. These developments were further evidence of the struggle for inclusiveness and diversity of the organization; as a result, it developed a new position, binational youth coordinator, and gave youth a vote and a voice in the organization's binational leadership council (see Oaxacalifornian Reporting Team 2013). Zapotec youth member Sarait Martinez, a cofounder of both Autónomos, an Indigenous migrant youth organization, and Oaxaqueño Youth Encuentro, became FIOB's first youth coordinator at that binational assembly. These developments reflected the emergence of new contours in the geography of difference, as age and generation emerged as markers of unity and difference within the Indigenous diasporas of what is now known as Latin America, specifically the Zapotec and Mixtec diasporas in California. This shift marked not when second-generation (or US-born and -raised) organizers and members joined FIOB's ranks in California, complementing the work of the first (migrant) and 1.5 (Oaxaca-born but US-raised) generations, but rather, when they advocated for their own forms of representation within the organization. These youth members not only recognize their Oaxacan Indigenous heritage within the context of the United States; they also work to keep alive and vibrant transborder ties to their own pueblos (peoples/towns) and a growing transborder civil society—all while asking organizations like FIOB to be more responsive to the needs and desires of youth members and to the different realities of the second generation.

In this chapter I illustrate how transborder Indigenous activists who engage in coordinated cross-border campaigns or programs, such as increasing women's participation and leadership, must translate these goals within geographies of difference, or specific arrangements of power and differential local realities, in order to be effective. Essentially, I examine how activists articulate demands, identities, and campaigns (trans)locally while creating resonance binationally within transborder Indigenous organizing. Although Indigenous women organizers face gender discrimination, it is the specific local expressions and configurations of that discrimination—and how it intersects with, and is often compounded by, other forms of oppression—that impact Indigenous women's activism in each region FIOB organizes. Indigenous women organizers in Oaxaca and their counterparts in California share organizing challenges related to the ways in which older forms of patriarchal exclusion— for example, the policing of women's participation in the public sphere (in terms of mobility, sexuality, and propriety)—collide with new realities as an increasing number of women and girls migrate from or organize within their own pueblos. Oaxaca has sixteen different Indigenous pueblos and a long history of Indigenous migration (Andrews 2018; Besserer 2002, 2004; Clarck-Alfaro 2003; Cruz-Manjarrez 2013; Fox and Rivera-Salgado 2004a; Gutiérrez Nájera 2010; Holmes 2013; Kearney 1995, 1998; Maier 2000, 2006a, 2006b; Rivera-Salgado 1999, 2006, 2014a, 2014b, 2016; Stephen 2007, 2009, 2012, 2014a, 2014b; Velasco 2002, 2005; Velasco and París Pombo 2014). Zapotecs, one of the largest groups to originate from the Northern Sierra or Central Valleys of Oaxaca, began migrating as braceros in the 1940s but only began settling in Los Angeles in the 1980s. Mixtecs also migrated internally within Mexico, worked as braceros, and began crossing the border to work in agriculture in California and Oregon (Velasco 2005). Oaxaca is one of the poorest states in Mexico and Indigenous people comprise 48 percent of its population, accounting for 53 percent of all Indigenous people in Mexico, according to the Mexican Comisión Nacional para el Desarollo de los Pueblos Indígenas (2008, 13).

"Geographies of difference" is an analytic that names how the political landscape of each region and scale, not to mention each country, in which Indigenous women organize is unique, with distinct colonialities and dynamic configurations of social, political, and economic power that differently animate axes of intersectional difference, such as race, gender, sexuality, or indigeneity. In this chapter I extend the conceptual framework of geographies of difference through an examination of the uneven and differential terrains of power that transborder activists navigate. I show how Indigenous migrant and nonmigrant women confront power differentials in various locales in Oaxaca and California, and thus must adopt their organizing strategies in accordance to those local realities while still crafting strategies that resonate binationally along their transborder membership. Geographies of difference help us to attend to the complexity and variety of power arrangements surrounding gender, indigeneity, migration, and globalization that shape these shared yet distinct struggles in differential ways. As a framework, geographies of difference are attuned to the way colonialism is organized differently across settler borders. The concept offers a way to see how organizers attempt to account for the ways the coloniality of power organizes patriarchal, racial, and capitalist logics differently in each context they work in. For example, the colonial logic of erasure enacted through different systems of racial management of classification differs between the United States and Mexico. Thus the very meaning of *indigeneity* shifts across national and regional settings, as well as colonial arrangements of power, requiring Indigenous people to develop distinct strategies related to how they are racialized in their pueblos, as internal migrants in Mexico, and as transborder migrants in the United States. The specific sociopolitical terrain that Indigenous women activists must navigate as migrant, Indigenous, poor women varies even within one country—from urban to rural settings; in differences in the ways national policies criminalize migrants, producing (il)legality (Ábrego 2013); and in the way illegality intersects with indigeneity, affecting language access, labor recruitment, education, health care, and life chances (Herrera 2016). Recognizing these differences, I explore here the uneven transnational terrains of power that structure Indigenous transborder organizing and the radically uneven geographies of difference that organizers must learn to navigate across multiple colonialities.

In my observations while accompanying FIOB for the past seventeen years, I've noted that these differences prove particularly true for gender arrangements, the way they intersect with race and indigeneity, and how they are organized differently in various parts of the migrant stream and are rearranged by migration. Although Indigenous peoples face ongoing colonialism, racism, and economic oppression in Mexico, which is compounded when they arrive to the United States, the ways these forms of oppression intersect with gender and are articulated through other processes of power, such as draconian immigration policies, class hierarchy, and labor segmentation, differ across national, regional, and translocal scales. These local complexities and entrapments of power shape how women and men experience different forms of discrimination, and they compel activists to innovate strategies to transform these inequalities. I explore how Indigenous women organizers navigate geographies of difference within the specific transborder Indigenous community that links Oaxaca and California in four ways: (1) the multiple scales of leadership and of economy that Indigenous women elaborate by organizing for economic livelihood; (2) the multiple generational strategies they develop to offset differential access to power and resources across geographies of difference; (3) gendered geographies and the way they are rearranged during migration; and (4) how political organizing around mobility and migration produce new forms of Indigenous consciousness.

Collaborative Methods and Other Knowledges

This chapter and the next are based on a collaborative research relationship that I have forged with FIOB activists over many years and draw on critical ethnography, participant observation, and more than twenty oral histories. I began my collaboration with FIOB in 2005 and served as a binational advisor to the organization for six years. Under the auspices of the Otros Saberes Initiative of the Latin American Studies Association, which funds Indigenous and Afro-descendant organizations and communities to partner with academics to design and carry out collaborative research projects, in 2006 FIOB leaders designed a study titled "Developing Binational Indigenous Leadership: Gender, Generation and Ethnic Diversity within the FIOB" and invited me to participate in the research. Our research team included Rufino Domínguez-Santos, the general coordinator of FIOB at the time; Centolia Maldonado, the then coordinator of the Juxtlahuaca region of Oaxaca; Odilia Romero Hernández, the Binational Coordinator of Women's Affairs at the time; Laura Velasco, a scholar of Indigenous migration from the Colegio de Frontera Norte; and myself. Throughout the next year and a half, we designed and implemented a study that included three statewide workshops and a binational encuentro addressing gender, generation, and ethnic diversity.

We worked with sixty-three activists who participated in the workshops in Tijuana, Baja California; Los Angeles, California; and Huajuapan de León, Oaxaca (figure 4.1). Among the participants, 59.5 percent were men and 40.5 percent were women, and their average age was 32 years old. A total of 56.8 percent of participants spoke an Indigenous language; the seven languages spoken by participants included Mixtec, Zapotec, Triqui, P'urépecha, Mixe, Spanish, and English (Romero Hernández et al. 2013). Interestingly, the Los Angeles workshop had the most linguistic diversity among Indigenous language speakers. While many people spoke some Spanish, English fluency was most prominent among migrant youth of the 1.5 and second generations. Our team presented all the results from the workshops and interviews to the FIOB's elected binational leadership in Mexico City in June 2007. There the leadership drafted a preliminary plan of action to address the findings and include more women, youth, and other Indigenous peoples. We presented our findings and this proposed plan to the general assembly of FIOB members in Juxtlahuaca, Oaxaca, in 2009. This chapter tells the story of the workshops and organizing campaign

Figure 4.1. The FIOB Otros Saberes workshop in Los Angeles, California, 2007. Photo by the author.

to diversify FIOB's leadership as a frame in which to understand what various actors at various times have called transnational, transborder, or binational organizing. In addition to building on the collaborative research conducted under the auspices of the Otros Saberes Initiative, this chapter and the next draw on other collaborative research projects and twenty oral histories I collected while accompanying women in FIOB as they organized leadership programs and sought to be heard at all levels of the organization. Since beginning my work with FIOB, I have spent the past seventeen years attending dozens of events and supporting the political organizing of members in Oaxaca City, Zanatapec, Juxtlahuaca, and, within California, in Fresno, Los Angeles, and Oceanside.

On a trip to the Mixteca region of Oaxaca in 2007, I traveled to Santiago Juxtlahuaca with Laura Velasco for the Otros Saberes project. As part of our work, Laura went to visit Triqui women artisans who organized to sell their work in the city center and the market. I traveled to the surrounding Mixtec pueblos, visiting FIOB's community credit unions and gastronomy projects with the organization's then statewide director, Centolia Maldonado, who served as a coresearcher and guide during that phase of the project. We visited Isabel Reyes, a mother who talked to me while making tortillas to sell at the market (figure 4.2). She moved quickly between the masa press on a small wooden table and the grill, with her baby in a rebozo on her back, and I asked whether I was bothering her while she worked. She laughed and said no, that talking while working was the best time to talk because it made the work go faster. She invited me to pull up the small child's chair in her outdoor kitchen, and there I sat, the recorder balanced on a brick to capture her words as she told me of how she was doing better now that she was organized with other women to save money and invest in her small tortillera business. Her words were punctuated with the quick rhythm of masa being pounded between fast hands and intermixed with the loud song of a turkey who stalked around the yard.

After piling back into the taxi with the yellow and green FIOB logo on the door, one of the compañeros from the FIOB taxi collective drove us to our next stop in Santa Maria to visit Doña Matilde, who organizes a gastronomy project with her sister (figure 4.3). At our first meeting, I was struck by her

Figure 4.2. Isabel Reyes, FIOB member, Oaxaca, 2007. Photo by the author.

fierce grassroots analysis of women's empowerment, which rapidly spilled out of her mouth before I could turn on the recorder. Centolia asked Doña Matilde what she has gained by participating in the organization. She quickly replied: "Value, giving input, learning about women's rights. [We are told] 'You are a woman. You don't study. You are a woman. You aren't worth anything. You are a woman, so you will marry. Nothing more. Period. Even if there is abuse.' Now, for me it is different. Things changed when I learned about this organization. I've been participating since 1999. Now [I know] we have the same value and the same worth [as men]. I think that we are worth the same because we women are hard workers" (Matlide Margarita Zurita Vásquez, interview with Maylei Blackwell, March 29, 2007). She went on to tell me about her small business making mole and how it helps her and her sister as they care for their elderly father. During subsequent visits, Doña Matilde has prepared tea from herbs growing in the yard to settle my stomach; upon each meeting I have found her to have an indomitable spirit and a generous smile. She introduced me to her elderly father. As his cloudy eyes looked out to the horizon beyond the fields of the sierra, he told me that nowadays people are getting sick because they have lost their connection to the land and stopped growing and preparing their own

Figure 4.3. Doña Matilde and her gastronomical products, Juxtlahuaca, Oaxaca, 2007. Photo by the author.

food. These collective activities of saving and lending through a small-scale community credit union or growing, grinding, and preparing food may seem like quotidian activities that have simply been collectivized, but they have become so economically and politically important during the past few years that they became part of a FIOB campaign for the "Derecho de No Migrar," or the right to remain (Bacon 2013; Rivera-Salgado 2014b).

On the other side of the border, women organizers within the FIOB face a different set of challenges. In California, where upward of an estimated 500,000 Indigenous Mexicans reside and 30 percent of all farmworkers are Indigenous migrants from Oaxaca, the most effective organizers are trilingual (Cengel 2013).[5] One such organizer fluent in Mixtec, Spanish, and English is Irma Luna, from San Miguel Cuevas, who began organizing in the 1990s after joining the FIOB in Fresno in 1996. Born in an agricultural work camp in Sinaloa in 1972, Irma Luna served at the FIOB's second Binational Coordinator for Women between 1999 and 2002 and worked for fifteen years for California Rural Legal Assistance (CRLA) where she was a fearless advocate for all farm workers on issues of unpaid wages, minimum wage violations, sexual harassment, discrimination, health and safety violations, housing rights, pesticides, and language access rights. Reflecting on the history of women's participation in FIOB on the occasion of the organization's twentieth anniversary, Irma Luna explained: "Many barriers that migrant Indigenous women face, especially those who work in agriculture, include the lack of transportation as many of them do not drive and more than that, they work from sun up to sun down. The families that do not have a license are limited in their participation in meetings and activities. Those who are mothers return from their jobs and arrive home to feed the kids, do household chores, and prepare food for the next day" (quoted in Rodriguez 2011, 16–17).[6] Although migrant Indigenous women in rural areas of California may face issues similar to those their counterparts face in rural Oaxaca in terms of transportation and access to political spaces, these differences are refracted through the violence of illegality that maintains migrant communities in the United States as the most vulnerable and exploitable. In many states in the United States, for many years undocumented immigrants could not obtain a driver's license because of an anti-immigrant backlash in the 1990s that resulted in restrictive legislation, voter propositions, and eventually mass mobilization of migrants in 2006.[7] Until California changed the law in 2015, many workers were forced to drive without a license to and from work or to pick up their families, increasing the daily fear that undocumented migrants face.

Whereas women in Oaxaca are organizing around their economic livelihood for the right to not migrate, Oaxacan Indigenous women in California face multiple exclusions based on layers of racism that include, on the one hand, extreme anti-immigrant rhetoric and political discourse against Latinos, and, on the other hand, anti-Indigenous prejudice from Mexicans and other Latinos in the United States. This compounded experience of oppression causes Indigenous migrants to pay more to migrate and to make less in the fields than their mestizo counterparts, and Indigenous migrant children often are bullied by other Latino kids. Despite these geographies of difference, migrant Indigenous women organizers have forged new forms of participation, leadership, and grassroots organizing on both sides of the US-Mexico border.

Traversing Uneven Terrains of Power in Transborder Organizing

Colonialism is organized differently across settler borders. Specifically, the ways the logics of colonialism are organized and articulated differently through intersecting forms of racial power, gender hierarchies and dichotomies, as well as class structures and labor segmentation in the United States and Mexico. In each context in which Indigenous women organize, gender is configured differently by race, indigeneity, class, sexuality, and the way migrants are criminalized. In other words, Indigenous women's experiences of racial and gender discrimination are shaped by local conditions and power configurations, and how those forms of discrimination intersect with, and often are compounded by, other forms of oppression in each region. Further, these local complexities and entrapments of power shape how both women and men experience these forms of discrimination, and the strategies activists may innovate to transform these inequalities.

In addition, colonial logics of race, class, and gender have been reinforced and reorganized by the globalization of labor, capital, and culture. Given the intensified flows of people, capital, and cultures unleashed by regional economic integration under the North American Free Trade Agreement, scholars have argued that US and Mexican civil society relationships are paradigmatic in the study of transnational organizing (Fox 2002).[8] Although Fox theorized that the density of transnational social movements relies on the idea that Indigenous activists as the "same social subject" (2002, 351), Teresa Carrillo's (1998) research on cross-border labor organizing efforts among Mexicana and Chicana garment workers adds a complex layer to this idea. Carrillo found that whereas Mexicana workers articulated their political demands in terms of survival and a class-based political consciousness, Chicana garment workers in the United States refracted their understanding of class oppression and labor segmentation through race. Indeed, Stephen (2011, 2012) observed that racial/

ethnic hierarchies shift from Mexico to regions in the United States. Despite a shared subjectivity, the distinct organization of power in each national context led to divergent forms of consciousness, material concerns, and frames of analysis—ultimately preventing a sustained transnational alliance between the two groups. This echoes my own earlier work in which I found that effective transnational social movements must cross not only the borders of nation-states but also the internal borders of race, class, gender, indigeneity, and citizenship created by differential relationships of power (Blackwell 2000, 2014, 2015).

Geographies of difference is a framework that allows us to see how multiple colonialities—that is, colonial power configured differently in each regional and national context—produce different but at times overlapping arrangements of power that activists not only negotiate but also seek to create transborder connections across. Even with a shared "social subjectivity" and a consciousness of Indigenous rights, forms of difference based on language, skin color, citizenship status, class, sexual orientation, and gender are part of the terrain of difference that transborder activists must navigate (trans)locally and (trans)nationally. Doing so requires no small amount of strategy in order to translate shared organizational goals for different geopolitical realities and to articulate forms of subjectivity that will make sense locally but still resonate binationally.[9]

FIOB organizes along the migrant stream from multiple regions of Oaxaca, Mexico City, and Baja California to several cities in California. It has built a base in Los Angeles to serve the numerous Oaxacans residing in the city and important allies from Guatemala within the Mayan diaspora. Migrant transit across Guatemala, Mexico, and the United States creates what Jonas and Rodriguez (2015) call a transregion. They argue that when migrants traverse expanses of territory, they shift the socio-spatial relationships of those spaces and are, in turn, transformed by them, thereby creating transregions. More specifically, they note that for "Maya and other Indigenous populations that currently live in and migrate from the southern reaches of the expanse, the socio-spatial reproduction has a history of more than two thousand years" (6). While they recognize the historic and precolonial nature of Indigenous migration and trade networks, Jonas and Rodriguez do not fully consider how the spaces that are traversed are already Indigenous lands and cosmovisions that orient us toward pluriverses (Byrd 2011; de la Cadena and Blaser 2018, Escobar 2020), and how Indigenous migrants create other transborder geographies of indigeneity on the homelands of other Indigenous peoples (Blackwell 2017a), which I explore further in chapter 5. For the purposes of this chapter, Indigenous transborder migration, organizing, civil society, and the life worlds that are reproduced across settler borders create a transregional scale that transverses not only the differential organization of power through intersecting colonial logics but other Indigenous territories and communities as well.

I build on the concept of transregion by retrofitting it in two ways. First, I acknowledge the Indigenous territories and homelands that Indigenous migrants work, settle, and build on in the transregion created by Indigenous diasporas. Second, I understand transregions not as unified spatial projects but as uneven terrains that encompass vastly different configurations and structures of power that Indigenous migrants must navigate. These differences in power and subject-making challenge transborder organizing. In chapter 3 I considered how meshworks link not only vertical scales but also horizontal ones. Indigenous migration not only creates a transregion, organizing within this region creates a transborder scale and yet even within that scale, differential power terrains create what I have been calling geographies of difference. Hence, Indigenous transborder organizers weave together multiple horizontal locales into a transborder scale with the intensity of their organizing as they create and participate in translocal ways of belonging to their pueblos through their rituals, foodways, music, collective labor, and civil society, while still negotiating the ways in which power is configured differently across those locales. In chapter 1, I discussed Aihwa Ong's (1996) formulation that even the labor of forging dissident subjectivities based on alternative forms of belonging or cultural citizenships does not stand outside of the way the state power creates subjects—what she calls subjectification. Her argument is an important reminder to be attentive to how the organizing to create Indigenous belonging across a transborder scale still occurs across two distinct state-projects of Indigenous elimination, not to mention the geographies of difference within those nations that form an Indigenous diasporic transregion.

Historically, part of the strength of FIOB derives precisely from its members' recognition of this diversity, and their commitment to cultivating leadership across different genders, ages, and Indigenous groups (Andrews 2018; Romero Hernández et al. 2013) in an attempt to negotiate geographies of difference. Cross-border movements are often motivated by a vibrant transnational imaginary that is broad enough to account for how actors come together across vastly different terrains of power—from Zapatismo to third world solidarity, feminism, Indigenous solidarity, or a shared sense of deterritorialized place and belonging (how those who are Oaxaqueño, serrano, or from the same pueblo construct a shared identity, for example) (Blackwell 2015).[10] The FIOB itself has deep roots. One source of these roots is grounded in the organizational processes among Indigenous migrants within Mexico during the 1980s, which, according to Laura Velasco Ortiz, stemmed from Mexico City, to Sonora, Sinaloa, the San Quintin

Valley, and Tijuana in Baja California, to California. "During those formative years, the 'hometown associations' were formed, including the Comité Cívico Popular Tlacotepense (CCPT), the Organización de Pueblo Explotado y Oprimido (OPEO), representing the village of San Miguel Cuevas, and the Asociación Cívica Benito Juárez (ACBJ)" (Velasco Ortiz 2005, 2). Other roots emerged from a shared hemispheric Indigenous activism born out of resistance to the quincentenary celebration of Columbus's arrival in the Americas. This Indigenous migrant movement, which has grown for over three decades, has been nourished by its diversity in terms of both membership and leadership. Furthermore, FIOB is a migrant rights organization that works from an Indigenous rights framework, but its parameters of Indigenous subjectivity are not given, fixed, or defined a priori.

Even the many changes to FIOB's name over the years reflect shifting understandings of broadening parameters of political subjectivity. Originally founded in 1991 in Los Angeles as the Mixtec-Zapotec Binational Front, representing two of the sixteen Indigenous pueblos in Oaxaca, the organization changed its name to the Binational Oaxacan Indigenous Front in 1994 in order to broaden its pan-Indigenous inclusion of Triquis and other Indigenous migrants from its home state.[11] Velasco Ortiz argues that the adoption of the "Oaxacan Indigenous" category not only allowed Triquis and Mixes to join Mixtec and Zapotec members, but that this shift was influenced by the January 1, 1994, Zapatista rebellion and the resurgence of Indigenous resistance movements throughout Latin America. She further points out that, "after years of association as migrants of Mixtec or Zapotec origin, or in separate groups representing other indigenous peoples, they now achieved unity as Oaxacan indigenous people straddling two nation-states" (Velasco Ortiz 2005, 2). FIOB changed its name again in 2005 to the Binational Front of Indigenous Organizations because of the increasingly diverse Indigenous diasporas—from the Mexican states of Oaxaca, Guerrero, Michoacán, and Hidalgo, as well as Maya migrants from Guatemala who reside in what is now the United States—that were participating in the organization's political movement.

Scales of Economy, Scales of Leadership

Oaxaca is known for the beauty of its landscapes, but despite its environmental and cultural richness, it is one of the poorest states in Mexico: 66.7 percent of women live in poverty, which is the second-highest such rate among the states of Mexico (Chiapas has the highest rate, at 76.8 percent). In addition, Mexico infamously has three tiers of poverty, so in addition to the 66.7 percent of women who live in poverty in Oaxaca, 44.1 percent live in moderate poverty, while 22.7 percent live in extreme poverty (INEGI 2019). Oaxaca is home to sixteen

Indigenous groups, each with their own language and culture, making it the most diverse state, with the most Indigenous language speakers; they are, however, structurally disadvantaged as a result of colonial racial relations of power. In addition to these class and racial disadvantages, Indigenous women face what activists call "triple oppression," which includes gender discrimination and structural inequality based on sexism. In 2015 Oaxaca had the third highest rate of illiteracy in Mexico, at 13.3 percent; Mexico's national average is 5.5 percent (Flores 2018). This rate is down from 21.5 percent in 2010 (Coordinación Genderal de Comunicación Social, n.d.). In addition, institutional gender inequalities have resulted in Oaxaca having high rates of infant and maternal mortality and domestic violence: 65 percent among women and 35 percent among men (Magaña 2010, 75). For example, in 2000, 48.6 percent of all married women reported having faced some form of emotional or physical abuse (INEGI 2019).

Yet, Indigenous women activists have navigated the lack of economic and educational opportunity and social capital (lack of access to education, lack of bilingual language skills, feeling uncomfortable speaking in public) by forging powerful multigenerational partnerships that invite willing youth into the ranks of the community's organizational life and into the ranks of FIOB (a process that is echoed, but in reverse, on the other side of the border, as I discuss later in this chapter). FIOB has spearheaded a number of collaborative projects with the goal of generating funds and increasing self-sufficiency: taxi collectives, a cement collective, agricultural projects, casas de ahorro (community credit unions), artisan collectives, and several gastronomical projects that feature women's food products such as mole, chile, or beans. Activists organize these community projects to raise money to supplement income from remittances, to earn funds for those who have no family members who have migrated, or simply to empower women with the choice to not migrate, as a recent FIOB campaign states. As much as FIOB was part of an emerging movement of Indigenous rights in the early 1990s, it was also part of a critical conversation about Indigenous-led economic development. Its members enacted their goal of Indigenous-led development via a nonprofit they established in 1993, the Binational Center for the Development of Indigenous Communities, which had offices in Fresno, Greenfield, and Los Angeles while I conducted this research.[12] The organization and effective spread of these projects across multiple communities and the coordination between them, not to mention the empowerment that people gain through the process of organizing, have led to a new generation of grassroots leaders.

In the pueblos of Vista Hermosa and Agua Fría, I visited several mother-daughter teams who talked with me about their work in the casas de ahorro. They pulled out notebooks in which the school-age daughters diligently recorded numbers to track the accounting while their mothers worked as community networkers and organizers. The interviews were often halting and slow because the moms did not necessarily feel comfortable talking with me, a non-Mixtec speaker and outsider. They would smile timidly and laugh nervously, and then prod their daughters to answer me with their better command of Spanish. After working with these women and girls later in a FIOB workshop in Huajuapan de León, I began to understand how mothers left behind by their migrating partners formed teams with their daughters, and how daughters' lives are changing as they are now staying in school longer—all the way into high school. Historically, many rural and poor students drop out before high school in order to help their families survive economically, either by working in the fields or joining in paid labor. Indigenous communities have even less access to educational opportunities because schools are far from their communities and because of structural racism, as Felicitas's story illustrated in chapter 1. In addition to economic marginalization and racial discrimination, girls are often told that their schooling is not important because they will "only" become mothers and thus will not need further education, as Monserrat's story illustrates later in this chapter. To organize for their survival, these mother-daughter teams build on their respective members' distinct skill sets and put them to work for community organizing. In her book *Undocumented Politics: Place, Gender, and the Pathways of Mexican Migrants* (2018), Abigail Andrews documents the women who began to participate in FIOB's development projects in the Mixteca region of Oaxaca, many whose husbands and family members are working and organizing with FIOB on the other side of the border. Andrews describes how, when the women in Oaxaca first began to participate, they often felt it was a burden and were often stigmatized and shamed as loose women for being out in the community organizing. Eventually, "despite the burdens of community service, many women who participated in politics felt a stronger capacity as women ... and that they would no longer tolerate abuse by politicians, employers or men" (190). She found that "while women in most Oaxacan villages still lacked recourse to report domestic violence, with the help of the FIOB, those in Retorno [the fictionalized name of the town of Andrew's study] regularly went to the district court to denounce abuse" (191). Despite setbacks and political battles, some of the women's empowerment strategies, along with community economic development, resulted in women beginning to vote in community assembly, run village committees, and attend meetings with the demand that they have a voice and vote like never before. "In short," Andrews argues, "migration drew women into politics not just through 'social remittances' from the United States but also through the pueblo's own mobilization" (195).

What became visible during our workshop in Huajuapan de León was that there are multiple scales of leadership (figures 4.4 and 4.5). Throughout the history of the FIOB in Oaxaca, women were not often in formal leadership positions, with the exception of the regional leadership of Centolia Maldonado, who not only actively cultivated women's participation within the pueblos over years and years of organizing but vocally expressed how male FIOB members in Oaxaca blocked her from assuming leadership in the organization's binational council (Centolia Maldonado, interview with Laura Velasco, March 30, 2007). Largely because of Maldonado's organizing work, women in FIOB Oaxaca held informal, grassroots leadership positions within their pueblos, while men tended to occupy the more formal political leadership roles. Laura Velasco Ortiz argues that "despite the notable visibility of women as activists in organizations on both sides of the border, this visibility diminishes considerably when one looks at the leadership" (2005, 161). Many outsiders would see this as a public/private gender dichotomy in terms of modes of production and civil duties, but this division of labor has never been completely static or fixed within Oaxacan Indigenous communities, according to ethnographic accounts (Stephen 1991). Challenging the way in which the cargo system was understood exclusively as public labor, and hence a male domain, Holly Mathews's ethnographic research in San Miguel—a mixed Zapotec and Mixtec village in the Central Valleys, where members refer to themselves as mestizos—found that "cargo service is undertaken not by individual men but by household units on the basis of wealth. Male and female household heads assume parallel roles and responsibilities for ritual, and the participation of each sex is crucial for successful service" (1985, 286). Mathews also points to other ethnographers who found that among diverse Indigenous communities such as the Mazahua (Iwanska 1966) and Zapotecs in the Isthmus of Tehuantepec (Chinas 1973), male and female household leaders held joint title to civic roles or ritual responsibilities by referring to themselves in the plural: "we are mayordomo." Mathews argues further "that many ethnographic descriptions of a domestic/public division in post contact societies may actually depict this more complex split in orientation between community and extracommunity institutions brought about by the penetration of state-level systems into formerly autonomous or semi-autonomous areas" (1985, 298). Initially, internal migration and the bracero program brought migrants into the cargo system for their acquired skills such as Spanish-language ability or experience negotiating with those outside community, shifting earlier criteria of wealth or prior experience. More recently, these roles have again been changing, albeit at an uneven pace, as women take up more and more civic and political cargos. For Indigenous migrant women,

Figure 4.4. FIOB Otros Saberes workshop in Huajuapan de León, Oaxaca, 2007. Photo by the author.

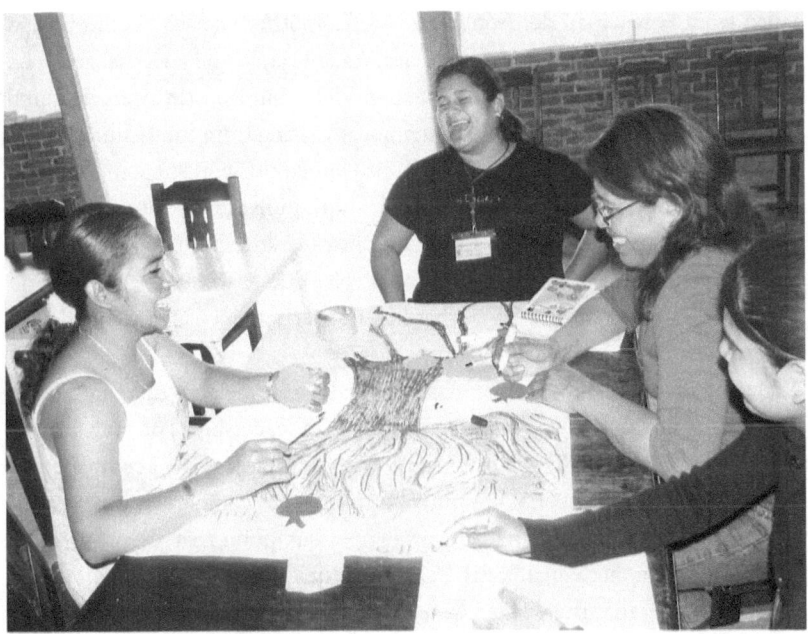

Figure 4.5. FIOB Otros Saberes workshop participants Rosie Mendez Moreno, Ana Ruth Mendez, and Maura Díaz, Huajuapan de León, 2007. Photo by the author.

Velasco Ortiz found the notion of public/private among Indigenous women street vendors and among FIOB members was disrupted as issues of domestic violence surfaced and were engaged within the organization. Critically, she reflects on the relationship of indigeneity and gender by saying, "The criticism and revision of ethnic identity taking place within the indigenous migration organizations is affecting gender relations; in this process, women's voices have played an important role" (Velasco Ortiz 2005, 181).

The dynamic nature of these gendered configurations of labor are often overlooked in writings about comunalidad (communality) (Aguilar Gil 2019; Worthen 2015). Yet migration is rearranging the relationship of women to formal cargos and extending informal community leadership positions (Andrews 2018; Velasco Ortiz 2005). Zapotec scholar Brenda Nicolás (2020) takes up this form of community building, which relies on women's labor (often made invisible) and their role in building transborder Indigenous communities, and theorizes transborder comunalidad. In the workshop in Huajuapan de León, we witnessed grassroots women activists, along with some male counterparts, leading productive projects and creating economic survival opportunities for themselves and their communities. They networked with other community members, organized participants, called for and facilitated meetings, and administered their projects or savings collectives. The collective wealth of experience was evident among the twenty-one participants in the workshop who hailed from Huajuapan de León itself and from other Oaxacan communities such as Santa Rosa de Juárez, Juxtlahuaca, Agua Fría, Vista Hermosa, San Juan Mixtepec, Santo Tomas Ocotepec, Rancho Viejo, San Agustín Atenango, and San Miguel Talcotepec. A few FIOB members visiting from the Isthmus of Tehuantepec and Tijuana, Baja California, also joined the workshop. In the room on the first day was FIOB's regional leadership—individuals who represented what could be seen as the more formal political leadership from the capital, Oaxaca City. Even with changes in gender roles due to women's activism and migration, the workshop revealed that historic patriarchal patterns of political leadership are linked to ideas of scale.

During the meeting, different gendered scales of leadership came into focus through the interaction between the two forms of leadership. The male leaders from Oaxaca City referred to the female grassroots leaders as their compañeritas (little comrades). Use of the diminutive form is quite complex; it can be used as an endearment, but it can also convey an assumption that the women are smaller, less than, not equal. Further, some of their comments had subtle overtones suggesting that the women were clients of the FIOB, passive recipients of project funds rather than organizers and generators of community knowledge and wealth. A few of the male leader's political discourse made it clear that women's participation was seen to be of a different order or scale—though, I must note that these paternalistic attitudes were less evident among the male community leaders who had traveled from the Mixteca and Sierra Norte regions.

In accompanying the Indigenous women's movement in Mexico for the past twenty years, I have witnessed how activists struggle for what they refer to as the right to "dar la palabra," to give their word. Beyond the right to literacy or education, organized women struggle for the right to voice their points of view during community deliberations and to have a space where what they have to say about their own lives and their communities matters. In the Indigenous women's movement in Mexico, the early slogan "No Mexico Sin Nosotras" (No Mexico Without Us) gendered the demand that Indigenous people dar su palabra (give their word), or help determine all economic, social, cultural, and political policies of the nation.[13] More recently, the slogan "Nada Sobre Nostras Sin Nosotras" (Nothing about Us without Us) has appeared and has been used in a range of demands such as for women's involvement in internal community deliberations, for consultation about external processes that affect their communities (e.g., development or extractive projects), and for their participation in crafting representations about themselves in scholarly and media sources.[14]

The power of the right to dar la palabra, to give one's voice, is documented in Lynn Stephen's 2013 study of the role of testimonio in the 2006 popular uprising in Oaxaca focusing on women's takeover of radio stations. Specifically, she examines how activists used the commandeered radio stations to broadcast testimonios of activists and communities in struggle, thereby enacting a more participatory form of democracy. Stephen identified a hybrid venacularization of human rights talk by women who had been marginalized on the basis of their gender and their racialized status as Indigenous and working class. Stephen argues, "If 'silence' was the norm for many of the women in grassroots movements they participated in and in their marginal political positions as poor, dark and working class, then 'speaking' as and with women was experienced as a 'women's right'" (2011, 177). In her book *We Are the Face of Oaxaca* (2013), Stephen found that "women who had previously been silenced and who characterized themselves as 'short, fat, and brown' and 'the face of Oaxaca' were now allowing new voices to be heard and new faces to be seen and permitting silenced modes of governance and democratic participation to move into the cultural and political mainstream" (146).

Within the formal political sphere in Mexico, and most especially within political gatherings, social movement actors take space when they stand to speak, and the power of their speech is often measured by its force of persuasion. This style of speaking as a político is a gendered practice. By referring to their female counterparts as compañeritas, male leaders assert the power of the políticos, while assigning their counterparts to the category of políticas lite.[15] Such speech practices are a way of signifying that cultural norms are governed by the unspoken rules of gendered power. When organized Indigenous women step outside of these prescribed roles to speak in public and take public space, they are often seen as gender deviant (masculinized) or sexualized (as promiscuous or loose women). Longtime FIOB activist Rosa Mendez Moreno, for example, told me in 2007 how difficult it was for women when she first began participating in FIOB (see figure 4.5): "And, well, really in the community they talk when you walk alone [gossiping] that you are seeing someone, that you are looking for a man—that's what they say.... It was a very difficult situation and at the same time, beautiful because our organizing showed us how to move forward as women and more than anything, to awaken that dynamism between women. To not be submissive in front of men" (Rosa Nava Méndez Moreno, interview with Maylei Blackwell, March 30, 2007). This culture shift work presents a seeming contradiction because when Indigenous women advocate for themselves, their communities, and Indigenous cultures, they travel, work in public spaces, and speak out in ways that can be seen to challenge gendered community norms. As has long been documented, women activists are often stigmatized, silenced, and controlled through gossip about their sexuality and morality.

These complex social relations reflecting the gendered geography that activists navigate also intersect with other social geographies that mark class distinction, such as who is from the city and who is from the more rural highlands. The Oaxaca City leaders did not return after the first day of the workshop. I observed how, with them absent, the space opened up for women to speak up and participate more actively, even as they participated with other male members from their own and other regions. The issue, therefore, concerns not only gender per se but how political power is wielded and how power relationships are mapped onto other social geographies such as rural versus urban divides. Women beginning to speak for themselves with their own voices also echoes an important political tradition within FIOB. Many of the organization's leaders have resisted clientelism (even under threats of violence), whereby one political figure stands in and becomes the voice for all those he claims to represent. As Stephen notes, by organizing and creating the space for others to speak and be heard—and more specifically, in her study, by taking over radio stations—Indigenous women are "moving far beyond their personal stories to share their analysis and put forward their demands—without interlocutors" (2013, 146).

The grassroots gendered leadership that women in FIOB are developing is important because it embraces change from the bottom up. These new practices illustrate how broader movement or organizational goals such as women's leadership development are emerging both as initiatives of the grassroots realities of Oaxaca and through transborder efforts of the binational coordinating council, FIOB's governing structure. Even with this push from above and below, organizing new forms of leadership for women and youth requires negotiating local geographies of difference to account for the complexities of shifting relationships of gendered power.

The Otros Saberes research project culminated in a binational meeting of the seventeen members of the FIOB leadership in June 2007 in Mexico City. The purpose of the meeting was to discuss the results of the research and to create a plan of action to address the findings and include more women, youth, and other Indigenous peoples.[16] These suggestions were then taken to FIOB's 2009 binational assembly in Juxtlahuaca, Oaxaca, where we sat in a circle within the lime green interior of the Juxtlahuaca municipal auditorium and shared with the delegates results from all three workshops and the binational meeting (figure 4.6); the delegates had gathered there to elect a new binational leadership. In the ensuing discussion, we developed the idea of women's leadership development programs, or what Odilia Romero Hernández dubbed the Mujeres Indígenas

Figure 4.6. Maura Díaz and Odilia Romero Hernández lead the discussion of findings from the Otros Saberes study at the Binational General Assembly, Juxtlahuaca, Oaxaca, 2009. Photo by David Bacon.

Figure 4.7. Mujeres Indígenas in Leadership (Indigenous Women in Leadership, MIEL) logo. Image courtesy of FIOB.

en Liderazgo (Indigenous Women in Leadership) program, whose acronym in Spanish is MIEL (honey) (figure 4.7).

The FIOB women's leadership from Oaxaca, California, and Baja California met at that meeting to begin brainstorming what MIEL trainings might look like in each region and identify who had the capacity to work on implementing them, and how FIOB could fund this binational women's leadership development. To that end, we met with Kay Cid, a staff member based at the then newly established Mexico City Office of the Rosa Luxemburg Foundation, to determine whether our project fit into their funding mission. It was agreed that because the foundation funding had to go to Mexico that the Oaxaca office of the FIOB in Juxtlahuaca.

Even with the shared goal of building women's leadership with an intensive process of community assessment and planning, creating programs across multiple (trans)locales with a shared understanding of Indigenous women's gender equity and the traditions it draws from was initially challenging. For example, when leaders from Oaxaca applied for funds from the Rosa Luxemburg Foundation, they wrote in the application that they wished to be neither "feminist" nor "machista," thereby suggesting equivalence between the two as forms of prejudice rather than recognizing feminism as an ideology of gender equality and machismo as an ideology of patriarchal superiority. Despite powerful organizational and leadership skills that allowed capacity building among the women in Juxtlahuaca and surrounding communities, leaders increasingly spoke very openly about their frustration with gender discrimination within the organization and how men in Oaxaca had blocked them from joining the binational leadership structure. Even with these frustrations and critiques of male dominance in their organizing, their political stance was one that refused a position of dominance by deploying a distorted stereotype of what feminism stands for.

Although the Rosa Luxemburg Foundation did not provide funding for the program at that point, it did offer funding for a training on the meaning of feminism and gender equity from the point of view of Indigenous women. Odilia Romero and I designed this gender rights training, which we called "Construyendo equidad al interior del FIOB y creando un camino compartido" (Constructing equity within the FIOB and creating a shared path) that both male and female leaders and members of FIOB's base communities attended. We facilitated the training with Gaspar Rivera-Salgado in Mexico City, December 5–7, 2008. A few dozen members engaged in exercises, activities, and discussions that focused on Indigenous women's rights and the intersection of indigeneity, gender, decolonization, and feminism.[17] One of the most powerful outcomes of these binational workshops on gender and women's rights was how activists found their own traditions of women's empowerment—what some openly embraced as Indigenous feminism and others saw as standing strong on behalf of one's community. In one of our trainings, Odilia Romero showed how patriarchal violence is linked to colonial violence in her presentation illustrating pre-Columbian gender arrangements. Rather than romanticizing the precolonial past, she asked her comrades within FIOB to consider overcoming gender hierarchies and binaries imposed by colonialism and the Catholic Church as part of their decolonizing work. This work creating shared narratives, or what social movement scholars call frame resonance, which motivate collective political action among diversely situated actors within the same social subjectivity, was part of how the women and men of the FIOB navigated geographies of difference around transregional, transborder, and translocal scales.

Migrant Indigenous Women and Multigenerational Political Engagement

I turn now to the United States to show how the goal of developing women's leadership was localized in California. In Los Angeles, FIOB built its base to serve the estimated 250,000 Oaxacans residing in the city, most of whom are

Zapotec (Vankin 2017). It also made important alliances with the increasingly Mayan diaspora from Guatemala. FIOB LA's activities during this time included organizing the first May 1, 2006, immigrant rights marches (what became known as the "mega marches") and building immigrant labor rights coalitions such as the Multiethnic Immigrant Workers Organizing Network; mobilizing in solidarity with Indigenous communities during the teacher's strike that turned into the 2006 Oaxacan popular movement (creating events such as the APPOsada);[18] advocating for Indigenous migrants in the courts by providing interpretation and organizing for language access and justice; and protesting the police shooting of Maya (K'iche') day laborer Manuel Jaminez Xum on September 5, 2010, in the Westlake neighborhood of Los Angeles. After receiving reports that a drunk man was wielding a knife, which witnesses dispute, the LAPD shot and killed Jaminez Xum even through it was not clear if he could understand their commands. Jaminez Xum's death spurred community protests, after which FIOB began to conduct annual cultural sensitivity training for the LAPD and other city agencies to educate them on Indigenous languages and the fact that many migrants do not speak Spanish or English as monolingual Indigenous language speakers. Other FIOB LA activities included working with cultural and civic organizations to create an Oaxacan corridor in Los Angeles; organizing educational forums for Oaxacan Heritage Month; mobilizing Mexican citizens to vote; organizing forums to meet with Oaxacan gubernatorial candidates; reinitiating and publishing the binational magazine *El Tequio* (Mercado 2015); and running a small-scale microlending operation. Such transborder organizing and community-building provided the vibrant context in which FIOB organizers carried out the collaborative Otros Saberes initiative to study how to renew their binational leadership in terms of ethnic diversity, gender, and generation, and to design and implement programs that would do just that. After the findings were discussed in Mexico City and later presented to the General Assembly in 2009, several FIOB sectors and regional offices began to focus on building the capacity of a new generation of leaders. In Los Angeles, a series of MIEL workshops were proposed. Activists and advisors met to plan the workshops and apply for funding. One of the key strategies to emerge from the process was to focus on organizing women as leaders in particular, with the assumption that encouraging their participation would ensure that of their whole family would become active, one of the hallmarks of Indigenous women's activism in Mexico discussed in chapter 2.

In the organizers' funding proposal, they stated that MIEL was developed in California in order to "increase immigrant Indigenous women's community involvement and build capacity for them to become advocates for their rights and the rights of their children. Overall, MIEL aims to reduce institutional, cultural, linguistic, and economic barriers that affect migrant Indigenous women."[19] The organizers, facilitators, and I organized a series of free monthly workshops around themes such as gender rights, health, immigration, Indigenous language, culture and storytelling, decolonization, leadership and capacity-building, and violence prevention. Over the course of six months, participants learned about human rights frameworks and Indigenous rights and eventually designed their own community project. MIEL was funded by FIOB, the Liberty Hill Foundation, Seventh Generation Fund for Indian Development, and Canicería Yalalateca.[20]

On January 31, 2010, in the community room of Koreatown Immigrant Workers Alliance in Los Angeles, about a dozen women gathered for the first day of the MIEL workshops. Odilia explained that they called the trainings MIEL, or "honey" in Spanish, to symbolize the wealth that results when women work together to gather knowledge and resources to serve their communities. On that crisp Los Angeles winter day, I could see the mountains surrounding the Los Angeles basin as I joined the local FIOB leadership, workshop participants, and facilitators, all of us full of excitement and hope. Also present were a half dozen undergraduate students from the honors section of my Chicana/o and Central American Studies introductory course at UCLA, titled "Latina/o Los Angeles and Globalization." That section focused on community-based research, and the students attended the first three months of the MIEL workshops to serve as the documentation team, taking notes, doing background research, conducting and editing entrance interviews.[21] The coordination team for MIEL included Zonia Robles, Cristina Lopez, and Luis Sánchez-López, three Oaxacan youth leaders who represent a multigenerational mode of empowerment.[22] The children of migrants often serve as mediators and translators/interpreters, helping their parents and grandparents navigate the world in English. This cohort represents how 1.5- and second-generation Oaxacan youth have used their education, language, and social capital to empower others in their communities, including their mothers, aunts, and other relatives. These youth activists, many of whom were attending college, represent a generation that has gone back to their cultural and linguistic roots precisely in order to help the prior generation by empowering them to become community leaders and access resources. These are not youth who became active though their parents, like their counterparts did in Oaxaca. Instead, they represent a new generation of young people who went to college and gained tools to organize, and then returned to their communities to empower their moms and aunts.[23]

Indeed, several MIEL participants were mothers, aunts, and female relatives of Robles and Sánchez. In the interviews with students, the participants spoke about the power of seeing these young people standing up and speaking in front of the group. The women described being inspired by their speaking skills, their commitment, and the knowledge that they could impart. This pride in their children also served as an impetus for them to get more involved. In fact, after completing the MIEL training, Doña Mari, Luis Sánchez-López's mother, became a local coordinator of FIOB in Los Angeles.

Multigenerational organizing took place on both sides of the border, but it took on different forms in each context. In California, it was generally the youth who recruited their parents, whereas in Oaxaca, parents recruited their children. This demonstrates a defining feature of contemporary immigrant organizing in LA—it is led by women and includes the full-scale participation of children and youth (Milkman and Terriquez 2012). These forms of kinship and sociality inform Indigenous migrant women activist's modes of organizing. It is important to consider the political implications of the feminization of immigration and to think of the possibilities that could be opened if this untapped power base would begin to mobilize on a mass scale.

Maria Sánchez, or Doña Mari as she is known in the community, was born in Valle de Tlacolula, Oaxaca. When we sat down in the FIOB office in Koreatown, Los Angeles, to talk, she was forty-four years old (born in 1968) and married with two children: a son, Luis, who was twenty-six at the time, and a daughter, Monica, who was ten. Growing up as the seventh of the eight children, Doña Mari's memories of her hometown were filled with nature, as most of the townspeople worked in the fields growing food. She recalled that her grandparents, Alfonso and Natalia Melchor, grew food, sold animals, and made baskets for a living (her grandfather would make them and her grandmother would sell them at the town's market). Her parents made candles to sell, and her father also worked at a government office before he passed away when she was only eight years old. Doña Mari worked at a clinic and was fifteen when she met her husband, Miguel Sánchez, then twenty. The pair soon fell in love and married. She explained to me that at that time it was normal for young women to marry at fifteen; indeed, if they weren't married by twenty, they were considered spinsters. By age seventeen, Maria was pregnant with Luis, and many of her goals changed.[24]

When Luis was four months old, Miguel told Doña Mari that he was planning to go to Los Angeles and would return for her. She was not sure whether to believe him—many men in the town had left and not come back for their wives—so she gave him an ultimatum: he was to come back for her in five months or forget her and Luis altogether. Sure enough, Miguel sent for her and Luis right at the five-month deadline. Migrating itself was extremely difficult because in addition to traveling with Luis, who was then only nine months old, Doña Mari was traveling with her sister and her twelve-year-old nephew. Doña Mari recounted feeling scared because their group would be traveling with strangers, whom they had to trust completely. The journey often involved walking or running through mountainous terrain—no small feat with such a young baby. There were times when Luis had to be prevented from crying, lest he give the group away. Luis later shared with me that his mother used the trick of putting small pieces of Oaxacan chocolate in his mouth so he would not cry during the crossing. After growing up in the United States, he became one of the facilitators of the workshops and an undergraduate student I mentored at UCLA and after completing his doctoral research on Indigenous autonomy and state formation, he has joined the faculty of the University of California, Irvine. In 2012, Doña Mari reflected back and said that had she known how hard it would be, she likely would not have crossed the border. She described their harrowing journey this way: "Because, well, there were times others would help carry him to the next place where they would tell us to go. Then came the time when they had to separate us because . . . four people fit in the trunk of a car but five do not. Then comes the time when you just have to make the decision even when you do not want to, you have no other alternative. . . . It is something you cannot imagine when you think of leaving the pueblo or the country" (Maria Isabel Sánchez, interview with Maylei Blackwell, May 21, 2012).

From the border, they traveled by car to Los Angeles and then went to Hollywood, where they lived with an aunt.[25] Doña Mari learned about the FIOB and got involved through Luis around 2010. Before participating in MIEL, she was involved in the Oaxacan community through her attendance at the Catholic church, which many other Oaxaqueños also attended. She remembered that at the first MIEL workshops, they were told not to be scared and encouraged to speak. Doña Mari is not shy or afraid to speak up, but when topics came up that she was unfamiliar with, she would stay quiet until she learned more. It was through this process, she told me, that she learned to speak up for herself.

When I asked Doña Mari about MIEL, she admitted that she was initially unaware that the workshops' goal was to train leaders, or that she herself was one of those taking on a leadership position. One of the most powerful experiences of the training was that her husband, Miguel, also began attending the women's leadership workshops and, despite being the only man, participated throughout the entire program. She feels that it has helped their relationship because he is now much more understanding.[26] After the MIEL workshops, Doña Mari began to get involved in other events like the May Day marches because, as she put it, folks who are documented "should support others who are still undocumented because everyone has the same dream" (Sánchez, interview, May 21, 2012). She went on to become the Los Angeles local coordinator for FIOB, and her responsibilities included looking at the needs of the community and finding creative strategies to address them. She worked, for example, with the youth coordinator to put on a workshop to help parents and students navigate the higher education system. Doña Mari's favorite work was helping coordinate community relations for the microloan program. This program loaned money at a low interest rate to community members, without the prohibitive requirements of other lending institutions. She has seen people use the funds to start small businesses and pay for Deferred Action for Childhood Arrivants applications, among other things.

Other participants in California were recruited from hometown associations, Los Angeles community organizations, and Oaxacan community events. Monserrat Bernardino, for example, met Luis, then the youth coordinator of the Los Angeles office of FIOB, that same year at another community training. When she introduced herself to him during lunch, he invited her to the MIEL workshops. The primary goal of the workshops was to encourage women's participation, but for many, the most long-lasting impact was the way the workshops transformed how they saw themselves. Through in-depth oral histories with several MIEL LA participants, I learned that the pedagogies of liberation and empowerment taught in the workshops not only serve to build women's leadership in transborder Indigenous organizing; they also intersected deeply with many of the women's lifelong aspirations for education, despite being denied it as young girls in Mexico and then struggling to access it as working migrant mothers in the United States. Monserrat, or "Monse" as she is called by friends, was born on April 27, 1968, in Santa Cruz Papalutla, a town of about one thousand inhabitants near Tlacolula, in the Central Valleys of Oaxaca. Her family grew corn, garbanzos, squash, beans, and maguey for mescal, and they raised goats, donkeys, cows, pigs, and chickens (Monserrat Bernardino, interview with Maylei Blackwell, September 17, 2011). She is the seventh of eight siblings (she has four brothers and three sisters). She recalled her mom taking care of the house and the domestic animals, and selling eggs and homemade tortillas in Oaxaca City and in the local market in Papalutla.

Although she loved going to the market with her mom, Monse's dream was to study and become a nurse "dressed in white." After her mother's untimely death when Monse was eleven, she enrolled in school by herself. She did not tell her father because he felt school was useless for girls because they would just grow up to stay at home and have kids. When he found out she had enrolled, he said, "Go, but you do not have my support. You still have to clean the house, cook and take care of pigs and chickens." As we sat in a park in Los Angeles on a Saturday, after her second job helping tenants to learn about their housing rights, tears started to well in Monse's eyes as she told me this part of this story. As she continued, we both sat on the bench, weeping. "I got up at three or four each morning to grind corn to make tortillas, collect the leña [wood] to cook breakfast, clean the house and go to school, walking one hour each way because there was not money for transportation. When school was done at three in the afternoon, I would then travel back home to make tamales, cut wood for dinner, wash, clean the house, and do homework" (Bernardino, interview, September 17, 2011). She told me that, looking back, she recognizes that those three years were difficult, but "I showed my dad I could . . . that I could go to school without getting pregnant or running off with a man [as he had feared]. It was so hard without support. There was no playing but it helped me mature and become responsible" (Bernardino, interview, September 17, 2011). Across the over seventy oral histories with women that I conducted over a span of twenty years, some of the most painful memories were when the women recalled being girls who were denied educational opportunities; who had to run away from home to pursue them, like Hermalinda Turbicio; or who were separated from their families and experienced racist treatment in order to be able to attend school, as Felicitas Martinez Solano did. (Hermalinda's and Felicitas's stories are shared in chapter 1.)

After losing her mother at a young age, Monse's life underwent yet another upheaval when her father and three brothers migrated to Mexico City. Despite her own strength and determination, her fate—like that of so many others—would be determined in the migrant stream. Months after their departure, her fathers and brothers finally sent for her; she was fourteen. She took secretary classes, but after three months she could no longer pay the tuition and had to quit. After the earthquake of 1985, her dad left Mexico City and Monse began to work as a nanny and domestic worker, cutting her educational goals short as she migrated first to Hermosillo, then to Tijuana, and finally to Los Angeles, as I detail in chapter 5. Monse's story represents that of many women forced by the migration process to defer their dreams. Monse was especially troubled that she was not able to return to school. Thus, for her and for other migrant women like her, the MIEL workshops provided an opportunity and a place to learn, often for the first time since they were girls.

Activists and social movement scholars might emphasize the workshops' role in raising consciousness or sharing resources. For many of the participants themselves, however, the workshops' most significant impact was through rekindling their love of learning. This outcome of their participation was unexpected, but it was the one the women valued most, particularly as their years, sometimes decades, in the United States have largely been dedicated to making sure that that their children get the education and opportunities that they had been denied.

Fighting for justice and access for Indigenous migrants has meant not only fighting the discrimination and exclusion they currently face in the United States, but addressing, even if unexpectedly, the conditions that have structured their exclusion as Indigenous women, which began in Mexico. After joining FIOB, Monse went on to participate actively in the decolonization workshop, which brought together activists to explore "decolonization as a historical process of indigenous peoples [in order] to reaffirm our identity and exercise our right to self-determination in the face of external domination."[27] The workshop facilitators use forms of popular education to share information about myriad topics. The participants' learning in the workshops included forms of *un*learning discrimination, prejudice, and hatred of themselves as Indigenous people. Mixtec scholar-activist and cofounder of the FIOB Gaspar Rivera-Salgado led the decolonization workshops. As the most successful and longest-running workshop series within FIOB, they were soon given in several other regions in California, including Oceanside, Madera, and Fresno.

Political Consciousness and Indigenous Diasporic Identities

Part of the geographies of difference that migrant organizers negotiate are multiple colonialities that have generated class, racial, and gender hierarchies that were not only established by colonial systems but continue to organize settler colonial structures and live on through the coloniality of power. I have observed that ideas of race and indigeneity shift through migration (both in the United States and Mexico) and that these shifting ideas allow migrants to reinterpret their experiences of marginalization. Whereas scholars of transnational migration would argue that mass migration from Oaxaca is creating a "transnational social field," I argue that this transborder social field, and even the transregion created by Indigenous migration, which I mentioned at the beginning of this chapter, is not homogenous or unified. Scholars have demonstrated that "transnational migration has significantly influenced culture, gender dynamics, and political practices in both immigrant-receiving and -sending communities" (Joseph 2015, 2). Joseph argues that "migrants first negotiate race transnationally by relying on racial ideals from their country of origin to understand and interpret race in their host society as immigrants. After their *return* migration, however, they draw on racial ideals acquired abroad to readapt to race at home" (2).

These systems of racial power are embedded in the coloniality of power. Indeed, María Josefina Saldaña-Portillo (2016) argues that empires, now nation-states, constructed "racial geographies" in what is now the US-Mexico borderlands to justify their conquest and colonization of the region. Her research, which spans the sixteenth to the twenty-first centuries, explores how Europeans, Mexicans, and Americans perceived Indigenous peoples and how they defined Indigenous peoples in relation to land in order to justify colonial occupation. Ultimately, she finds that modern US and Mexican national projects are based on inherited colonial and postcolonial constructions of indigeneity—"that the racial geographies of these two countries are indeed Indian given" (Saldaña-Portillo 2016, 11). Whereas some scholars argue that the meaning of race shifts whereby migrants take on "American" notions of race (Joseph 2015), others discuss how "foreign" racial notions become localized in the United States (Roth 2012). Oral histories and life trajectories of Indigenous migrants reveal that although continuities exist in the fact that Indigenous migrants face poverty, discrimination, and marginalization in both Mexico and the United States, the ideologies that support these phenomena are organized differently by Mexican and US racial hierarchies and colonial projects. My argument is that these colonialities that create racial geographies are part of systems of power that not only merge but also hybridize during migration. This understanding of multiple colonialities contributes to and expands the conversation on race and migration in that it sees constructions of race and indigeneity, and for that matter gender, as processes of two national systems that not only collide but hybridize, producing what I have called "hybrid hegemonies" (Blackwell 2010).

Indigeneity is commonly understood as being rooted in place and grounded in relationships to land and place—so much so that in Mexico, and in many parts of Mesoamerica, a person is no longer considered Indigenous if they do not live in that place, speak the language, or historically, wear traditional dress. Yet, Indigenous migrants are uprooted and displaced by colonial design. For Indigenous migrants, it is precisely the process of being dislocated, coupled with the experience of racism and discrimination through migration, that leads many to develop new forms of Indigenous consciousness and to claim an Indigenous identity—one that has been shaped by racism on both sides of the border as they transit different racial geographies in Mexico and the United

States (Saldaña-Portillo 2016). Before migrating, many identify as belonging to a particular pueblo or region, and as Laura Velasco Ortiz (2005) notes, many Indigenous leaders, specifically in the Mixtec organizations she studied, draw from the political and communal identities based on the scale of their hometowns: "For centuries, towns and villages of the Mixteca have maintained an intense community political life" (194). Especially for the municipalities in the district of Juxtlahuca that she researched, and from which many FIOB activists hail, "migration to the United States has added to the already rich history of activism of those interviewees in their hometowns; recognizing this is fundamental to understanding the migrants' present political activism" (194).

Although some activists draw on long histories of communality and some have experiences of social activism, by and large many Indigenous women activists I interviewed were not traditionally seen as leaders in their communities before migrating as they migrated at a young age. Yet the experience of racism and discrimination from mestizos shapes their consciousness as Indigenous peoples, which, in addition to the forms of solidarity they build with others from their hometown, region, or state (in this case, Oaxaca), propels them to participate in Indigenous rights movements and organizations. Many find that the framework of Indigenous rights gives them a language to name their Oaxacan roots and lifeways *as* Indigenous. For example, when I asked Monserrat Bernardino what it was like to join an Indigenous rights organization, she said that even though her parents speak Zapotec, "It never occurred to me that I am Indigenous. I would just say, I am from Oaxaca. I eat chapulines [grasshoppers] or whatever. I know how to make mole but I never identified as Indigenous. Then, when I began to participate in the FIOB, it struck me, 'Wow, I *am* Indigenous.'"

In a similar fashion, Doña Mari learned to identify herself as Indigenous when she joined FIOB and attended the workshops:

> Well, before, I never identified myself [as Indigenous]. I would only say I am Oaxaqueña from the Central Valley . . . because I didn't know. But then it came to me that this always existed with the fear of rejection from people. One could be seen badly [in a negative light] just because they are dark [in complexion], because they are short, because they have black hair—it's like they already profile you. So it was better to just say that I am from any other place other than Oaxaca. If people are going to laugh at me or hurt me then it seemed better to say nothing. But after some of the workshops happened, I was learning about my identity and that I do not have to be ashamed or anything. On the contrary, I could

feel very proud because we all have a history, a past, an identity so that is how I began to grow as a person and to feel more comfortable around people, to no longer feel ashamed nor to walk or speak as if I am. (Sánchez, interview, May 21, 2012)

Like Monse, Doña Mari experienced a profound shift in consciousness. Her process of concientización was shaped not only by her own experience but also by coming to identify with a collective identity, as Indigenous people and Indigenous women. As she explained: "I also learned from the other women talking about their histories and because they had experienced discrimination—being called oaxaquita [little Oaxacan/little Indian] or worse . . . they shared how they felt about [it] and that [the discrimination] had been happening since they lived in Mexico. . . . They told how it was to fight living in Mexico and the discrimination that they suffered" (Bernardino, interview, September 17, 2011).

Doña Mari explained that she felt that other Indigenous migrants could be easily intimidated by structural barriers like language access in both Mexico and the United States. Many Indigenous migrants are monolingual speakers of Indigenous languages and speak no English and only a little Spanish. This makes them vulnerable targets, easily taken advantage of, because, as she put it, "even people who understand and can communicate are taken advantage of, so . . . people who do not understand what is being said will be abused even more. They are only going to do things they are told or obey because they do not know or understand well what is happening, as I see it" (Sánchez, interview, May 21, 2012). Doña Maria described a brutal system of human trafficking and labor exploitation, in which Indigenous migrants pay up to three times more than other migrants to cross the border, get paid less when and if they do find work in the United States, they are often relegated to the more difficult and dangerous jobs in an already racially segmented labor market, as Mines, Nichols, and Runsten (2010), for example, have documented.

In other work, I use the term *hybrid hegemony* to describe when two racial systems collide, mapping onto each other and becoming hybridized through migration. These multiple systems that collide and merge are part of what form the geographies of difference that Indigenous migrants learn to negotiate. I have found that Indigenous migrants are learning not only how to navigate multiple racial hegemonies but also how local, national, and transnational systems of power shift, overlap, and hybridize during the process of migration (Blackwell 2010). Building on earlier transnational feminist understandings of how global forces intersect with local ones, such as Inderpal Grewal's (1994) notion of scattered hegemonies, hybrid hegemony allows us to understand the migrating meanings of race in relation to indigeneity that are both historic and new, the ways in which racial power is signified and utilized to create structures of disempowerment, and how labor segmentation relies on the exploitation of Indigenous migrants in the increasingly global economy. Historic racial hierarchies from Mexico that marginalize Indigenous peoples are not just imported; they are hybridized and get mapped onto American race, class, gender, and sexual relations. In earlier work (2010) with Mixtec women farmworkers, I showed how Indigenous migrant women work in an already racially segregated labor market and that the dangerous, low-paying jobs they perform are further stratified among mestizo and Indigenous workers. Other researchers such as Juan Herrera (2016) have also noted how indigeneity functions intersectionally to further complicate categories of power and exclusion, such as illegality. Adding to this intersectionality uniquely for women migrants, and unlike their male counterparts, this collision of new and old racial systems of power intersects with gendered forms of oppression, as seen in the feminization of the global division of labor, including an increase in women entering the migrant workforce. The complexities of at least two systems of race, gender, and class then hybridize during the process of migration and are compounded by citizenship status—created the geographies of difference that activists are navigating.

Challenging how indigeneity is fixed in time and place, it is often the process of displacement and mobility that lead to new forms of Indigenous consciousness. Migrants gain new awareness when they encounter new forms of racial discrimination, prejudice, and hatred from mestizos and others in Mexico and the United States. Furthermore, these new forms of consciousness give migrants different tools to understand relationships of power in Mexico that they did not have the language for before, or that they previously categorized as simply the difference between the rich and the poor or the urban and the rural. Activists engage in the political work of building consciousness around indigeneity as a political stance, shared discourse, and international framework for rights, and they elaborate their own forms of analysis within Mixtec, Zapotec, Triqui, and other Indigenous cosmovisions. Their indigeneity and its potential political meaning are discussed, debated, and discovered—as FIOB members have done throughout the organization's history. It is part of the transborder and transregional imaginary that connects activists together in order to craft a shared political project across radically uneven terrains of power or geographies of difference. Over the years of the FIOB's history, indigeneity, and its potential political meaning is discussed, debated, and discovered. The implication of my research is that migration and complex migrant civil society organizing navigate geographies of difference in ways that produce new gendered arrangements and new forms of indigeneity that are transforming US Latinidad[28]—processes that will be explored further in chapter 5.

As Monse's and Doña Mari's reflections reveal, many migrant activists start off describing their cultural roots as Oaxacan but, through their participation in FIOB workshops, they come to name their experiences of racism, discrimination, marginalization, and poverty as part of their analysis of being Indigenous. In addition, they perform the gendered work to reproduce Indigenous lifeways and social and political worlds during migration. After the first MIEL cohort graduated, another class was initiated. MIEL was both about developing leaders in FIOB and about participants coming to consciousness regarding the racial geographies of Mexico and the United States, learning to navigate hybrid hegemonies that merge the dual discrimination of being Mexican and Indigenous, as well as new gendered forms of exploitation. The process of forging a political consciousness based on Indigenous rights has also led to the revitalization of other Indigenous artisanal and culinary practices. The FIOB's historic bases have been along migrant streams and in the Mixteca, Sierra Norte and Central Valleys regions of Oaxaca, yet organizing efforts have been happening in the Isthmus of Tehuantepec as well. There, in Zantepec, the women of the FIOB gather for workshops that focus on Indigenous women's rights and (re)learning local traditions of embroidery on velvet huipiles famous in that region (Maria Antonieta Martinez, interview with Maylei Blackwell, October 6, 2011)—an art that they tell me has been forgotten since their grandmothers' time. The revitalization of this Indigenous art has accompanied a growing Indigenous consciousness and a form of economic development in their arts that aligns with the "right to not migrate," or the right to stay home. Members who hosted me during my visit to Zanatepec told me that the workshops helped them to stop domestic violence in their homes and that even husbands are learning to embroidery, which they practice between customers in their taxi collective.

This shift in consciousness is making an impact in communities in California where Oaxacans live in large numbers—not just in LA, but throughout the state, where Indigenous laborers are predicted to comprise 45 percent of the farmworker population (Mines, Nichols, and Runsten 2010, 8). The increasing Indigenous diaspora from Latin America is also raising new conversations about the discrimination Indigenous people face from their mestizo and Ladino counterparts both in the United States and in their homelands. For example, in schools in Oxnard, California, after suffering many years of bullying, Indigenous students and families started an antidiscrimination campaign and won a victory when the school board recognized that using the word *Oaxaquita/o* is a form of racial taunting and would be considered hate speech (Barrillas-Chón 2010; Esquivel 2012).

These experiences point to the fact that Indigenous migrants navigate multiple colonialities. The coloniality of Mexican race relations produces anti-Indigenous hatred and prejudice. The settler colonial logic of the United States attempts to eliminate Indigenous populations, and then US capitalist imperialism dislocates these populations to extract labor and natural resources. To understand the intersectional implications of these racial hybrid power relations, we can recall the gendered struggles for education that Monse faced in Mexico. Grewal's (1994) original formulation of scattered hegemonies asserts that global capitalist hegemonies are arranged through local patriarchies. My use of hybrid hegemonies considers how those scaled systems of power collide and hybridize in the lived experiences and life chances of Indigenous migrant women. For example, before migrating, migrant Indigenous women like Monse were denied access to education because of patriarchal arrangements of power, poverty, and being Indigenous; this denial shaped their life chances and, in Monse's case, pushed her into the migrant stream. Once in the United States, Indigenous migrant women face the harrowing demands of women's work as domestic workers, where sexual harassment and assault and wage theft are rampant, where work hours are not standard, and where they experience prolonged exposure to dangerous chemicals, often dangerous working conditions, and precarious living situations. For Monse, both gendered/racial hierarchies and exclusion existed in Oaxaca and in her experiences of internal migration to Mexico City, Hermosillo, and Tijuana. These systems of oppression were built on and exacerbated by her experience in the US labor market, but her consciousness of them changed—topics I take up in chapter 5.

Concluding Reflections

At the FIOB Binational Assembly in 2017, twelve years after I first met Odilia Romero, she was elected by the FIOB membership to serve as the organization's first female general coordinator, its highest position of leadership. She was elected to this position after serving two terms as the binational coordinator for women's affairs and one term as the vice general coordinator of the organization. While this can be seen as a result of her long-term leadership in and commitment to the organization, as well as the work of members and leaders to diversify their leadership structure, it was also a painful process that revealed the misogyny of some members and leaders who resisted having a woman leader. The election process was tumultuous, and a competitor even left the organization. Yet Odilia told me, "This has been the most ugly, yet the most successful three years of the FIOB for me personally." Despite the contentious divisions and debates, building on her earlier work, she worked tirelessly to provide trainings for Indigenous interpreters during the crisis at the border produced by then president Donald Trump's immigration policies, caging children and breaking up families amid mass migration of Indigenous people from Central America. She tells me that she did all this "with a very small group of supporters." Women have a long history within the FIOB, and the organization prides itself on including gender justice in its principal demands. Yet, these wins have not been without challenges. This chapter has focused on the organization's journey toward leadership development for women and more equitable leadership opportunities and structures, and it theorizes the uneven transnational, transborder, and transregional terrains of power around which gender and indigeneity are organized. The FIOB allows us to see how new forms of transborder organizing and community making navigate geographies of difference, and even how new geographies of indigeneity are emerging.

The density of FIOB's transborder organizing forges the transregion, which is a scale of organizing that recalls the idea of Indigenous organizing, epistemologies, and knowledges, conjuring the new scales that we explored in chapter 2. FIOB's dense networks of communication, kinship, and political organizing, along with the intense work of hometown associations, which I explore in the next chapter, produce binational communal citizenship through tequio (voluntary, communal labor). Indigenous transborder forms of belonging are forged through collective cultural, musical, and religious forms—all part of the work of building sociocultural, political, and economic spatial relationships that conjure the transregional scale. Although the idea that transborder organizing creates a unity across borders has much appeal, my goal in this chapter has been to show how scales are conjured by building transborder projects that effectively navigate geographies of difference to build such unity.

5. Translocal Geographies of Indigeneity

A map of Los Angeles does not tell the story of its people. Most maps of the city obscure Indigenous geographies. The Gabrieleño/Tongva peoples whose homeland includes the Los Angeles basin and southern Channel Islands have their own geography shaped by their own sense of place and relationships, as they continue to struggle for land, self-determination, protection of sacred spaces, and revitalization of their cultures (Alvitre 2015). Tongva cartographies and surviance have endured what I have called multiple colonialities, the enduring spatial, cultural, economic and political organization of power that is the result of how United States settler colonialism overlays Spanish and Mexican colonial structures in the city. Layered on Tongva geographies and multiple colonialities are other Indigenous spatial imaginaries created by the sedimented histories of the largest urban Indigenous population in the United States.[1] Other Native Americas have called Los Angeles home since earlier migrations that brought native artists to Hollywood in the 1920s (Raheja 2011), during the World War II industrial and manufacturing boom in the region, and during what are known as the "relocation days" of the 1950s, when US government policies of termination and "detribalization" led to the removal of reservation-based populations to urban centers (Blackhawk 1995; Rosenthal 2012). These Indigenous geographies also include large diasporas of Indigenous peoples from Latin America and Oceania who have histories of displacement by imperialism, militarism, and neoliberal policies, and have subsequently made their home in Los Angeles. The city has become a "transnational hub" (Ramirez 2007) for many cultures and migrant streams within an increasingly Indigenous diaspora from Mexico and Guatemala during the past forty years, which includes the estimated 250,000 to 300,000 Indigenous Oaxacans (largely Zapotec) who are settling and working in Los Angeles, not to mention the growing presence of Mayas (largely Kanjobal and K'iche) from Guatemala (Batz 2014; Bermudez 2010a; Vankin 2017). Based on my over seventeen years of collaborative research with Indigenous migrant women, in this chapter I examine the geographies of indigeneity, community formation, and translocal politics of place-making with a focus on Indigenous migrant women's political organizing.

Throughout this book I have analyzed how Indigenous women activists navigate geographies of difference—how global and local power is configured differently at each scale, region, or locale, or across the national and transborder contexts in which they organize. My research challenges how migration scholars fail to see "receiving countries" as Indigenous territories and nations, reenacting the terra nullius of settler colonialism. Similarly, Leti Volp (2015) argues, "the critique of exclusion fails to note how the nation-state in which an immigrant seeks membership relies tacitly on the dispossession of already existing populations" (291). Understanding Indigenous mobility as a global process of settler colonialism means understanding displacement—be it through war, ecological destruction, or extractive capitalist schemes to remove the earth's resources or to leverage human labor and ingenuity—as part of its logic of elimination. Carpio, Barnd, and Barraclough (2022) invite us to think about "mobility sovereignty," which "refers equally to the right to move and the right to stay put" (5). Geographies of difference capture the ways in which indigeneity is produced differentially by multiple colonialities and by the various Indigenous diasporas that may exist on the homelands of other Indigenous nations, while simultaneously working against erasure of Indigenous peoples, and of the homelands they transit and settle on (Byrd 2011).

Whereas indigeneity has historically been rooted in land-based notions of place, one of the unexpected outcomes of Indigenous migration is that it is the very process of being uprooted, deterritorialized, and displaced, often by political and economic design, that leads some some migrants to an develop Indigenous political consciousness. It is when people experience racism, gendered violence, and economic injustice during the process of migration and within labor segmentation that many of them begin to develop an Indigenous political identity, as I explored in chapter 4. Dislocation makes Indigenous identity and language a matter of cultural survival, and many migrants aim to build translocal notions of Indigenous place that tie them and their children back to their pueblos of origin, to its feast days, and to civic responsibilities and cultural practices. Indigenous activists consistently point to the fact that Indigenous peoples migrated before colonization and call for the need to decolonize borders that create false colonial divisions. Many Indigenous cosmovisions center interrelationships with land, but both Indigenous peoples' forced displacement from it and static notions of place fixed through confinement that create falsely bounded spaces are both settler colonial projects. Part of settler colonialism is the imposition of spatial immobilization and dispossession of Indigenous peoples along with the state's exercise of sovereignty determining who is deportable through carceral and border technologies and discourses that, through their very enforcement, assert settler sovereignty. In fact, as Monisha Das Gupta (forthcoming) illustrates "the state's claim on the right to deport is bound up with the continuous effort to dispossess Indigenous people of their material and cultural base. Setter colonialism, then, undermines Indigenous sovereignty and determines deportability. It is a two-in-one deal" (12).

In contrast, in this chapter I examine how Indigenous mobility and community organizing, labor circuits, and spiritual practices are forms of Indigenous place-making that are reorganizing socio-spatial relations in Los Angeles creating geographies of indigeneity (Lefebvre 1991; Soja 1989). The culinary, political, and communal spatial projects and musical soundscapes of the Latin American Indigenous diaspora in Los Angeles provide a deep context for understanding how women have created translocal, transborder, and transregional Indigenous social worlds. Then I go deeper into exploring the production of sacred geographies and mobile circuits of labor through oral histories with migrant Indigenous women organizers. Finally, I consider how the increasingly Indigenous Latin American diaspora compels activists and scholars in the fields of Latinx studies and Native American/Indigenous studies to think in increasingly unbordered and unsettled ways. Building on collaborative work with colegas, I elaborate Critical Latinx Indigeneities as a framework that helps me to situate Indigenous migrant spatial projects in relation to existing Indigenous homelands and multiple settler/colonialist logics, which include forms of Oaxacan and Maya Indigenous belonging that are spatialized into LA neighborhoods through soundscapes and foodways, spiritual geographies, labor circuits of mobility, and respatialized political cartographies. These diasporas compel us to think about categories such as indigeneity and Latinidad in complex, comparative, and compounding ways. Although the density of transborder Indigenous communities may be unique to Los Angeles, this phenomenon helps us to think more capaciously and critically about indigeneity and Latinidad, as multiple Indigenous migrant streams flow from Latin America to the United States, including Mayas in Houston, P'urépecha in North Carolina, Garífuna in New York, and Nahuas and Quechas along the Eastern Seaboard, to name just a few.

Here I explore translocal place-making and transregional ways of being Indigenous that are creating multiple Indigenous geographies in Los Angeles, reflecting on how Indigenous migrants' spatial projects come into complex play with the region's multiple colonialities on Tongva territory. My work builds on Renya Ramirez's (2007) work on transnational hubs, a concept she uses to describe how urban Indigenous communities create relationships among themselves in the urban "hub" while still being linked via "spokes" to their Indigenous homelands, their nations and pueblos of origin. Drawing on Paiute community activist Laverne Roberts's notion of how urban native communities create a sense of communal belonging, what she calls a "hub," Ramirez argues that transnational hubs are "a native woman's vision of urban and rural mobility, her suggestion of a mechanism of cultural and identity transmission, as well as social change" (24). I ground transnational hubs of Indigenous people who are linked not only to their nations/pueblos of origin, as Ramirez (2007) suggests, but also to the Indigenous homelands they reside on in order to open up conversations about relationalities and responsibilities amid uneven terrains of power; such terrains are produced by multiple colonialities, racializations, and statuses that federal recognition confers onto some but not onto others, like the Tongva. To understand the multiple indigeneities in LA, we must disrupt the city's settler and prior colonial geographies to grasp the original Tongva and Tatavium geography as the base map that locates all other arrivants through a web of relations and responsibilities. For this reason, I draw on Jodi Byrd's theorization of Afro-Caribbean poet Kamau Braithwaite's concept of arrivant, which helps us to open up the native/settler dichotomy (Byrd 2011). I also consider the conflicts, responsibilities, and opportunities to build solidarity with the native communities whose land we are working and residing on. Critical Latinx Indigeneities is a framework that allows me to think about how Indigenous migration forms diasporic geographies that are mapped onto multiple colonial and settler geographies and, even more importantly, on Indigenous geographies of those who are native to this land (Vicenti Carpio 2011). These geographies of land and water are central to Charles Sepulveda's (2018) work on water and the Tongva concept of guest, or Kuuyam, which he posits as decolonial possibility. Sepulveda argues that "this concept of Kuuyam can continue to be applied today. Settlers in California, and elsewhere, can be guests on the lands they live on. Kuuyam to the local Indigenous, but more importantly, to the land itself which contains spirit and is willing to provide" (54). This reframing allows for a "re-centering of place," rather than a division of people on the basis of a settler/Indigenous binary; Kuuyam "allows all people to understand themselves as guests of the land—either they behave appropriately, or they do not" (55). The power of Sepulveda's argument is based on a relationship with and responsibility to the land and the Indigenous peoples of that land. "Forming relationships has continuously been an Indigenous method to easing and avoiding confrontation and violence. Relationships form responsibility and protocol . . . [and thus] Kuuyam can assist in the abolition of white supremacist logics that demand domestication and submission" (55).

Organizers of the Frente Indígena de Organizaciones Binacionales (Indigenous Front of Binational Organizations, FIOB) LA allow us to see how transborder organizing (Stephen 2007) creates translocal and transregional ways of being Zapotec. As I described in the introduction, Indigenous migrants create transnational community, families, and identities (Glick Schiller, Basch, and Blanc-Szanton 1992), and even binational (Indigenous) civil societies (Fox 2005; Rivera-Salgado 2006). Yet we also can deploy the notion of Indigenous transborders (versus transnational ones) to denaturalize multiple colonial borders, colonialities of power (systems that have colonial arrangements of meaning and power at the center), and settler colonial structures (designed to eliminate the native). Immigration scholars overlook the idea that the US-Mexico border is not only a colonial border being crossed by migrants, their translocal cultures, and binational civil societies, but also a border that maps over other Indigenous nations' borders that are also crossed, divided, and traversed, though far less frequently acknowledged (Schaeffer 2022; Simpson 2014; Tamez 2013). A Critical Latinx Indigeneities framework provides a way to read multiple colonialities and complex geographies of difference as Indigenous geographies. For me, Stephen's (2007) notion of transborder is an important tool in this analytic repertoire. I use it to account for the ways in which transborder organizers and Indigenous migrants must also cross multiple borders of social and political power. This perspective then opens up what *transnational* means, to include Indigenous nation-to-nation relationships and to account for the multiple configurations of power within nations. For me, the concept of transborder is also useful, following Anzaldúa's notion of borderlands (1987), to call attention to the multiple colonial, racial, class, and gender borders that transborder migrants and organizers navigate. The Latin American Indigenous diaspora creates transborder forms of belonging to maintain within Los Angeles cultural and civic ties to pueblos of origin, and by acknowledging these multiple border crossings, we can further expand the notion of transborder.

Activist women in the Latin American Indigenous diaspora navigate violence, discrimination, gendered exclusion, and racism in workplaces, schools, and the city itself, all while practicing the resilience and recovering Indigenous cultures. As members of Indigenous communities that have survived both the long history of discrimination and marginalization in Mexico and the cultural and structural dislocation of the migrant experience, Oaxacan Indigenous people face institutional, cultural, linguistic, and economic barriers that affect their access to health care, education, safe jobs, dignity, and life chances (Fox and Rivera-Salgado 2004b; Kearney 1995; Stephen 2007; Velasco Ortiz 2005). With the added layer of gender discrimination, Indigenous women often have little formal education and are more likely to be monolingual Indigenous-language speakers when they arrive to the United States. While many FIOB members also belong to hometown associations (HTAs), which create new spaces of belonging and transborder communities, women's participation within HTAs has sometimes limited to the reproductive labor of nostalgia (cooking, organizing fiestas or celebrations for patron saints) (Rivera-Salgado 2016). Although scholarship on the gendered labor of social reproduction of indigeneity is emerging, especially in the work of Zapotec scholar Brenda Nicolás (2020), who explores women's role in founding her HTA, civic and political organizations like FIOB have been important sources of women's binational political participation and mobilization on behalf of themselves and their communities (Rivera-Salgado 2014b). Indigenous women arrivants carry out gender-specific roles in creating and maintaining tradition. At the same time, they are shifting narratives of tradition by becoming organizers on behalf of their communities.

Mapping Multiple Scales of Transborder Communities and Place-making

Within geographies of indigeneity in Los Angeles, Indigenous migrant women navigate multiple scales even within one city. Whereas the city itself, like other levels of governance (the nation, the state), is usually understood as a single scale, the regions of Oaxaca are recast onto the geography of Los Angeles, remapping the city through the multiple scales of regions or transregions of Oaxaca. Researchers have documented that communities in migration tend to settle where they have family and connection, but they have paid less attention to how migrants cast Indigenous geographies in the city. Through Indigenous migrants' social practices of place-making, the regions of Oaxaca are recast onto the Los Angeles geography, remapping the city through the scales of pueblo and region. These dense localities of belonging and kinship have made Pico Union and Koreatown the epicenter of migration from the Northern Sierra region, whereas Westside neighborhoods such as Mar Vista and Venice are the primary receiving communities for people from the Central Valleys.[2]

The eight regions of Oaxaca are named for geographic regions, and each is celebrated for its distinctive cultural and geographic features during festivals like Guelaguetza ("offering"), reflecting Zapotec notions of reciprocity (Flores-Marcial 2015).[3] Guelaguetza is largely attended by tourists in Oaxaca City, but in migration it has become a vehicle for Oaxacan pride, social and cultural reproduction, and migrant civil society (X. Chavez 2013). Indeed, Los Angeles has been called the ninth region of Oaxaca. Migrants often identify by the region they are from, and their work building social, economic, political, and spiritual links creates Indigenous transregions. Scaling down even deeper, beyond regions or transregions, the main spatial unit of identification for many Oaxacan migrants is their pueblo, meaning that they identify as being from Tlacolula, for example, rather than as being Oaxacan, Zapotec, or Indigenous. What is less understood is that many Indigenous migrants maintain citizenship in their pueblos or hometowns through civic responsibilities and a traditional collective labor system known as the cargo system (Ventura Luna 2010). In addition to these political and civic duties, social and cultural reproduction occurs translocally across generations, as exemplified by Brenda Nicolas's (2016) research with second-generation US-born Oaxacans who learn the dances of their pueblos or perform in a hometown brass band; often they must perform for the elders back in their pueblos in Oaxaca first before they gain permission to perform publicly in the United States. Because the primary form of belonging for most Indigenous Oaxacans is based on their pueblos back home, the scale of "pueblo" is re-created in HTAs in Los Angeles (at backyard parties, patron saints' days, and events in parks, for example) that create translocal or, better said, transpueblo structures, socially reproducing religious, civic, social, and cultural life. These geographies of indigeneity not only are mapped onto neighborhoods but also, in the density of that resettlement, create micro-zones where many residents of a particular Oaxacan pueblo may live together on one block or even in one apartment building. These multiscalar experiences are largely invisible to outsiders, as Indigenous communities are folded into other racial formations wherein Mayas or Zapotecs, for example, often undergo a process of Indigenous disappearance or erasure through Hispanicization, becoming Mexican or Latino. This process makes invisible the high rate of Indigenous migration from Mesoamerica that has happened since the 1980s, building on earlier migrants within the bracero program that started in the 1940s.[4] Even the most racially and ethnically diverse neighborhoods of Los Angeles—the Spanish- or even Korean-dominant spaces of Koreatown, MacArthur Park, or Westlake—hold within them linguistic and cultural micro-zones of Zapotec or Kanjobal (Popkin 2005).

To understand how civic, cultural, and religious practices spatialize indigeneity within neighborhoods, we can look most weekends to backyards, driveways, and dance halls that host community gatherings, meetings, HTA events, patron saint day celebrations, and processions for each hometown (many of which have multiple saint's days). These place-making practices have led even more recently to the migration of the patron saints themselves to Catholic churches throughout Los Angeles. For example, St. Anne's on the west side now houses seven patron saints from Oaxaca and the dark-skinned Virgen de Juquila, patron saint of Santa Catarina Juquila in Oaxaca, is revered, celebrated, and receives petitions in the city at Saint Thomas the Apostle Church and Our Lady Queen of the Angels Church in the historic plaza.[5] Indeed, anthropologist Lourdes Guitérrez Nájera (2010) has done ethnographic research on how Yalalaltecos create belonging not only through formal events that maintain and reproduce community but also during everyday acts of being together. For example, she argues that "home gatherings are important community-building practices that, while spanning the distance between LA and Yalalag, also foster a sense of belonging" that affirm their identity as Zapotecs; such practices include sharing photos, sharing gossip, and dancing (71). In Gutiérrez's study of these affective, embodied practices of belonging, Felipe shared that being at a community dance was like being transported home, serving "as a reminder that the body has a history, a memory that in this case is linked to his natal community" (75). For Gutiérrez, "ultimately, dancing provides a way to express ethnic identity. Sentiments of joy, sadness, and love shared with family, friends, and paisanos at public bailes reaffirm their collectivity" (76). Belonging is mapped not only across pueblos, regions, borders, and neighborhoods but is located in the scale of the body.

Indeed, the patterns of place-making and social organization, and the cultural practices of Oaxacan dance troupes and brass bands, inspired early migrants to begin organizing an annual Guelaguetza festival at Normandie Park in the late 1980s (Alberto 2018). Normandie Park, just south of Koreatown and east of the Pico Union neighborhood, also became a well-known site of Zapotec basketball, which was initially organized informally as a league between different HTAs but eventually led to tournaments such as the Juarez Cup organized by the Union of Highland Communities of Oaxaca for numerous years (Fox and Rivera-Salgado 2004a, 18; see also Alberto 2018).[6] The park became a nexus for community and cultural gatherings, leading some community members to mount a campaign to rename the park after Benito Juárez, the only Indigenous (Zapotec) president of Mexico, on the occasion of his two-hundredth birthday, by gathering more than two thousand signatures (Quinones 2006). Though their campaign was not successful, a Oaxacan Indigenous sense of place has been made in relation to settler and immigrant geographies, as the park is adjacent to the newly named El Salvador Community Corridor. Eventually, because of the growth of the Guelaguetza festival each year and the emergence of other such festivals throughout the state of California, the original festival was moved to the Los Angeles Memorial Sports Arena in 2002, drawing from six thousand to ten thousand participants. Since then the festival has grown even larger and has been moved outdoors to Lincoln Park in East Los Angeles.

The growth of the Guelaguetza festival into the Oaxacan Heritage Month calls attention to an emerging soundscape that has developed over the past twenty-five years and accompanies these geographies. Isaí Pazos, president of the Organización Regional de Oaxaca (Regional Organization of Oaxaca, ORO), an organization founded in 1988, spoke with me about this cultural history and soundscape at a recent community event. He told me that more than forty bands and dance troupes represent the various pueblos of Oaxaca. Only twenty-four are currently active and performing, but he pointed out that each hometown has its own philharmonic band (some forty members strong) and Oaxacan dance groups, so their practices, performances, fundraisers, and gatherings create other Indigenous soundscapes and places within Los Angeles. Indeed, Guelaguetza has grown from a single event to a series of events spread over Oaxacan Heritage Month to include a calenda, or community procession featuring all the dancers, musicians, and community members, before the Guelaguetza; a proclamation from the mayor's office; a basketball tournament; an encounter of the bands; a beauty contest; at one point an Indigenous literatures conference; and other civic and political events (X. Chavez 2013; Escala Rabadán and Rivera-Salgado 2017) (see figures 5.1 and 5.2).[7]

Figure 5.1. Mayoral proclamation on Oaxacan Heritage Month in Los Angeles. Pictured here at the Los Angeles City Hall are (*left to right in the front row*) Gaspar Rivera-Salgado, Isaí Pazos, City Council Representative Curren D. Price Jr., Odilia Romero Hernández, and Janet Martinez. Photo by Mauro Hernandez.

Figure 5.2. Maritza Sanchez, 2014 Queen of the Vela Muxe LA at the annual calenda, Los Angeles, 2015. Photo by the author.

These cultural forms of place-making complement a wealth of spatial projects based on culinary practices and the distinctive regional foodways of Oaxaca that feature mole, tamales wrapped in banana leaves, tlayudas, and totopos.[8] The fast-paced growth of Oaxacan restaurants in the South LA, Pico Union, Koreatown, and Westside neighborhoods of Los Angeles is outpaced only by independent food that is home-crafted and sold through informal street vendors and neighborhood caterers who provide a diverse array of delicacies including homemade tamales, champurrado (a chocolate drink with a ground-corn base), corn, blood sausage, or raspados (ice cones) with homemade flavors and sauces.[9] These small-scale entrepreneurs have changed both the face and the flavor of neighborhoods, making them cultural gateways for the broader community to learn about Oaxacan Indigenous communities. These changes have brought with them unexpected developments, as declared by the *Los Angeles Times* headline "Eat Your Crickets: Los Angeles Is the Chapulin Capital of the US" (Cabral 2013).

Perhaps one of the most significant reflections of this growing visibility in the city is the restaurant Guelaguetza, which in 2015 won the prestigious James Beard Award for being an American classic (Parsons 2015). After a year of street vending, owner Fernando Lopez originally opened Guelaguetza Restaurant with his wife Maria Monterrubio in 1994 on Eighth Street, a vibrant center of Oaxacan life in Los Angeles. Several years later, the restaurant relocated to a much larger space in Koreatown, and it is now run by the Lopez children, Bricia, Fernando Jr., and Paulina. The iconic restaurant features Korean-style architecture but functions as a hub of Oaxacan cultural life in the city. It features a mural from the artist-duo known as Los Tlacolulokos, Dario Canul and Cosijoesa Cernas, who hail from Tlacolula, Oaxaca (Gutiérrez Nájera and Maldonado 2017; Morales 2020; Vankin 2018). As for Fernando Lopez, he retired in 2013 and returned to Mitla, Oaxaca (Virbila 2014). Having already found such great success selling Oaxacan food to homesick paisanos in Los Angeles, he opened a new restaurant in 2014 called Pink Burger that catered to return migrants who miss American food.[10]

One of the more dramatic spatial projects involves Oaxacan civic and political geographies of dissent. FIOB LA was one of the convening organizations for the first protest against HR 4437 (also known as the Sensenbrenner Bill) in March 2006, which then grew into the May 1 protests (or what became known as mega-marches).[11] The marches were organized by a wide range of organizations such as FIOB LA and the Multiethnic Immigrant Workers Organizing Network (to which the FIOB belongs), along with the Coalition for Humane Immigrant Rights of Los Angeles (CHIRLA) and other organizations (A. Gonzalez 2013). These mass protests shifted the geography of dissent in the city, which before 2006 had been organized around the Federal Building in Westwood, occasionally at City Hall, or at the intersection of Hollywood and Highland, specifically for the antiwar protests leading up to the invasions of Afghanistan and Iraq. After the mega-marches, the geography of dissent in the city was oriented toward the immigrant epicenter of MacArthur Park, which was the starting point for the marches in 2006 and the end point of the 2007 march. This site also became a space of state violence, as the police brutally beat protesters and their families (and journalists) after trapping people in the park (Costanza-Chock 2014; Santa Ana, López, and Munguía 2010).

The year 2006 was intense, as it was also when Oaxacan communities in Los Angeles mobilized in solidarity with the teacher's strike in Oaxaca, which was violently put down by then governor Ulises Ruiz and the Federal Preventive

Police. In response to the repression, a full-scale popular movement was born as the Asamblea Popular de los Pueblos de Oaxaca (Oaxacan Popular People's Assembly, APPO). FIOB was one of the main political actors and transborder communities that mobilized support, forming APPO LA as APPO's counterpart in the United States. Throughout the autumn of 2006, protests took place in Los Angeles in the MacArthur Park area and ended each time in the park across from the Mexican Embassy at Sixth and Park View Ave (see figure 5.3). Indeed, a series of events led up to an encampment in front of the consulate, which activists occupied in November 2006 (Gringo 2006a). These geographies of dissent are part of the creation of transborder Indigenous diasporic communities, movements, and spatial relations that, in this case, were dramatically illustrated as LA demonstrators called activists from Oaxaca speaking from cell phones held up to a microphone to share messages of solidarity and direct material aid. During an interview at one of the November protests, Odilia, then of the FIOB, was asked by a journalist how the uprising in Oaxaca was connected to Oaxacan communities in LA; she pointed to the power of transnational, transborder organizing in the Indigenous diaspora:

Figure 5.3. FIOB LA after a protest in solidarity with the APPO at Macarthur Park, in front of the Mexican Embassy in Los Angeles, 2006. Photo by the author.

> There is a direct relationship from APPO LA. We have direct contact because within the Frente [FIOB] our members are in the leadership in the APPO who are members of Section 22 [the teachers union in Oaxaca]. Everybody here within the community has a brother, a sister, a cousin [involved in the movement] so we have more contact and direct relationships. We know what is happening before the news comes out....
> It is not just in Oaxaca City, but it is Sierra Norte, the Sierra Sur, the Isthmus, the Mixteca, and the Mixe region. All sixteen ethnic groups in the seven regions are involved. (Gringo 2006b)

With her words and the community's actions, Odilia demonstrated that the Oaxacan diaspora in LA has emerged as another transregion of Oaxaca that, despite being deterritorialized, stood up against the human rights violations occurring in their hometowns. They raised funds throughout the uprising to help buy phone cards and other necessities for organizers, even going so far as to transform the posada, the traditional December ritual that symbolizes Mary and Joseph's search for lodging, into an "APPOsada" in which community members raised funds at each stop along the route, serving Oaxacan hot chocolate and food for a donation to the cause (Stephen 2013).

These networked geographies and the growing political and economic power of migrants have not gone unnoticed by the elite in Mexico. The Mexican state has capitalized on the funds generated by HTAs by offering the 3×1 Program, which matches three dollars for every one dollar HTAs contribute for infrastructure projects (Duquette-Rury 2014). Likewise, political candidates have also begun to campaign for political office in Oaxacalifornia in an effort to win the votes of those migrants who are Mexican citizens and those who hold dual citizenship (Gutiérrez 2010) thereby further creating what Fox and Rivera-Salgado (2004a) called binational civil society and reinforcing transborder forms of citizenship in both the nation-states of Mexico and the United States, as well as in the Indigenous pueblos I describe. Finally, these geographies of protest are also linked to state violence and the creation of pan-Indigenous solidarity within the Latin American Indigenous diaspora in Los Angeles. For example, the police shooting death of Maya (K'iche') day laborer Manuel Jaminez Xum on September 5, 2010, at Sixth and Union in the Westlake district of Pico Union spurred community members to create a geography of remembrance: a makeshift memorial was created at the location of the shooting, and people gathered there for candlelight vigils (Blackwell 2017a; Blackwell, Boj Lopez, and Urrieta Jr. 2017; Estrada 2017). The vigils eventually evolved from a space to remember Jaminez Xum's death into a place to give testimonio, as residents of the neighborhood began speaking out about their experience of regular police harassment and violence. Their collective frustration with the LAPD-caused death ignited three days of intense protest and resulted in more than thirty arrests. The chief of police eventually called a community meeting to which more than four hundred people attended ("LAPD Murders Again" 2010).

Jaminez Xum came to the United States right before the great recession, and his debt had tripled by the time of his murder. He lived in a small studio apartment with eleven other men. Research has shown that Indigenous migrants are often charged more by coyotes to migrate and pay much higher rates of interest on the loans most of them must take in order to risk crossing the border. Part of this tragedy is transnational, as the debt that Jaminez Xum incurred to come work in the United States passed to his widow, Isabel Marroquin Tambriz, in a small Maya pueblo called Xexac in Guatemala (Bermudez 2010a).[12] Following this tragedy, the FIOB began to conduct annual cultural sensitivity training for the LAPD and other city agencies. It also worked with other cultural and civic organizations to create an Oaxacan corridor in Los Angeles. As part of a broader Latino coalition, following the success of the Salvadoran community corridor in Pico Union, the Latino Empowerment Roundtable came together to create visibility for the increasingly diverse Latino population in Los Angeles, similar to how Asian Americans have a historic Chinatown, Japantown, Koreatown, Thai Town, and Cambodia Town in the City of Los Angeles. This recognition by the city signals a potential change in its official geography and raises important questions about multiracial neighborhoods and communities, as the proposed corridor includes areas of Koreatown. FIOB and the coalition that has formed to create the Oaxacan corridor have begun to work with civic organizations and leaders in Koreatown (Trinh 2014). It will be critical to see whether these emergent geographies and spatial projects forge relationships, solidarities, or responsibilities toward the Indigenous people of Los Angeles.

Indigenous women migrants navigate not only a collision of new and old racial systems that intersect with gendered forms of oppression, as seen in the feminization of the global division of labor, including the feminization of immigration; the complexities of at least two colonial systems of race, indigeneity, gender, and class also hybridize during the process of migration and are compounded. Building on the context of spatial practices, in the following sections I discuss how Indigenous migrant women's organizing creates sacred geographies and, through the mobilities of labor, new circuits of organizing.

Spaces of Violence: Geographies of the Sacred

One of the most important things I have learned through working with Indigenous migrants is their attention to new ideas of scale that move beyond the notions of space assumed by Western cartography and the ways in which scale is theorized in conventional geography. For the Indigenous migrants whom I work with, the scales of the body, the home, and the spiritual world profoundly affect the conditions of their labor and the possibilities of their own liberation. Los Angeles–based Zapotec activist Odilia Romero Hernández has been at the heart of many spatial projects of resistance and community organizing, some of which I've discussed earlier, but her participation in creating new Indigenous geographies of the sacred within Los Angeles has been especially powerful. Through her healing and spiritual community in Los Angeles, she has been part of a pan-Indigenous community that is creating new geographies of the sacred through the work of the Mayan Day Keepers Association.

Born in May 1971, Odilia Romero Hernández is from Zoogocho in the Northern Sierra of Oaxaca; her strongest memory is the smell of earth at her grandmother's adobe home there. As the oldest of four sisters, Odilia remembers the freedom she had to play and run in nature since there were few cars.[13] Her parents earned a living by slaughtering pigs to sell at the weekly market. The town was so small, they needed only one pig per week. Odilia's father was the first of her family to migrate in 1974, but he soon returned to Zoogocho because of the isolation he experienced in Los Angeles. Later, in 1979, both of Odilia's parents migrated together with her younger sisters, who were then small children. They left Odilia in the care of her grandmother. Recounting her family's history of migration, Odilia began by telling me about the sexual violence she experienced as a child. Although I had been aware of this part of her history before us sitting down to formally record her testimonio, I began to realize how powerful this part of her life was in shaping her narrative of healing and political awareness.

Odilia has a kind of fearless bravery that is hard to describe. It's like she bears the most painful scars while looking you in the eye, daring you to blink (figure 5.4). Her decision to share her story with me and to publish the testimonial in Spanish meant that her story would not only go public; it would also be public within the community. The testimonio was a collaborative project we created as part of a binational research conversation with other Indigenous women and scholars (Blackwell 2009a). The details of her experiences are painful to hear, but in witnessing this pain, and in turn by doing so publicly, Odilia demands justice for what happens to young people who are left behind during migration.[14]

Figure 5.4. Odilia Romero Hernández. Photo by Antonio Nava.

Odilia's experience of sexual molestation is inextricably linked to her memory of migration. She began the migration story this way: "I remember my dad came here [to the United States] for a time before we all stayed here with my mom. I have really clear visions of one of the stepbrothers of my dad touching me sexually, but I don't remember if that was when I was with my mom or after when both my parents migrated, but the image is very clear" (Odilia Romero Hernández, interview with Maylei Blackwell, January 31, 2009).

Trauma shapes memory, leaving some things, like the perception of time, fuzzy and others razor sharp. When I ask how she survived something so painful and how it shaped who she is today, she replied, "At first I had so much anger toward my parents for having left me because if they could have borrowed the passage for three daughters, why not four? I didn't understand economic issues that impact your life as an immigrant and as an Indigenous person." Her sense of abandonment was seared into her mind, and she vividly remembers the date of their departure as February 28, 1979, when she was eight years old. She stayed behind because her parents couldn't afford for everyone to migrate, and while they looked for work and established themselves, she lived in her grandmother's house, where her three step-uncles repeatedly molested her. When Odilia's parents finally sent for her and she was reunited with her family in Los Angeles at the age of eleven, she initially did not remember her mother, even though it had been only three years since they had last seen each other.

Her trauma was compounded by the disorientation of being in a new urban environment with new forms of racism. Along with the trauma, Odilia experienced multiscalar violence once she came to the United States, disrupting the narrative of US exceptionalism that claims migrant women and children experience less oppression and have more freedom in this country. Once in the United States, Odilia felt profound alienation and isolation because, in addition to facing economic exploitation, marginalization, and racism, the mestizo Latino neighbors would make fun of them because, as one of the Oaxaqueño families living in the building and on their block, they spoke Zapotec. Her mother worked at a factory as a seamstress where she was treated badly because of the language barrier. Her father worked as a busboy and then as a cook. They then decided to make moronga, a blood sausage based on a recipe that her father knew how to make, and that is how they made a living no longer having to work for others. Although Pico Union, a neighborhood just west of downtown Los Angeles, has the largest and most historic Oaxacan settlement community in Los Angeles, it is just one ethnic enclave inside multiple others, as Pico Union is also home to both Salvadorans and Guatemalans who arrived during the wars in those countries in the 1980s. In addition, it is adjacent to Koreatown, where over time the borders have become blurred geographically, so Oaxacans commonly work as cooks and busboys in Korean restaurants, and ethnic and civic organizations are in communication and coalition with each other.

When Odilia attended a school in Los Angeles on Union Ave, she had a really hard time because she did not speak Spanish or English and only knew "si" y "tu" and she was reprimanded for not speaking proper Spanish. At school, Odilia got suspended for hitting a kid with a stapler. Her parents had a hard time helping her because they simply could not understand. At the age of fifteen, Odilia dropped out of ninth grade. As much as schooling has been a site of racism, it was also a site of possibility and change. Odilia told me, "Things began to change for me because I then went to City College and took a class with a teacher of Irish descent. She was always talking about women's rights and I liked it because she was very sarcastic about the double standards of society. Then she began to talk a lot about the issue of gender balance, the issue facing African American communities here in South Central Los Angeles, and about systematic inequities at the global level" (Romero Hernández, interview, January 31, 2009). When I asked her if her process of coming into social and political consciousness was through schooling, she explained, "Yes, it was a process of access to education more than anything that allowed me to realize all the things that were going on, about the people who made ugly faces or mocked you when you spoke Zapotec, or because you didn't speak Spanish well. In the class, I learned how to name the positive and negative things that were going on, especially when you experience discrimination, racism, and inequality in your own flesh. You know it's not right, but you don't know how to call it. Imagine everything a simple literature class gives" (Romero Hernández, interview, January 31, 2009).

When I asked her about work, Odilia told me that she basically kept switching jobs that mistreated her or abused her until she arrived at the Frente (the FIOB). She heard about FIOB through a television announcement and wanted to participate because she felt a connection. She wanted them to be more political as she noticed that the work that they were doing provided only band-aid solutions to what she saw as the larger problem. She spoke to Rufino, a Mixtec community leader and co-founder of the FIOB, who told her to create a Frente committee that would take care of these issues. She started out at the Union Social de Zoogochense, the hometown association from her pueblo, attempted to organize there, but she was rejected mainly because she did not follow traditional gender roles. Odilia explains how most of the backlash came from her own family. She tells me, "Sure, it was difficult. And worst of all was my family who was saying, 'You neither cared for your house, nor were you a good wife to your husband. How are you going to want to help us? That won't do.' I thought why it was my family said this, that since I was not good wife, then somehow could I not contribute to the growth of the organization of my pueblo's association. And yes, I was very sad because I said, 'Well, I can't cook or I can't be the best wife, true. But I can do many other things.' But they were always throwing the past in my face. Even though it had been a long time, when I started at the Frente it was there. The Fresno office was too far away to have the workshops we have today on how to conduct a meeting and all that. Then, when I began the first meeting with my pueblo, it was a disaster" (Romero Hernández, interview, January 31, 2009).

While she went on to organize with other Oaxacan activists in Los Angeles, Odilia explained that she felt that her hometown association did not support her because they are not political and exist to create events to raise funds for the infrastructure of the towns they come from or to organize cultural forms and fiestas for the town's patron saints, the work of nostalgia, as she called it.[15] She told me that the Frente, on the other hand, is a consciousness raising organization that teaches members to analyze the political situation and to be proud to speak the Zapoteco or their Indigenous language. She observed that the success of the Frente varies by experience but she was inspired, for instance, that some women left the fields and went to work in offices, other women have left their abusive husbands. What she liked about the FIOB was they conducted workshops in Indigenous languages, they have interpreters who will speak to the court and to the hospitals on behalf of community members, they have *El Tequio* magazine. At the time she began organizing the office in Los Angeles, there had been an office in Fresno and the FIOB had committees throughout California in San Diego, Santa Maria, Santa Rosa, and Madera as well as an office in Hollister that was shared with other organizations. They also had an offices in Oaxaca in the central valleys region, in Huajuapan de Leon, and in the mixteca region, in Juaxtlahuaca, and members would later start an office in the isthmus of Tehuantepec, in the city of Zanatepec. They also had committees in Mexico City and Tijuana. Odilia started out working with the sister organization, the Binational Center for Oaxacan Indigenous Development (Centro Binacional para el Desarrollo Indígena Oaxaqueña, CBDIO), and that is how she got involved with the Frente coordinating the local Los Angeles committee. Odilia was nominated to be a local leader, she explains, "because they said that they needed a woman but I said that if they were going to give me the title they also needed to let me do what I needed to and not have just have me sitting there" (Romero Hernández, interview, January 31, 2009). She tells me that is how the decolonization workshops (discussed in chapter 4) began explaining that she felt decolonization was an important process that needed to happen along with including women's participation and ensuring their rights. Her vision at the time was to create a space in the organization that would account for precolonial Indigenous traditions of gender egalitarianism. At the time of our first interview, Odilia shared that the Frente was the only space where she was able to truly organize for women's issues because she felt it was the only space that really created support beyond paying lip service, a view that she later would find challenged by a process I describe in the coda of this book.

As we concluded our testimonio, I asked Odilia how she has healed as a survivor of sexual violence. She told me she found peace by breaking her silence about the violence she experienced and by confronting one of her uncles. "It has been a very intense spiritual process and I learned the history of my Indigenous pueblo. I believe education has a lot to do with it. Learning to read and finding books about how to survive these forms of violence." Odilia began this healing journey, she recalled, while attending a Native American mental health conference, where she met Cecilia Fire Thunder, who gave her books about native women in the United States healing themselves and their communities from violence. This exchange illustrates the importance healing historic trauma led by Northern native feminists over the past three decades and of work by women of color to understand how intimate violence is tied to larger colonial and institutional structures of violence.[16]

Indeed, Odilia tells me that her healing has been linked to her intense involvement in ceremony. After getting to know FIOB activists who met regularly at her parents' Oaxacan restaurant, where she was a waitress, Odilia became active in Indigenous politics and immigrant rights. Odilia served as the binational vice coordinator of FIOB and has gone on to organize women's leadership development workshops, empowering other Indigenous women in Oaxaca, Baja California, and Los Angeles during her two terms as the binational coordinator of women's affairs. There is a growing spiritual community of Mayas, Zapotecs, Mixtecs, and mestizos from the Latin American diaspora, as well as Anglos and Chicanos who have been trained as Maya day keepers.[17] Akin to the way many Lakota ceremonies became part of a pan-Indian cultural identity and formation for urban Indians in the decades after relocation days, there is an increasing pan-Indigenous consciousness among the Latin American Indigenous diaspora. Members of the Los Angeles–based Mayan Day Keeper Association, and many others, have been trained by Julio Puac, a spiritual teacher who comes from Quetzaltenango, Guatemala, several times each year to do healings, hold ceremonies, and train new day keepers. In his oral history, Puac explained that his elders speak of this time as one in which the Earth needs her sacred portals reawakened through fire ceremonies (Julio César Puac Gutiérrez, interview with Maylei Blackwell, April 25, 2012). To this end, several ceremonial sites are now spread throughout Northeast, East, and South Los Angeles. But while establishing these new sacred geographies can be seen as part of a transregional production of the sacred and a vital part of healing individual and collective trauma, it also opens up complicated questions about Indigenous sacred geographies in the Los Angeles basin, coast, and islands taking their place on preexisting sacred sites of the Tongva, the original peoples of Los Angeles (Alvitre 2015; Jurmain and McCawley 2009).[18] Diverse Indigenous traditions of land stewardship and spiritual connection to the Earth can serve as an opportunity for connection and responsibility as guests, or Kuuyam as Sepulveda suggests, on Tongva territory, or Tovaangar.

Many of the struggles of the Tongva (Gabrieleño), Acjachemen (Juaneño), and Tataviam (Fernandeño) have been organized in order to protect their land and water, including their sacred sites.[19] Among the Tongva, it is their guardianship of lands, waters, and relationships to those places, ranging from Kurvungna Springs to Puvuu'ngna to Pimu to the annual ancestor walk organized in order to bring attention to the struggle for the protection of sacred sites. Providing a way for multiple Indigenous communities in LA to be visible to each other, and facilitating conversations about solidarities and responsibilities within these complex relationships, is at the heart of the Mapping Indigenous LA Project.[20] The platform features Tongva, Tatavium, relocated American Indians, and the Latin American and Pacific Islander diasporas through digital storytelling projects with community members. We have followed an Indigenous protocol of privileging the original peoples of the land and working with them, and through this process we have found a way for other Indigenous arrivants to engage with the histories and places of the Tongva and grapple with ideas of settler colonial structures and histories. These histories shared by Tongva community scholars help us see that the spatial and place-making practices of Indigenous migrant communities are overlaid onto settler colonial geographies, and that those in turn are imposed on Tongva Indigenous geographies of place, history, and community.

Organizing and Survival across Circuits of Mobility and Zones of Containment

Although Odilia's testimonio illustrates how violence and healing shaped her participation in geographies of the sacred, Monserrat Bernardino's story illustrates how circuits of labor transit the city. These forms of mobility—buses, for example—are also becoming spaces of organizing as what was thought of as hidden, informal, and precarious labor creates new spaces of mobilization. I met Monserrat Bernardino, or Monse as she is known, after she completed the Mujeres Indígenas en Liderazgo (Indigenous Women and Leadership, MIEL) training and was on her way to becoming a regional FIOB leader in Los Angeles and throughout the state of California (see figure 5.5). Hailing from Santa Cruz Papalutla, a small town of a thousand inhabitants near Tlacolula in the Central Valleys of Oaxaca, Monse dreamed of going to school and becoming a nurse. But her dream was disrupted by gendered expectations, exacerbated by poverty and the death of her mother due to lack of access to health care, as she shared in

Figure 5.5. Monserrat Bernardino and her "We are on Indian Land. Legalization Now!" sign at the May 1 march for immigrant and worker rights. Photo by the author.

chapter 4. Here, I discuss how her fate was decided through migration and the circuits of immigrant women's labor that remap the city.

After the loss of her mother, Monse struggled to wake up at three or four each morning and gather wood to cook and feed the animals before walking the long distance to school. During that time, Monse's dad and three brothers migrated to Mexico City and finally sent for her when she was fourteen. She took secretary classes but, but after three months, her family could no longer pay the tuition and she had to quit. Her dad left Mexico City after the 1985 earthquake, so she started to work in a house as a maid, then at a restaurant where she cooked, and then at a clothing factory where she did ironing—all within one year. At fifteen years old, Monse left Mexico City with her sister for Hermosillo, Sonora, where she did housekeeping and worked as a nanny. Monse's migration story north continued when, at age sixteen, she decided to accompany her sister, who wanted to migrate to Los Angeles. They attempted to cross the border but kept getting caught, so they worked as domestic workers in

Tijuana for six months to make enough money to try crossing again. Even then, while waiting to cross, they were running out of money, so they decided to go back to work as domestic workers in Hermosillo for another six months. They finally saved enough to come to Los Angeles in 1987. Monse recalls that the crossing was very difficult, but she remembers that she arrived in Hollywood by car.

I share this circuitous story to illustrate the perilous crossings and the multiple internal migrations that can characterize one migrant's or one family's journey, and that illustrate what Gaye Theresa Johnson (2013) has called "spatial immobilization"—a strategy of racial containment she links to militarization and anti-immigration policies. State strategies of containment, fixing Indigenous people to rural locales or reservations thereby disrupting broader mobilities and territories, as well as displacement and dispossession are both settler strategies of eliminating the native. The transborder community-making practices and transregional geographies in Los Angeles that are analyzed through this research are even more critical, given state-sponsored spatial immobilization that supports capital-driven labor mobility and control. Jonas and Rodriguez remind us that "regions need to be considered within the world divisions of capital" (2015, 6) and call attention to the profound contradiction of labor mobility (7). Structural adjustment and neoliberal policies, as well as military interventions, have created a mobile supply of labor by pushing laborers to more affluent core countries. Meanwhile, the demands of capitalism and colonialism obscure the reliance of industry and global cities on cheap labor through schizophrenic policies and discourses that criminalize migration and produce illegality.

Like Odilia, Monse's story revels that not all violence that women migrants face happens en route. After Monse arrived in Los Angeles, she lived in Hollywood in a crowded apartment with her brothers and some other men who were also migrants. One day, one of the men who lived at the apartment asked her to go into a room and watch a film. When she sat down she saw the film was pornographic, so she immediately ran out, and she no longer felt safe staying in the apartment. She had heard of jobs for domestic workers in Ohio, so she left to be a live-in domestic working for a family. What she found there, though, were miserable conditions, as the family made her live in the garage, made her clean the floor on her knees, and denied her any days off. In addition to wage theft issues, her sense of stigmatization and isolation was increased because of the family's religious beliefs—they were Brahmins—she could not touch any of their plates, cups, or towels. Because she was so far away from her family, she felt very lonely and had to wait three months before she had saved enough to be able to leave. When she returned to LA, it was through working at the Hollywood Job Center that Monse was able to meet with other women who worked as domestic workers. In 1998 they began organizing themselves into a cooperative that initially had about twenty members. She found that the benefit of belonging to the co-op was that everyone was an owner, and together they would organize to receive benefits and health insurance.

Monse's story illustrates new circuits of mobility produced by the labor routes that migrant women travel on crosstown buses from Central to West LA (or from Palms to Santa Monica within the Westside) to clean houses, serve as nannies, or work in dry cleaners or elder care. These mobilities are part of migrant women's empowerment, as they learn to face the big city with multiple levels of linguistic and racial discrimination and to navigate complex bus systems that move the invisible populations of migrant workers in the global city of LA's massive service sector (Sassen 1991). Such mobility creates new circuits of possibility that happen during informal conversations on buses and while waiting at bus stops. The crosstown buses on Sunset or Wilshire are full of students and workers crossing into more affluent neighborhoods to work and study and attend classes. These new mobilities are not just circuits of labor, they are also circuits of collectivity, and organizers within CHIRLA have used them to create the Household Workers Collective. Further, Oaxacan communities are mapping new Indigenous geographies of labor and belonging through their settlement patterns in Pico Union, Koreatown, South LA, West LA, and in unexpected places like Hollywood.

The control of labor and mobility is a long strategy of colonial management, as was evident in the building of the historic pueblo of Los Angeles itself. Tongva, Tatavium, and other California Indigenous peoples were often arrested under so-called vagrancy laws that colonial administrators used to produce an incarcerated supply of Indigenous workers who resided at Yaagna, close to downtown Los Angeles (Lytle Hernandez 2017). Now, transnational corporations within global cities maintain settler colonial structures, and recently migrated Indigenous laborers reside in neighborhoods adjacent to downtown Los Angeles.

Implications of the Latin American Indigenous Diaspora for Indigenous and Latinx Studies

Indigenous migrant women navigate social geographies of cultural dislocation that occur within the immigrant experience. Many women not only navigate the geography of a new city but also deal with the different ways colonial logics are organized across borders, adding layers of discrimination around race and the criminalization of migration as well as the intimate, gendered geographies of labor and care work as household workers (maids, nannies, elder care workers). In addition, their cultural and political organizing and translocal community-making are producing new spatial relationships and geographies in Los Angeles and transforming US Latinidad. These multiple layers of coloniality and indigeneity help us understand how spatial projects such as Odilia's and Monse's sacred geographies, circuits of labor, and spaces of dissent, along with the organizing within the Latin American Indigenous diaspora, are shifting the spatial politics of Los Angeles. Furthermore, by blending critical, comparative, and hemispheric Indigenous studies approaches (Castellanos, Gutiérrez Nájera, and Aldama 2012), Critical Latinx Indigeneities allows us to see how these changes take place always already in relation to the first peoples of that land, presenting members of the Latin American Indigenous diaspora with new possibilities for colluding with settler colonialism and creating new forms of solidarity as they settle into the existing relations of colonial power in the city, becoming Kuuyam, or guests as Sepulveda suggests.

These diasporas raise new questions about the responsibilities and relationships Indigenous migrants will have with the Indigenous people of Los Angeles. The May Day parade has been a de facto immigrant rights event since 2006, and at the 2011 parade, many of the FIOB women organizers mentioned in this chapter participated in a contingent of Zapotec and Mixtec marchers who carried protest art that included a large-scale puppet of an Indigenous woman in a traditional Indigenous Mexican huipil. She carried a sign that read, "We are on Indian Land. Legalization Now!" (figure 5.5), revealing the many complex layers of indigeneity in Los Angeles. Some American Indian and native Californian activists have been wary of increasing immigration to already existing settler structures and of new populations that may burden their already taxed territories and relatives, which is how Tongva community educator Craig Torres refers to what dominant society see as natural resources. Pointing out the relatively recent immigration histories of European settlers who have, ironically, been at the forefront of the xenophobic backlash against immigrants has been a strategy of Indigenous and Chicanx activists, as illustrated by Yolanda López's famous 1978 poster showing an Indigenous warrior and reading "Who's the Illegal Alien, Pilgrim?" Chicano alliance with American Indians in the United States is based an anti-colonial stance that sees Europeans are newcomers to this land, whereas they have long histories of migration, trade, and diplomacy among Indigenous nations. Arguing that Indigenous migrants have landed relations and millennial relations to the land now known as the Americas speaks to the ways immigrant rights activists have tried to naturalize migration as a human right and part of the long past that precedes European arrival, as symbolized by the monarch butterfly that migrates annually between California and Michoacán.[21] These strategies of connection do not override the fact that Los Angeles in not only part of the Indigenous Americas; it is also the specific homeland of the Tongva. Indigenous diasporas create forms of multiterritorial belonging on other Indigenous homelands, scales, and lands.

Migration from Mexico and Central America has become increasingly Indigenous over the past forty years as witnessed by the 250,000 to 300,000 Zapotecs and Mixtecs who live and work in Los Angeles (Bermudez 2018; Vankin 2017) and the fact that approximately 40 percent of the California farmworker population are estimated to be Indigenous, mostly Mixtec and Triqui (Fox and Rivera-Salgado 2004b; Mines, Nichols, and Runsten 2010; Ramirez 2007; Stephen 2007). There also has been considerable Maya migration to Los Angeles, the San Francisco Bay Area, and Houston, Texas (Jonas and Rodriguez 2015), and Garifuna migrations to New York and Los Angeles. These migrations raise the question of the role of Indigenous migrants in settler colonial projects, following the important work of Hokulani Aikau (2010). While Jodi Byrd (2011) complicates the settler/Indigenous dichotomy and Verancini's (2010) triad of Indigenous–settler–immigrant with the idea of the arrivant, naming the fact that some migration occurs through forced displacement/enslavement, there is still much work to do in order to understand how Indigenous migrants interact with settler colonial projects. If we consider, for example, Patrick Wolfe's mantra that settler colonialism is a structure and not an event (2006), we can complicate this argument by seeing that someone still needs clean that structure. In the current capitalist system, because settler colonialism does not operate in a vacuum, those who comprise the surplus labor force are often those who have been dislocated by imperialist projects and neoliberal policies. While Indigenous migrants cannot (yet?) access settler privilege, it is not yet clear what work the positionality of arrivant does and how it might make possible the kind of responsibility (or kuleana) that Aikau (2010) speaks of in relation to the Tongva, Tativium, Chumash, Ohlone, or the Indigenous people of California, for example, many of whom are not federally recognized. Tongva/Acjachemen scholar Charles Sepulveda builds on a Tongva protocol of Kuuyam, or guests, as a decolonizing philosophy and proposal for action. He suggests that "residents of Tongva land (Tovaangar), for example, can be Kuuyam and not act as colonizers or seek to further domesticate the environment for their own benefit. They can be welcomed guests, and not looked at by the Native community as settler colonizers—no matter their skin color, histories, or origins. The status of Kuuyam is neither demanded or ordered. It is instead a relationship offered and chosen" (2018, 54). Adopting the stance of being "Kuuyam can disrupt settler colonialism. It can support bringing balance back to the environment, re-centering Indigenous peoples, and in decolonial struggles to revitalize cultural elements such as the respect for those who transcend gender binaries" (54–55). Critically, Sepulveda's theorization of the Tongva notion of Kuuyam serves as a repair to how the institutionalization of settler colonial studies has erased Indigenous people (Kauanui 2016) and how this field has ignored both their views of nonnative peoples on their land and their approaches in defining who is a settler.

These critically important conversations are just starting to take place. Modes of translocal community formation in the Latin American Indigenous diaspora are based on hometown affiliations. Yet within politically active sectors of the Latin American diaspora, there is also a pan-Indian identity that echoes earlier mid-twentieth-century pan-Indian urban identities that formed because of native relocation and termination in the United States, and that served as precursors to the American Indian movement. Because federal recognition grants uneven power to Indigenous people of the United States, many Indigenous people of California are rendered invisible in their own territories by institutions that see federally recognized, relocated American Indians as the only Indigenous people of Los Angeles. Although pan-Indian identities are generally positive in terms of Indigenous solidarity, both American Indian activists and other Indigenous migrants are increasingly recognizing that whether they are Indigenous to the Americas or to Oceania, they are still visitors to Tongva land. Through a transindigenous dialogue, they can also choose to create relationships as Kuuyam with all the responsibilities that being a good guest implies.

Through the lens of Critical Latinx Indigeneities, we can begin to think about how these multiple colonialities produce multiple indigeneities vis-à-vis colonial management enacted through racial projects of nation-making. In Critical Indigenous Studies, this gives us a framework for understanding divergent indigeneities (what it means to be Indigenous in different colonial contexts), and how those systems hybridize during migration and collide with other colonialities. It allows us to interrogate how, in the fields of Chicano/Latino studies, indigenismo has been conflated with indigeneity, and uninterrogated celebrations of mestizaje have been the order of the day (Blackwell 2017b). Uncritical deployments of mestizaje echo the ways in which the Chicano movement and Chicana feminisms have recycled the Mexican state projects of eugenics based on whitening and erasure in terms of mestizaje discourses (Castellanos, Gutiérrez Nájera, and Aldama 2012; Contreras 2008;

Guidotti-Hernández 2011; Saldaña-Portillo 2001). In the case of indigenismo, recycling these discourses upholds the Mexican state's project of celebrating the grandeur of a mythological Aztec past, while denying the present and future of the country's sixty-eight Indigenous groups—the largest Indigenous population in the hemisphere. A new generation of Zapotec and Maya scholars is challenging the ways in which the Chicano movement and Chicana feminists have uncritically adopted these Aztec imaginaries historically deployed by the Mexican state to reclaim their Indigenous roots (Alberto 2012, forthcoming). By occupying the space of the mythological or the indigenista, Chicano/a scholars not only replicate the state project of indigenismo, they also fail to name the often powerful loss of or sometime disconnection from their indigeneity that is itself a product of coloniality and mestizaje. Further, by going Aztec, indigenists occupy a mythologized indigeneity rather than the historical, colonized one that can foreclose settler and arrivant forms of analysis and solidarity with the Indigenous peoples of this land. A Critical Latinx Indigeneities framework recognizes multiple colonial regimes of racial management that produce "Indigenous" subjects as well as attempts to deindigenize them. To generate solidarities means to understand these differing yet connected histories and the places where the coloniality of power (the maintenance of colonial hierarchies in current relations of power, discourses, and institutions) meets settler colonialism (the structure of settlement that requires the continual elimination of the native).

Coda: The Subterranean Life of Seeds

Now we have a voice. We live in a context of extreme violence and repression. It seems difficult to hold those two historical trajectories together and make meaning out of them. While there is no linear history of progress that can be ascribed to processes of social change for Indigenous women, their gains have been made in tremendous times of structural realignment and social and political repression.—ERNESTINA ORTIZ

• • •

At the twentieth-anniversary celebration of the Coordinadora Nacional de Mujeres Indígenas de México (National Coordinator of Indigenous Women, CONAMI) in Mexico City in August 2017, I sat listening to a speech by Ernestina Ortiz, an early member of CONAMI. I was moved by her powerful summary of the challenges of the past twenty years of Indigenous women's organizing—challenges I'd long been struggling to describe in my own writing. When I began to write this book in 2012, I recalled the despair of witnessing the mass violence of the narcostate through feminicides, extrajudicial assassinations linked to extractivism, and state repression of social protest that affected Indigenous communities in Mexico and left them feeling increasingly devastated and powerless. These feelings only intensified with an increase in mass deportation under the Obama administration and in the numbers of refugees and asylum seekers fleeing from violence in Central America, including many Mayas. It then spiraled to a new low with the xenophobic, anti-Mexican political discourses in the United States with the 2016 election of Donald Trump as president, which translated into inhumane "zero tolerance" policies of caging children and separating families, largely Indigenous migrant families from Central America. Many Indigenous activists on both sides of the border argued that this practice amounts to child theft, as the United States used family separation as a deterrent to migration, deporting parents and losing hundreds of children in the system. Many Indigenous children died while in the custody of US Customs and Border Protection. North of the border, Indigenous and First Nations peoples mourned and offered their solidarity as they recognized these carceral practices of death and the physical, emotional, and sexual abuse of children as part of the long history of boarding schools run by the US and Candadian governments and churches.

The historical context that produced this crisis includes neoliberal economic policies that mandated deregulation, privatization—including the privatization of lands held in ejidos, the collective land tenure system implanted during the Mexican revolution that lies at the heart of many Indigenous communities—and elimination of the social safety net, including cuts to education, health care, and infrastructure. These policies increased poverty, economic insecurity, and precarity, which in turn led to more migration and to the steady growth of the informal economy. This development was coupled with the militarization of the drug war, the collusion of law enforcement and military, and their corruption by drug and human traffickers, leading many social analysts to talk of a narcostate (Fregoso 2003, 2006). Along with this economic desperation, weakened juridical institutions and wide-scale impunity has created a context of mass violence. Violence dramatically increased throughout Mexico during the 2006–12 sexenio of Felipe Calderón, who heightened the war on drugs while cracking down on social protest. Chickasaw feminist anthropologist Shannon Speed argues there has been a "significant shift in the form in the state itself and its forms of governance. Since the 1990s, free market economies in Mexico and Central America quickly expanded and grew out of the control of legal regimes. Meanwhile, the nascent democratic tendencies and fledgling rights regimes, however limited, were quickly sucked into the vortex of mass-scale illegal economies. Drug, gun, and human trafficking expanded as cartels grew in Mexico, feeding on widespread corruption of the government and military and the deregulated flows of capital. Cartels also found a reserve in those newly impoverished under neoliberal reforms" (2019, 4). Yet, as Aida Hernández Castillo (2014) argues, there are racialized geographies linked "to the specific ways in which the violence of militarization, parmilitarization, and organized crime has affected indigenous territories" (2). Further, she argues these "semantics of patriarchal violence" that assert control of "women's bodies through sexual violence and incarceration is a way of demonstrating control over colonized people's territories" (2). This line of analysis echoes the modes of analyis by Indigenous women leaders, discussed below, that see the connection between Indigenous women's bodies as territory and the exertion of violence as a continuation of colonization, which, according to Hernández Castillo (2014), represents a new phase of accumulation by dispossession. The increased sexual violence related to the the (para)militarization of Indigenous territories due to the "War on Drugs" is exacerbated by the way the state has used sexual and gender violence to repress social protest. Hernández Castillo points out that the "use of sexual violence as a counterinsurgency tool is present in the historical memory of recent decades in many regions where indigenous women have actively participated in the struggle for the defense of their lands and territories" (5).

In this context Ernestina so powerfully describes above, how do we hold the space for hope? It was against this context that I felt compelled to tell the story of powerful Indigenous women organizers as I started writing this book, even as the broader Indigenous movement and many Indigenous women's organizations were struggling to find their way in a period of seeming demobilization. I knew their story was too important not to tell, so I put my hopes in the subterranean organizing I saw happening at the time. To those on the outside, there might have appeared to be little movement, but as CONAMI was reorganizing internally, it was simultaneously seeding leadership among the next generation of activists. Activists have long understood this cycle of growth that takes place even when things seem the most dire. When things are darkest, some communities mobilize—often those that have nothing to lose. The resilience of Indigenous people in the face of colonial legacies and mass violence echoed bravely in the chant that many movements used, including in the powerful struggle against impunity of forty-three Indigenous students forced disappearance and mass murder in Iguala, Mexico, in 2014, all from the Ayotzinapa Rural Teachers' College: "Nos quisieron enterrar, pero no sabian que eramos semilla [They tried to bury us but they didn't know we were seeds]."[1] The power of this image is scalar: the seed, germinating below the surface, unfolds its shoots in the soil before surfacing, just as Indigenous people—who have, in their own words, been buried by the forces of colonialism, capitalism, and patriarchy—endure, grow unseen, and emerge into the sun. Like the strategy of weaving scales that I have described throughout this book, the resurgence of Indigenous women's organizing is made possible by their labor of cultivating, organizing, and preserving hope at scales that are not always visible on the surface. What is woven disappears to root into unseen scales before emerging to connect with visible ones, creating a beautiful pattern of interconnection. The Indigenous women organizers I have accompanied used their own epistemologies, knowledges, labor, organizing, communal care, and the fight against the exploitation, pain and struggle of their communities as the hope, sun, water, and nutrients to grow these new seeds of rebellion.

During this seemingly dormant period, for those inside CONAMI it was a period of germination as they reorganized and emerged with a new decentralized leadership structure that included many younger regional leaders. Like so many other organizations that are challenged to grow beyond the founding generation, CONAMI overcame that challenge by taking root in their founding and second-generation leaders while supporting the bloom of a newer, younger generation of Indigenous women leaders. In 2017, in an unexpected turn, the CNI announced it would be running a candidate for the upcoming 2018 presidential election. María de Jesús Patricio, a founding member of CONAMI, was named the vocera (the voice or spokesperson) of the newly founded CIG. As women and men of the CIG, including Marichuey, traveled throughout Mexico to gain enough signatures to get on the ballot, many witnessed the seeds of decades of Indigenous women's leadership at the grassroots level, with roots in a radical democratic movement guided by Indigenous feminist vision, beginning to sprout. Again in 2017, the FIOB nominated the first woman for general coordinator, Odilia Romero Hernández, to represent the binational organization. A few years later, Odilia and her daughter, Janet Martinez, went on to establish the Comunidades Indígenas en Liderazgo (Indigenous Communities in Leadership, CIELO), an Indigenous-woman led nonprofit. Amid these important shifts and developments, the results of Indigenous women's leadership above and below the surface of multiple organizations at multiple scales, the epidemic of violence against Indigenous women continued unabated alongside narcostate terror, the criminalization of protest and migration, and dispossession and repression due to extractivism and megaprojects in Indigenous territories.

In this chapter's epigraph, Ernestina Ortiz, an early member of CONAMI who returned to participate in the twenty-year anniversary, eloquently articulates CONAMI's progress on behalf of Indigenous women, while also acknowledging the devastating context of extreme social, political, and state violence within which those gains have been made. Indeed, the organization itself had named this tension. In a 2016 press release, CONAMI announced its new structure after a series of re-visioning and reorganization meetings. The statement laid out its analysis of the organization's history and the shifting context in which it found itself. The press release opened:

> Today we are marking the anniversary of twenty years of the signing of the San Andrés Accords, where our founding sisters of CONAMI constructed, elbow to elbow with our sisters of the Zapatista movement, where we recognize Comandanta Ramona, Esther and Trini, among other sisters for their strength to include women in decision-making. Today,

we close the circle strengthening CONAMI, taking as fundamental to the struggle, the denunciation and visibilization of femicidal, structural, institutional and political violence. This is a social, political and cultural context where our undeniable exclusion as Indigenous women [is coupled with] the criminalization of struggle and social protest, like in the case of our sister Néstora Salgado [and] the forced disappearances as an act of state terrorism, like the case of the 43 teacher's college students of Ayotzinapa and thousands more. Where the dispossession of Indigenous People's territories is legitimized by the State; where we are made into migrants in our own territories; and the media create and reproduce stereotypes about us as people that disrupt our being, dignity and identity.[2]

Over the past twenty years, organizing has become much more digital, as electronic missives travel at lightning speed. Unlike past generations of CONAMI leaders whom I met at large gatherings, I met Norma Don Juan over email, in her new role as CONAMI's coordinator of communication and logistics, before we met in person. When we did meet in person, it was in Peru, where she was to present on the Emergencia Comunitaria de Género (Gender Community Emergency) network. At the time, CONAMI was using new media to call attention to the ways those counting feminicides in Mexico overlook the widespread gendered racial violence against Indigenous women. The vast majority of feminicides in Mexico are against Indigenous women, yet analysts frame the issue as one of only gendered violence. Norma opened her presentation by mentioning that her pocket was full of seeds from her pueblo and that she was wearing the rebozo her political comrades had gifted her. She literally carried the seed technology of Indigenous Earth science, love, and cultivation and was wrapped in a rebozo, a weaving of horizontal affiliation and solidarity among activist friends that represents Indigenous women's care work. In reflecting on CONAMI's history, she argued that Indigenous women organizers were, and should continue to be rebels, that they deserve recognition not only for raising critiques and questions but also for envisioning and enacting real-world proposals and solutions. She ended her presentation by saying, "We live in a country [Mexico] where we think things cannot get worse . . . and then they do. At the same time, I see we are advancing with the steps of a turtle. We have to plant our seeds. Hay que cosechar. . . ." During our subsequent conversations, Norma framed the strategic planning processes of CONAMI in past years as planting the seeds for the continued work of rebellion. Through that process, she related, they decided on CONAMI's new collective leadership structure in order to break up the centralism of the former structure, share the network's organizational labor and power among several people, and let the orientation of their work emerge from their own Indigenous communities and regions, "from where we build." Indeed, there was determination and quiet reflection during our 2018 interview that took place on Maya territory after leadership of CONAMI stayed to have a closing ceremony to their VI encuentro, debrief and swim together in the sacred lagoon. Norma reflected on the work reseeding rebellion—the work of "rearticulating" the work of CONAMI as a national network; one with a powerful history, roots in storied Indigenous regional histories and struggles. Yet, at the time she came to lead the organization the ground looked largely fallow, although she, along with her predcessor Fabiola Jurado, had been gathering seeds and nurturing the soil to "create the conditions," she told me (Norma Don Juan, interview with Maylei Blackwell, August 12, 2018). The work of CONAMI I described in chapter 3 that nurtured local and regional formations, such as Felicitas leaving the leadership of CONAMI to join the leadership of the CRAC-PC, meant that much of the continuity of their work and their connections had to be rebuilt (Don Juan, interview, August 12, 2018). Their new structure had an elders council and a committee on youth and children so along with the work done at the twentieth anniversary they had begun to bridge the founding generations with the younger ones that were emerging and forge a connection that would help them reorganize and thrive in the future.

The organization announced that it would continue its political work "against the current" by changing the leadership structure from a general coordinator and coordinating council of "representatives of the northern, central and southern regions, of the national territory" to a collective structure that includes two "compañeras from each region." In an open letter "to the founding organizations, members and allies of CONAMI, the national Indigenous movement, and brothers and sisters of the Indigenous pueblos of Mexico," the CONAMI (2016) leadership team explained the thinking behind such restructuring:

> With this new structure we intend to let go of inherited, vertical, patriarchal structures and recover the horizontal structures of collaboration and accompaniment, [thereby] integrating the way of doing politics from the vision of [Indigenous] pueblos. Respect for our ancestral forms will allow us to take decisions together, horizontally and collectively. We materialize the resignification of our identity formally by integrating a council of elders [mayoras] who will guide us with their experience and wisdom to orient the work . . . recognizing these founding sisters and coordinators who have given their lives in the struggle for indigenous women.

The earlier seeding CONAMI did to cultivate new leadership is taking root and the intergenerational conversation has been powerful to witness. In a coauthored essay, Dolores Figueroa and Laura Hernández Pérez (2021) document the critical work of building a multigenerational organization. They show the "struggle for autonomy from the experience of young women has several interconnected scales: The body/person; the community/socio-political; and the organizational/praxis-strategy dimensions" (16). Critically, they argue that young Indigenous women activists add sexuality beyond reproduction to the dialogue, dream of communal imaginaries that add fluidity to urban/rural, physical/virtual, and local/global dichotomies, and fight for a world where individuality is not a pretext for exclusion but the possibility of a collectivity of "others" (17). For them, the community is more porous, fluid, and multisituated (11).

Turning the Soil and Seeding Change: The National Indigenous Congress and Marichuey's Presidential Candidacy

Patriarchy and capitalisms are ruining the world and we have to do away with them. *We* are the answer. We know that these elections are a party of the rich that happen on our backs so we decided to show up uninvited and ruin their party. To find a different mode to govern ourselves according the principals of the CNI that visualizes and creates another world of many worlds.—VALIANA AGUILAR, 2017

As I noted above, the CNI, in a surprise turn, decided to field a candidate for the 2018 presidential election in Mexico. In a move of radical democracy based on Indigenous principals of governance, they ran a collective called the Concejo Indígena de Gobierno (CIG), which comprised one male and one female representative from the 523 communities active in the CNI across twenty-five states, rather than one individual. María de Jesus Patricio (whom many know by her nickname, Marichuey), a traditional healer from Jalisco who was a founding member of CONAMI and a longtime activist in the CNI, was selected by the CIG to be the vocera to represent them and their collective candidacy. Marichuey described how they decided to use the electoral process to tour and consult Indigenous communities throughout Mexico, specifically how the group engaged the process of gathering signatures to get their candidate on the ballot. She explained,

After the meeting we had in May 2017, they proposed me ... actually since October, we decided to run for the 2018 campaign. Those that were present in CNI understood that the circumstances of Indigenous communities had serious problems. It had to go beyond just a simple declaration (which is what usually comes out of those meetings). We have to think beyond. Our communities are being dispossessed of the little we have. We decided to participate [in the elections and to use them] to consult with other communities not present at the CNI. They decided to participate—there's no alternative. Our goal: visibility of indigenous communities' issues. (Patricio 2017b)

The CNI and the EZLN established the CIG via Indigenous grassroots participatory governance called consulta (discussed in chapter 1), and it was approved in December 2017. The CIG includes one male and one female representative from each of the forty-two Indigenous pueblos that participate, a significant representation of the sixty-eight pueblos recognized in Mexico. The CIG organizes for self-government, health, education, and self-defense in Indigenous and non-Indigenous communities.[3] Marichuey recounted: "We decided to have both men and women [serve as representatives] in this council. Women are usually seen as a second, third[-class] citizen. We decided to have a woman and man [serve as representatives] selected by their regions. We wanted to run the Indigenous Governing Council [for office] but since a group cannot run for presidency, we decided to have a vocera and we decided to have a woman [serve in that capacity]. The National Indigenous Congress and the EZLN decided to name me the vocera" (Patricio 2017b). The idea of the vocera emerged because the CIG proposed to run a representative body of hundreds of Indigenous leaders for office, but because a collective body could not run for president of Mexico, they chose instead a vocera for that collective. While on the election trail, Marichuey shared the process described above with news outlets. Yet in meetings with communities, members of the CIG went deeper, sharing the political process and analysis that led to the CIG's formation and its selection of a vocera.

When the CIG toured Los Angeles (Marichuey herself could not travel to California) in 2017, I met Valiana Agulilar Hernández, a Maya representative of the CIG who was traveling with Ángel Rafael Kú Dzul; both are with the Center for Encounters and Intercultural Dialogues and the Universidad de la Tierra, Oaxaca. Valiana explained how the CNI's decision to run an Indigenous presidential candidate came to be:

The CNI turned twenty years old—it was founded as the house of the Indigenous people—before convening for the twentieth-year anniversary, we convened meetings to ask ourselves what we want [now]. For the last twenty years we served as a department of complaints and we [realized that if we] only continued to denounce, we would disappear as the CNI. The first meetings of the CNI were convergences—thousands would come from the communities—and in this one only five hundred people came so we decided to take the offensive. After much discussion and debate, we saw that the only way for CNI to stay alive was for CNI to organize ourselves. . . . So we devised a different strategy to let us travel the country [to] organize ourselves. We formed the Consejo Indígena de Gobierno (CIG) made of one man and one woman from each indigenous community . . . we also choose a vocera for the council. We decided, very clearly, that it needed to be a women even though it was very clear to see the patriarchy was very present [in the process of making that decision]. There was a proposal to select a man and woman vocera, but the women said 'it has to be a woman spokesperson.' It was a long process that was all year long . . . there was a process of consultation in the communities about this process. It was decided that Marichuey would be the vocera and that she would register for the elections [in] 2018 because we couldn't register two hundred delegates from the council. It was a hard decision to use this apparatus that they call elections but we saw it as a strategy to travel the country and not disappear in the attempt to do that [organize Indigenous communities on the campaign trail].

Valiana contextualized the urgency of using the electoral process as a mechanism to organize and as a pretext to call attention to the critical issues facing Indigenous survivance in Mexico. She explained that their strategy extended beyond elections:

So, it is not just a [presidential] campaign but we are gathering our communities' pain and struggles to share. While the proposal was to get to 2018 and win the election, really for the Indigenous peoples of Mexico [the goal was] to continue to exist and live. This proposal was developed from different angles and perspectives and it has received many critiques from the institutional Left exposing its machismo and racism. This is a proposal that emerges in a context of war against Indigenous peoples and against everyone . . . so we cannot stay neutral. The Indigenous communities in Mexico are being forgotten. [We realized] that the country is destroyed and . . . that after 2018, it is going to get worse. The process

[of] displacement, dispossession, the attacks, and massacres is getting worse... we also realized that it is not only coming from above. That the system of democracy is falling apart. The system and institutions are rotten. If we don't want these institutions, we have to do something else.... It is not a problem of Peña Nieto or Lopez Obrador.

Valiana pointed to patriarchy and capitalism as world-destroying forces and argued that "we ourselves are the answer" to building an alternative world. She then went on to describe how the women of CNI and the EZLN decided that the vocera must be a woman and that the structure of the CIG would have a male and female representative from each region.

In this context of war and death, with respect to the compañeros here, it is the moment to listen to Indigenous women and women in general. Indigenous women in Mexico are the symbol of all the unvalued in Mexican society—to be women, to be Indigenous, to be poor, to not speak Spanish. We are not looking to have power to impose ourselves but to walk in the struggle for life—for the organization and dignity of our communities—to walk shoulder to shoulder with women from the countryside and the cities to dismantle the power from above... dismantle the need for the state and these institutions. This is only possible by dismantling the system of patriarchy that is killing us.

Using this powerful vision of women walking shoulder to shoulder to dismantle "power from above," Marichuey speaks of the vision Valentina laid out describing how capitalism "has designed structures of death for our pueblos, that are machista (sexist)" (Patricio 2018). Further, Marichuey shared how Indigenous women's antipatriarchal practices emerge from their daily lives within their communities of resistance. "Women have always been [in the movement], although they have not been visible, they may not appear as much, but they have been [active]. It's been my turn to travel to places and I've seen women make their own decisions [by saying that even] 'if they [men] don't want to [change], we ourselves will move forward.' And then that decision encourages everyone and from there, they walk the path of struggle together" (Patricio 2018).

As she traveled through Mexico to consult with and gather the voices of Indigenous communities without homogenizing them, Marichuey said, "One of the intentions to participate in this process is to visit some of the sister communities that have walked with us in the CNI, to listen to their palabra (word), their problems, and also to lay out our proposal. If they agree, then we will walk together, we invite them" (quoted in Muñoz Ramírez 2018, 165). The route to gather signatures for the National Electoral Institute was paved by the voluntary organizational labor of communities, as the CIG and Marichuey's campaign had no funding, and yet they came together to "speak of impossible things, because too much has been said from the possible" (Patricio, quoted in Muñoz Ramírez 2018, 170). Of listening to the communities and gathering signatures, Marichuey said, "They are not signatures, they are sorrows" (Patricio 2018). Even the process of gathering the signatures illustrates how the system was not designed to allow non-elite Mexicans to have their democratic rights. The official app used to collect signatures was only available on late-model phones and tablets and required wireless internet, which was largely unavailable in rural communities. Gathering signatures was an act of grassroots democracy aimed at spotlighting the urgent issues Indigenous communities in Mexico face. The CIG delegation met with community leaders and Indigenous women who spoke out against the multiple forms of violence against women, which Marichuey framed as a collective violence against Indigenous people—a form of violence that colonizes the heart of the community for capitalist domination. In one of the communiques from "the walk with Marichuey" in Neza (short for Nezahualcoyotl, one of the world's largest mega-slums in the northeast of Mexico City), she shared not only the notion that violence against women was collective violence against Indigenous peoples, but also an expanded notion of relations and connectivity that interconnects violence against any woman to all men and women, the earth, and future generations.

> When they rape, disappear, imprison or murder a woman, it is as if the whole community, the barrio, the town or the family has been raped, disappeared, imprisoned or murdered, seeking in the midst of that mourning and fear to colonize and pervert the fabric that is in our collective heart, to take over all who we are and turn it into the goods they need for the insatiable accumulation of money and power that makes the capitalists what they are. A hate crime is a capitalist crime, so we don't shut up about it and [we] respond with dignified rebellion and organizing because in truth, when the blood is of a woman, it is a wound to all men and women, it is a wound to our mothers, our daughters, to our grandmothers, and of Mother Earth, that is the light that guides us to birth a new autonomous and rebellious civilization that today asks us to rise up for those who are not yet born. (Patricio 2017a)

While the CIG and their supporters were ultimately unable to gather all the necessary signatures to put Marichuey/the CIG on the ballot, the response to an Indigenous woman as presidential candidate revealed the depths of misogynistic racism within Mexican society. The process revealed the depth of the knowledge and vision for building a world in which all forms of social justice could be honored and healed within Indigenous communities and within Mexico. The communiques issued at various stops along the consulta with rural and urban Indigenous communities throughout Mexico were an exercise in grassroots democracy that used the electoral system to break the marginalization of Indigenous peoples in Mexico. On a profound level, the exchange between the CIG delegates and the communities revealed a deepening reconceptualization of social relations and forged new forms of social analysis and political theory that are urgently needed in the time of mass violence. The decision to form the CIG with a female and male representative from each community and to specify that the vocera had to be a women represents the profound effect Indigenous women's organizing and analysis has had on the national Indigenous movement in general and on the CNI specifically.

This book started with a vignette set at the 2001 Congreso Nacional Indígena (CNI) where women in attendance attempted to meet in a mesa de mujeres and were blocked. Chapter 1 also described a prior CNI meeting where, after meeting for a year to deliberate the constitutional reform to article 4, women brought forward their analysis from the perspective of Indigenous women and were denied a space to discuss it. With quick thinking they changed their proposal to have their findings discussed during each working session, rather than in just one, yet the struggle to find space for Indigenous women's voices in those early meeting shows how powerful the growth has been of those voices, and their analyses and organized presence. Almost every statement that has emerged from the CIG and the CNI explicitly critiqued patriarchal violence and systemic racism, capitalism, and colonialism. These forms of intersectional analysis that understand the interconnection between colonial/racial, capitalist, and patriarchal systems of power have emerged within US third world women's organizing (Beal 1970; Blackwell 2011; Burnham 2001; Combahee River Collective 1971; Hancock 2016; Hill Collins 1990, 2019; NietoGomez 1974; Taylor 2017). Yet Indigenous women's understanding of intersectional analysis in Mexico and its diaspora put those forms of intersectional analysis in the realm of Indigenous cosmovisions that honor the interconnection of the Earth, multiple beings, and generations.

Marichuey is a curandera (healer) who comes from a genealogy of curanderas, and she has worked for twenty years as an expert on Indigenous healing knowledges and plant medicines. She has participated in forums to support traditional medicine and to challenge the 2016 ban on traditional medicine that was designed to benefit pharmaceutical companies. Being a healer has led Marichuey to defend traditional knowledges, and it gives her insights into the needs of a diverse spectrum of her community. The consulta with Indigenous communities throughout Mexico also foregrounded issues such as multiple forms of dispossession due to mining companies and megaprojects; agrarian issues and land disputes; and health problems caused by contaminated water and deforestation. In turn, the electoral process allowed these communities to shine a light on the radical forms of violence, injustice, and impunity Indigenous communities in Mexico confront. For example, after seeing the issues communities are facing, Marichuey cried out: "Land is being given to foreign companies, [yet] when people protest, there are jailings, disappearances and death. Violence comes with dispossession and the police, military, [and] sometimes organized crime are working against us" (Patricio 2017c).

Breaking through the media representations that she believes folklorize Indigenous communities and disguise its problems, Marichuey's report "Desde el Totonacapan" highlighted the extraction of gas and petroleum by a corrupt government and its transnational bosses. Using a scalar analysis linking what happens at the local level of Totonacapan, Veracruz to the regional and national levels, she connected the violence of water contamination, deforestation, and the privatization of electricity to narco violence, feminicide, and violence against migrants. Marichuey also detailed how representations of Indigenous people so often rely on negative stereotypes that blame them for their own poverty and the violence on their lands; instead, she frames Indigenous territories through ancestors, language, culture, and resistance:

> The capitalists want to make us believe that our territory is the miles of oil wells, dozens of mining concessions, assassinated women, and the disappeared. But we know that this is not our territory, just like violence, deforestation, high tariffs on water and light, water controlled by regional caciques, and extractive megaprojects are not part of the Indigenous territory of Veracruz. Our territories are the original languages, ancestral cultures, our resistances, community organization that invites us to not sell out, to never give up, to not forget what we've inherited from our ancestors to be protected, that invites us to organize and govern ourselves, exercising that which we decide collectively. (Patricio 2017b)

She spoke out against extractivism and the violence it brings to Indigenous communities. "We are seeing a state of war declared against the pueblos in order to implement the megaprojects that will only bring territorial destruction to entire pueblos and communities. It's a dispossession carried out by the government by means of repressive forces, like the Army, police, although narco groups also submit to corporate interests" (Patricio, cited in Tejada 2019). The presidential candidacy of María de Jesús Patricio revealed the deep racism of Mexican society, as she was continuously dismissed and diminished on the campaign trail. Around the same time, Alfonso Cuarón's 2018 film *Roma* featured the day-to-day life of a middle-class Mexican household, foregrounding the experience of two Mixtec domestic workers. The film made visible the invisible labor of Indigenous women and how normalized forms of racism and classism are in daily patterns of discrimination and belittlement. When Yalitza Aparicio, a Mixtec schoolteacher from Tlaxiaco, Mexico, with no acting experience, was nominated for an Academy Award for her leading role in *Roma*, social media exploded with racist comments denigrating her racial and class background, while others argued that an Indigenous woman was not worthy to represent Mexico (Aparicio 2020). A broader conversation about race, class, and the rights of domestic workers—who are overwhelmingly Indigenous women in Mexico—led the Mexican Congress to unanimously approve a bill granting 2 million domestic workers in Mexico their rights to social protections, written contracts, benefits, and paid vacation.[4] The unexpected presidential candidacy of the CIG, and of Marichuey as their vocera, illustrated how when there was a stagnancy in the Mexican political system, the CNI used the electoral process to turn the soil and plant new seeds. The growth of activist Indigenous women's voice and analysis, both in the Indigenous movement and within national debate, are evidence of how the seeds of their organizing, planted over decades and generations, are sprouting above ground to demand justice for themselves, their communities, and the Earth.

Multiple Harvests: The Campaign for Women's Leadership in FIOB and the Founding of CIELO

Early morning on Sunday, August 4, 2019, I pull into the UCLA Labor Center across the street from MacArthur Park where a few families are gathering to be together on a Sunday. Yet, I see noticeably fewer people in the park due to the palpable fear of many in the community caused by the ICE raids of the poultry plants in the city along with the White supremacist shooting spree that killed 23 Chicanxs and Mexicans, injuring 23 more, at a Walmart in El Paso, Texas the day before. Even with the somber mood, in the parking lot, I greet friends and longtime activists as they change out of huaraches into tennis shoes, pulling strollers and a wheelchair out of the white minivan they have been driving in since the middle of the night all the way from the central valley. Inside, I greet

Gaspar Rivera-Salgado, the Mixtec co-founder of the FIOB, who was the driving force behind getting the INPI (National Institute of Indigenous Peoples) of Mexico to hold a "consulta" or popular consultation in "the exterior" of the country in California so that migrant Indigenous people and Afro Mexicans in the diaspora could participate a trans/national discussion on a Mexican constitutional reform. Seventy-five activists pack the room and I recognize organizers from Mixtec/Indigenous Community Organizing Project (MICOP) from Oxnard, Triqui women from Greenfield, as well as historic leaders of the FIOB from Santa Maria, Northern San Diego County, and Fresno (see figure C.1). All have gathered to participate in the "Free, Prior, and Informed Consultation on the Legal and Constitutional Reform on the Rights of Indigenous and Afromexican Peoples"—an initiative the Mexican president Andrés Manuel López Obrador (AMLO, as he is known popularly by his initials) has been pushing. Once people settle in with coffee, pan dulce, and champurrado, I am asked to help facilitate and take notes for "Session 2: On the Rights of Indigenous Women." Gathered in our smaller breakout room, the questions are projected on a white board. They read: What rights of Indigenous women should be recognized and protected? How should the effective participation of Indigenous women be ensured at the community, municipal, and regional levels? What effective means should be implemented to guarantee the participation of Indigenous women at the federal and state levels?

As the conversation begins, I type notes trying to keep up with the fast-paced discussion but since someone has placed a digital recorder on the table, I stop typing to just listen. I am caught by how strident the women gathered in the room are about the need for Indigenous women to have women's rights. After more than a decade attending grassroots discussions on similar topics, I sense there is no hesitation or the cautious debate I had seen before. The pace and tenor of the conversation is deep, thoughtful, and far ranging. The conversation turns to the limitations of the Mexican government, even though there is general support of the initiative. One woman says that if they had these rights when they lived there (another quips, "you mean if the government cared about us"), then they would not have had to migrate and uproot their lives. As they grapple with the questions, they analyze the challenges to women's rights in their homes, communities and in diaspora. The two frameworks that ground the discussion become clear—there are the political claims to Indigenous autonomy in Mexico, but this group of women is also deeply steeped in immigrant rights. They move on to discuss the second question. There is agreement that within Indigenous systems of governance, they feel women should have the right to participate fully, hold office but also to not

Figure C.1. Consulta on Indigenous and Afro-descendant Reform of the Mexican Constitution, Los Angeles, 2019. Photo by Anamar López, courtesy of Gaspar Rivera-Salgado.

work so much—to have the labor they do count. They discuss the need for economic rights, not just cultural rights for Indigenous women. They want the right to land, to fair wages, and education and health care that is not racist and services that reach them and their communities. As the conversation continues, I note the difference in the kind of discussion now versus just five or ten years before in terms of how the Indigenous women gathered in the room address the question and advocate for their rights without hesitation. I think about all the organizing that has happened, the workshops, and lived experiences that might shape the views of women around the room and the honor it has been accompanying this movement (see figure C.1).

Some seeds of resistance germinate and grow within one organization, whereas others branch off into new organizations. Much of the dynamism of FIOB Los Angeles has been a result of the leadership by the mother-daughter team of Odilia Romero Hernandez and Janet Martinez. After working to relaunch *El Tequio* with a team of seven others who assembled the publication, Odilia served as the general director of *El Tequio*, working with Bertha Rodríguez, who worked as the lead editor. While they struggled to raise the funds to publish each issue—they would sometimes have yard sales to fundraise—the print magazine ran five thousand copies per issue (Mercado 2015). After years of building a women's leadership training program and continued challenges with FIOB, Janet and Odilia began sharing their dream of launching CIELO, a nonprofit that would be led by Indigenous women. They seeded this dream over many years, but once it took flight in 2019, they were in a fight for their lives: the years in which they were launching the organization coincided with the migration crisis, engineered by then US President Donald Trump and former US Attorney General Jeff Sessions, with Central American Indigenous migrants and families at the center. The COVID-19 pandemic hit in 2020 and heavily affected frontline workers, many of whom are Indigenous workers from Mexico who were exempt from receiving governmental aid because they are often undocumented. Janet and Odilia not only stepped up to meet these dire needs, they organized the first National Indigenous Interpreters Conference, the only one of its kind organized in the United States. Their work was featured in *Vogue* magazine, where Odilia shared the experiences that motivate her organizing around language justice:

> What many people don't realize is that there is a lot of racism toward Indigenous people, even within the Latinx community. When we come here not speaking English or Spanish, not knowing the system, and we end up at a hospital or court of law, we're given a Spanish-English interpreter. However, those interpreters are usually not aware of our language diversity—there are 68 different [Indigenous] languages spoken in Mexico alone. My parents came here speaking very little Spanish. I came here speaking very little Spanish. We've gone through this firsthand—we have firsthand experience of the institutional racism toward Indigenous people and also the racism of other Latinx people. (Rucker 2020)

The FIOB began its Indigenous Interpreters program in 1997, focusing on Indigenous language interpretation for Zapotec, Mixtec, Maya, and Triqui members of the community in medical and legal settings; this program served as a model for many Indigenous organizations in the United States. In the early days, the program aimed to support farmworkers and service workers who often experienced injustices because they spoke neither Spanish nor English.

Much of the work was galvanized when the Los Angeles Police Department killed Manuel Jaminez Xum, a Maya K'iche day laborer, in the Westlake neighborhood. Bicycle police responded to a report of an inebriated man who had threatened people with a knife. Witnesses dispute that account, insisting that Jaminez Xum had no knife and that he was not a violent person. When the officers shot and killed him, they did not realize that he may not have understood what they were asking of him, as he did not speak English or Spanish well, but Maya K'iche. He had moved to Los Angeles from Xexac, a small village in southwestern Guatemala, but the Great Recession had started, his debt from crossing had tripled, and he was having a hard time finding work and paying rent on a small apartment he shared with eleven other people. The LAPD shooting death of Jaminez Xum set off a long-simmering set of grievances within the community surrounding the Rampart police station, which was rife with corruption and violence, and led to protests, street memorials for Jaminez Xum, and police cars being set on fire. Following the incident, FIOB initiated an annual cultural competency training for police about Indigenous migration to Los Angeles and invited Mixtec, Zapotec, and Maya activists, experts and academics to lead the training. Training the police was controversial and there was criticism. Some have questioned the efficacy of trainings about cultural diversity and competencies—illustrated most recently by the 2020 death of George Floyd at the hands of the Minneapolis Police Department, which had received numerous diversity trainings. Others have been calling attention to the ways cultural competency training that does not analyze power can often reinforce the inequalities it seeks to overturn (Hester 2015), and to how cultural competence can facilitate cultural dominance (Hester 2016). Others argue for the need for structural competency of the underlying structures of power, especially in medical field (Holmes 2020; Metzel and Hansen 2013; Neff et al. 2020). Acknowledging that working with the LAPD has been controversial, Janet Martinez has argued that members of FIOB do not have the privilege of sitting on the sidelines while members of their community are being harmed. Yet as she points out, "That's the difference with our training. It's [done] by Indigenous people to bring cultural awareness and cultural competency to the LAPD. We want to make space for people to bring cultural awareness and cultural competency to the LAPD. We want to make space for people [so they can] speak for themselves and not just have us speak about them" (Tseng 2019, n.p.). One victory FIOB feels its members have gained with this work is that police officers in the Rampart division now carry with them a pocket card that shows translations of common phrases in Indigenous languages. Odilia Romero has commented that in light of recent events, Indigenous language interpreters' phones should be ringing off the hook because of how many community members of the Latin American diaspora live in that precinct. While initially they were disappointed to have just received one call for many years after the program started, in 2022 they are receiving regular calls.

Odilia tells me that the Indigenous Interpreters program had gone dormant by the time she was elected as binational vice coordinator of FIOB in 2014 (Odilia Romero Hernández, interview with Maylei Blackwell, September 9, 2020).

Odilia's first memory of serving as an interpreter during her youth was when she helped a man from her community with the state barber's exam. However, it was not until after she went to interpreter's school that she was motivated to relaunch the FIOB's interpreters program because she realized that Indigenous language interpreters were not being fully trained. She joined with others who dedicated themselves to learning all the rules of the court and medical systems. Yet she realized what others calling for structural competency understood: that to be effective as an interpreter, she would have to become a language access activist and work to expose the implicit, structural, institutionalized forms of racism and colonial violence that underlie language access. As she has continued her work with CIELO, she worked with others to make Indigenous language interpreting an act of rebellion. She and Janet, under the banners of FIOB and CIELO, organized a second annual National Indigenous Interpreters conference, held December 14-15, 2019, and more recently a third conference in 2021. Given the immigration crisis, such interpreters have become even more urgent given the high demand for trained interpreters who speak Indigenous languages. "Building upon Title VI of the 1964 Civil Rights Act, Executive Order 13166 (2000) purports to require all federally funded agencies to provide those who receive their services with 'meaningful access' to information, including legal proceedings" (Newdick and Romero 2019, 30). Despite language access plans published by the Departments of Homeland Security and Immigration and Customs Enforcement, widespread documentation indicates that detainees receive almost no interpretation. Newdick and Romero describe these "failures" as "overwhelming and nightmarish: interpretation is delivered mostly by telephone, which misses all visual cues and is subject to technological interruption" (31). When interpretation is delivered via video, the video calls are plagued with technological problems. Newdick and Romero continue: "Hastily recruited indigenous interpreters are rarely screened, trained, or proficient in legal terminology. Most language providers are incapable of matching indigenous detainees with interpreters who verifiably speak their language" (31).

CIELO organized a variety of workshops that are tailored to real-life interpreting in Indigenous communities. It provides trainings led by professionals in law, health care, and government. Odilia tells me that they want to begin to offer workshops on issues like secondary trauma, as so many interpreters are working with refugees and asylum seekers fleeing violence and with Indigenous women who confront violence before leaving home, on the journey, and while in detention, not to mention with families and children who are separated and left in horrible conditions (Speed 2019). CIELO's work recognizes Indigenous

Figure C.2. Janet Martinez, Indigenous Literature Conference. Photo courtesy of CIELO.

language interpretation as not only translation but also cultural mediation. As CIELO (n.d.) put it, "Histories of neglect and dispossession, therefore, do not simply inform interpretive practices, but *actively frame* and *structure* the ways in which people organize themselves and how they relate to one another—both institutionally and personally."

Much of CIELO's work has organized around the fight for the revitalization of Indigenous languages and cultures. Their work has bridged Odilia's passion for language justice as an interpreter and Janet's passion for literature, words, and books. Janet worked tirelessly to launch two of their signature projects in 2016. That year, hundreds of people gathered for the first Indigenous Literature Conference, which was organized as a joint project of FIOB and CIELO; the conference now in its fifth year takes place annually in late July at the Central Library of Los Angeles (see figure C.2). The event was initially organized as part of Oaxacan Heritage Month (described in chapter 5) that featured the Guelaguetza and had expanded to include a basketball and Oaxacan band tournament, a Miss Oaxaqueña beauty pageant, the calenda, and an opening event at the Los Angeles city hall.[5] Janet says that the conference was "created to provide a space for Indigenous people to showcase and share their work with a wider public, a possibility that is often undermined by mainstream assumptions of what gets to count as 'Literature.'" Creating a space for Indigenous literatures was initially meant to promote language revitalization, because "many [languages] are in danger of being extinct. By incorporating issues of language into non-traditional spaces, the conference is also pioneering new forms of identity formation for a new generation."[6] Critically, the conference turned into an annual event and a venue in which Indigenous literatures that may not have wide circulation can be seen, and a space for Indigenous writers to share and think together. Importantly, for Janet, "The conference aims to break away from mainstream understandings of literature by creating a space for Indigenous writers to share their work and speak for themselves, without the need to have outsiders, including academics and researchers, legitimize their work or knowledge." The Indigenous Literature Conference is also intensely personal for Janet (who studied literature and gender studies at the University of California, Berkeley) because she has witnessed Indigenous language loss as a member of the second generation of the Oaxacan diaspora (Janet Martínez, interview with Maylei Blackwell, November 6, 2015). Although some migrant Indigenous parents do transmit their language as a source of pride, many more take a more pragmatic approach and want their children to focus on learning English in order to survive in the United States. Some of the writers who have been featured at the conference include Sol Ceh Moo (Maya Yucatan), Enriqueta Lunez (Tsotzil), Natalia Toledo (Zapotec), Pergentino Jose Ruiz (Zapotec), Javier Castellanos (Zapotec), Mardonio Carballo, Francisco Lopez Barcenas, Gloria Muñoz Ramirez, Adelfo Regino, Irma Pineda, Celerina Sanchez (Ñuu Savi/Mixtec), Filemon Beltran (Zapotec), Jorge Cocom Pech (Maya), Yasnaya Elena Aguilar (Ayuujk/Mixe), Jennifer Vest (Seminole/Black), Victoria Bomberry (Muscogee), Juan Gregorio Regino (Mazatec). To support the Indigenous Literature Conference, Janet also organized the "Weaving Words and Rhymes" concert, first in March 2016 and then in subsequent years, to promote the use of Indigenous languages and traditional art forms in rap and music. The inaugural event attracted more than two hundred people from a multigenerational Indigenous community. In addition, Janet has gone on to produce, with Luis Lopez-Resendiz, the podcast called *Tu'un Dali*, which they describe as "a podcast for Indigenous people by Indigenous people. Our love letter to Oaxacalifornia." Odilia Romero and Gaspar Rivera-Salgado have contributed as well. The work of CIELO and FIOB LA show transborder horizontal interweaving across the Oaxacan diaspora that creates important scales of Indigenous women's organizing—ones that have had frustrations and trials but have also led to an expansive growth in organizing.

As I was talking with Odilia while writing this coda in 2020, she asked me whether the original testimonio that we collaborated on could be published in English. As we were in the midst of the coronavirus pandemic, we planned a socially distanced meeting. She called me because she couldn't get onto the Zoom platform and was just leaving a food distribution center—an urgent need because of the financial downturn due to COVID-19. I reflected on the changes in our work, as we used to meet and cook food and have long talks. We do a quick check-in about key developments in our lives, about how our kids and her granddaughter are doing during the pandemic, and she tells me that Poncho, her partner who runs the famous pop-up Poncho's Tlayudas, had a kimchi-making lesson with one of the organizers of the food distribution center (Tseng 2019). She tells me that she needs the longer form of the testimonio we did translated into English because she is getting many requests from the press after CIELO's work was featured in *Vogue* and in Mexican actor Diego Luna's *Pan y Circo*, a series on Amazon Prime, so I work on the translation. Although she is uncomfortable in the spotlight, she tells me that she is learning to occupy these spaces, as she is focused on raising funds for the Undocu-Indigenous fund, which supports those who, despite being frontline workers, are unable to receive assistance during COVID-19 because they are undocumented (CIELO 2020). When CIELO did its 2020 budget, Odilia's advisors told her to lower her expectations—they would not hit the $1 million mark she dreamed of. On the day we talked in September, they had raised $967,000 and had now set their sights on raising $2 million, as CIELO had been selected to be one of the beneficiaries of funds raised during a telethon for El Grito on Mexican Independence Day; they hoped to feed six thousand families. By August of 2022, Odilia shared that the organization had raised and distributed 2.3 million in cash solidarity and 1.8 in grocery cards. CIELO has been on the front lines, holding numerous Zoom-based trainings regarding the correct translation of the COVID-19 virus medical settings for interpreters and providing broader education on the impact of the coronavirus on Indigenous diasporic communities from Latin America—effects that range from a lack of translation for those taking a COVID-19 test to the economic crisis of many Indigenous communities with members who are unable to access the government's relief funds to the manufactured crisis of family separation and caging children, making the Undocu-Indigenous project even more critical (Romero Hernández, interview,

September 9, 2020). Throughout the shutdown of the COVID-19 pandemic, they even continued their Indigenous language justice work launching numerous new Indigenous language classes on Zoom.

This work is urgent and life-sustaining and an important outlet for Odilia since she stepped down as FIOB'S binational general coordinator in October 2020; that same day, she resigned from the organization completely when a member who had been stripped of his political rights within the FIOB as a result of accusations of sexual harassment was not only reinstated but elected the next general coordinator. "On May 5th of 2019, the ex magisterial leader Ezequiel Rosales Carreño was detained and later accused of sexual abuse against a woman who was traveling aboard a bus en route from Mexico City to Oaxaca" (Sirenio 2020). He was eventually acquitted because the woman who accused him was unable to produce further evidence. In October 2020 the FIOB binational assembly, which normally takes place every three years when delegates from the FIOB base communities in Oaxaca, California, and Baja California come together to elect new binational leadership, took place online because of the COVID-19 pandemic. The virtual gathering included reports from the outgoing coordinators, and "then came the discussion to reinstate Rosales Carreño, former leader of the Sección 22 Sindicato Nacional de Trabajadores de la Educación (Section 22 of the National Union of Educational Workers), who already had the support of the delegates from Baja California and Oaxaca" (Sirenio 2020, n.p.). The structure of the debate on whether Ezequiel Rosales Carreño should have political rights was that Odilia, as the outgoing binational general coordinator, argued against it for five minutes and then Rosales Carreño spoke on his own behalf for five minutes, after which two delegates spoke in his favor and two spoke against him, each for two minutes. "I believe the compañera who denounced (accused) Ezequiel Rosales. I believe her because in Mexico women are killed and we don't see justice, for this reason my vote is against the restitution of the political rights of the professor (teacher)" (n.p.). Miguel Villegas argued, "We expel the compañero for the damage he caused the organization with his bad conduct. In Mexico, they exhibited the video where he received money from Ulises Ruiz (the governor who violently put down the teachers strike of Sección 22 which led to a popular uprising), he was given amnesty and after came the accusations of sexual abuse while on public transportation, and for this reason I will not vote that he return to the organization" (n.p.).

In his defense, Ezequiel Rosales argued: "I am a victim within the interior of Section 22, because in 2018 I was a candidate for the PRD and those of MORENA accused me of being in cahoots (nexo) with former governor Ulises Ruiz. In the case of sexual harassment, it was unfair, moreover, the judge who heard the case acquitted me of the crime I am accused of" (Sirenio 2020, n.p.). Rubén Eleuterio Santillán spoke in favor of Ezequiel Rosales by stating, "Compañeros, we must not believe the information in the newspapers because it was in excess, we must not judge what was already judged. Since women have more rights than men, now they accuse without reason (fundamento), it now turns out they can no longer be touched because they accuse one when they do not even tell the truth." Mixtec activist Oralia Maceda, a longtime FIOB member who had joined the organization in 1997, stated categorically, "We do not believe Mexican justice, nor do I believe Ezekiel because they exonerated him only on September 7, just a few months ago. I do believe the woman who was the victim of Ezekiel, because in Mexico women are raped and killed. I believe that women do not speak out (denucian) because of fear and because Mexican justice is sexist [machista]" (n.p.).

For his part, the outgoing statewide coordinator for FIOB in California, Luis López, defended the position of the delegates from California that Ezequiel not be permitted to return to the FIOB: "We believe in the voice of women, we believe that in Mexico, they rape and kill women, we believe that there is no justice for women because of the machismo that is imposed on women who do not have money to buy justice." Ezequiel received sixty votes in favor from Baja California and Oaxaca, whereas California voted fourteen against and one in favor; three abstained. In the end, delegates voted to reinstate Rosales Carreño's political rights, after which they presented a unity platform for new leadership with Ezequiel Rosales Carreño as the general binational coordinator. He was ultimately voted in as the new binational leader.

When Odilia Romero resigned from the FIOB, her communique read:

> I leave happy with the actions achieved in these three years, especially those obtained in the indigenous interpreters program, necessary and fundamental labor in our community for the importance of linguistic and political rights of indigenous migrants. From now on my time and energies will be dedicated to working for Comunidades Indígenas en Liderzgo (CIELO), a nonprofit, led by indigenous women, who have struggled and will continue to struggle for migrant indigenous peoples and women. Our labor in CIELO has already born fruit. In these difficult times of the pandemic, we have mobilized to raise 1.7 million dollars, money that has been directly given to indigenous migrants as financial support to confront the adversities of COVID-19.

Oralia Maceda, outgoing binational women's coordinator, said, "I expressed what I have lived and felt as a woman, I've lived these abuses for that reason I refuse to believe that in Oaxaca they have normalized violence against indigenous women. The return of Ezequiel to the FIOB represents a setback of human rights and those of women. There are women in the organization, but not in decision making [positions], which means that women are just adornments in the assembly. In California, Ezequiel is not welcome" (Sirenio 2020, n.p.)!

The mother-daughter team at the center of CIELO went on to publish *Diža' No'ole* (translated from Zapotec as *Palabra Mujer* in Spanish, literally *Word Woman* in English), a book of oral histories with undocumented Indigenous women with accompanying photographs of the women in which their faces are obscured because of their undocumented status. These women are anonymous; they are identified only by the places they are from—Bartolomé Zoogocho, Villa Alta; Tamazulapam del Espíritu Santo, Sierra Mixe; Cajolá, Quezaltenango; to name a few. The project, a collaboration between photographer June Canedo de Souza, Janet, and Odilia, documents the undocumented, telling Indigenous stories of migration and place, of the sorrow of leaving children behind for their own economic survival, of food and textiles, of mutual aid, communal survival, and exchange. The book plays along the razor edge between visibility and invisibility, between what is revealed and what is hidden, between who and what are inside and who is on the outside. For example, the book includes poems by the famed Zapotec poetess Natalia Taledo and the Mixtec writer Celerina Patricia Sánchez Santiago, in the original languages, untranslated: "We wanted to push people to feel uncomfortable, not knowing exactly what's being said, making you feel like an outsider," Janet said of the decision to publish the poems without translation (quoted in Stromberg 2021, n.p.). For the book, the Oaxacan artist duo Tlacolulokos designed a map in the shape of Los Angeles County showing the eighteen indigenous languages spoken by the book's participants, which include Zapoteco, K'iche, Mixteco, and Nahuatl, among others. With the data from the surveys of 2,500 undocumented Indigenous fund recipients, that represent 11,000 members of their households from thirty different Indigenous communities of Mexico and Central America, Bene Xogsho (Zapotec) cofounder and vice executive director of CIELO Janet Martinez created the *We Are Here* storymap alongside Diné cartographer and GIS specialist Mariah Tso. The map visualizes Indigenous language speakers and communities that have been historically undercounted in Los Angeles County because they are subsumed under the Hispanic/Latino category.[7]

Mobile Indigenous Community Archives (MICA): Rematriating Seed Knowledges for Community Access and Control

Drawing on decades of community-engaged research, teaching digital storytelling and collaborating with Indigenous communities in Los Angeles on community story maps, I created the Mobile Indigenous Community Archive (MICA) project as an Indigenous memory project in 2018. As it was dreamt, and is still evolving, MICA (archivo móvil de las comunidades indígenas) is an Indigenous memory project that seeks to build a digital archive or seed bank of the rich histories of Indigenous organizing in Mexico and the Latin American Indigenous diaspora, with a special focus on women who are often left out of the documenting and archiving process. It is guided by community designed protocols, and a commitment to rematriate knowledges that are gathered. We aim to be of service and provide training and labor for Indigenous organizations and community members to collect and digitize their documents, videos, photos, and ephemera to build and catalogue their collections in ways that make sense to them. The memory projects have community control over what is collected, how it is collected, how it is organized and catalogued, how and it is preserved, and ultimately, how it is used. We are creating an online digital platform that is open to the public guided by community protocols that each organization develops. Within the resurgence of Indigenous activism in Abyiyala in the 1990s, some members of the founding activist and migrant generation have passed on, several due to COVID-19, while others want to use the archival materials to organize and revitalize and seed new leadership and consciousness within their movements, organizations, and communities.

The Mobile Indigenous Community Archive (MICA) aims to rematriate knowledge just as Indigenous nations and community organizations, like the Indigenous Seed Keepers Network, are building their own Indigenous seed banks and seed exchange programs to gather, protect, grow, teach about, and ultimately rematriate seeds that have been missing from Indigenous lands for generations. Historically, academic research has removed Indigenous knowledge from its community context, extracting knowledge and resources to produce reports, policy, and scholarship by and for those external to the community, never returning to invest or give back; never repatriating that knowledge and stories back into the communities or organizations. Seeds, plant medicines, Indigenous science and technologies have endured despite colonial attempts at extermination through a wide range of historic practices that have included the dispossession of land, enslavement, beating and physical punishment when knowledge was shared and languages were spoken, and institutions that enforce not only settler colonial narratives and eurocentrism but white knowledge supremacy. This dispossession and theft continues today through corporate biopiracy, biocolonialism, and capitalist greed that aims to thieve Indigenous plant technologies, science, and seeds to profit off them by genetically modifying them, killing their ability to propagate future generations (so consumers have to purchase seeds from the same companies), monocropping (where genetically modified seeds kill the rich variation of ancestral knowledge/seeds of corn, for example), and patenting Indigenous technologies of plant care and medicinal knowledges to monopolize that knowledge for profit. These actions can be seen in the ways many academic disciplines were created through the colonial endeavor and continue to practice extractivism, decontextualizing and cutting off stories and knowledge from future Indigenous generations, and creating and participating in knowledge systems and modes of knowledge production and distribution that monoworld and monopolize knowledge and knowledge validation procedures, and ultimately profit from Indigenous dispossession. The institutionalization of knowledge, knowledge validation, and organization in archives replicates settler colonial logics and nationalist narratives, categories and hierarchies of knowledge based on ideas and informational logics of conquest, expansion, white supremacy, heteropatriarchy, imperialism, US exceptionalism, to name a few (Adams-Campbell et al. 2015). Ultimately, MICA is conceptualized as a knowledge and memory rematriation, rather than a repatriation, project because what I have witnessed accompanying Indigenous women's organizing for over twenty-five years, and other women of color social movements for longer than that, is that women's (and feminine embodied people's) stories, memories, genealogies of struggle, and histories of movement are often ignored and minimized so they are not transmitted, documented, and archived. Just as Indigenous feminists, food sovereignty activists, and seed justice advocates have shifted the narrative of repatriation to rematriation to decolonize knowledge and rightly returning land, stolen ancestors and material culture to the Indigenous communities they belong to, as well as to return to ways that honor and restore our sacred relationship the Earth, MICA is an Indigenous memory and knowledge project of rematriation. What Indigenous healers and spiritual guides have taught me about rematriating seeds and plant medicines informs our community guided archival practices of gathering (known in the archival world as collecting), storing (organizing, developing metadata, cataloging and indexing), planting and harvesting (giving access, curation, exhibition), teaching (skill sharing, trainings and pedagogical philosophies), and communal labor (partnering with Indigenous community and students to tend to the processes above).

I began dreaming of MICA with Indigenous activists and organizers in 2018. As we dreamt together and built the vision of the project with Indigenous community organizers throughout 2019, it became clear the project we wanted to build was not just as a repository for memory, story, and knowledge but rather a digital, community, and pedagogical space and process for multiple generations of organizers and knowledge holders to contribute, store, organize, and teach with these memories, stories, documents, images, and ephemera. It is a space to exchange knowledge, train and share skills, and offer research and student assistance to organizations and individual knowledge keepers to help them systematize, build, and digitize their collections as well develop metadata, curate, exhibit and distribute this memory work. Initially, I wanted to give community control and access to the knowledge that had been gifted to me over the last twenty years, including organizational documents, photos, ephemera and oral history transcripts. I realized that many younger generations of activists did not have access to many of the organizational and founding documents that had been shared with me over the years. While there is no organizational archive for either CONAMI or FIOB, even if there was, there are challenges to institutional archives in terms of community access to those spaces, the slow speed at which institutions organize their holdings, and the ways they organize the materials according to institutional logics and needs, rather than community ones. Beyond those challenges, both organizations are networks with activists spread across Mexico and the largely Oaxacan (but also P'urépecha and Maya) Indigenous diaspora respectively, which makes decentered digital knowledge sharing and archiving even more urgent. When I started talking with both the organizations and community knowledge holders I work with, the project grew even larger as they wanted to include their own personal and organizational archives, publications, photographs and other materials like the aging VHS tapes Zapotec and Mixtec migrants used to document their own community organizing and lives to mail back and forth to Oaxaca. Moreover, I saw that MICA could not only be a platform that housed the seed banks of memory and story but one that facilitates the memory work of Indigenous social movements. As community collaborators shared their dreams, it also became clear that they wanted to have their own sand boxes and garden plots to nurture and play with their own knowledge and story seeds, using memory work to form seed bombs to plant, germinate, and organize with their communities—working together our seed bank is growing the capacity to be a community memory garden.

In 2019 I began meeting with Maya K'iche scholar and community organizer Floridalma Boj Lopez, who was collaborating with Maya youth organizations, cultural projects and other members, organizations, and projects of the Maya diapora in Los Angeles, to discuss building the archive together with the community organizations we worked with and our students. At the time she was an Assistant Professor at California State University, Los Angeles (before joining the UCLA faculty and becoming my colleague) and that fall we wrote our first grant to fund a digital Indigenous community archive that could be built by community members in diapora, meaning it would be a mobile archive. We were inspired by her notion that Indigenous migrants, refugees and their children carry what she calls a "mobile archive of indigeneity" in their cultural, community, and knowledge practices that include a wide range of stories, weavings, dress, food, art (theater, film, and photos), organizing, children's coloring books and other materials (Boj Lopez 2017). Her concept of mobile archives of indigeneity emerged from her in-depth research accompanying Maya families, youth, and community organization who are documenting and analyzing their own experiences of war, genocide, survival, communal belonging and indigeneity. Her collaborative research with the Comunidad Ixim, which includes members from the K'iche', Kaqchikel, Q'anjob'al, and Xinca Maya peoples, analyzes how members draw together family histories with political insights from their participation in social justice organizing to create mobile archives of indigeneity and challenge mainstream notions of value and what counts as a "cultural artifact." In fact, Boj Lopez (2017) argues, "Mobile archives of indigeneity challenge institutionalized archives because they document Maya epistemologies and experiences through mobile materials that move with migrants to support Maya community formation in diaspora. Institutionalized archives are instead entangled in the consolidation of national power because they are repositories for accumulated information that facilitates a greater legibility in the service of governmentality" (203). Boj Lopez's mobile indigenous archives make several key moves that ground MICA. First, she centers indigeneity to consider memory and knowledge transfer in the contexts of displacement, diaspora, and deterritorialized Indigenous belonging without avoiding the issue of Native land claims. While MICA is mobile, it aims to attend to Indigenous memory of movement and organizing while tending to the responsibilities of place and relation of those whose land we are on. Second, Boj Lopez theorizes how, despite the process of erasure, Maya continuity is based on "multidirectional, intergenerational memory and a nonlinear relationship to categories of Latinidad and indigeneity" (203) and that these qualities produce important new aspects of geographic and spatial knowledges and a sexual diversity and queer knowledge in diaspora.

In the spring of 2019, I was invited to apply for the UCLA Chancellor's Award for Community Engaged Research, which came with funding and the opportunity to build a community engaged class guided by a year-long seminar organized by the Center for Community Partnership in the academic year of 2019-20. For the class to be successful, the community protocols and partnerships as well as the platform had to be up and ready to pilot so I spent that academic year continuing to meet with community partners as they determined which community groups would want to be the first to pilot the MICA and what collections and protocols we would create together. As we approached the spring quarter of the year building the community partnerships and protocols and we started thinking about how to involve Indigenous youth and students, the world shifted on its axis and shut down almost overnight due to the COVID-19 pandemic, which made us realize we would need to work with materials that were already digitized. While I had a dozen or so conversations with individual and groups who wanted to work with the project, a set of Indigenous community archival projects moved to the fore in our rapidly changing context. Zapotec community organizer Janet Martinez of CIELO and the FIOB at the time, was to lead a process of archiving all the Indigenous Literature Conferences and Indigenous Hip Hop Beats and Rhymes concerts she had organized in Los Angeles, as much of the archive that existed at the time, she told me, was housed on social media platforms. Gaspar Rivera-Salgado, Mixtec research/scholar and the first editor of *El Tequio* and FIOB's newsletter (*boletin informartivo del FIOB*) as Coordinator of Propaganda and Press, was working to digitize *El Tequio* and we began a conversation with longtime FIOB ally, the photojournalist and writer David Bacon, so those became the first collections we would work with.

In the fall of 2019, I conducted a landscape analysis, with the support of the UCLA Center for Digital Humanities, meeting weekly with Indigenous archivists and data sovereignty experts as well as an array of Information and Library Studies and Archival and Digital Humanities professionals on Zoom, all the while prototyping the Mobile Indigenous Community platform on Murkutu and building a portal that was housed at UCLA to pilot the project with community partners. In the fall of 2020, I also taught a course I have been teaching since the 1990s, "Women's Movements in Latin America," for the first time on Zoom. My students were thrilled to learn about the Indigenous women's movement of Mexico and wanted to learn more about the members of CONAMI. Since the classroom has shifted to a fully virtual reality, we shifted to working on digital assignments as the pandemic ground on that year. During the shutdown, members of the class began developing a timeline of CONAMI's history and writing biographies of CONAMI members with the idea of writing a series of Wikipedia entries. Working with this team of students, I started digitizing some of the early documents and photos of CONAMI that I had, along with oral histories, and then founding members such as Margarita started to send me their photos. I began consulting with Martha Sánchez and Margarita Gutiérrez about their collections. Fabiola Jurado and Norma Don Juan attended the class via Zoom to speak to the students and view the presentation of the final projects. In the winter of 2021, when I launched the "Indigenous Histories and Community Archives" class, students studied ideas of Indigenous archiving, collaborative research, and data sovereignty and began to process both the CONAMI and FIOB collections. One of the joys and challenges of long-term collaborative research with Indigenous organizations is not just building and learning from activists but rebuilding and learning from each new generation—at least three generations in CONAMI's history. Laura Hernández Pérez helped us see that as much as we had materials from the founding generations dating back twenty years, we needed to include newer materials, documents, and photos that were "born digital," which allows for easier transfer and storage. Yet, digital materials can present other challenges as files spread over multiple computers, hard drives, and phones, this presented another challenge may be lost or inaccessible as technology becomes outdated.

One student team worked to systematize and develop metadata for the CONAMI documents and photographs as well as refine the biographies and timeline that the prior class of students had started. Taking the lead from FIOB leaders Gaspar Rivera-Salgado and Mixtec historian Jorge Ramirez, along with dozens of members, another three teams worked with Zapotec digital humanities scholar Michelle Vasquez Ruiz, who served as the project's teaching assistant, and myself to process the *El Tequio* collection and create popular education modules with the materials; process the FIOB's David Bacon Photographic collection; and develop materials for the FIOB website. In addition to countless hours developing metadata and working to upload documents, we organized a series of viewing parties in Spanish where more than a dozen FIOB members talked story and shared memories of the meetings and events as well as identified members and shared the histories they saw depicted in the photographs. These talking/memory circles allowed students to build metadata collaboratively in real time and allowed FIOB members to do the intergenerational memory work of sharing knowledge about organizational histories, stories of people, and reflections on the campaigns, relationships, and places that appeared in the photographs. Another team worked with Dr. Sarit Martinez, a Zapotec immigrant daughter of Indigenous farmworkers, co-founder of Oaxaqueño Youth Encuentro, the Fresno-based Indigenous youth group "Autonomos," the first Binational Youth Coordinator for the FIOB (discussed in chapter 4) and current executive director of the CBDIO. They worked to develop an organizational timeline, materials and photos as well as helped to create a new website for the FIOB. Their last website had been lost, along with decades of documents and information, an informal archive in itself, when the past leadership did not renew the domain site, showing the members and students the fragility of digital storage. The third student team worked with Jorge Ramirez to develop metadata and organize popular education materials for the FIOB members to use their own history to organize and develop their own analysis of their history. Despite the strength of Indigenous women's organizing in the FIOB, which I have documented, in part, in chapters 4, 5, and the coda, Sarait, along with longtime FIOB grassroots organizers Oralia Maceda and Irma Luna, discussed the specific need for Indigenous women's history of the FIOB to be preserved so the students organized histories, documents, and materials, along with popular education materials for them to use in the FIOB's women's circles. This call to document women's histories within the FIOB feels even more urgent given the untimely death of Irma Luna in April 2022, a year after she made this call to action. In the spring of 2021, I taught a Digital Humanities senior capstone class and the students launched the platform for MICA, continued scrubbing the metadata, and built both the CONAMI and FIOB portals. The students presented their initial work back to the FIOB and CONAMI and we piloted the digital archives with the organizations, having them use them in the ways they wanted, to organize and share knowledge, and this is an evolving process.[8] As we continue to the next phases of the development of the Mobile Indigenous Community Archive, we worked closely with CONAMI to develop their archival materials into an exhibition to celebrate both the twenty-fifth anniversary in August 2022 and honor the life of Martha Sánchez, who died of COVID complications in 2021. As a way to preserve and share seeds of Indigenous knowledge, women's stories, and community memories, MICA will continue to work with activists and organizers to rematriate their seeds of knowledge as they have transformed and interwoven colonial and Indigenous scales across settler borders and Abyiyala.

By Way of Conclusion

Scales of Resistance has highlighted the ways Indigenous women organizers in Mexico and its diaspora have organized and collaborated across scales—both those configured as we traditionally think of scale and those conjured by Indigenous epistemologies of land, practices of solidarity, and pluriversal conceptions of spatial relationships (de la Cadena 2015; de la Cadena and Blaser 2018; Escobar 2020). This project illustrates how Indigenous women's activism in Mexico and its diaspora scales vertically, up and down, but also horizontally, connecting locales, territories, and regions. I have shown how Indigenous women organizers interweave different types of scale that include the formal political arena of Western, hegemonic spaces and discourses as well as Indigenous scales, spatial practices, knowledges, and epistemologies. Strategic movement in and between scales is a form of interweaving that blends various ideologies and standpoints and can also produce a third space. Indigenous women activists weave scale in order to navigate geographies of difference, or how power is configured differently at each scale and space in which they organize. This movement in and between scales also produces a form of *differential consciousness*, a term coined by Chela Sandoval (1991) to theorize how US third world women read power and strategically shift between forms of feminist consciousness like shifting between gears in a car. Beyond feminist consciousness, I have used *differential consciousness* throughout this book to help us understand how shifts between scalar formations produce differential consciousness and how Indigenous women shift strategically between multiple forms of consciousness in the multiple scales of power they organize and weave.

This book centers on how organizers have transformed Indigenous autonomy from political discourse to embodied practice by scaling down to the intimate scales of the body, the home, and the community. Through the mass mobilization following the 1994 Zapatista uprising, Indigenous women activists came together through a process of consulta to deliberate on Indigenous autonomy and create a world in which many worlds fit. Through this process of consulta they grounded Indigenous autonomy in, or scaled it down into their own forms of embodiment and their own lived traditions of dress, weaving, and medicinal knowledges. The practice of autonomy at the scale of the body and the family allowed organized Indigenous women to claim their own bodily autonomy, such as the right to decide if and when to bear children and how many, whom to partner with, and how to live a life free of violence. Tying these practices to a formal claim to Indigenous autonomy has led to a more profound transformation of community life and Indigenous world-making and has sustained their movement in times of demobilization, selective neoliberal incorporation, state repression, recalcitrance and outright negation, as well as increased narcostate violence.

Chapter 1 illustrated how the country's only nationwide network of Indigenous women was built through roots to scales above and below. They built on the strength of local and continental organizing to shape and articulate CONAMI and sustain their organizing when blockages occurred at the national level. Through their organizing, Indigenous women navigated geographies of difference by negotiating the various political traditions, histories, and differences among Indigenous communities and organizations, and across regions, as they built their national network. Whereas Indigenous women activists' strategies for gaining dignity for women and Indigenous autonomy have been focused largely outside of the state, they are interpolated and subjectified by the state, as they do not stand outside power. As the most marginal of the marginalized within Mexican society, Indigenous women activists scaled up and down to leverage new spaces of participation, discourses, and practices of Indigenous autonomy; then they interwove those strategies, knowledges, and discourses translocally or horizontally to build with other Indigenous men and women and with allies in Mexican civil society more broadly. CONAMI restructured its leadership structure and has been recruiting younger Indigenous women leaders, renewing its leadership and membership after twenty years of struggle. To confront the way Indigenous women have been made invisible during the feminicide epidemic in Mexico, CONAMI launched a digital community gender emergency alert and database.

In *Scales of Resistance* I have detailed how Indigenous women activists from Mexico traveled to participate in the 1994 Latin American and Caribbean regional preparatory meeting for the Fourth United Nations Conference on Women in Beijing. Chapter 2 analyzes the way they immediately dealt with stark power differentials at the heart of the concept of geographies of difference, as they had to overcome their marginalization as women and as Indigenous people at the national level of politics even before they arrived at the continental and transnational network, where they felt deeply excluded by the racism, paternalism, and exclusion of its mestiza feminist organizers. Even within work with the global Indigenous movement and their own continental network, Indigenous women organizers must circumvent geopolitical differences between various members of their coalition and their differential access to power, privilege, and money—what Adrienne Rich (1986) called the politics of location (see also Blackwell 2000, 2014; Grewal and Kaplan 1994). They then organized their own meeting in Ecuador to develop an Indigenous women's agenda for Beijing and launched the Continental Network of Indigenous Women of Abya Yala (ECMIA) in 1995, which was renamed the Continental Network of Indigenous Women of the Americas two years later.

Heeding the call to use the Guna land episteme of Abiayala, Indigenous women activists conjured an Indigenous scale of connection, solidarity, and responsibility throughout the hemisphere through their organizing. Through it they created a scale of action that centered their own knowledges, needs, and cosmovisions. They used this Indigenous scale of Abiayala to generate their own alternative form of connection and organizing and to counter colonial regional, hemispheric, and continental names, and the knowledges and political formations meant to eliminate them and their communities as Indigenous people. Ultimately, they found Abiayala to be unscalable as a way both to enter and resonate within the international system and to encompass the great diversity of Indigenous women from northern Canada to Tierra del Fuego. Though Indigenous women organizers in what is now the Americas could not scale Abiayala in that setting, they were able to cast a broad transnational imaginary that has the possibility of transcending colonial nation-state borders and creating forms of affinity and connection with Indigenous women throughout the continent. This transborder and transindigenous political imaginary of solidarity connected to earlier work done in 1992 to unite much of the continent in a resistance movement against the celebration of the five-hundredth anniversay of Columbus and built toward the 2007 passage of the UNDRIP.

Building on what Martha Sánchez Néstor (2005), an Amuzgo activist and founding member of CONAMI, calls the "doble mirada" (double look), and Gloria Chacón (2018) theorizes as Kab'awil strategies, Indigenous women's activism moves between Indigenous knowledge systems, scales, shared political projects, and dominant Western systems and scales to form a doubleweave, or what Qwo-Li Driskill (2016) calls a "third space epistemology." Sonia Alvarez (2000) identifies two logics within Latin American and Caribbean feminist organizing: an identity solidarity logic and a policy advocacy logic. The negotiations and interweaving of Indigenous epistemologies and more pragmatic concessions toward aligning to the regions within the international system are an interweaving of these two logics. This interweaving both contests Western hegemonic feminism and centers forms of Indigenous feminist struggle that not only demand the decolonization of concepts of gender and sexuality, but also are grounded in communal struggle—within their own families and communities, not outside of them. This insistence on working within Indigenous communities, families, and organizations demands that the community at large be accountable for women's well-being (such as their right to live free of violence) and foregrounds the interconnection of women's health and well-being and the well-being of the Earth and community. Indigenous women's activism challenges their historic servitude to mestiza women and the idea that others can speak for them, foregrounding instead Indigenous notions of balance, territory, and collectivity—such as the collective right to breathe healthy air and drink clean water. Invoking Abiayala was an Indigenous feminist strategy to call forward the interconnection to land and other nonhuman relations. This lived, embodied solidarity reminds us that we are connected wherever our feet touch the Earth, and that the well-being of all women is interrelated with the well-being of all people, the Earth, and other beings. Indigenous women's organizing across Abiayala has inspired new Indigenous theories and practices of feminism and has pushed some of the region's feminist movement toward a decolonial stance.

In this book I have explored how Indigenous women's activism takes place within and across multiple locales. I challenge the frozen representations of Indigenous women as outside of time or backward, emphasizing instead their roles in linking and networking Indigenous territories, municipalities, and regions to national, transregional diasporic, and global/transborder/transindigenous networks. In *Scales of Resistance* I engage the idea of meshworks as grounded networks to describe how activists cast multiscalar strategies to move in and between vertical scales while building horizontally to organize transregional linkages of Indigenous political projects and lifeworlds. Specifically, activists in CONAMI recast the local by building networks of connection along different kinds of scale including community, territory, or Indigenous municipality. While they do organize along the dominant scales of nation-states, when that scale collapses or become untenable, they also scale down to state-, region-, and municipal-wide Indigenous women's networks, localizing their knowledge, training, and capacity from national organizing in their home communities and regions. They also weave scale horizontally (translocally) by sharing Indigenous knowledges of autonomy in ways that spark new local, national, and global political imaginaries and networks of organizing, as was the case of Oaxacan Indigenous rights activists influencing the Zapatistas to frame their demands through Indigenous autonomy. Further, activists have organized women's networks that cross municipal borders but honor Indigenous territorial integrity, recognizing the land-based relationships that connect people despite existing colonial borders.

Grounded in communities' traditions and practices of Indigenous autonomy, policing in Guerrero and governance in Oaxaca, chapter 3 illustrated how the roots of the contemporary Indigenous movement and its call for autonomy stem from local practices and knowledges which roots grew horizontally to support other trees and networks of autonomy. Within Indigenous autonomy regimes, women have struggled for their labor, dignity, and well-being, and for their voices to be heard, by scaling down community care and economic well-being to their homes, gardens, communities, and municipalities. These struggles for Indigenous women's dignity and voice have emerged within and through Indigenous organizing and communities, proposing a form of gender activism and feminism that centers communal, rather than individual, well-being and rights. In chapter 3 I illustrated the long histories and intersections of women's community organizing for both Indigenous rights and women's rights. I highlighted how women articulate their own successes in gender-based organizing in ways that foreground a main methodology of Indigenous women's organizing and Indigenous feminisms that is grounded in forming connections or relationality.

This project highlights the experiences of Indigenous women migrant organizers who are building transborder, binational organizations and communities across colonial borders and systems of power. Indigenous migration creates what Jonas and Rodríguez (2015) call a transregion, a scale conjured by Indigenous mobility and, I would argue, by Indigenous community-making and political organizing. Organizing across an Indigenous transregion ties together the multilocal nodes of the Oaxacan Indigenous diaspora, and yet this concept also suggests a unity of time, place, and subjectivity that I hold in tension with geographies of difference. If, as Aída Hernández Castillo (2010b) argues, indigeneity is a field of power, we must acknowledge that such fields are constituted differently across multiple colonialities, scales and borders, from pueblo to cities like Hermosillo, Fresno, and Tijuana to megacities like Mexico City and Los Angeles to agricultural zones both big and small that span the San Quintin and San Joaquin Valleys in Baja California and California, respectively. Neoliberalism accelerated earlier migrations and the current displacement of Indigenous peoples, leading transborder organizers to simultaneously coordinate campaigns for the right to stay home and for recognition of human, workers', women's, and migrant rights—in other words, the right to a dignified life on either side of the border. Indigenous people are displaced by economic and political design, and organizers find themselves coordinating actions across multiple borders and colonialities in ways that account for the differential experiences of Indigenous migrant women, who are racialized and gendered and face economic oppression ways in distinct ways. The women at the center of organizing leadership development for Indigenous women and youth navigated geographies of difference as they organized transregionally, building campaigns that resonated binationally while attending to specific configurations of power in their communities locally. Further, Indigenous identities have been portrayed as static and tied to land; through political and economic design, settler governments and their global capitalism often force Indigenous people to migrate, what Shannon Speed (2017) calls settler capitalism, one of many strategies of deindigenization. The women's oral histories at the center of chapter 4 illustrate how mobility and political organizing has led them to embrace Indigenous political consciousness and work to decolonize their own histories, identities, and life experiences through decolonization workshops and by building spiritual and political communities in diaspora.

Finally, this book centers on the Latin American Indigenous diaspora in Los Angeles, including the political and cultural work of FIOB. I have explored transregional place-making and ways of being Indigenous that are creating multiple Indigenous geographies in Los Angeles. In chapter 5 I reflected on how Indigenous migrants' spatial projects come into complex play with the multiple colonialities of the region that overlay a Tongva homeland. Using Byrd's (2011) formulation of arrivant, I asked how Indigenous migrants transit Tongva territory, opening up the idea that Indigenous arrivants position themselves as Kuuyam, or guests, in the homelands of other Indigenous peoples (Sepulveda 2018). The chapter explored spiritual geographies and responsibilities as well as the labor circuits and gendered geographies of Indigenous women's labor and care work as maids, nannies, and elder care workers. Oaxacan Indigenous place-making is recasting political cartographies, foodways, and soundscapes in Los Angeles. Geographies of difference that I describe in chapter 5 include the multiple colonialities of Los Angeles and how racial and gendered hegemonies collide and hybridize. Indigenous migrants confront a labor market segmented by race, citizenship, and class exploitation and within which mestizo foremen deploy anti-Indigenous prejudice that leads to lower wages, dangerous conditions, and wage theft. I proposed a Critical Latinx Indigeneities framework to attend to those overlapping and colluding forms of racial, colonial, and gendered forms of power, what I have called geographies of difference throughout this study.

Notes

INTRODUCTION

1. In 2010 the Congreso Guna General (Guna General Congress) and Congreso de la Cultura (Congress of Guna Culture) voted to officially change the spelling of Abya Yala to Abiayala. They worked for more than ten years to build a dictionary and subsequently published the gayamar sabga: diccionario escolar gunagaya—español (Gayamar Sagba: Gunagaya—Spanish Scholastic Dictionary). The dictionary, released in 2013, was part of a larger Congreso Guna General initiative called Proyecto de Educación Bilingue Intercultural de Gunayala (Guna Intercultural Bilingual Education Project). I thank Dule scholar Sue Hagland for drawing my attention to this change in spelling and the important political work of cultural autonomy and language.
2. I developed this concept to describe a set of conditions I witnessed as I conducted interviews with Indigenous women in the 1990s (Blackwell 2000). In accompanying an array of women's social movement since then, I continue to see its relevance as an analytic to describe other organizing (Blackwell 2014).
3. Following Lynn Stephen (2007), I do not translate the word *pueblo* to leave intact the simultaneous meaning of a people and a town or place, revealing the socio-spatial relationship between place and peoplehood.
4. Brenner (2011) further argues: "We are dealing not with a nested political economy of fixed, discrete, singular and nested scales, but rather with a multiplicity of scaled political economies that are implicated in, and are in turn productive of, diverse, tangled patterns of scale-differentiation and scale-redifferentiation" (12).
5. In deploying differential consciousness, I retrofit Sandoval's model (in homegirl homage). In her original formulation, she fought against the erasure of US third world women in typologies of US feminism by describing the ways women of color feminists move in between modes of consciousness like a differential on the gears of a car. Rather than getting stuck in narrow forms of consciousness (liberal, radical, cultural, separatist), her fifth gear, or mode of consciousness, overrides and reconstructs the other modes it moves between. She acknowledged how differential consciousness would be transformed by multiply situated actors in diverse contexts, arguing that it was not bound but "a theory and method of oppositional consciousness that rose out a specific deployment, that is, out of a particular tacti-

cal expression of US third world feminist politics that more and more became its overriding strategy" (Sandoval 1998, 368; italics in the original).

6   Feminist scholar Sonia Alvarez (2000, 2010) has explored this key challenge of Latin American social movements, theorizing the selective co-optation of women's rights discourse and two distinct logics of organizing that have emerged in the context of neoliberal governance, increased "ngo-ization," and the transnationalization of social movements.

7   See also Inda (2006) and Ong (2006).

8   Lemke (2001) argues that this is a technique of power that harmonizes collective and individual bodies, corporations, states, universities to be "lean," "flexible," and "autonomous" as well as an "integral link between micro- and marco-political levels of analysis (e.g., globalization or competition for 'attractive' sites for companies and personal imperatives as regards beauty or a regimented diet)" (203). Critically, what he doesn't mention is how both these processes are gendered and are seen upon recruitment of transnational capital to maquiladoras (export processing zones) in Mexico, and the forms of beauty pageants and gendered surveillance and regulation that are widespread in such industries.

CHAPTER 1. THE PRACTICE OF AUTONOMY

1   Unless otherwise noted, all translations by author.

2   For a history of the way autonomy developed as a shared framework of meaning, see Carlsen (1999, 45–70) and Stephen (2003).

3   Melissa Forbis (2003) found a similar pattern in which Indigenous women collectively engage in autonomy as part of Zapatista base communities and at the individual level of their daily lives.

4   Whereas many Indigenous communities in Chiapas, Oaxaca, Guerrero, and Michoacán have declared themselves autonomous, many other communities that are not specifically Indigenous have also adopted the Zapatista philosophy of autonomy to protest the lack of social services under neoliberalism. See, for example, Tellez (2005, 2021).

5   The "right to have rights" was invoked in 1994 both by Dagnino (1994) and by the Zapatistas. See also N. Harvey (1998), and for an earlier formulation of the right to have rights, see Arendt (2000).

6   IUP Cultural Studies Working Group (1987); Rosaldo (1994); Flores and Benmayor (1997).

7   Ong (1996, 737) sees citizenship as "a cultural process of 'subject-ification'" in the Foucaldian sense of self-making and being-made by power relations that produce consent through schemes of surveillance, discipline, control, and administration (Foucault 1989, 1991).

8   Because research is a relational activity, it is important to note that I met most of these activists when I was in my twenties, and at that time, I was generally the same age as the younger generation. Our proximity in age, class, and indigeneity brought us closer as we built our shared sense of collaborative and activist research. I hung out with organizers while we created photocopies, put together folders, picked up food, and performed other tasks for the national meetings CONAMI hosted.

At that time, we were all young, unmarried women in the movement. Whereas some of those activists are now national and international leaders, some did go on to marry, while many others stayed unmarried. For most of this twenty-year period, I was still considered a young woman because I am queer and was, until recently, without children. In the context of migrant Indigenous women's organizing, women I work with are my age and yet they are referred to as "Doña" because they have grown children. In the life cycle of those whom I work with, I am often seen as a perpetually young woman because of my delayed motherhood and my unmarried, queer femininity. Finally, well into my fifties I can say that is changing.

9 "Indian from the hills" is a racial slur that refers to stereotypes of the Indigenous, rural poor as ignorant, backward, and dirty.

10 See Palomo (1996), which includes the "Conclusiones de Encuentro Nacional de las Mujeres de ANIPA," "El Mesa de Mujeres del Foro Nacional Indígena (convocado por los Zapatistas y la COCOPA)," and "La Mesa del Diálogo." See also "Encuentro Nacional de Mujeres de la Asamblea Nacional Indígena para la Autonomía (ANIPA)," in Lovera and Palomo (1999, 363).

11 The dialogues focused on Indigenous rights and culture were subdivided into six aspects: (1) autonomy; (2) justice; (3) political representation and participation; (4) situation, rights, and culture of Indigenous women; (5) means of communication; and (6) promotion and development of Indigenous culture.

12 Convention 169 of the International Labor Organization, passed in 1989, is important because it is the only international treaty open for ratification that deals exclusively with the rights of Indigenous peoples. The law recognizes Indigenous peoples as collective subjects with the right to self-determination and right to control their own institutions, ways of life, and economic development. It has two important components: it recognized (1) the right to prior consultation on any projects that affect Indigenous peoples and (2) Indigenous peoples' right to maintain and strengthen their identities, languages, and religions. With its forty-six articles, Convention 169 sets minimum standards of respect for Indigenous peoples' rights including collective land ownership, management of natural resources on their territories, and preservation of traditional knowledges.

13 I was initially scheduled to interview Margarita in 1999, while she served at the Secretariat of Indigenous Peoples for the PRD in Mexico City. After waiting for hours in the office, I left, hoping that I would meet her another time. That time came in Durban, South Africa, at the UN World Conference against Racism. After our interview, I stowed my backpack under the table at our group's booth and we went to see Fidel Castro address the NGO forum and the thousands of antiracism activists gathered there. Unfortunately, my backpack was stolen, so I relied on my notes from our first interview. After many years of working together, we joked many times about these false starts and had a long interview session in 2014, when we completed two interviews as she was visiting Los Angeles. We edited those interviews together when I stayed with her in San Cristobal de las Casas in 2018 before the EZLN Encuentro Internacional de Mujeres que Luchan.

14 See, for example, "Mujeres indígenas de Chiapas: Nuestros derechos, costumbres y tradiciones," a pamphlet originally published by K'inal Ansetik and the Unión

Regional de los Altos de Chiapas (republished in Lovera and Palomo 1999, 65). For a rich discussion of women's organizing in Chiapas before 1994, the impact of the Zapatista uprising, and women's organizing after 1994, including the National Convention of Women, see Stephen (1998).

15 Hernández Castillo (1998b, 131) discussed the State Convention of Chiapanecan Women in September 1994 as an important space where women working in mixed organizations could reflect on the way in which the issues they deal with in peasant and Indigenous organizations, and it brought together urban mestizas, members of NGOs, feminists and nonfeminists, and members of ecclesiastical base communities, as well as Tzetzal and Tzotzil women from the highlands, members of weavers' and artisans' cooperatives, midwives, and Tojola'bal, Chol, Mam, and mestiza women from the jungle and the coast.

16 This wording comes from an early national Indigenous women's meeting in August 1995 at the third Asamblea Nacional Indígena Plural por la Autonomía. For examples of these discussions, see Lagarde (1999); Palomo, Castro, and Orci (1999); and *Propuestas de las mujeres indígenas al Congreso Nacional Indígena: Seminario Legislación y Mujer: Reformas al artículo 4 constitucional*. These discussions took place in many arenas, including the Encuentro con Mujeres Zapatistas during the Consulta nacional por el respeto de los derechos indígenas y para el termino de la guerra de exterminación, Foro Cultural Azcapotzalco, March 16, 1999; Taller Nacional: Las Mujeres Indígenas en el Proceso Autonómico, organized by CONAMI, August 20 and 21, 1999, México, DF; and Segundo Encuentro Nacional de Mujeres Indígenas, organized by CONAMI, Chilpancingo, Guerrero, March 31–April 2, 2000.

17 ANIPA was formally established after the second National Indigenous Convention in Juchitán, Oaxaca, and after the dissolution of the National Democratic Convention, to unite Indigenous organizations as a sector. In April of 1995, ANIPA met in Mexico City for the first time to discuss proposals for constitutional reform and the creation of autonomous regions in Mexico. They participated in the San Andrés Accords, supported the COCOPA, attended the Democratic National Convention convened by the EZLN. They have had political alliances with the PRD and previously participated with the CNI.

18 After some years, there was a split between those who wanted to work independently from K'inal Antsetik Distrito Federal (K'inal DF), arguing that Indigenous women should be autonomous, and those who wanted to stay affiliated. The coordinator of K'inal DF at the time, Nellys Palomo, found the debate painful because of her close relationship with many of the Indigenous women activists and her own Colombian Afro-descendant identity, which she noted was an Afro-Indigenous one. CONAMI eventually became independent, although several founding members continued to work with K'inal DF through their maternal mortality work and early work accompanying the founding of CAMI in Guerrero.

19 The seminar, organized by K'inal Antsetik and the Servicio Desarrollo y Paz Huasteca Potosina (Development and Peace Service Huasteca Potosina), was held from May to December 1996; meetings on two days of each month brought together Indigenous women leaders, legal scholars, and women's rights experts.

20 Speech republished in *La Jornada Perfil*, March 29, 2001. Other essays also analyze Comandanta Esther's speech: see Hernández Castillo (2005), which includes an important summary of the critiques of Indigenous normative systems, or usos y costumbres; and Marcos (2005).
21 *La Jornada Perfil*, March 29, 2001.
22 The Institutional Revolutionary Party (known as PRI, the acronym of its Spanish name, Partido Revolucionario Institucional) was the hegemonic political force in Mexico for more than seventy years until the center-right PAN won the presidency in 2000. Those on the Left, however, also have perspectives that are informed by deeply embedded forms of cultural racism and coloniality.
23 Comments given at the 10th Latin American and Caribbean Feminist Encuentro where Martha Sánchez challenged the racism of mestiza feminists, arguing that they replicated the logic of racist legislators in México when the denied Indigenous people their right to autonomy based on a false concern for gender.

CHAPTER 2. ABIAYALA AS SCALE

1 By the tenth gathering of ECMIA in 2013, the network counted twenty-three organizations from nineteen countries, as membership changes from gathering to gathering. The Guna Intercultural Bilingual Education Project of the General Guna Congress published a new dictionary in 2013—in which they proposed the new spelling of Abiayala. In a section of the dictionary titled "Reglas básicas de escritura y lectura de gunagaya" ("Basic Rules of Gunagaya Reading and Writing"), the authors explain the purpose the new spelling of *Abiayala*: in dulegaya (the Guna language), "the elision of letters and/or syllables in a word is very common. . . . This permits the union of words for the formation of more precious concepts. For a better conceptual definition, it is also common to unify entire terms. For example, Abiayala (Abia + Yala), Gunayala (Guna + Yala); gunadule (guna + dule); sagladummad (sagla + dummad); igwawala (igwa + wala); dulegaya (dule + gaya)" (Orán and Wagua 2010, 14).
2 I borrow the concept of the wellspring from Linda Burnham (2001) who, after our conversations about how the social movement roots of concepts like intersectionality of the 1960s and 70s are often erased in academic knowledge production, wrote an important article recentering women of color, theorizing simultaneous and intersecting forms of oppression and multiple fronts of struggle.
3 "The Road to Huairou" (1996).
4 Sofía Robles H., Women's Commission of Servicios del Pueblo Mixe (SER), news release, August 4, 1995. Document archived at CIMAC, Communicación y Información de la Mujer, Mexico City. The press release was sent to Mexico from the First Continental Encuentro.
5 With financial support from the UN Population Fund of Ecuador, encuentro participants worked for five days to present their petition to Virginia Vargas, NGO coordinator of Latin America and the Caribbean. See Vargas (1998) for further information on the Beijing process in Latin America.
6 For a full discussion of results, see *Declaración del Sol* (1995). In addition to interviews conducted with Robles, Gutiérrez, and Sánchez in the late 1990s and early 2000s,

I conducted new interviews with all three during 2014–17. The wording "First Nations of Abya Yala" signals an important bridging of Northern and Southern traditions of Indigenous women's organizing. It uses the verbiage *First Nations*, a reference to how Indigenous nations are referred to in the settler colonial Canadian context. Use of *First Nations*, along with *Abya Yala*, the Guna word that refers to the land of all that is now the Americas, is an important intervention in asserting nation-to-nation relationships among Indigenous nations and states, especially in Latin America, where Indigenous people are often referred to as ethnicities subsumed by nations.

7   A copy of both the English and Spanish versions of the Beijing Declaration of Indigenous Women, Huairou, 1995, published for the Global Conference of Indigenous Women in Lima, Perú, in 2013 in preparation for Beijing+20 global process can be found at the Mobile Indigenous Community Archive: https://mica.pre.ss.ucla.edu.

8   Although this definition comes from the dictionary developed by the Guna Congress, the Abiayala spelling had also been previously published by Aiban Wagua in his 2007 book, *Así lo vi y así me lo contaron: Datos de la revolución Kuna*.

9   I thank Emil Keme for his time and generosity, and for always willing to be in dialogue with me about his conceptualizations of Abiayala and to share his writings as they developed. We met and have collaborated as founding members of the Abiayala Working Group in the Native American and Indigenous Studies Association.

10 The Guna land struggle involved the US investor Thomas M. Moody, who prohibited the Guna from fishing after he "bought" the island of Pindertupi in the Guna Yala territory in 1977. After a protracted struggle, which included Guna demands to the then president that went ignored, young Guna militants attacked Moody and his wife, burned down their hotel and yacht, and killed two policemen. The Guna won a legal claim to defend their territories and autonomy, and the island of Pidertupi passed to the General Guna Congress (Keme 2018).

11 "About Abya Yala Net," NativeWeb, accessed September 21, 2017, http://abyayala.nativeweb.org/about.html.

12 Translations are mine unless otherwise noted.

13 Pamphlet, Enlace Continental de Mujeres Indígenas, collection of the author, n.d.

14 After attempting to be in the Northern network for several years, Mexico broke off and became its own region. Years later, the Caribbean also became a region within the network, so now regions include North, Mexico, Caribbean, Central, and South America. The working commissions are Central Commission, Commission on Commercialization and Intellectual Property, Commission on International Instruments (which works on conventions and treaties that affect Indigenous women), and the Communications Secretariat.

15 "Enlace Continental de Mujeres Indigenas de las Americas," organizational documents, 2015, collection of the author.

16 "Enlace Continental de Mujeres Indigenas de las Americas."

17 For a history of the encuentros and questions of diversity, see Alvarez et al. (2002); organizers of the tenth encuentro used that piece to think through questions of difference. The theme of the tenth encuentro engaged questions of feminism and democracy. One central way to deal with axes of difference was through Diálogos

Complejos, which included "Feminism and Strategies to Confront Racism in a Democratic Latin America," "Feminism against Ethnocentrism for Latin American Democracy," "Feminism Youth and Power: Alternatives to Commercialization and Marginalization in Search of Democratic Perspectives," and "Feminism and Lesbian Sexualities and Democracy."

18 Myrna Cunningham, a Miskita leader from Nicaragua, details two examples of this difficulty: "Recently, I was invited to give a lecture in the US to a group of feminist studies students. I was in the middle of describing how resource privatization threatens Indigenous Peoples on the North Atlantic Coast of Nicaragua, where I am from, when the professor stopped me. 'We were really hoping you could speak from your experience as a woman, not so much as an Indigenous person,' she said in a tone meant to be encouraging" (2006, 55). In chapter 2 of her book *Multiple InJustices* (2016), Rosalva Aída Hernández Castillo also reports painfully being invited to sit on a panel that repeatedly did this to Indigenous women community leaders.

19 This document entitled "Dualidad y Complementaridad" is available in the Mobile Indigenous Community Archive: https://mica.pre.ss.ucla.edu.

CHAPTER 3. REBELLION AT THE ROOTS

1 See, for example, the 2015 ECMIA report, "Nada Sobre Nosotras Sin Nosotras. Beijing+20 y Las Mujeres Indígenas de las Américas: Avances, Vacíos y Desafíos."

2 When we originally met in 1999, Sofía shared her experiences building CONAMI and ECMIA (detailed in chapter 2). We met up again in 2011 in Oaxaca City and then in 2015 in Los Angeles.

3 A cargo is a position of responsibility, and sometimes leadership, within an Indigenous governance system.

4 In Mexico, some professional and technical degrees require a year of "social service" to the nation in order for students to receive their license and title. It is seen as a remuneration to society in the form of social service for the benefits students received during their training, usually in public universities.

5 At the time, Rodolfo Stavenhagen was a research professor at El Colegio de Mexico who served as part of the mediation between the Mexican government and the EZLN and had been appointed special rapporteur of the UN Human Rights Commission on the rights and fundamental freedoms of Indigenous people.

6 Law 701 of Recognition, Rights, and Culture of the Indigenous Pueblos and Communities of the State Guerrero (Ley 701 de Reconocimiento, Derecho, y Cultural de los Pueblos y Comunidades Indigenas del Estado de Guerrero) was approved in April 2011. According to Sierra, the law has "innovative aspects in its formulation," (Sierra 2015, 141) because it recognizes the CRAC and auxiliary community police in its chapter 37.

7 Hailing from Santa María Alotepec, Regino Montes was a founder of SER, an advisor to the EZLN, and Secretary of Indigenous Affairs for the State of Oaxaca under Governor Gabino Cué. Most recently, in 2018 he was tapped to head the Instituto Nacional de los Pueblos Indígenas by Mexican President Andrés Manuel López Obrador.

8   When I first arrived in Mexico to conduct research, I met with a feminist academic in Mexico City who told me that Sofía Robles was no "professional Indian." She went on to suggest that this meant that Sofía did not live in the city and may not even have a phone. It was true that at that time Sofía did live in Tlahuitoltepec, a municipal center, rather than in Oaxaca City or Mexico City, but she certainly had a phone, a fax machine, and a computer. This interaction illustrated a certain disdain for Indigenous activists, especially those who do not stay in their "place," these bounded locales that stereotypically signify Indigenous authenticity, but are in reality a form a what Gaye Theresa Johnson (2013) calls "spatial immobilization."

9   Sofia married Floriberto Díaz, a Mixe anthropologist and political activist who created Comité de Defensa de los Recursos Humanos y Culturales Mixes (Committee in Defense of Mixe Human and Cultural Resources, CODREMI) in the early 1980s. CODREMI's demands included land reform and transportation and access to markets for their products, and they emphasized communal self-determination of territory (land and natural resources) and autonomy for Indigenous pueblos. CODREMI's work has continuity in the Asamblea de Autoridades Mixes (Assembly of Mixe Authorities) and in SER. Díaz was an early theorist of comunalidad (communalism), an Indigenous philosophy of collective identity based on communal labor and belonging. For more on Díaz's writings, see Robles Hernández and Cardoso Jiménez (2007).

10 SER was always a multiscalar organization focusing on local issues such as economic development and community-based credit and organizing producers to build regional networks, for example, the 2001 organizing effort with seventeen Mixe communities to create the Assembly of Mixe Producers, as well as building a national Indigenous rights movement. For more about SER, see Mejía Pinneros and Sarmiento (1987).

11 Since the time of this interview, one municipality has changed to election by political party rather than by Indigenous normative systems.

12 The ritual transfer of power bestowed by the sacred bastón de mando (staff of rule) that symbolically represents that the care of the people is entrusted to the leader.

13 "The school of leña" refers to the school of women's work that involves not only cooking but also gathering water and firewood, or leña. It refers to the idea that women may not have the same educational opportunities as men, but they have the experience they gain after many years at the school of hard work.

14 Jeffery Rubin (1997) has previously argued that many in Indigenous communities such as those in the isthmus of Oaxaca have lived in de facto regional autonomy because of their distance from, and the highly centralized form of, the Mexican government in the capital, which has produced the context in which Indigenous social movements such as the Coalición Obrera, Campesina, Estudiantil del Istmo emerge.

15 REDMMI was supported by SER in collaboration with the Consoricio para el Diálogo Parlamentario y la Equidad Oaxaca (Consortium for Parlimentary Dialogue and Equity Oaxaca) and the Red por los Derechos Sexuales y Reproductivos en México (Network for Sexual and Reproductive Rights of Mexico), and had the backing of the municipal and communal authorities of each of the regions where the encuentros have been.

16 *Red de Mujeres Mixes*, pamphlet, n.d., in the author's collection.
17 *Red de Mujeres Mixes*, pamphlet.
18 *Red de Mujeres Mixes*, pamphlet.

CHAPTER 4. GEOGRAPHIES OF DIFFERENCE

1 For that meeting, I had been charged with video-recording the event and serving as one of the scribes documenting the proceedings for FIOB—one of the many roles I have been assigned while collaborating with FIOB during the the past seventeen-plus years. I have also helped design and support implementation of the women's leadership development programs (the Mujeres Indígenas en Liderazgo [MIEL] program described here), applied for funding, created before-and-after videos of participants, and developed collaborative research projects including Otros Sabres and Mapping Indigenous LA, discussed in this chapter.
2 A few exceptions include Maura Diaz who was elected to the binational vice coordinator position in 2009, and Odilia Romero Hernández, who was later elected to serve as coordinator general of the organization in 2014, the only woman to hold this position.
3 Cargos are part of the positions of responsibility within the collective labor, or tequio, that helps define Oaxacan Indigenous forms of community belonging.
4 The literal saying is "Cuando un mujer advanza, ningún hombre retrocede" ("When a woman steps forward, no man steps back [or is left behind]"). This saying has been used as the title of a film about Zapotec feminist rapper Mare and is a common slogan among Zapatista autonomous communities which is even woven into their artesania (artisanal weavings, bags, blouses, and even tortilla warmers).
5 For more information on Indigenous farmworkers, see Mines, Nichols, and Runsten (2010). For a wealth of information and to access the Indigenous Farmworker Study, see "Indigenous Mexicans in California Agriculture," accessed September 14, 2014, http://Indigenousfarmworkers.org/.
6 Tragically, Irma Luna died in April of 2022 as this book was going to press. For more on her life, see https://www.centrobinacional.org/post/irma-luna-ortega-presente.
7 Recent state strategies for controlling and regulating human mobility have scholars examining the ways in which mobility and migration have been criminalized through discourses of illegality and how they have produced legal violence. See, for example, De Genova (2004). Menjívar and Abrego argue that immigration law and its implementation at the federal, state, and local levels are a form of legal violence "that not only restricts immigrant women's ability to mother their children but also brings suffering to these women as mothers" (2011, 9).
8 In his 2002 essay "Lessons from Mexico-U.S. Civil Society Coalitions," Jonathan Fox differentiates between transnational networks, coalitions, and social movements in a sobering analysis of what had, up to that point, been quite celebratory claims about the possible power of civil society as a counterweight to global capitalism. Briefly, Fox argues that networks are comprised of civil society actors who are connected and in communication but not necessarily coordinated, whereas coalitions are networks in action mode with shared targets, goals, and mutual

trust. Fox states that migrant Indigenous organizing is emblematic of transnational social movements in terms of the higher density and cohesion possible when an organization such as FIOB literally crosses borders. Lynn Stephen (2007, 2013) also developed these insights with rich ethnographic detail.

9   I first elaborated the idea "geographies of difference" in my 2000 dissertation to describe how effective transnational social movements cross not only the borders of nation-states but also configurations of power such as race, class, gender, and sexuality. Other researchers have made similar arguments, noting that migrants navigate multiple borders of nation-states and categories of power, for example, Lynn Stephen's (2007) concept of the transborder. Edward McCaughan has likewise approached the study of art and social movements through a comparative framework across three different locations—Oaxaca, Mexico City, and California—by analyzing how "the particularities of each movement were shaped by local variations in the prevailing regimes of accumulation, representation, and signification" (2012, 2).

10 One unexplored aspect of transnational social movements is not the efficacy of framing across borders or the coordination of multisited mobilization but the power of diaspora and diasporic subjectivities in combination with a powerful political imaginary. In earlier diasporic histories, émigrés were pivotal in mobilizing solidarity abroad for social justice or decolonization movements in the home country, but the current conditions of mass migration and displacement wrought by neoliberal globalization have changed the nature and scale of transborder organizing.

11 FIOB is a community-based organization that, at the time of this study, had local committees in Santa Rosa, Los Angeles, San Diego, Oceanside, Santa Maria, and Fresno in California; in Tijuana and the San Quintin Valley in Baja Calfornia; and in Juxtlahuaca, Huajuapan de León, and Zanatepec, Oaxaca, and in Mexico City. Four offices—those in Juxtlahuaca, Santa Maria, Fresno, and Los Angeles—coordinate a coalition of Indigenous organizations, communities, and individuals in the states of Oaxaca and Baja California, in Mexico City, and in the State of California in the United States. The FIOB unity statement reads: "FIOB is an Indigenous organization of migrants and non-migrants united by a strong desire to help Indigenous communities and individuals. We are independent of governments, political organizations, and religious organizations. We are united by the conviction, ideal and necessity of bettering community life unites us." (Communique in author's collection).

12 In the early years, the first office was in San Jose and later, Santa Cruz, before moving to Fresno; see Centro Binacional para el Desarrollo Indígena Oaxaqueño (Binational Center for the Development of Oaxacan Indigenous Communities, accessed September 15, 2014, http://centrobinacional.org/en/.

13 In a provocative twist, Yasnaya Aguilar Gil (2018) suggests, in her article "Nostros sin México: naciones indígenas y autonomía" (Us without Mexico: Indigenous Nations and Autonomy), that Mexico is not only a nation but a state in which many oppressed nations exist. Aguilar Gil, a Mixe scholar-activist from Oaxaca, proposes

that Mexico be reimagined by disarticulating nationalist discourses and practices to find a confederation of autonomous communities capable of generating collective life without the intervention of state institutions.

14   See the 2015 report from the Continental Network of Indigenous Women of the Americas on Beijing+20, edited by then president Tarcila Rovera Zea: *Nada sobre nosotras sin nosotras: Beijing +20 y las mujeres indígenas de las Américas: avances, vacíos y desafíos.* The Free, Prior and Informed Consent is a right of Indigenous peoples enshrined in the Convention 169 of the International Labor Organization signed by Mexico in 1989. While the implementation and enforcement has been inconsistent, Indigenous peoples in Mexico have pushed for this right.

15   Many female authors in Latin America were overlooked in the so-called Latin American literary boom because women's themes were seen as literatura lite (light literature).

16   The results of this research can be found in Romero Hernández et al. (2013).

17   Later, when we returned to Los Angeles, women staff members of the National Day Laborer Organizing Network heard we had designed this training and invited us to facilitate a gender training for their staff in Los Angeles. We did a one-day workshop and a follow-up session several months later.

18   After the annual encampment of the Oaxacan teacher's union (Section 22 of the National Educational Workers Union) in the zócalo (public square) to negotiate their wages was violently evicted by then governor Ulises Ruiz and 3,500 municipal police and Federal Preventive Police, a popular uprising began called the Asamblea Popular de los Pueblos Oaxaca (Popular People's Assembly of Oaxaca, APPO). The APPO was a mass-based coalition of labor, Indigenous, neighborhood, and youth organizations that challenged governmental corruption and demanded fair negotiations with the teachers, an end to state repression of dissents, and the governor's resignation. Playing on the term *posada*, which refers to the Latin American Christmas festivity of reenacting Mary and Joseph's search for lodging, Oaxacan community members living in Los Angeles organized an "APPOsada" to raise funds and express solidarity with what was happening back home. They formed APPO LA, held protests, and staged their own encampment in front of the Mexican embassy. For further descriptions of the FIOB's APPOsada, see Costanza-Chock (2014); and Stephen (2013).

19   Draft of funding proposal, "Indigenous Women in Leadership/Mujeres Indígenas en Liderazgo (MIEL), January–June 2010."

20   MIEL Recruitment flyer, 2010.

21   A second group of students edited the exit interviews, and leaders of FIOB asked them to create "before and after" video testimonials for funders. I thank Thenmozhi Soundararajan for her innovative digital storytelling pedagogy and assistance editing the students' work.

22   All three had been, or were at that time, college students; two had been my students at UCLA. Robles initially served as the facilitator of the workshops, and Sánchez López later took over the role. In my role as advisor to the organization, I met with the team to assist them in organizing the next month's workshop.

23   Many parents are afraid that their kids will be raised in the United States and become Chicano/Mexicano, forgetting their Zapotec/Mixtec roots, so this road to community empowerment is especially rewarding.
24   She also wanted me to know that Miguel's family was very traditional but he is very open-minded, so he did not expect Maria to move into his house and help with the family business of making tortillas.
25   In the early 1990s, Maria's employer at a drycleaner sponsored her citizenship, and she, Miguel, and Luis became US citizens.
26   When MIEL was designed, our goal was to have a youth component come together as well. Having husbands participate was an added bonus.
27   Flyer for the workshop "Decolonization: Resistance and Liberation of the Indigenous Movement," led by Dr. Gaspar Rivera-Salgado, February 6, 2010, Madera, California. Collection of the author.
28   First used by Latino sociologist Felix Padilla (1985) to refer to what Juana María Rodriguez would later theorize as "a particular geopolitical experience [that] also contains within it the complexities and contradictions of immigration, (post)(neo)colonialism, race, color, legal status, class, nation, language and the politics of location" (2003, 10).

CHAPTER 5. GEOGRAPHIES OF INDIGENEITY

1   According to 2010 US census data, New York City has the largest American Indian population. If we include the approximately 250,000 Indigenous Oaxacans and the 50,245 Indigenous peoples of Oceania with the cited 54,263 American Indians in Los Angeles, LA far surpasses the 111,749 American Indians of New York. For the purposes of this research, I use the definition of Indigenous peoples according to the United Nations Permanent Forum on Indigenous Issues (United Nations 2007). These numbers will be eclipsed by the 2020 US census which showed an 86.5 percent increase in the US Indigenous population, the vast majority of which is due to the influx of Latin American Indigenous diaspora (*Indian News Today* 2020). The percentage change in those who identify as Indigenous among Latinos also increased 115.3 percent between the 2010 and 2020 census (Jones, Marks, Ramirez, and Ríos-Vargas, 2021).
2   The Mid-Wilshire neighborhood became home to large numbers of South Korean immigrants in the 1960s, following the relaxation of federal immigration rules after passage of the 1965 Immigration and Nationality Act, who took advantage of the numerous vacant storefronts and homes in the area. In 2008 the City of Los Angeles designated the area centering from Eighth Street and Western Avenue as the Koreatown district. This historic ethnic enclave has since become the most densely populated district in the city, and the most racially and ethnically diverse, and the population is more than 50 percent Latino. See "Koreatown," Mapping L.A., *Los Angeles Times*, accessed November 11, 2016, http://maps.latimes.com/neighborhoods/neighborhood/koreatown/.
3   Over time, the number of regions of Oaxaca has increased from seven to eight by dividing the Sierra into northern and southern regions. The eight geographic

regions of Oaxaca include the Istmo (isthmus), Costa (coast), Papaloapan (river basin), Sierra Norte (northern mountains), Sierra Sur (southern mountains), Mixteca (Mixtec territory), Valles Centrales (central valleys), and Cañada (woodlands). Many claim Los Angeles as the newest region of Oaxaca.

4   This process of Hispanicization occurs through external forces that tend to Mexicanize and erase Indigenous difference invisibilizing whole communities in a process community organizers call "statistical genocide—the erasure of Indigenous communities from public records [which] creat[e] major barriers to accessing basic human rights like interpretation in institutions (CIELO, UCLA AISC, UCLA Promise Institute for Human Rights, UCLA Bunche Center, 2022). It also is a strategy of survival that occurs through internal forces of a community responding to racial prejudice and bullying that often lead people to closet themselves in order to avoid violence and discrimination (i.e., not speaking their languages outside of the house, not wearing huaraches or huipiles outside the community context). See Alberto (2017) and Sánchez-López (2017) in the special issue of *Latino Studies* that focuses on Critical Latinx Indigeneities, coedited by Urrieta and Blackwell.

5   See the entries on the Latin American Indigenous Diasporas map I created in collaboration with community members that detail the history of Indigenous migrants organizing to bring their hometown saints to St. Anne's Church based on research that I conducted with Brenda Nicolás: "Latin American Indigenous Diasporas," a Mapping Indigenous LA (MILA) UCLA project, accessed September 24, 2017, http://www.arcgis.com/apps/MapTour/index.html?appid=31d1100e9a454f5c9b905f55b08c0d22.

6   See Lourdes Albertos's entries on Zapotec Basketball and Normandie Park on Mapping Indigenous LA's "Latin American Indigenous Diasporas" map, http://www.arcgis.com/apps/MapTour/index.html?appid=31d1100e9a454f5c9b905f55b08c0d22.

7   Oaxacan Heritage Month was started by the Oaxacan Association of Businesses (Asociación Oaxaqueña de Negocios, AON) and eventually came to be organized by a committee that included ORO, FIOB, AON, and COLIBA/Raza Unida. The first proclamation was drafted by Janet Martinez in collaboration with the Oaxacan Heritage Month Committee. The FIOB, the ORO, the calenda, and the proclamation that begins Oaxacan Heritage Month are among the points I created for the "Latin American Indigenous Diasporas" map through the Mapping Indigenous LA (MILA) UCLA project.

8   Oaxacan cuisine is renowned throughout the world for its rich variety of pre-Hispanic ingredients. It is thought that corn and many beans were first cultivated in Oaxaca, and the cuisine includes ingredients such as chocolate (often drunk as a hot liquid with spices and other flavorings) and delicacies like Oaxacan cheese, mezcal (an alcohol made of agave), and grasshoppers (chapulines). Many dishes start with labor-intensive hand-ground corn, spices, and chocolate, which rely on Indigenous women's labor. Mole is a sauce made from roasted ingredients (at least two different chiles, chocolate, spices, herbs like hoja santa, nuts and seeds, tomatoes or tomatillos, and sometimes fruits) that are then ground and allowed to simmer together for many hours to create a rich, complex, complementary flavor in which no one ingredient

dominates. Whereas black mole is most common, Oaxaca is known as the "land of seven moles," which were born out of the different mountainous terrains and microclimates, and the diversity of Indigenous peoples who live there. Tlayudas, affectionately called the Oaxacan pizza, consist of a dinner plate–sized thin, crunchy tortilla, usually seared on a comal or grill, covered with beans, lettuce or cabbage, avocado, Oaxacan cheese, and salsa, and served with chicken, beef, or pork toppings. Totopos are generally baked in a clay oven known as a comixcal to form a large, round, moon-shaped cross between a baked tortilla cracker and a flatbread.

9   Neighborhood favorites like the renowned raspado street vendor who makes his own syrups from fresh fruit and other flavors daily often become the vehicle for opening a storefront. For example, see Janet Martinez's project *Zapotecs: The Journey to Success*, a photo exhibit for the 2015 Oaxacan Heritage Month, that tells several of these stories. Several of her interviews from this project were featured in the 2016 Latin American Indigenous Diaspora map of the Mapping Indigenous Los Angeles project: https://www.arcgis.com/apps/MapTour/index.html?appid=31d1100e9a454f5c9b905f55b08c0d22. See also the Los Angeles Street Vendor Campaign, accessed February 11, 2016, http://streetvendorcampaign.blogspot.com/.

10 Pink Burger was opened in Mitla but was a short-lived venture (Baker 2017; Virbila 2014).

11 HR 4437 was the Border Protection, Antiterrorism and Illegal Immigration Control Act of 2005, a bill that was passed by the House of Representatives on December 16, 2005, but did not pass the Senate. Its provisions ranged widely, from building a seven-hundred-mile-long fence along the US-Mexico border to increasing the penalties for employing, and making it a felony to house, undocumented immigrants, with a punishment of no less than three years in prison plus fines.

12 This shooting and the community response is also featured on the "Latin American Indigenous Diasporas" map; the entry is written by Floridalma Boj Lopez.

13 The Sierra Norte (or the Sierra Juarez) is one of the four Zapotec regions of Oaxaca that also include the Isthmus of Tehuantepec, the Southern Sierra, and the Central Valleys. In 2008 it was estimated that 1,500 Zoogochenses were living in Los Angeles, and many community members have remarked on how more residents are living in LA than in the pueblo. "Los Angeles Immigrant Community Pushes to Keep Zapotec Language Alive," The World from PRX, August 9, 2013, accessed March 20, 2015, https://theworld.org/stories/2013-08-09/los-angeles-immigrant-community-pushes-keep-zapotec-language-alive.

14 We produced this testimonio (Blackwell 2009a) as part of our long-term collaboration but specifically in relation to a UC MEXUS collaborative grant I had with Aída Hernández Castillo at the time. I find it emotionally difficult to work with this material, and I have regularly checked in with Odilia since our interview to find out how she feels about having shared her story and to ensure that I still have her permission to share it. She confesses that she has never read the interview, but she thinks that telling her story is part of the healing of her community. She recently asked me to have it translated so we could update it and publish in English.

15 Odilia has come full circle. As we did our final check-in as this book was going to press in the fall of 2022, she was serving as the treasurer for her HTA and was busy

preparing for a multiday celebration of the patron saint. She shared that her work in the HTA is still untraditional but she was happy to have recently organized a workshop for her paisanos to learn how to access government funds in partnership with migrant organizations.

16 See INCITE! Women of Color Against Violence (2006) and the work of Sarah Deer (2009, 2015) and the report she created with other Native American grassroots activists (Deer et al. 2007). See also Amnesty International USA (2007); and Robertson (2012).

17 In the highlands of Guatemala, the Ajq'ijab' are spiritual guides who keep for their communities the calendar days according to the Maya sacred calendar and provide offerings, ceremonies, consultations, and cultural teachings.

18 For Tongva histories of what is now Los Angeles and community stories of place, see Craig Torres's work with the Mapping Indigenous LA Project: http://www.arcgis.com/apps/MapJournal/index.html?appid=4942348fa8bd427fae02f7e020e9876. Maya Vision, established in 1988 by Maya refugees in Los Angeles, is also an important organization. Longtime Maya Vision community organizer, K'iche interpreter, spiritual leader, and friend Policarpo Chaj worked in collaboration with FIOB and unfortunately, was among the Indigenous leaders who succumbed to the COVID-19 pandemic. In addition to Maya-based spiritual practices, a widespread geography of the sacred has been folded into immigrant Catholic churches in Los Angeles and is richly illustrated in the migration of the saints from Oaxacan hometowns. For example, St. Anne's is home to nine patron saints from three towns in Oaxaca. For further information about Maya Vision, Chaj, and St. Anne's, as well as many other organizations, visit the Mapping Indigenous LA Project's "Latin American Indigenous Diasporas" map.

19 As part of their struggle for survival and self-determination, many Indignous nations have reclaimed their own names for themselves, shedding colonial names like those of the missions the Spanish established to serve, along with presidios (military garrisons), as the center of colonial life in terms of missionization. This system was part labor extraction, part religious conversion, and attempted to turn Indigenous societies into dependent wards of the missions.

20 I am a cocreator of this project, and I codirect it with Mishuana Goeman and Wendy Teeter. We have collaborated with our colleague Keith Camacho at UCLA and with many Indigenous community scholars in Los Angeles.

21 More recently undocuqueer Indigenous (Q'anjob'al Maya descent) artist Mario Alvarado Cifuentes has produced an image of the monarch bleeding with tattered wings that pushes back on the immigrant rights movement's slogan "Migration is Beautiful." See www.marioalvaradocifuentes.com.

CODA

Epigraph: Ernestina Ortiz, speech at the twentieth-anniversary celebration of the Coordinadora Nacional de Mujeres Indígenas, Mexico City, August 9, 2017.

1 Although there are many origin stories for this chant, according to Xiao (2018) it is linked to the Greek poet Dinos Christianopoulos who, in 1978, wrote the couplet, "What didn't you do to bury me, but you forgot that I was a seed," published in his

collection *The Body and the Wormwood* (1960–93), which apparently was aimed at the Greek literary community who criticized his work, some claim because of his homosexuality.

2 CONAMI. 2016. Open Letter to founding organizations, members and allies of CONAMI, the national Indigenous movement, and brothers and sisters of the Indigenous pueblos of Mexico. In the author's possession.

3 The CIG proposes to govern the country collectively in accordance with the EZLN'S seven principles of "mandar obeciendo" (translated as to rule by obeying). These principals of ruling or leading while obeying are: lead by obeying; represent, don't replace; serve, don't serve oneself; construct, don't destroy; propose, don't impose; convince, don't defeat; from below, not from above.

4 In the United States, the National Domestic Workers Alliance wrote an open letter dedicated to the women in the movie and held screenings nationwide to build support for the National Domestic Workers Bill of Rights being considered in the US Congress.

5 Despite much of their labor creating signature events, Odilia and Janet were ousted from the Oaxacan Heritage Month organizing committee after the split, described below, as local LA FIOB activists no longer wanted to share space with CIELO on the committee.

6 A collaboration with the UCLA American Indian Studies Center and the Bunch Center for African American Studies, the Indigenous language storymap We Are Here can be found at: https://storymaps.arcgis.com/stories/618560a29f2a402faa2f5dd9dedocc65.

7 Janet Martinez, n.d., unpublished paper, 2014.

8 It is still a work in progress as the FIOB team, for example, found that the Murkutu platform was difficult for community members to navigate. While designed with Indigenous communities in mind, and specifically for differential access for different kinds of users, Murkutu was too cumbersome and not user friendly. We had already been creating work arounds since the entire back end was English only, but the community partner found it was just not accessible and practical to use for the mostly migrant, Indigenous, working-class participants, many of whom were from farmworker backgrounds who have access only to very limited educational resources and connect to digital technology on their smart phones.

References

ORAL HISTORIES

Ancheita, Alejandra. Interview with Maylei Blackwell. March 15, 1998. Cassette recording.
Bernardino, Juanita. Interview with Maylei Blackwell. December 11, 2010.
Bernardino, Monserrat. Interview with Maylei Blackwell. September 17, 2011. Digital recording, transcript.
Cristancho, Daris. Interview with Maylei Blackwell. May 18, 2004. Cassette recording.
Delgado, Gloria. Interview with Maylei Blackwell. December 11, 2010.
Diaz Altamirano, Genoveva. Interview with Maylei Blackwell. October 19, 2011. Digital recording, transcript.
Don Juan, Norma. Interview with Maylei Blackwell. August 12, 2018. Digital recording.
Garcia, Veronica. Interview with Maylei Blackwell. December 11, 2010.
Gutiérrez, Margarita. Interview with Maylei Blackwell. September 3, 2001. Cassette recording.
Gutiérrez, Margarita. Interview with Maylei Blackwell. October 20, 2014. Digital recording, transcript.
Gutiérrez, Margarita. Interview with Maylei Blackwell. October 21, 2014. Digital recording, transcript.
Henriquez, Sonia. Interview with Maylei Blackwell. November 19, 2014. Digital recording, transcript.
Henriquez, Sonia. Interview with Maylei Blackwell, November 20, 2014. Digital recording, transcript.
Jímenez, Cándida. Interview with Maylei Blackwell. August 23, 1999. Cassette recording, transcript.
Jurado, Fabiola. Interview with Maylei Blackwell, June 30, 2015.
López Galindo, Cenobia, and Irais Sandra Sánchez López. Interview with Maylei Blackwell. March 29, 2007. Cassette recording, transcript.
"Lorena." Interview with Maylei Blackwell. April 1, 2000. Cassette recording.
Maldonado, Centolia. Interview with Laura Velasco, March, 2007. Digital recording, transcript.
Martinez, Ivón. Interview with Maylei Blackwell. December 11, 2010.
Martinez, Janet. Interview with Maylei Blackwell. November 6, 2105. Video recording.

Martinez, Maria Antonieta. Interview with Maylei Blackwell. October 1, 2011. Digital recording, transcript.

Martinez, Maria Antonieta. Interview with Maylei Blackwell, October 6, 2011. Digital recording, transcript.

Martinez, Minerva. Interview with Maylei Blackwell. December 11, 2010.

Martinez Solano, Felicitas. Interview with Maylei Blackwell. November 19, 2015. Digital recording, transcript.

Méndez Moreno, Rosa Nava. Interview with Maylei Blackwell. March 30, 2007. Cassette recording, transcript.

Mendoza, Fabiola del Jurado. Interview with Maylei Blackwell. June 30, 2015. Digital recording, transcript.

Mendoza Roriguez, Susana, and Blanca Flor Mendoza. Interview with Maylei Blackwell. March 29, 2007. Cassette recording, transcript.

Miguel, Marisela. Interview with Maylei Blackwell. December 11, 2010.

Ortiz Peña, Ernestina. Interview with Maylei Blackwell. August 17, 2017. Digital recording, transcript.

Palomo, Nellys. Interview with Maylei Blackwell. August 24, 1999. Cassette recording, transcript.

Patricio, Maria de Jesús. Interview with Maylei Blackwell. April 1, 2000. Cassette recording, transcript.

Puac Gutiérrez, Julio Cesar. Interview with Maylei Blackwell. April 25, 2012. Digital recording, transcript.

Ramos Reyes, Isabel. Interview with Maylei Blackwell. March 29, 2007. Cassette recording, transcript.

Robles, Sofía. Interview with Maylei Blackwell. March 13, 2015. Digital recording, transcript.

Robles, Sofía. Interview with Maylei Blackwell. October 6, 2011. Digital recording, transcript.

Robles, Sofía. Interview with Maylei Blackwell. August 31, 1999. Cassette recording, transcript.

Romero Hernández, Odilia. Interview with Maylei Blackwell. July 13, 2021. Digital recording, transcript.

Romero Hernández, Odilia. Interview with Maylei Blackwell. September 9, 2020. Digital recording, transcript.

Romero Hernández, Odilia. Interview with Maylei Blackwell, January 31, 2009. Digital recording, transcript.

Salvador, Edith. Interview with Maylei Blackwell. 2010.

Sánchez, Maria Isabel. Interview with Maylei Blackwell. May 21, 2012. Digital recording, transcript.

Sánchez, Maria Isabel. Interview with Maylei Blackwell. December 11, 2010.

Sánchez, Miguel. Interview with Maylei Blackwell. December 11, 2010.

Sánchez Nestor, Martha. Interview with Maylei Blackwell. November 18, 2015. Digital recording, transcript.

Sánchez Nestor, Martha. Interview with Maylei Blackwell. March 24, 2002. Cassette recording, transcript.

Sánchez Nestor, Martha. Interview with Maylei Blackwell. March 10, 2001. Cassette recording, transcript.

Sanchez Oriano, Griselda. Interview with Maylei Blackwell. December 11, 2011. Digital recording, transcript.

Sandoval, Patty Torres. Interview with Maylei Blackwell. June 28, 2015. Digital recording, transcript.

Sandoval, Patty Torres. Interview with Maylei Blackwell. June 27, 2015. Digital recording, transcript.

Sandoval, Tomasa. Interview with Maylei Blackwell. August 22, 1999. Cassette recording, transcript.

Tello, Gloria. Interview with Maylei Blackwell. March 3, 1999. Cassette recording.

Turbicio, Hermalinda. Interview with Maylei Blackwell. March 31, 2000. Cassette recording, transcript.

Vargas, Virginia. Interview with Maylei Blackwell. December 8, 1999. Cassette recording.

Villa, Doña Rufina. Interview with Maylei Blackwell. April 1, 2000. Cassette recording, transcript.

Zurita Vásquez, Matlide Margarita. Interview with Maylei Blackwell. March 29, 2007. Digital recording, transcript.

PRIMARY SOURCES

Aguilar Gil, Yásnaya Elena. 2019. "Mujeres Indígenas, Fiesta y Participación Política." *Cultura unam, Feminismos/Dossier*. November 2019. Accessed January 15, 2020. https://www.revistadelauniversidad.mx/articles/1157b614-c696-4872-9b14-c48b1c8680b5/mujeres-indigenas-fiesta-y-participacion-politica.

Aguilar Gil, Yasnaya Elena. 2018. "Nosotros Sin México: Naciones Indígenas y Autonomía." *Nexos*, May 18. https://cultura.nexos.com.mx/nosotros-sin-mexico-naciones-indigenas-y-autonomia/.

Amnesty International USA. 2007. *Maze of Injustice: The Failure to Protect Indigenous Women from Sexual Violence in the USA*. New York: Amnesty International.

Aparicio, Yalitza. 2020. "In Mexico, 'Roma' Lit a Fire for Workers' Rights." *New York Times*, May 23. Accessed September 15. https://www.nytimes.com/2020/05/23/opinion/roma-mexico-workers-rights.html.

Asociación Femenina para el Desarrollo de Sacatepéquez (Afedes) y Movimiento Nacional de Tejdoras Maya de Guatemala. 2020. *Nuestros tejidos son los libros que la colonia no pudo quemar: El camino del Movimiento Nacional de Tejedoras Mayas de Guatemala*. Santiago, Scatepéquez, Guatemala: Asociación Femenina para el Desarrollo de Sacatepéquez (Afedes).

Baker, Katie. 2017. "Mole Means Love." *The Ringer*. March 3. https://www.theringer.com/2017/3/3/16046194/guelaguetza-lopez-family-los-angeles-oaxacan-cuisine-ringer-last-meal-on-earth-a61422bab42b.

Bermudez, Esmeralda. 2010a. "Protests over Police Shooting Resonate All the Way to Guatemala." *Los Angeles Times*, September 26.

Bermudez, Esmeralda. 2010b. "Trying out Indigenous Languages." *Los Angeles Times*, October 11.

Blackwell, Maylei, and Maureen White-Eagle. 2007. "Desde Estados Unidos Las Mujeres Indígenas Ante La Violencia Sexual." *La Jornada*, May 21.

Burguete Cal y Mayor, Araceli. 2021. "Martha Sánchez Néstor: una historia de éxito desdeñada por el sistema de partidos políticos." *Pie de Página* August 4. https://piedepagina.mx/martha-sanchez-nestor-una-historia-de-desarrollo-desdenada-por-el-sistema-de-partidos-politicos/.

Cabral, Javier. 2013. "Eat Your Crickets: Los Angeles Is the Chapulin Capital of the U.S." *Los Angeles Times*, July 9.

Camacho, Zóismo. 2019. "Cárteles, en guerra contra puebla indígenas." *Contralínea*. October 9, 2019. Accessed November 11, 2020. https://www.contralinea.com.mx/archivorevista/2019/10/09/carteles-punta-de-lanza-contra-los-pueblos-indigenas-del-/.

Cengel, Katya, 2013. "The Other Mexicans: Indigenous People Come from a World Apart from Spanish-Speaking Mexicans." *National Geographic*, June 25. Accessed August 3, 2016. https://www.nationalgeographic.com/culture/article/130624-mexico-mixteco-indigenous-immigration-spanish-culture.

Chavez, Lourdes. 2016. "Celebra la CRAC Su 21 Aniversario." *El Sur: Periodico de Gurrero*, October 16.

CIELO. n.d. "Interpreter Project." Accessed May 1, 2020. https://mycielo.org/interpreter-project/.

CIELO. 2020. "Undocu-Indigenous Fund." CIELO. April 9. https://mycielo.org/undocu-indigenous-fund/.

CIELO, UCLA AISC, UCLA Promise Institute for Human Rights, UCLA Bunche Center. 2022. "We Are Here." ArcGIS StoryMaps. January 31. https://storymaps.arcgis.com/stories/618560a29f2a402faa2f5dd9dedocc65.

Combahee River Collective. 1979. *The Combahee River Collective Statement*. "A Black Feminist Statement." In *Capitalist Patriarchy and the Case for Socialist Feminism*, edited by Zillah Eisenstein. New York: Monthly Review Press.

Comisión Nacional para Desarrollo de los Pueblos Indígenas (CDI). 2008. *Región Sur. Tomo 1 Oaxaca: Condiciones Socioecónomicas y Demográficas de la Población Indígena*. Mexico City: CDI.

CONAMI. 2016. Open Letter to founding organizations, members and allies of CONAMI, the national Indigenous movement, and brothers and sisters of the Indigenous pueblos of Mexico.

Construyendo nuestra historia. 1997. Encuentro Nacional de Mujeres Indígenas. Oaxaca de Juárez, August 29–31. Mexico City: K'inal Antsetik, 1998.

Coordinación General de Comunicación Social. n.d. "En dos años IEEA alfabetiza a más de 19 mil oaxaqueños." Accessed May 23, 2022. https://www.oaxaca.gob.mx/comunicacion/en-dos-anos-ieea-alfabetiza-a-mas-de-19-mil-oaxaquenos/.

Del Jurado Mendoza, Fabiola, Norma Don Juan Pérez, and Coordinadora Nacional de Mujeres Indígenas (CONAMI). 2019. "Emergencia comunitaria de género. Respuesta de las mujeres indígenas a las múltiples violencias y el despojo del territorio." *Ichan Tecolotl*, February 5. https://ichan.ciesas.edu.mx/emergencia-comunitaria-de-genero-respuesta-de-las-mujeres-indigenas-a-las-multiples-violencias-y-el-despojo-del-territorio/.

Encuentro Nacional de Mujeres de la ANIPA, December 1995. San Cristobal de las Casas. Chiapas.

Enlace Continental de Mujeres Indígenas de las Américas (ECMIA). 2010. *Dualidad y Complementariedad*, edited by Margarita Gutiérrez. Geneva, Switzerland: University College Foundation Henry Durant.

Enlace Continental de Mujeres Indigenas de las Americas (ECMIA) and Centro de Culturas Indigínas del Peru (CHIRAPAQ). 2015. *Nada Sobre Nosotras Sin Nosotras Beijing +20 Las Mujeres Indigenas de Las Americas: Avances, Vacios y Desafios*. Lima: Gama Graficas S.R.L.

Esquivel, Paloma. 2012. "Epithet That Divides Mexicans Is Banned by Oxnard School District." *Los Angeles Times*, May 28.

Figueroa Romero, Dolores, Vivian Jiménez Estrada, Stéphane Guimont Marceau, and Roberta Rice. 2017. *Foro Virtual: Violencia contra Mujeres Indígenas de las Américas*. March 6–10, 2017. Final report. Asociación Canadiense de Estudios de América Latina y el Caribe (ACELC).

Flores, Lizbeth. 2018. "Registra Oaxaca cerca de 400 mil analfabetas." *El Universal*, September 9. https://oaxaca.eluniversal.com.mx/estatal/09-09-2018/registra-oaxaca-cerca-de-400-mil-analfabetas.

Front Line Defenders. 2017. *Annual Report on Human Rights Defenders at Risk in 2017*. Dublin, Ireland: Front Line, the International Foundation for the Protection of Human Rights Defenders.

Garcia Martínez, Anayeli. 2015. "Darán a defensora indígena Reconocimiento Ponciano Arriaga." *Cimacnoticias Periodismo con Perspectiva de Género*, November 15. https://cimacnoticias.com.mx/noticia/daran-a-defensora-indigena-reconocimiento-ponciano-arriaga/.

Grau Villa, Carment, and Mailen Manga Urkizu. 2018. "Tarcila Rivera: Indigenous Women Have to Build Our Own Concept of Feminism." *El Salto*, March 20.

Gringo, Rogue. 2006a. "11/01 Demonstration of Oaxacans and Supporters at Mexican Consulate, with Audio Interview." *Los Angeles Indymedia: Activist News*, November 3. Accessed July 20, 2015. https://la.indymedia.org/news/2006/11/186082.php.

Gringo, Rogue. 2006b. "Interview with Coalition Leader Odilia [sic] Romero." *Los Angeles Indymedia: Activist News*, November 3. Accessed July 20, 2015. http://la.indymedia.org/news/2006/11/186082_comment.php.

Hernández Castillo, Rosalva Aída. 2013. "Recuerdo Atenco. La Memoria Como Resistencia." *La Jornada*, May 5.

Hernández Castillo, Rosalva Aída. 2007. "La Guerra Sucia, Contra Las Mujeres." *La Jornada*, May.

Indian Country Today. 2021. "2020 Census: Native population increased by 86.5 percent." *Indian Country Today*. August 13. https://ictnews.org/news/2020-census-native-population-increased-by-86-5-percent.

"The Indigenous World 2021: Mexico." 2021. International Work Group for Indigenous Affairs. March 18. https://www.iwgia.org/en/mexico/4232-iw-2021-mexico.html.

INEGI. 2020. "Indigenous Language." Demography and Society. INEGI. https://en.www.inegi.org.mx/temas/lengua/#General_Information.

INEGI. 2019. *Censo Nacional de Transparencia, Acceso a la Información Pública y Protección de Datos Personales 2019*. Mexico City: El Censo Nacional de Gobierno Federal.

Jones, Nicolas, Rachel Marks, Roberto Ramirez, and Merarys Ríos-Vargas, 2021. "2020 Census Illuminates Racial and Ethnic Composition of the Country" August 12.

https://www.census.gov/library/stories/2021/08/improved-race-ethnicity-measures-reveal-united-states-population-much-more-multiracial.html.

K'inal Antzetik. 2007. "Campaña Por Una Atención de Calidad y Buentrato Para Las Mujeres Indígenas." Mexico City: K'inal Antzetik.

K'inal Antzetik. 1998. "Carpeta de Derechos y Salud Reproductiva." Mexico City: K'inal Ansetik.

"LAPD Murders Again—Basta Ya! No More! Justice for Manuel Jaminez." 2010. *Revolution: Voice of the Revolutionary Communist Party, USA*, September 26. https://revcom.us/a/212/LAPD_murder-en.html.

NietoGomez, Anna. 1974. "La Feminista." *Encuentro Femenil* 1 (2): 34–37.

Martinez, Janet. 2014. "Unpublished Paper."

Morales, Areli. 2020. "After Being Deported, These Oaxacan Muralists Are Back and Now Have a 'Permanent' Show at MOLAA." *L.A. Taco*, March 5.

Muñoz Ramírez, Gloria. 2018. "Flores En El Desierto." *DesInformemonos*, January 2018. https://floreseneldesierto.desinformemonos.org/.

Oaxacalifornian Reporting Team/Equipo de Cronistas Oaxacalifornianos (ECO). 2013. *Voices of Indigenous Oaxacan Youth in the Central Valley: Creating Our Sense of Belonging in California*. Research report no. 1. Santa Cruz: Center for Collaborative Research for an Equitable California.

Orán, Reuter, and Aiban Wagua, eds. 2010. *Gayamar Sabga: diccionario escolar gunagaya español*. Panama City: Proyecto EBI Guna.

Ortiz, Teresa. 2001. *Never Again a World without Us: Voices of Mayan Women in Chiapas, Mexico*. Washington, DC: Ecumenical Program on Central America and the Caribbean (EPICA).

Palomo, Nellys. 1996. *Influencias Del Zapatismo En Las Mujeres Indigenas*. Comision de Seguimiento de Mujeres de La ANIPA. K'inal Ansetik, A.C.

Parsons, Russ. 2015. "Guelaguetza's Bricia Lopez on the 'Overwhelming Happiness' of a James Beard Award." *Los Angeles Times*, February 27.

Patricio, María de Jesus. 2018. "Marichuy, Vocera Del Concejo Indígena de Gobierno. Comunidad Nahua, Tuxpan, Jalisco." YouTube. Video, 11:07. Desinformémonos. https://www.youtube.com/watch?v=jQ6jXMnfTB0.

Patricio, María de Jesus. 2017a. "Palabra de Marichuy en Neza. Sobre las Mujeres y los feminicidios." *Congreso Nacional Indígena*. November 27. https://www.congresonacionalindigena.org/2017/11/27/palabra-marichuy-neza-lasmujeres-los-feminicidios/.

Patricio, María de Jesus. 2017b. "Palabra de vocera Marichuy en el Totonacapan." *Congreso Nacional Indígena*, November 15. https://www.congresonacionalindigena.org/2017/11/15/palabra-la-vocera-marichuy-totonacapan/.

Patricio, María de Jesus. 2017c. "Entrevista con María de Jesús Patricio, Vocera del Congreso Indígena de Gobierno." WRadio 969, August 8. https://www.youtube.com/watch?v=F40f_omvSkg.

Petrich Enviada, Blanche. 2006. "Comunidades de la Sierra Juárez se unen a la lucha por derrocar a Ulises Ruiz." *La Jornada*, March 21. Accessed August 8, 2020. https://www.jornada.com.mx/2006/11/21/index.php?section=politica&article=024n1pol.

Quinones, Sam. 2006. "Group Seeks to Name Park after a Mexican President." *Los Angeles Times*, May 30.

Robles Hernández, Sofía. 2015. "8 de Marzo Día Internacional de la Mujer: Mujer Indígena y Resistencia Cultural en las Americas." Unpublished paper delivered in Los Angeles, March 8.

Rodriguez Santos, Bertha. 2011. "El FIOB: 20 años de lucha por los derecho's de indigenas y migrantes." *Revista El Tequio: La Presencia Hecha Palabra* 10: 2–24.

Rucker, Gabrielle Octavia. 2020. "When COVID-19 Hit the Indigenous Communities in L.A., This Group Stepped In." *Vogue*, August 18. Accessed August 18, 2020. https://www.vogue.com/article/indigenous-women-la-cielo.

Sanchez, Rocio. 2014. "Entre la tradición y el cambio: mujeres jóvenes indígenas de Chiapas." *La Jornada*, June 5.

Santamaria, Maya. 1996. "Two Watershed Encounters for Indigenous Women in Mexico." *Abya Yala News* 10: 6–7.

Sirenio, Kau. 2020. "Frente Indígena de Organizaciones Binacionales elige como dirigente a profesor acusado de abuso sexual." *Pie de Página*, October 26, 2020.

Solis, Nathan. 2021. "Indigenous Leader Taken by Covid-19 Caught Between Two Countries in Death." *Courthouse News Service*, March 13. https://www.courthousenews.com/indigenous-community-leader-taken-by-covid-19-leaves-lasting-impression-in-los-angeles/.

Stromberg, Matt. 2021. "Honoring the Stories of Undocumented Indigenous Women in Los Angeles." *Hyperallergic*, April 20. http://hyperallergic.com/639146/diza-noole-stories-of-undocumented-indigenous-women-in-los-angeles/.

Subcomandante Marcos. 1994. "Heroismo cotidiano hace possible que existan los detallos." *La Jornada*, January 26.

Tejada, Armando G. 2019. "Ha crecido represión indígena desde que llegó la 4T: Marichuy." *La Jornada*, October 12. https://www.jornada.com.mx/ultimas/politica/2019/10/12/hacrecido-represion-indigena-desde-que-llego-la-4t-marichuy-2622.html.

Torres, Craig, Cindi Alvitre, Allison Fischer-Olson, Mishauna Goeman, and Wendy Teeter. n.d. "Perspectives on a Selection of Gabriele.o/Tongva Places." Mapping Indigenous LA. Accessed November 28, 2022. http://www.arcgis.com/apps/MapJournal/index.html?appid=4942348fa8bd427fae02f7e00e98764.

Trinh, Jean. 2014. "Latinos Petition for Official Neighborhoods, like Peru Village, Little Venezuela." *LAist*, April 4. https://laist.com/news/latinos-petition-for-official-neigh.

Tseng, Esther. 2019. "A Tlayuda Pop-Up Speaks the Language of South LA's Indigenous Community." *LAist*, September 17. Accessed September 11, 2020. https://laist.com/news/food/ponchos-tlayudas-language-interpretation-odilia-romero.

United Nations. 2007. *Permanent Forum on Indigenous Issues: Report of the Sixth Session*. May 14–25. Accessed December 14, 2021. https://www.un.org/development/desa/indigenouspeoples/unpfii-sessions-2/sixth.html.

Vankin, Deborah. 2018. "Oaxacan Muralists' L. A. Works Give Voice to Indigenous Peoples—But the Artists Cannot Travel to the U.S. to View Them." *Los Angeles Times*, August 29.

Vankin, Deborah. 2017. "Oaxacalifornia Dreaming: L.A. Library Mural Project Looks at Visual Language That Transcends Borders." *Los Angeles Times*, September 20.

Virbila, Irene. 2014. "Pink Burger: Guelaguetza Founder's Burger Spot in Oaxaca for Those Homesick for Los Angeles." *Los Angeles Times*, June 10.

Wood, Stephanie, ed. 2018. "Welcome to the Mapas Project!" University of Oregon. Accessed May 1, 2017. http://mapasuoregon.edu/.

Xiao, An. 2018. "On the Origins of 'They Tried to Bury Us, They Didn't Know We Were Seeds.'" *Hyperallergic.* July 3. http://hyperallergic.com/449930/on-the-origins-of-they-tried-to-bury-us-they-didnt-know-we-were-seeds/.

SECONDARY SOURCES

Ábrego, Leisy J. 2013. "Latino Immigrants' Diverse Experiences of 'Illegality.'" In *Constructing Immigrant "Illegality": Critiques, Experiences, and Responses*, edited by Cecilia Menjívar and Daniel Kanstroom, 139–60. New York: Cambridge University Press.

Ábrego, Leisy J., and Cecilia Menjívar. 2011. "Immigrant Latina Mothers as Targets of Legal Violence." *International Journal of Sociology of the Family* 37: 9–16.

Acosta, Georgina Cárdenas, and Rita Bell López Vences. 2021. "El Bastón de Mando en Las Presidentas Municipales de Oaxaca." *Revista Inclusiones* 8: 57–71.

Adams-Campbell, Melissa, Ashley Glassburn Falzetti, and Courtney Rivard. 2015. "Introduction: Indigeneity and the Work of Settler Archives." *Settler Colonial Studies* 5, (2): 109–16.

Aikau, Hokulani K. 2012. *A Chosen People, a Promised Land: Mormonism and Race in Hawai'i.* Minneapolis: University of Minnesota Press.

Aikau, Hokulani K. 2010. "Indigeneity in the Diaspora: The Case of Native Hawaiians at Iosepa, Utah." *American Quarterly* 62 (3): 477–500.

Alberto, Lourdes. Forthcoming. *Mexican American Indigeneities.* New York: New York University Press.

Alberto, Lourdes. 2017. "Coming Out as Indian: On Being an Indigenous Latina in the US." *Latino Studies* 15: 247–53.

Alberto, Lourdes. 2012. "Topographies of Indigenism: Mexico, Decolonial Indigenism, and the Chicana Transnational Subject in Ana Castillo's *Mixquiahuala Letters*." In *Comparative Indignities of the Américas: Toward a Hemispheric Approach*, edited by M. Bianet Castellanos, Lourdes Gutiérrez Nájera, and Arturo J. Aldama, 38–52. Tucson: University of Arizona Press.

Alexander, Jacqui M., and Chandra Talpade Mohanty, eds. 1997. *Feminist Genealogies, Colonial Legacies, Democratic Futures.* New York: Routledge.

Allen, Chadwick. 2012. *Trans-Indigenous: Methodologies for a Global Native Literary Studies.* Minneapolis: University of Minnesota Press.

Altamirano-Jiménez, Isabel. 2013. *Indigenous Encounters with Neoliberalism: Place, Women, and the Environment in Canada and Mexico.* Vancouver: University of British Columbia Press.

Alvarez, Sonia. 2010. "Advocating Feminism: The Latin American Feminist NGO 'Boom.'" *International Feminist Journal of Politics* 1 (2): 181–209.

Alvarez, Sonia E. 2000. "Translating the Global Effects of Transnational Organizing on Local Feminist Discourses and Practices in Latin America." *Meridians: Feminism, Race, Transnationalism* 1 (1): 29–67.

Alvarez, Sonia E. 1998. "Latin American Feminisms 'Go Global': Trends of the 1990s and Challenges for the New Millennium." In *Cultures of Politics/Politics of Cultures: Re-Visioning Latin American Social Movements*, edited by Sonia E. Alvarez, Evelina Dagnino, and Arturo Escobar, 293–324. Boulder, CO: Westview.

Alvarez, Sonia E., Evelyn Dagnino, and Arturo Escobar, eds. 1998. *Cultures of Politics of Cultures: Re-Visioning Latin American Social Movements*. Nashville, TN: Westview.

Alvarez, Sonia E., Claudia de Lima Costa, Veronica Feliu, Rebecca Hester, Norma Khlan, and Millie Thayer, eds. 2014. *Translocalities/Translocalidades: Feminist Politics of Translation in the Latin/a Américas*. Durham, NC: Duke University Press.

Alvarez, Sonia E., Elizabeth Friedman, Erika Beckman, Maylei Blackwell, Norma Stoltz Chinchilla, Nathalie Lebon, Marysa Navarro, and Marcela Ríos Tobar. 2002. "Encountering Latin American and Caribbean Feminisms." *Signs: Journal of Women in Culture and Society* 28 (2): 537–80.

Alvarez, Sonia E., Jeffrey Rubin, Millie Thayer, Gianpaolo Baiocchi, and Agustin Lao-Montes. 2017. *Beyond Civil Society: Activism, Participation, and Protest in Latin America*. Durham, NC: Duke University Press.

Alvitre, Cindi Moar. 2015. "Coyote Tours." In *Latitudes: An Angelino Atlas*, edited by Patricia Wakida, Glen Creason, and Luis Alfaro, 43–52. Berkeley, CA: Heyday.

Anderson, Jane. 2010. *Indigenous/Traditional Knowledge and Intellectual Property*. Durham, NC: Duke University School of Law, Center for the Study of the Public Domain.

Andrews, Abigail. 2018. *Undocumented Politics: Place, Gender, and the Pathways of Mexican Migrants*. Berkeley: University of California Press.

Andrews, Abigail. 2014. "Women's Political Engagement in a Mexican Sending Community: Migration as Crisis and the Struggle to Sustain an Alternative." *Gender and Society* 28 (4): 583–608.

Anzaldúa, Gloria. 1987. *Borderlands/La Frontera: The New Mestiza*. San Francisco: Spinster/Aunt Lute.

Appadurai, Arjun. 1990. "Disjuncture and Difference in the Global Cultural Economy." *Public Culture* 2 (2): 1–24.

Aquino Moreschi, Alejandra, 2013. "La comunalidad como epistemología del Sur Aportes y retos. " *Cuaderno del Sur, Revista de Ciencias Sociales* 18 (34): 7–19.

Aquino Moreschi, Alexandra, 2012. *De las luchas indias al sueño americano: Experiencias migratorias de jóvenes zapotecos y tojolabales en Estados Unidos*. México: Centro de Investigaciones y Esudios Superiores en Antropología Social.

Aquino Moreschi, Alejandra. 2010. "La Generación de la 'Emergencia Indígena' y el Comunalismo Oaxaqueño: Genealogía de un Proceso de Descolonización." *Cuadernos Del Sur* 15 (29): 7–21.

Arendt, Hannah. 2000. "The Perplexities of the Rights of Man." In *The Portable Hannah Arendt*, edited by Peter Baehr, 31–45. New York: Penguin.

Arrizón, Alicia. 2006. *Queering Mestizaje: Transculturation and Performance*. Ann Arbor: University of Michigan Press.

Artía Rodríguez, Patricia. 2001. "Desatar las voces, construeir las utopias: la coordinadora nacional de mujeres indígenas en Oaxaca." Master's thesis, CIESAS, Mexico City.

Arvin, Maile, Eve Tuck, and Angie Morrill. 2013. "Decolonizing Feminism: Challenging Connections between Settler Colonialism and Heteropatriarchy." *Feminist Formations* 25 (1): 8–34.

Bacon, David. 2013. *The Right to Stay Home: How US Policy Drives Mexican Migration*. Boston: Beacon.

Bacon, David. 2006. *Communities without Borders: Images and Voices from the World of Migration*. Ithaca, NY: ILR Press.

Barillas-Chón, David W. 2010. "Oaxaqueño/a Students' (Un)Welcoming High School Experiences." *Journal of Latinos and Education* 9: 303–20.

Barker, Joanne. 2015. "Indigenous Feminisms." In *Handbook on Indigenous People's Politics*, edited by José Antonio Lucero, Dale Turner, and Donna Lee VanCott. New York: Oxford University Press.

Barker, Joanne. 2011a. *Native Acts: Law, Recognition, and Cultural Authenticity*. Durham, NC: Duke University Press.

Barker, Joanne. 2011b. "Why 'Settler Colonialism' Isn't Exactly Right." Accessed September 28, 2015. https://tequilasovereign.wordpress.com/2011/02/14/why-settlercolonialism-isntexactlyright/.

Barker, Joanne. 2006. "Gender, Sovereignty, and the Discourse of Rights in Native Women's Activism." *Meridians: Feminism, Race, Transnationalism* 7: 127–61.

Barrera-Bassols, Dalila. 2006. "Indigenous Women in the Representation System for Elective Posts: The Case of Oaxaca." *Agricultura, Sociedad y Desarrollo* 3 (1): 19–37.

Barrera-Bassols, Dalia, and Cristina Oehmichen Bazán, eds. 2000. *Migración y relaciones de género en México*. Mexico City: Instituto de Investigaciones Antropológicas, Universidad Nacional Autónoma de México, GIMTRAP.

Basch, Nina, Linda Glick Schiller, and Cristina Blanc, eds. 1993. *Nations Unbound: Transnational Projects, Postcolonial Predicaments, and Deterritorialized Nation States*. New York: Routledge.

Bastos, Santiago, comp. 2008. *Multiculturalismo y futuro en Guatemala*. Facultad Latinoamericana de Ciencias Sociales, Guatemala.

Batz, Giovanni. 2014. "Maya Cultural Resistance in Los Angeles: The Recovery of Identity and Culture among Maya Youth." *Latin American Perspectives* 41 (3): 194–207.

Bauerkemper, J., and H. K. Stark. 2012. "The Trans/national Terrain of Anishinaabe Law and Diplomacy." *Journal of Transnational American Studies* 4 (1): 1–21.

Beal, Frances. 1970. "Double Jeopardy: To Be Black and Female." In *The Black Woman: An Anthology*, edited by Toni Cade, 90–100. New York: Signet/Times Mirror.

Berrio Palomo, Lina Rosa. 2006. "Liderazgos femeninos indígenas en Colombia y México: una mirada a sus procesos." Master's thesis, Universidad Nacional Autónoma de México. https://ru.dgb.unam.mx/handle/DGB_UNAM/TES01000603514.

Besserer, Federico. 2004. *Topografías transnacionales hacia una geografía de la vida transnacional*. Mexico City: Plaza y Valdés y UAM.

Besserer, Federico. 2002. *Contesting Community Cultural Struggles of a Mixtec Transnational Community*. Stanford, CA: Stanford University Press.

Besserer, Federico. 2000. "Sentimientos (In)Apropiados de las Mujeres Migrantes: Hacia una Nueva Ciudadanía." In *Migración y Relaciones de Género en México*, edited by Dalia Barrera-Bassols and Cristina Oehmichen Bazán, 371–89. Mexico City: GIMTRAP-UNAM/IIA.

Blackhawk, Ned. 1995. "I Can Carry on from Here: The Relocation of American Indians to Los Angeles." *Wicazo Sa Review* 11 (2): 16–30.

Blackwell, Maylei. 2017a. "Geographies of Indigeneity: Indigenous Migrant Women's Organizing and Translocal Politics of Place." *Latino Studies* 15: 156–81.

Blackwell, Maylei. 2017b. "Indigeneity." In *Keywords in Latina/o Studies*, edited by Deborah Vargas, Nancy Raquel Mirabal, and Lawrence La Fountain-Stokes, 100–104. New York: New York University Press.

Blackwell, Maylei. 2015. "Geographies of Difference: Transborder Organizing and Indigenous Women's Activism." *Social Justice* 42: 137–54.

Blackwell, Maylei. 2014. "Translenguas: Mapping the Possibilities and Challenges of Transnational Women's Organizing across Geographies of Difference." In *Translocalities/Translocadidades: Feminist Politics of Translation in the Latin/a Americas*, edited by Sonia E. Alvarez, Claudia de Lima Costa, Veronica Feliu, Rebecca Hester, Norma Khlan, and Millie Thayer, 299–320. Durham, NC: Duke University Press.

Blackwell, Maylei. 2012. "The Practice of Autonomy in the Age of Neoliberalism: Strategies from Indigenous Women's Organizing in Mexico." *Journal of Latin American Studies* 44: 703–32.

Blackwell, Maylei. 2011. *¡Chicana Power! Contested Histories of Feminism in the Chicano Movement*. Austin: University of Texas Press.

Blackwell, Maylei. 2010. "Líderes Campesinas: Nepantla Strategies and Grassroots Organizing at the Intersection of Gender and Globalization." *Aztlán: A Journal of Chicano Studies* 35 (1): 13–47.

Blackwell, Maylei. 2009. "Mujer Rebelde: Testimonio de Odilia Romero Hernández." *Desacatos* 31: 147–56.

Blackwell, Maylei. 2007. "Engendering the 'Right to Have Rights': The Indigenous Women's Movement in Mexico and the Practice of Autonomy." In *Women, Ethnicity, and Nationalisms in Latin America*, edited by Natividad Gutierrez, 193–222. Hampshire, UK: Ashgate.

Blackwell, Maylei. 2006. "Weaving in the Spaces: Indigenous Women's Organizing and the Politics of Scale in Mexico." In *Dissident Women: Gender and Cultural Politics in Chiapas*, edited by Shannon Speed, Rosalva Aída Hernández Castillo, and Lynn Stephen, 115–56. Austin: University of Texas Press.

Blackwell, Maylei. 2004. "(Re)Ordenando el discurso de la nación: El movimiento de mujeres indígenas en México y la práctica de la Autonomia." In *Mujeres y nacionalismo: De La independencia a La nación del nuevo milenio*, edited by Natividad Gutiérrez Chong, 193–234. Mexico City: Universidad Nacional Autónoma de México.

Blackwell, Maylei. 2000. "Geographies of Difference: Mapping Multiple Feminist Insurgencies and Transnational Public Cultures in the Americas." PhD diss., University of California, Santa Cruz.

Blackwell, Maylei, Floridalma Boj Lopez, and Luis Urrieta. 2017. "Special Issue: Critical Latinx Indigeneities." *Latino Studies* 15 (2): 126–37. https://doi.org/10.1057/s41276-017-0064-0.

Blackwell, Maylei, Laura Briggs, and Mignonette Chiu. 2015. "Transnational Feminisms Roundtable." *Frontiers: A Journal of Women Studies* 36 (3): 1–24.

Blackwell, Maylei, Rosalva Aída Hernández Castillo, Juan Herrera, Morna Macleod, Renya Ramírez, Rachel Sieder, María Teresa Sierra, and Shannon Speed. 2009. "Cruces de fronteras, identidades indígenas, género y justicia en las Américas." *Desacatos* 31: 13–34.

Blackwell, Maylei, and Edward McCaughan, eds. 2015. "Introduction: New Dimensions in the Scholarship and Practice of Mexican and Chicanx Social Movements." *Social Justice* 42: 1–9.

Boj Lopez, Floridalma. 2017a. "Mobile Archives of indigeneity: Building La Comunidad Ixim through organizing in the Maya diaspora. *Latino Studies* 15: 201–18.

Boj Lopez, Floridalma. 2017b. "Weavings That Rupture: The Possibility of Contesting Settler Colonialism through Cultural Retention among the Maya Diaspora." In *U.S. Central Americans: Reconstructing Memories, Struggles, and Communities of Resistance*, edited by Karina Oliva-Alvarado, Alicia Ivonne Estrada, and Ester E. Hernández, 188–203. Tucson: University of Arizona Press.

Bonfil Sanchez, Paloma, Dalia Barrera Bassols, and Irma G. Aguirre Pérez. 2008. *Los Espacios conquistados: Participación política y liderazgo de las mujeres indígenas de México*. México City: Programa de las Naciones Unidas para el Desarrollo.

Bonfil Sanchez, Paloma, and Marcó del Pont Lalli. 1999. *Las mujeres indígenas al final del milenio*. Mexico City: Secretaria de Gobernación and Comisión Nacional de la Mujer.

Boone, Elizabeth. 2000. *Stories in Red and Black: Pictorial Histories of the Aztecs and Mixtecs*. Austin: University of Texas Press.

Brady, Mary Pat. 2022. *Scales of Captivity Racial Capitalism and the Latinx Child*. Durham, NC: Duke University.

Braman, Sandra. 1996. "Interpenetrated Globalization: Scaling, Power and the Public Sphere." In *Globalization, Communication, and Transnational Civil Society*, edited by Sandra Braman and Annabelle Sreberny-Mohammadi, 21–35. Cresskill, NJ: Hampton Press.

Brenner, Neil. 2011. "The Urban Question and the Scale Question: Some Conceptual Clarifications." In *Locating Migration: Rescaling Cities and Migrants*, edited by Nina Glick Schiller and Ayse Çağlar, 23–41. Ithaca, NY: Cornell University Press.

Brysk, Alison. 2000. *From Tribal Village to Global Village: Indian Rights and International Relations in Latin America*. Stanford, CA: Stanford University Press.

Brysk, Alison. 1993. "From Above and Below: Social Movements, the International System, and Human Rights in Argentina." *Comparative Political Studies* 26: 259–85.

Burguete Cal y Mayor, Araceli. 2021. "Martha Sánchez Néstor, Una lucha por los derechos de autodeterminación de las mujeres indígenas y afromexicanas" *Autonomias hoy Pueblos Indigenas en América Latina* 3: 11–16.

Burguete Cal y Mayor, Araceli. 2007. *Cumbres indígenas en América Latina: recuento de una tradición política*. Mexico City: Revista Memoria, CEMOS.

Burnham, Linda. 2001. "The Wellspring of Black Feminism." Working Paper Series, no. 1. Oakland, CA: Women of Color Resource Center.

Burnham, Linda. 1994. "Race and Gender: The Limits of Analogy." In *Challenging Racism and Sexism: Alternatives to Genetic Explanations*, edited by Ethel Tobach and Betty Rosoff, 143–62. New York: Feminist Press.

Byrd, Jodi A. 2011. *The Transit of Empire: Indigenous Critiques of Colonialism*. Minneapolis: University of Minnesota Press.

Cabnal, Lorena. 2010. "Acercamiento a la Construcción de la Propuesta De Pensamiento Epistémico de las Mujeres Indígenas Feministas Comunitarias de Abya Yala". In *Feminismos Diversos: El Feminismo Comunitario*. Guatemala: Acsur.

Cabrera Pérez-Armiñan, María Luisa, and Morna Macleod. 2000. *Faces without Masks: Mayan Women on Identity, Gender and Ethnicity in Guatemala*. Guatemala City: Oxfam Community Aid Abroad.

Carlsen, Laura. 1999. "Autonomía indígena y usos y costumbres: La innovación de la tradición." *Chiapas* 7: 21–70.

Carneiro, Sueli. 2016. "Women in Movement." Translated by Regina Camargo. *Meridians: Feminism, Race, Transnationalism* 14 (1): 30–49.

Carneiro, Sueli. 2000. Raca e Etnia No Contexto da Conferencia de Beijing. In *O Livroda Saude das Mulheres Negras: Nossos Passos Vem de Longe*, 2nd ed., edited by Jurema Werneck, Maisa Mendonca, and Evelyn C. White, 247–56. Rio de Janeiro: Impresso no Brasil.

Carpenter, Kristen A., Sonia K. Katyal, and Angela R. Riley. 2010. "Clarifying Cultural Property." *International Journal of Cultural Property* 17: 581–98.

Carpio, Genevieve, Natchee Blu Barnd, and Laura Barraclough. 2022. "Introduction to the Special Issue: Mobilizing Indigeneity and Race within and against Settler Colonialism." *Mobilities* 17 (2): 179–95.

Carrillo, Theresa. 1998. "Cross-Border Talk: Transnational Perspectives on Labor, Race and Sexuality." In *Talking Visions: Multicultural Feminism in Transnational Age*, edited by Ella Shohat, 391–411. Cambridge, MA: MIT Press.

Castañeda Salgado, Martha Patricia, Fabiola Del Jurado Mendoza, Norma Don Juan Pérez, Beatriz Gómez Barrenechea, Lizbeth Hernández Cruz, and Laura Hernández Pérez. 2022. "Construyendo Relaciones de Igualdad Desde La Práctica Comunitaria Indígena: La Experiencia Política de La Coordinadora Nacional de Mujeres Indígenas (Mexico)." In *Nudos Críticos de Las Desigualdades de Género En América Latina y El Caribe*, 1–11. Buenos Aires: CLACSO.

Castellanos, M. Bianet, Lourdes Gutiérrez Nájera, and Arturo J. Aldama. 2012. *Comparative Indigeneities of the Américas: Toward a Hemispheric Approach*. Tucson: University of Arizona Press.

Caudillo Félix, Gloria Alicia. 2012. "Reflexciones Sobre el Buen Vivir o Vivir Bien (Suna Qamaña; Sumal Kawsay, Balu Wala)." *Temas De Nuestra América. Revista De Estudios Latinoamericanos*, Número Extraordinario dedicado al XII Congreso de SOLAR: 185–98.

Chacón, Gloria Elizabeth. 2018. *Indigenous Cosmolectics: Kab'awil and the Making of Maya and Zapotec Literatures*. Chapel Hill: University of North Carolina Press.

Chancoso, Blanca. 2014. "El Sumak Kawsay desde la visión de mujer." In *Sumak Kawsay Yuyay. Antología del pensamiento indigenista ecuatoriano sobre Sumak Kawsay*, edited by Antonio Luis Hidalgo Capitán, Alejandro Guillén García, and Nancy Deleg Guazha, 221–28. Cuenca, Ecuador: Centro de Investigación en Migraciones (CIM), Universidad de Huelva and Programa Interdisciplinario de Población y Desarrollo Local Sustentable (PYDLOS).

Chavez, Xochitl Consuelo. 2013. "Migrating Performative Traditions: The Guelaguetza Festival in Oaxacalifornia." PhD diss., University of California, Santa Cruz.

Chinas, Beverly L. 1973. *The Isthmus Zapotec: Women's Roles in Cultural Context*. New York: Holt, Rinehart and Winston.

Clarck-Alfaro, Victor. 2003. *Los Mixtecos en la Frontera (Baja California)*. San Diego, CA: Montezuma.

Cohen, Cathy J. 1997. "Punks, Bulldaggers, and Welfare Queens: The Radical Potential of Queer Politics?" *GLQ: A Journal of Lesbian and Gay Studies* 3 (4): 437–65.

Contreras, Sheila M. 2008. *Blood Lines: Myth, Indigenism, and Chicana/o Literature*. Austin: University of Texas Press.

Costanza-Chock, Sasha. 2014. *Out of the Shadows, into the Streets! Transmedia Organizing and the Immigrant Rights Movement*. Cambridge, MA: MIT Press.

Coulthard, Glenn S. 2014. *Red Skin, White Masks: Rejecting the Colonial Politics of Recognition*. Minneapolis: University of Minnesota Press.

Crenshaw, Kimberle. 1991. "Mapping the Margins: Intersectionality, Identity Politics, and Violence against Women of Color." *Stanford Law Review* 43 (6): 1241–99.

Cruz-Manjarrez, Adriana. 2013. *Zapotecs on the Move: Cultural, Social, and Political Processes in Transnational Perspective*. New Brunswick, NJ: Rutgers University Press.

Cumes, Aura. 2021. "La Dualidad Complementaria y el Popul Vuj: Patriarcado, Capitalismo y Despojo.'" Interview with Yásnaya A. Gil. *Revista de la Universidad de Mexico*, Universidad de Mexico, April, 2021.

Cumes, Estela Aura. 2014. "Multiculturalismo, género y feminismos: mujeres diversas, luchas complejas." In *Tejiendo de otro modo: Feminismo, epistemología y apuestas descoloniales en Abya Yala*, edited by Yuderkys Espinosa Miñoso et al., 237–52. Cauca, Colombia: Editorial Universidad del Cauca.

Cunningham, Myrna. 2006. "Indigenous Women's Vision of an Inclusive Feminism." *Development* 49 (1): 55–59.

Dagnino, Evelina. 2007. "Citizenship: A Perverse Confluence." *Development in Practice* 17: 549–56.

Dagnino, Evelina. 1994. "Os Movimentos Sociais e a Emerência de Uma Nova Noção de Ciodadania." In *Os Anos 90: Política e Sociedade no Brasil*, edited by Evelina Dagnino, 103–15. São Paulo: Brasiliense.

Dalton, Margarita. 2012. *Democracia e igualdad en conflicto: las presidentas municipales en Oaxaca*. Mexico City: Tribunal Electoral del Poder Judicial de la Federación.

Dalton, Margarita. 2005. "La Participación Política de las Mujeres en los Municipios Llamados de Usos y Costumbres." In *Diez Voces a Diez Años: Reflexiones Sobre los Usos y Costumbres a Diez Años del Reconocimiento Legal*, 51–84. Oaxaca: EDUCA.

Dalton, Margarita. 2004. "Democracia y equidad de género. La voz de las presidentas municipales zapotecas." In *Los retos culturales de México frente a la globalización*, edited by Lourdes Arizpe, 215–39. Mexico City: Cámera de Diputados/Miguel Ángel Porrúa.

Das Gupta, Monisha. Forthcoming. *Settling Migration: Migrant Organizing in an Era of Deportation and Dispossession*. Durham, NC: Duke University Press.

Deer, Sarah. 2015. *The Beginning and End of Rape: Confronting Sexual Violence in Native America*. Minneapolis: University of Minnesota Press.

Deer, Sarah. 2009. "Decolonizing Rape Law: A Native Feminist Synthesis of Safety and Sovereignty." *Wicazo Sa Review* 24: 149–67.

Deer, Sarah, Bonnie Clairmont, Carrie A. Martell, and Maureen L. White Eagle. 2007. *Sharing Our Stories of Survival: Native Women Surviving Violence*. Lanham, MD: AltaMira.

De Genova, Nicholas. 2004. "The Legal Production of Mexican/Migrant 'Illegality.'" *Latino Studies* 2: 160–85.

De la Cadena, Marisol. 2015. *Earth Beings: Ecologies of Practice across Andean Worlds*. Durham, NC: Duke University Press.

De la Cadena, Marisol. 2010. "Indigenous Cosmopolitics in the Andes: Conceptual Reflections beyond 'Politics.'" *Cultural Anthropology* 25: 334–70.

De la Cadena, Marisol, and Mario Blaser. 2018. *A World of Many Worlds*. Durham, NC: Duke University Press.

Del Valle Escalante, Emilio. 2018. "For Abiayala to Live, the Americas Must Die: Toward a Transhemispheric Indigeneity." *Native American and Indigenous Studies* 5: 42–68.

Del Valle Escalante, Emilio. 2014. "Self-Determination: A Perspective from Abya Yala." In *Restoring Indigenous Self Determination: Theoretical and Practical Approaches*, edited by Marc Woons, 101–9. Bristol, UK: E-International Relations Publishing.

De Sousa Santos, Boaventura. 2002. "Towards a Multicultural Conception of Human Rights." In *Moral Imperialism. A Critical Anthology*, edited by Berta Hernández-Truyol, 39–60. New York: New York University Press.

De Sousa Santos, Boaventura. 1998. "La globalización del derecho. Los nuevos caminos de la regulación y la emancipación." Bogotá: International Law Students Association, Universidad Nacional de Colombia.

Díaz Gómez, Floriberto. 2004. "Comunidad y Comunalidad." In *Culturas Populares e Indígenas*, 365–73. Mexico City: CONACULTA.

Dove, Atrick. 2004. *The Catastrophe of Modernity: Tragedy and the Nation in Latin American Literature*. Lewisburg, PA: Bucknell University Press.

Downing, John D. 2000. *Radical Media: Rebellious Communication and Social Movements*. Los Angeles: SAGE.

Driskill, Qwo-Li. 2016. *Asegi Stories: Cherokee Queer and Two-Spirit Memory*. Tucson: University of Arizona Press.

Driskill, Qwo-Li. 2010. "Doubleweaving Two-Spirit Critiques: Building Alliances between Native and Queer Studies." *GLQ: A Journal of Lesbian and Gay Studies* 16 (1–2): 69–92.

Duarte Bastian, Ángela Ixkic. 2002. "Conversación con Alma López, autoridad guatelmateca. La doble mirada del género y la etnicidad." *Estudios Latinoamericanos* 9 (18): 16–24.

Dunbar-Ortiz, Roxanne. 2021. *Not a Nation of Immigrants: Settler Colonialism, White Supremacy, and a History of Erasure and Exclusion*. New York: Beacon.

Dunbar-Ortiz, Roxanne. 1984. "The Fourth World and Indigenism: Politics of Isolation and Alternatives." *Journal of Ethnic Studies* 12 (1): 79–105.

Duquette-Rury, Lauren. 2014. "Collective Remittances and Transnational Coproduction: The 3×1 Program for Migrants and Household Access to Public Goods in Mexico." *Studies in Comparative International Development* 49: 112–39.

Eber, Christine Engle, and Christine Marie Kovic. 2003. *Women of Chiapas: Making History in Times of Struggle and Hope*. London: Routledge.

Eisenstadt, Todd. 2013. "Introduction: Reconciling Liberal Pluralism and Groups Rights: A Comparative Perspective on Oaxaca, Mexico's Experiment in Multiculturalism." In *Latin America's Multicultural Movements: The Struggle Between Communitarianism, Autonomy, and Human Rights*, edited by Todd A. Eisenstadt, Michael S. Danielson, Moises Jaime Bailon Corres, and Carlos Sorroza Polo, 3–17. Oxford: Oxford University Press.

Eisenstadt, Todd. 2011. *Politics, Identity, and Mexico's Indigenous Rights Movements*. New York: Cambridge University Press.

Escala Rabadán, Luis, and Gaspar Rivera-Salgado. 2017. "Festivales, comunidades migrante oaxaqueñas y espacios culturales entre México y Estados Unidos: las Guelaguetzas en California." *Migraciones Internacionales* 9: 37–63.

Escárcega, Sylvia. 2013. "The Global Indigenous Movement and Paradigm Wars: International Activism, Network Building, and Transformative Politics." In *Insurgent Encounters: Transnational Activism, Ethnography, and the Political*, edited by Jeffrey S. Juris, and Alex Khasnabish, 129–50. Durham, NC: Duke University Press.

Escobar, Arturo. 2020. *Pluriversal Politics: The Real and the Possible*. Translated by David Frye. Durham, NC: Duke University Press.

Escobar, Arturo. 2008. *Territories of Difference: Place, Movements, Life, Redes*. Durham, NC: Duke University Press.

Escobar, Arturo. 2001. "Culture Sits in Places: Reflections on Globalism and Subaltern Strategies of Localization." *Political Geography* 20: 139–74.

Espinosa Damián, Gisela. 2010. "Por un Mundo de libertades y derechos: La Coordinadora Guerrerense de Mujeres Indígenas." In *La Coordinadora Guerrerense de Mujeres Indígenas: Construyendo le equidad y la ciudadanía*, edited by Gisela Espinosa Damián, Libni Iracema Dircio Chautula, and Martha Sánchez Néstor, 30–130. Coyoacán, Mexico: Universidad Autonoma Metropolitana.

Espinosa Damián, Gisela. 2009a. *Cuatro vertientes del feminismo en México: Diversidad de rutas y cruce de caminos*. Mexico City: Universidad Autónoma Metropolitana.

Espinosa Damián, Gisela. 2009b. "Movimientos de Mujeres Indígenas y Populares En México Encuentros y Desencuentros Con La Izquierda y El Feminismo." *Laberinto* 29 (1): 9–28.

Espinosa Miñoso, Yuderkys, Diana Gómez Correal, Karina Ochoa Muñoz. 2014. *Tejiendo de otro modo: Feminismo, epistemología y apuestas descoloniales en Abya Yala*. Popayán, Colombia: Universidad de Cauca.

Estrada, Alicia Ivonne. 2017. "(Re)claiming Public Space and Place: Maya Community Formation in Westlake/MacArthur Park." In *U.S. Central Americans: Reconstructing Memories, Struggles, and Communities of Resistance*, edited by Karina O. Alvarado, Alicia I. Estrada, and Ester E. Hernández, 166–87. Tucson: University of Arizona Press.

Featherstone, David, Richard Phillips, and Johanna Waters. 2007. "Introduction: Spatialities of Transnational Networks." *Global Networks* 7 (4): 383–91.

Figueroa Romero, Dolores. 2019. "Políticas de Feminicidio En México: Perspectivas interseccionales de mujeres indígenas para reconsiderar su definición teórica-legal y las metodología de recolección de datos." *Journal of International Women's Studies* 20 (8): 64–86.

Figueroa Romero, Dolores, Laura Hernández Pérez. 2021. "Autonomía, interseccionalidad y justicia de género: de 'la doble mirada' de las mayorías a las violencias que no sabemos cómo nombrarlas." In *Autonomías y Autogobierno en la América Diversa* by Miguel González, Araceli Burguete Cal y Mayor, José Marimám, Pablo Ortiz-T., Ritsuko Funaki, 349-380. Quito, Ecuador: Editorial Universitaria Abya-Yala.

Flores, William V., and Rina Benmayor. 1998. *Latino Cultural Citizenship: Claiming Identity, Space, and Rights*. Boston: Beacon.

Flores-Marcial, Xóchitl Marina. 2015. "A History of Guelaguetza in Zapotec Communities of the Central Valleys of Oaxaca." PhD diss., University of California, Los Angeles.

Forbis, Melissa. 2003. "Hacia la Autonomía: Zapatista Women and the Development of a New World." In *Women of Chiapas: Making History in Times of Struggle and Hope*, edited by Christine Eber and Christine Kovic, 231–52. New York: Routledge.

Foucault, Michel. 1991. " On governmentality." In *The Foucault Effect*, edited by Graham Burchell, Colin Gordon, and Peter Miller, 87–104. Chicago: University of Chicago Press.

Foucault, Michel. 1989. "The Subject and Power." In *Michel Foucault: Beyond Structuralism and Hermeneutics*, edited by Hubert L Dreyfus and Paul Rabinow, 208–28. New York: Harvester Wheatsheaf.

Fox, Jonathan. 2006. "Reframing Mexican Migration as a Multi-Ethnic Process." *Latino Studies* 4: 39–61.

Fox, Jonathan. 2005. "Unpacking 'Transnational Citizenship.'" *Annual Review of Political Science* 8: 171–201.

Fox, Jonathan. 2002. "Lessons from Mexico-U.S. Civil Society Coalitions." In *Cross-Border Dialogues: U.S.-Mexico Social Movement Networking*, edited by David Brooks and Jonathan Fox, 341–418. La Jolla: Center for U.S.-Mexican Studies, University of California San Diego.

Fox, Jonathan, and Gaspar Rivera-Salgado. 2004a. "Building Civil Society among Indigenous Migrants." In *Indigenous Mexican Migrants in the United States*, edited by Jonathan Fox and Gaspar Rivera-Salgado, 101–15. La Jolla: Center for U.S.-Mexican Studies, University of California San Diego.

Fox, Jonathan, and Gaspar Rivera-Salgado. 2004b. *Indigenous Mexican Migrants in the United States*. La Jolla: Center for U.S.-Mexican Studies, University of California San Diego.

Fregoso, Rosa-Linda. 2014. "For a Pluriversal Declaration of Human Rights." *American Quarterly* 66: 583–608.

Fregoso, Rosa-Linda. 2006. "'We Want Them Alive!' The Politics and Culture of Human Rights." *Social Identities* 12 (2): 109–38.

Fregoso, Rosa-Linda. 2003. *meXicana Encounters: The Making of Social Identities on the Borderlands*. Berkeley: University of California Press.

Fujikane, Candace. 2008. "Introduction: Asian Settler Colonialism in the U.S. Colony of Hawai'i." In *Asian Settler Colonialism: From Local Governance to the Habits of Everyday Life in Hawai'i*, edited by C. Fujikane and J. Y. Okamura, 2–42. Honolulu: University of Hawai'i Press.

Fujikane, Candace, and Jonathan Y. Okamura. 2008. *Asian Settler Colonialism: From Local Governance to the Habits of Everyday Life in Hawai'i*. Honolulu: University of Hawai'i Press.

García Sánchez, Nayeli. 2018. "Comunidad y comunalidad. Claves para una lectura de la narrativa documental." *Acta poética* 39 (1): 45–65.

Gargallo Celetani, Francesca. 2014. *Feminismos desde Abya Yala: Ideas y proposiciones de las mujeres de 607 pueblos en nuestra américa*. Mexico City: Editorial Corte y Confección.

Gibson, Charles. 1964. *The Aztecs under Spanish Rule: A History of the Indians of the Valley of Mexico 1519–1810*. Stanford, CA: Stanford University Press.

Gil-García, Óscar F. 2015. "Gender Equality, Community Divisions, and Autonomy: The Prospera Conditional Cash Transfer Program in Chiapas, Mexico." *Current Sociology* 64 (3): 447–69.

Glick Schiller, Nina. 2005. "Transnational Social Fields and Imperialism: Bringing a Theory of Power to Transnational Studies." *Anthropological Theory* 5 (4): 439–61.

Glick Schiller, Nina, Linda Basch, and Cristina Blanc-Szanton, eds. 1992. *Towards a Transnational Perspective on Migration: Race, Class, Ethnicity and Nationalism Reconsidered.* Annals of the New York Academy of Sciences. New York: New York Academy of Sciences.

Goeman, Mishuana. 2013. *Mark My Words: Native Women Mapping Our Nations*. Minneapolis: University of Minnesota Press.

Goeman, Mishuana. 2009. "Notes toward a Native Feminism's Spatial Practice." *Wicazo Sa Review* 24 (2): 169–87.

Goeman, Mishuana. 2008. "(Re)Mapping Indigenous Presence on the Land in Native Women's Literature." *American Quarterly* 60 (2): 295.

Goeman, Mishuana, and Jennifer Nez Denetdale. 2009. "Guest Editors' Introduction: Native Feminisms: Legacies, Interventions, and Indigenous Sovereignties." *Wicazo Sa Review* 24 (2): 9–13.

Gonzalez, Alfonso. 2013. *Reform without Justice: Latino Migrant Politics and the Homeland Security State*. Oxford: Oxford University Press.

Gonzalez, Martha. 2020. *Chican@ Artivistas: Music, Community, and Transborder Tactics in East Los Angeles*. Austin: University of Texas Press.

Grande, Sandy. 2015. *Red Pedagogy: Native American Social and Political Thought*. Lanham, MD: Rowman and Littlefield.

Grande, Sandy Marie Anglas. 2000. "American Indian Geographies of Identity and Power: At the Crossroads of Indigena and Mestizaje." *Harvard Educational Review* 70 (4): 467–98.

Gregory, Derek. 2009. *The Dictionary of Human Geography*. 5th ed. Chichester, UK: Wiley Blackwell.

Grewal, Inderpal. 1994. "Autobiographic Subjects and Diasporic Locations: Meatless Days and Borderlands." In *Scattered Hegemonies: Postmodernity and Transnational Feminist Practices*, edited by Inderpal Grewal and Caren Kaplan, 231–54. Minneapolis: University of Minnesota Press.

Grewal, Inderpal. 1992. "The 'Post-Colonial' Question: South Asia Studies and Feminist Research in a Multinational World." Paper delivered at the South Asia Conference, University of California, Berkeley.

Grewal, Inderpal, and Caren Kaplan, eds. 1994. *Scattered Hegemonies: Postmodernity and Transnational Feminist Practices*. Minneapolis: University of Minnesota Press.

Guidotti-Hernández, Nicole M. 2011. *Unspeakable Violence: Remapping U.S. and Mexican National Imaginaries*. Durham, NC: Duke University Press.

Gutiérrez, Margarita, and Nellys Palomo. 1999. "Autonomía con Mirada de mujer." In *México: experiencias de autonomía indígena*, edited by Araceli Burguete Cal y Mayor, 55–86. Copenhagen: International Working Group on Indigenous Affairs.

Gutiérrez, Marisol Raquel. 2010. "The Power of Transnational Organizing: Indigenous Migrant Politics in Oaxacalifornia." *NACLA Report on the Americas* 43: 32–35.

Gutiérrez Nájera, Lourdes. 2010. "Hayandose: Zapotec Migrant Expressions of Membership and Belonging." In *Beyond El Barrio: Everyday Life in Latina/o America*, edited by Gina M. Pérez, Frank A. Guridy, and Adrian Burgos Jr., 63–80. New York: New York University Press.

Gutiérrez Nájera, Lourdes, and Korinta Maldonado. 2017. "Transnational Settler Colonial Formations and Global Capital: A Consideration of Indigenous Mexican Migrants." *American Quarterly* 69 (4): 809-21.

Hale, Charles R. 2008. *Engaging Contradictions: Theory, Politics, and Methods of Activist Scholarship*. Berkeley: University of California Press.

Hale, Charles R. 2005. "Neoliberal Multiculturalism." *Political and Legal Anthropology Review* 28: 10-19.

Hale, Charles R. 2004. "Rethinking Indigenous Politics in the Era of the 'Indio Permitido.'" NACLA *Report on the Americas* 38: 16-21.

Hale, Charles R. 2002. "Does Multiculturalism Menace? Governance, Cultural Rights and the Politics of Identity in Guatemala." *Journal of Latin American Studies* 34: 485-524.

Hale, Charles R., and Lynn Stephen. 2013. *Otros Saberes: Collaborative Research on Indigenous and Afro-Descendant Cultural Politics*. Santa Fe, NM: School for Advanced Research Press.

Hall, Bud L. 1983. "Investigación participativa, conocimiento popular y poder: una reflexión personal." In *La investigación participativa en América Latina Antología*, 15-34. Pátzcuaro, Michoacán: CREFAL.

Hall, Lisa Kahaleole. 2009. "Navigating Our Own 'Sea of Islands': Remapping a Theoretical Space for Hawaiian Women and Indigenous Feminism." *Wicazo Sa Review* 24 (2) (Fall): 15-38.

Hamilton, Nora, and Norma Stoltz Chinchilla. 2001. *Seeking Community in a Global City: Guatemalans and Salvadorans in Los Angeles*. Philadelphia: Temple University Press.

Hancock, Ange-Marie. 2016. *Intersectionality: An Intellectual History*. Oxford: Oxford University Press.

Harcourt, Wendy, and Arturo Escobar. 2005. *Women and the Politics of Place*. Boulder, CO: Lynne Rienner.

Harcourt, Wendy, and Arturo Escobar. 2002. "Women and the Politics of Place." *Development* 45: 7-14.

Hardt, Emily. 2013. "In Transition: The Politics of Place-based, Prefigurative Social Movements." PhD diss., University of Massachusetts Amherst.

Harvey, David. 2003. *The New Imperialism*. Oxford: Oxford University Press.

Harvey, David. 2000. *Spaces of Hope*. Oakland: University of California Press.

Harvey, David. 1997. *Justice, Nature and the Geography of Difference*. Malden, MA: Blackwell.

Harvey, Neil. 1998. *The Chiapas Rebellion: The Struggle for Land and Democracy*. Durham, NC: Duke University Press.

Hennessy, Rosemary. 2011. "Gender Adjustments in Forgotten Places: The North-South Encuentros in Mexico." *Works and Days* 29: 57-58.

Hernández Ávila, Ines. Forthcoming. "Retornos: A Meditation on the Indigenous Americas—A Personal History." In *Critical Latinx Indigeneities*, edited by Lourdes Alberto, Maylei Blackwell, Floridalma Boj Lopez, and Luis Urrieta.

Hernández Castillo, Rosalva Aída. 2016. *Multiple InJustices: Indigenous Women, Law, and Political Struggle in Latin America*. Tucson: University of Arizona Press.

Hernández Castillo, Rosalva Aída. 2013. "¿Del estado multicultural al Estado penal? Mujeres indígenaspresas y criminalización de la pobreza en México." In *Justicias Indí-*

genas y Estado: Violencias Contemporáneas, edited by María Teresa Sierra, Rosalva Aída Hernández Castillo, and Rachel Sieder, 299-335. Mexico City: FLACSO-CIESAS.

Hernández Castillo, Rosalva Aída. 2010a. "The Emergence of Indigenous Feminism in Latin America." *Signs: Journal of Women in Culture and Society* 35 (3): 539-45.

Hernández Castillo, Rosalva Aída. 2010b. "Indigeneity as a Field of Power: Multiculturalism and Indigenous Identities in Political Struggles." In *The SAGE Handbook of Identities*, edited by Margaret Wetherell and Chandra Talpade Mohanty, 379-402. London: SAGE.

Hernández Castillo, Rosalva Aída. 2008. "Introducción. Descentrando el feminismo. Lecciones aprendidas de las luchas de las mujeres indígenas de América Latina." In *Etnografías e historias de Resistencia: Mujeres indígenas, procesos organizativos, y nuevas identidades políticas*, Rosalva Aída Hernández Castillo, editora, 15-44. México City: Centro de Investigaciones y Estudios Superiores en Antropología Social.

Hernández Castillo Rosalva Aída. 2006. "The Indigenous Movement in Mexico Between Electoral Politics and Local Resistance." Translated by Victoria J. Furio. *Latin American Perspectives* 33 (147): 115-31.

Hernández Castillo, Rosalva Aída. 2005. "Gender and Differentiated Citizenship in Mexico: Indigenous Women and Men Reinvent Culture and Redefine the Nation." In *Citizenship, Political Culture and State Transformation in Latin America*, edited by Willem Assies, Marco A. Calderon, and Tom Salman, 323-41. Amsterdam, Netherlands: Dutch University Press-COLMICH.

Hernández Castillo, Rosalva Aída. 2002a. "Indigenous Law and Identity Politics in Mexico: Indigenous Men's and Women's Struggles for a Multicultural Nation." *PoLAR: Political and Legal Anthropology Review* 25 (1): 90-109.

Hernandez Castillo, Rosalva Aída. 2002b. "National Law and Indigenous Customary Law: The Struggle for Justice of Indigenous Women in Chiapas, Mexico." In *Gender Justice, Development, and Rights*, edited by Maxine Molyneux and Shahra Razavi, 384-481. Oxford Studies in Democratization. New York: Oxford University Press.

Hernández Castillo, Rosalva Aída. 2001. "Entre el etnocentrismo feminista y El esencialismo étnico. Las mujeres indígenas y sus demandas de género." *Debate Feminista* 24 (October): 206-29.

Hernández Castillo, Rosalva Aída. 1998a. "Indígenas y Religiosas en Chiapas: ¿Una Nueva Teología India desde las Mujeres?" In *Cristianismo y Sociedad* 36 (137): 79-96.

Hernández Castillo, Rosalva Aída. 1998b. *La Otra Palabra: Mujeres Y Violencia En Chiapas, Antes Y Después De Acteal*. Textos Urgentes. Mexico City: CIESAS, Grupo de Mujeres de San Cristóbal, Centro de Investigación y Acción para la Mujer.

Hernández Castillo, Rosalva Aída. 1997. "Between Hope and Adversity: The Struggle of Organized Women in Chiapas since the Zapatista Uprising." *Journal of Latin American Anthropology* 3: 102-20.

Hernández Castillo, Rosalva Aída. 1994. "Reinventing Tradition: The Women's Law." *Akwe:kon A Journal of Indigenous Issues* 11 (2): 15-23.

Hernández Castillo, Rosalva Aída, and Hector Ortiz Elizondo. 2005. "Different but Equal: Indigenous Peoples and Access to Justice in Mexico." In *Reforming the Administration of Justice in México*, edited by Wayne Cornelius and David Shirk, 369-93. Notre Dame, IN: University of Notre Dame Press.

Hernández, Rosalva Aída, Rachel Seider, and María Teresa Sierra. 2013. "Introducción." In *Justicias Indígenas y Estado: Violencias Contemporáneas*, edited by Maria Teresa Sierra, Rosalva Aída Hernández, and Rachel Sieder, 13-41. Mexico City: FLACSO-México.

Hernández Castillo, Rosalva Aída, and Liliana Suarez Navaz. 2008. *Descolonizando El Feminismo: Teorias Y Practicas desde Los Márgenes*. Valencia, Spain: Ediciones Cátedra.

Hernández Díaz, Jorge. 2014. "Discurso y práctica del liderazgo feminino en la política local en un ámbito multicultural." In *Repensando la participación política de las mujeres: Discursos y prácticas de las costumbres en el ámbito comunitario*, edited by Charlynne Curiel, Holly Worthen, Jorge Hernández-Díaz, Josefina Aranda Bexaury, and Evelyn Puga Aguirre-Sulem, 47-86. Mexico City: Plaza y Valdés.

Hernández Navarro, Luis. 1999. "The San Andrés Accords: Indians and the Soul." *Cultural Survival Quarterly* 23: 30-32.

Hernández Navarro, Luis, and Laura Carlsen. 2004. "Indigenous Rights: The Battle for Constitutional Reform in Mexico." In *Dilemmas of Political Change in Mexico*, edited by Kevin J. Middlebrook. 440-65. London: Institute of Latin American Studies, University of London.

Hernández Navarro, Luis, and Ramón Vera Herrera. 1998. *Acuerdos de San Andrés*. Mexico City: Ediciones Era.

Herrera, Juan. 2016. "Racialized Illegality: The Regulation of Informal Labor and Space." *Latino Studies* 14: 320-43.

Hester, Rebecca. 2016. "Culture in Medicine: An Argument against Competence." In *The Edinburgh Companion to the Critical Medical Humanities*, edited by Angela Whitehead and Angela Woods, 541-58. Edinburgh: Edinburgh University Press.

Hester, Rebecca. 2015. "Cultural Competency Training and Indigenous Cultural Politics in California." *Latino Studies* 13 (3): 316-38.

Hidalgo, Alex. 2019. *Trail of Footprints: A History of Indigenous Maps from Viceregal Mexico*. Austin: University of Texas Press.

Hill Collins, Patricia. 2019. *Intersectionality as Critical Social Theory*. Durham, NC: Duke University Press.

Hill Collins, Patricia. 1990. *Black Feminist Thought: Knowledge Consciousness, and the Politics of Empowerment*. New York: Routledge.

Hindley, Jane. 1996. "Towards a Pluricultural Nation: The Limits of Indigenismo and Article 4." In *Dismantling the Mexican State*, edited by Rob Aitken, Nikki Craske, Gareth A. Jones, and David E. Stansfield, 225-43. New York: St. Martin's.

Holmes, Seth. 2013. *Fresh Fruit, Broken Bodies: Migrant Farmworkers in the United States*. Berkeley: University of California Press.

Hong, Grace Kyungwon. 2015. *Death beyond Disavowal: The Impossible Politics of Difference*. Minneapolis: University of Minnesota Press.

Hong, Grace Kyungwon. 2006. *The Ruptures of American Capital: Women of Color Feminism and the Culture of Immigrant Labor*. Minneapolis: University of Minnesota Press.

Hong, Grace Kyungwon, and Rodrick A. Ferguson, eds. 2011. *Strange Affinities: The Gender and Sexual Politics of Comparative Racialization*. Durham, NC: Duke University Press.

Horn, Rebecca. 1989. "Postconquest Coyoacan: Aspects of Indigenous Sociopolitical and Economic Organization in Central Mexico." PhD diss., University of California, Los Angeles.

Huhndorf, Shari M. 2009. *Mapping the Americas: The Transnational Politics of Contemporary Native Culture*. Ithaca, NY: Cornell University Press.

Hunt, Sarah. 2015. "Violence, Law and the Everyday Politics of Recognition." Comments on Glen Coulthard's "Red Skin, White Masks," presented at the Native American and Indigenous Studies Association (NAISA) Annual Meeting, Washington, DC, June 3-6.

Hunt, Sarah. 2014. "Ontologies of Indigeneity: The Politics of Embodying a Concept." *Cultural Geographies* 21: 27-32.

INCITE! Women of Color against Violence. 2006. *Color of Violence: The INCITE! Anthology*. Cambridge, MA: South End.

Inda, Jonathan Xavier. 2006. *Targeting Immigrants: Government, Technology, and Ethics*. Malden, MA: Blackwell.

IUP Cultural Studies Working Group. 1987. "The Concept of Cultural Citizenship." Working paper no. 1. Los Angeles: UCLA Chicano Studies Research Center.

Iwanska, Alicja. 1966. "Division of Labor among Men and Women in a Mazahua Village of Central Mexico." *Sociologus* 16: 173-86.

Jacquelin-Andersen, Pamela. 2018. *The Indigenous World 2018*. Copenhagen: Eks-Skolens Trykkeri.

Johnson, Gaye T. 2013. *Spaces of Conflict, Sounds of Solidarity: Music, Race, and Spatial Entitlement in Los Angeles*. Berkeley: University of California Press.

Jonas, Susanne, and Nestor Rodríguez. 2015. *Guatemala-U.S. Migration: Transforming Regions*. Austin: University of Texas Press.

Joseph, Tiffany D. 2015. *Race on the Move: Brazilian Migrants and the Global Reconstruction of Race*. Stanford, CA: Stanford University Press.

Jung, Courtney. 2003. "The Politics of Indigenous Identity: Neoliberalism, Cultural Rights, and the Mexican Zapatistas." *Social Research: An International Quarterly* 70: 433-61.

Juris, Jeffrey S., and Alex Khasnabish. 2013. *Insurgent Encounters: Transnational Activism, Ethnography, and the Political*. Durham, NC: Duke University Press.

Jurmain, Claudia K., and William McCawley. 2009. *O, My Ancestor: Recognition and Renewal for the Gabrielino-Tongva People of the Los Angeles Area*. Berkeley, CA: Heyday.

Kampwirth, Karen. 2002. *Women and Guerrilla Movements: Nicaragua, El Salvador, Chiapas, Cuba*. University Park: Pennsylvania State University Press.

Kauanui, J. Kēhaulani. 2016. "A Structure, Not an Event": Settler Colonialism and Enduring Indigeneity." *Lateral: Journal of the Cultural Studies Association* 5 (1). https://csalateral.org/issue/5-1/forum-alt-humanities-settler-colonialism-enduring-indigeneity-kauanui/.

Kauanui, J. Kēhaulani. 2008. *Hawaiian Blood: Colonialism and the Politics of Sovereignty and Indigeneity*. Durham, NC: Duke University Press.

Kearney, Michael. 2000. "Transnational Oaxacan Indigenous Identity: The Case of the Mixtecs and Zapotecs." *Identities: Global Studies in Culture and Power* 7 (2): 173-95.

Kearney, Michael. 1998. "Mixtec Political Consciousness: From Passive to Active Resistance." In *Rural Revolt in Mexico: U.S. Intervention and the Domain of Subaltern Politics*, expanded edition, edited by Daniel Nugent, 113-24. Durham, NC: Duke University Press.

Kearney, Michael. 1995. "The Effects of Transnational Culture, Economy, and Migration on Mixtec Identity in Oaxacalifornia." In *The Bubbling Cauldron: Race, Ethnicity, and the Urban Crisis*, edited by Michael Peter Smith and Joe R. Feagin, 226-43. Minneapolis: University of Minnesota Press.

Kearney, Michael, and Federico Besserer. 2004. "Oaxacan Municipal Governance in Transnational Context." In *Indigenous Mexican Migrants in the United States*, edited by Jonathan Fox and Gaspar Rivera-Salgado. La Jolla, CA: Center for U.S.-Mexican Studies/Center for Comparative Immigration Studies.

Keck, Margaret E., and Kathryn Sikkink. 1998. *Activists beyond Borders: Advocacy Networks in International Politics*. Ithaca, NY: Cornell University Press.

Keme, Emil. 2018. "For Abiayala to Live, the Americas Must Die: Toward a Transhemispheric Indigeneity." *Native American and Indigenous Studies* 5: 42-68.

Keme, Emil. 2015. *Teorizando las literaturas Indígenas contemporáneas*. Chapel Hill: University of North Carolina Press.

Klein, Hillary. 2015. *Compañeras: Zapatista Women's Stories*. New York: Seven Stories Press.

Lamas, Martha. 1991. "Nationalism and Latin America. Identity as women? The Dilemma of Latin American Feminism." In *Being América: Essays on Art, Literature, and Identity from Latin America*, edited by Rachel Weiss and Alan West, 129-41. New York: White Pine.

Latham, Alan. 2002. "Retheorizing the Scale of Globalization: Topologies, Actor-Networks, and Cosmopolitanism." In *Geographies of Power*, edited by Andrew Herod and Melissa W. Wright, 115-44. New York: Malden, MA: Blackwell.

Leal, Alejandra. 2001. "La Identidad Mixteca en la Migración al Norte: El Caso del Frente Indígena Oaxaqueño Binacional." *Amérique Latine Histoire et Mémoire. Les Cahiers ALHIM* 2.

Lefebvre, Henri. 1991. *The Production of Space*. Oxford: Blackwell.

Lemke, Thomas. 2001. "'The Birth of Bio-Politics': Michel Foucault's Lecture at the Collège de France on Neo-Liberal Governmentality." *Economy and Society* 30 (2): 190-207.

Levitt, Peggy, and Sally Merry. 2009. "Vernacularization on the Ground: Local Uses of Global Women's Rights in Peru, China, India and the United States." *Global Networks* 9 (4): 441-61.

Lovera, Sara, and Nellys Palomo. 1999. *Las Alzadas*. 2nd ed. Mexico City: CIMAC and Convergencia Socialista A.P.N.

Lugones, Maria. 2010. "Toward a Decolonial Feminism." *Hypatia* 25 (4): 742-59.

Lugones, Maria. 2008. "Colonialidad y género." *Tabula rasa (Bogotá, Colombia)*, 9: 73-102.

Lytle Hernández, Kelly. 2017. *City of Inmates: Conquest, Rebellion, and the Rise of Human Caging in Los Angeles, 1771-1965*. Chapel Hill: University of North Carolina Press.

Macleod, Morna, and María Luisa Cabrera Pérez-Armiñan, eds. 2000. *Identidad: Rostros sin máscara (Reflexiones sobre cosmovisio´n, ge´nero y etnicidad)*. Guatemala City: Oxfam Australia.

Magaña, Maurice R. 2020. *Cartographies of Youth Resistance: Hip-Hop, Punk, and Urban Autonomy in Mexico*. Oakland: University of California Press.

Magaña, Maurice R. 2010. "Analyzing the Meshwork as an Emerging Social Movement Formation: An Ethnographic Account of the Popular Assembly of the Peoples of Oaxaca (APPO)." *Journal of Contemporary Anthropology* 1 (1): 72-87.

Maier, Elizabeth. 2006a. "Territorial Transits and Identity of Indigenous Migrant Women." *Papeles de población* 12 (47): 201-25.

Maier, Elizbeth. 2006b. "The Unsettling, Gendered Consequences of Migration for Mexican Indigenous Women." In *Women and Change at the U.S.-Mexico Border*, edited by Doreen J. Mattingly and Ellen R. Hansen, 19–35. Tucson: University of Arizona Press.

Maier, Elizbeth. 2000. "La migración como mediación en las relaciones de género de obreras agrícolas de Oaxaca residentes en Baja California." In *Migración y relaciones de género en México*, 229–52. Mexico City: Gimtrap-UNAM.

Maldonado Alvarado, Benjamín. 2015. "Perspectivas de La Comunalidad En Los Pueblos Indígenas de Oaxaca." *Bajo El Volcán* 15 (23): 151–69.

Maldonado Alvarado, Benjamín. 2013. "Comunalidad y responsabilidad autogestiva," *Cuaderno del Sur, Revista de Ciencias Sociales* 18 (34): 21–27.

Maldonado Alvarado, Benjamín. 2010. "Comunidad, Comunalidad y Colonialismo En Oaxaca, México: La Nueva Educación Comunitaria y Su Contexto." PhD diss., Leiden University.

Maldonado Alvarado, Benjamín. 2002. *Autonomía y comunalidad india: enfoques y propuestas desde Oaxaca*. Mexico City: CONACULTA-INAH.

Mani, Lata. 1998. *Contentious Traditions: The Debate on Sati in Colonial India*. Berkeley: University of California Press.

Marcos, Sylvia. 2005. "The Borders Within: The Indigenous Women's Movement and Feminism in Mexico." In *Dialogue and Difference: Feminisms Challenge Globalization*, edited by Sylvia Marcos and Marguerite R. Waller, 81–112. New York: Palgrave Macmillan.

Marston, Sallie A. 2000. "The Social Construction of Scale." *Progress in Human Geography* 24: 219–42.

Martinez, Víctor. 2007. *Autoritarismo, movimiento popular y crisis política: Oaxaca 2006*. Oaxaca: Instituto de Investigaciones sociológicas, Universidad Autónoma "Benito Juarez" de Oaxaca (IISUBAJO).

Martinez Cruz, Alicia. 2016. "Weaving Strategic Identities: Oaxaca Assembly of Indigenous Women." *Nómadas* 45: 170–87.

Martínez Luna, Jaime. 2013. "Origen y ejercicio de la comunalidad." *Cuadernos del Sur: Revista de Ciensas Sociales* 18 (34): 83–90.

Martínez Luna, Jaime. 2010. *Eso Que Llaman Comunalidad*. Oaxaca, Mexico: CONACULTA.

Martinez Luna, Jaime. 1993. ¿*Es la comunidad nuestra identidad? In movimientos indígenas contemporáneos en México*, edited by Arturo Warman and Arturo Argueta, 157–70. Mexico City: CIIH; Porrúa.

Massey, Doreen. 1999. "Imagining Globalization: Power-Geometries of Time-Space." In *Global Futures: Migration, Environment and Globalization*, edited by Avtar Brah, Mary J. Hickman, and Máirtín Mac an Ghaill, 27–44. London: Palgrave Macmillan UK.

Massey, Doreen. 1994. *Space, Place, and Gender*. Minneapolis: University of Minnesota Press.

Massey, Doreen. 1993. "Power-Geometry and a Progressive Sense of Place." In *Mapping the Futures Local Cultures, Global Change*, edited by Jon Bird, Barry Curtis, Tim Putnum, George Robertson, and Lisa Tickner, 59–69. London: Routledge.

Mathews, Holly F. 1985. "'We Are Mayordomo': A Reinterpretation of Women's Roles in the Mexican Cargo System." *American Ethnologist* 12 (2): 285–301.

Mattiace, Shannan. 2003. *To See with Two Eyes: Peasant Activism and Indian Autonomy in Chiapas, Mexico*. Albuquerque: University of New Mexico Press.

McCaughan, Edward. 2012. *Art and Social Movements: Cultural Politics in Mexico and Aztlán*. Durham, NC: Duke University Press.

Mejía Pinneros, María Consuelo, and Sergio Sarmiento. 1987. *La lucha indígenas: Un reto a la ortodoxia*. Mexico City: Universidad Nacional Autónoma de México.

Menjívar, Cecilia, and Leisy Abrego. 2012. "Legal Violence: Immigration Law and the Lives of Central American Immigrants." *American Journal of Sociology* 117 (5): 1380–421.

Mercado, Antonieta. 2015. "El Tequio: Social Capital, Civic Advocacy Journalism and the Construction of a Transnational Public Sphere by Mexican Indigenous Migrants in the US." *Journalism* 16 (2): 238–56.

Merry, Sally Engle. 2006. *Human Rights and Gender Violence: Translating International Law into Local Justice*. Chicago: University of Chicago Press.

Metzl, Jonathan M., and Hansen, Helena. 2014. "Structural Competency: Theorizing a New Medical Engagement with Stigma and Inequality." *Social Science and Medicine* 103: 126–33.

Milkman, Ruth, and Veronica Terriquez. 2012. "'We Are the Ones Who Are out in Front': Women's Leadership in the Immigrant Rights Movement." *Feminist Studies* 38: 723–52.

Millán, Márgara. 2014. *Desordenando el género ¿Descentrando la nación? El zapatismo de las mujeres indígenas y sus consecuencias*. Coyoacan, Mexico: Universidad Nacional Autónoma de México.

Millán, Márgara. 1996. "Las zapatistas de fin del milenio. Hacia políticas de autorrepresentación de las mujeres indígenas." *Chiapas* (3): 19–32.

Miller, Francesca. 1990. "Latin American Feminism and the Transnational Arena." In *Women, Culture, and Politics in Latin America*, edited by the Seminar on Feminism and Culture in Latin America, 10–26. Berkeley: University of California Press.

Million, Dian. 2014. *Therapeutic Nations: Healing in An Age of Indigenous Human Rights*. Tucson: The University of Arizona Press.

Mines, Richard, Sandra Nichols, and David Runsten. 2010. "California's Indigenous Farmworkers: Final Report of the Indigenous Farmworker Study to the California Endowment." California Rural Legal Assistance. Accessed December 11, 2021. https://www.alrb.ca.gov/wp-content/uploads/sites/196/2018/05/IFS_Mines_Final_2010.pdf.

Miranda, Deborah A. 2010. "Extermination of the Joyas: Gendercide in Spanish California." *GLQ: A Journal of Lesbian and Gay Studies* 16 (1–2): 253–84.

Mogrovejo, Norma. 2000. *Un Amor que se Atrevío a Decir su Nombre: La Lucha de las Lesbianas y sus Relaciones con los Movimientos Homosexuales y Feminista en American Latina*. Mexico City: Centro de Documentación y Archivo Histórico Lésbico (CDAHL).

Moller Okin, Susan. 1999. "Is Multiculturalism Bad for Women?" In *Is Multiculturalism Bad for Women?*, edited by Joshua Cohen, Matthew Howard, Martha C. Nussbaum, 7–24. Princeton, NJ: Princeton University Press.

Moller Okin, Susan, Joshua Cohen, Matthew Howard, and Martha Craven Nussbaum. 1999. *Is Multiculturalism Bad for Women?* Princeton, NJ: Princeton University Press.

Mora, Mariana, and Jaime García Leyva. 2020. "Racist Criminalization, Anti-Racist Pedagogies, and Indigenous Teacher Dissidence in the Montaña of Guerrero, Mexico." In *Black and Indigenous Resistance in the Americas: From Multiculturalism to Racist Backlash*,

Mora, Mariana. 2021. "Gender-Territorial Justice and the 'War against Life': Anticolonial Road Maps in Mexico." In *Indigenous Women and Violence: Feminist Activist Research in Heightened States of Injustice*, edited by Lynn Stephen and Shannon Speed, 157–83. Tucson: University of Arizona Press. edited by Juliet Hooker, translated by Giorleny Altamirano Rayo, Aileen Ford, and Steven Lownes, 217–48. New York: Lexington.

Mora, Mariana. 2017a. "Ayotzinapa and the Criminalization of Racialized Poverty in La Montaña, Guerrero, Mexico." *PoLAR: Political and Legal Anthropology Review* 40: 67–85.

Mora, Mariana. 2017b. *Kuxlejal Politics: Indigenous Autonomy, Race, and Decolonizing Research in Zapatista Communities*. Austin: University of Texas Press.

Mora, Mariana. 2017c. "Voices within Silences: Indigenous Women, Security and Rights in the Mountain Region of Guerrero." In *Demanding Justice and Security: Indigenous Women and Legal Pluralities in Latin America*, edited by Rachel Sieder, 197–219. New Brunswick, NJ: Rutgers University Press.

Mora, Mariana. 2015. "The Politics of Justice: Zapatista Autonomy at the Margins of the Neoliberal Mexican State." *Latin American and Caribbean Ethnic Studies* 10 (1): 87–106.

Moraga, Cherríe, and Gloria Anzaldúa, eds. 1981. *This Bridge Called My Back: Writings by Radical Women of Color*. Watertown: Persephone.

Moreton-Robinson, Aileen. 2016. *Critical Indigenous Studies: Engagements in First World Locations*. Tucson: University of Arizona Press.

Mundy, Barbara E. 1996. *The Mapping of New Spain: Indigenous Cartography and the Maps of the Relaciones Geográficas*. Chicago: University of Chicago Press.

Muñoz Ramírez, Gloria. 2018. *Flores en el Desierto: Mujeres del Concejo Indígena de Gobierno*. Mexico City: desInformémmonos and Rosa Luxemburg Stiftung.

Muyolema, Armando. 2001. "De la 'cuestión indígena' a lo 'indígena' como cuestionamiento. Hacia una crítica del latinoamericanismo, el indigenismo y el mestiz(o)aje." In *Convergencia de tiempos: Estudios subalternos/contextos latinoamericanos estado, cultura, subalternidad*, edited by Ileana Rodríguez, 1–32. Amsterdam: Rodopi.

Nava Morales, Elena. 2013. "Comunalidad: Semilla Teórica En Crecimiento." *Cuaderno Del Sur Revista de Ciencias Sociales* 18 (34): 57–70.

Neff, J., S. M. Holmes, K. R. Knight, S. Strong, A. Thompson-Lastad, C. McGuinness, L. Duncan, N. Saxena, M. J. Harvey, A. Langford, K. L. Carey-Simms, S. N. Minahan, S. Satterwhite, C. Ruppel, S. Lee, L. Walkover, J. De Avila, B. Lewis, J. Matthews, and N. Nelson. 2020. "Structural Competency: Curriculum for Medical Students, Residents, and Interprofessional Teams on the Structural Factors That Produce Health Disparities." *MedEdPORTAL: The Journal of Teaching and Learning Resources* 16: 10888.

Newdick, Vivian. 2005. "The Indigenous Woman as Victim of Her Culture in Neoliberal Mexico." *Cultural Dynamics* 17 (1): 73–92.

Newdick, Vivian, and Odilia Romero. 2019. "Interpretation Is an Act of Resistance: Indigenous Organizations Respond to 'Zero Tolerance' and 'Family Separation.'" *LASA Forum: The Languages and Literature of Abiayala* 1 (50): 30–34.

Nicolás, Brenda. 2021. "'Soy de Zoochina': Transborder Comunalidad Practices among Adult Children of Indigenous Migrants." *Latino Studies* 19 (1): 47–69.

Nicolás, Brenda. 2020. "Zapotec Generations across Settler Colonial Borders: Gendering Belonging and Identity." PhD diss., University of California, Los Angeles.

Nicolás, Brenda. 2016. "Soy de Zoochina: Zapotecs Across Generations in Diaspora Re-Creating Identity and Sense of Belonging." Master's thesis, University of California, Los Angeles.

Olesen, Thomas. 2005. *International Zapatismo: The Construction of Solidarity in the Age of Globalization*. London: Zed.

Olivera Bustamante, Mercedes. 1994. "Aguascalientes y el movimiento social de las mujeres chiapanecas." In *A propósito de la insurgencia en Chiapas*, edited by Silvia Soriano Hernández. Mexico City: Asociación para el Desarrollo de la Investigación Científica y Humanística en Chiapas.

Ong, Aihwa. 2006. *Neoliberalism as Exception: Mutations in Citizenship and Sovereignty*. Durham, NC: Duke University Press.

Ong, Aihwa. 1996. "Cultural Citizenship as Subject-Making: Immigrants Negotiate Racial and Cultural Boundaries in the United States." *Current Anthropology* 37 (5): 737–62.

Padilla, Felix M. 1985. *Latino Ethnic Consciousness: The Case of Mexican Americans and Puerto Ricans in Chicago*. Notre Dame, IN: University of Notre Dame Press.

Palomo, Nellys. 1998. "La ausencia de las mujeres indígenas en las iniciativas sobre derechos y cultura indígena." *Cuadernos Feministas* 5: 22–27.

Palomo, Nellys, Yolanda Castro, and Cristina Orci. 1999. "Mujeres indígenas de Chiapas: nuestros derechos, costumbres y tradiciones." In *Las Alzadas*, 2nd ed., edited by Sara Lovera and Nellys Palomo, 65–81. Mexico City: CIMAC and Convergencia Socialista.

Paredes, Julieta. 2008. *Hilando Fino: Desde el Feminismo Comunitario*. La Paz, Bolivia: CEDEC.

Paris Pombo, Maria Dolores. 2010. "Youth Identities and the Migratory Culture among Triqui and Mixtec Boys and Girls." *Migraciones Internacionales* 5: 139–64.

Pérez, Laura E. 2010. "Enrique Dussel's *Etica de la Liberación*, U.S. Women of Color Decolonizing Practices, and Coalitional Politics amidst Difference." *Qui Parle: Critical Humanities and Social Sciences* 18 (2): 121–46.

Pessar, Patricia R., and Sarah J. Mahler. 2003. "Transnational Migration: Bringing Gender." *The International Migration Review* 37 (3): 812–46

Picq, Manuela Lavinas. 2012. "Between the Dock and a Hard Place: Hazards and Opportunities of Legal Pluralism for Indigenous Women in Ecuador." *Latin American Politics and Society* 54 (2): 1–33.

Pons Cardoso, Cláudia. 2016. "Feminisms from the Perspective of Afro-Brazilian Women." Translated by Miriam Adelman. *Meridians: Feminism, Race, Transnationalism* 14 (1): 1–29.

Popkin, Eric. 2005. "The Emergence of Pan-Mayan Ethnicity in the Guatemalan Transnational Community Linking Santa Eulalia and Los Angeles." *Current Sociology* 53 (4): 675–706.

Postero, Nancy Grey. 2007. *Now We Are Citizens: Indigenous Politics in Postmulticultural Bolivia*. Stanford, CA: Stanford University Press.

Povinelli, Elizabeth A. 2002. *The Cunning of Recognition: Indigenous Alterities and the Making of Australian Multiculturalism*. Durham, NC: Duke University Press.

Pratt, Mary Louise. 2008. "In the Neocolony: Destiny, Destination, and the Traffic in Meaning." In *Coloniality at Large*, edited by Mabel Morana, Enrique Dussel, and Carlos A. Jauregui, 459-78. Durham, NC: Duke University Press.

Quijano, Anibal. 2000. "Coloniality of Power, Eurocentrism, and Latin America." *Nepantla: Views from South* 1 (3): 533-80.

Quijano, Anibal. 1997. "Colonialidad de Poder, Cultura y Conocimiento en América Latina." *Anuario Mariáteguiano* 9: 113-22.

Radcliffe, Sarah A. 2020. "On Decoloniality and Geographies." *Postcolonial Studies* 23 (4): 584-88.

Radcliffe, Sarah A. 2015. *Dilemmas of Difference: Indigenous Women and the Limits of Postcolonial Development Policy*. Durham, NC: Duke University Press.

Radcliffe, Sarah. 2008. "Las Mujeres Indígenas Ecuatorianas Bajo La Gobernabilidad Multicultural y de Género." In *Raza, Etnicida y Sexualidades. Ciudanía y Multiculturalism En América Latina*, edited by Peter Wade, Fernando Urrea Giraldo, and Mara Viveros Vigoya, 105-36. Bogotá, Colombia: Universidad Nacional de Colombia, Facultad de Ciencias Humanas. Centero de Estudios Sociales (CES), Escuela de Género.

Raheja, Michelle H. 2011. *Reservation Reelism: Redfacing, Visual Sovereignty, and Representation of Native Americans in Film*. Lincoln: University of Nebraska Press.

Ramirez, Renya K. 2007. *Native Hubs: Culture, Community, and Belonging in Silicon Valley and Beyond*. Durham, NC: Duke University Press.

Razack, Sherene. 2002. *Race, Space, and the Law: Unmapping a White Settler Society*. Toronto: Between the Lines.

Recondo, David. 2001. "Usos y costumbres, procesos electorales y autonomía indígena en Oaxaca." In *Costumbres, leyes y movimiento indio en Oaxaca y Chiapas*, edited by Lourdes de Leon Pasquel, 91-113. Mexico City: Miguel Angel Porrua.

Rich, Adrienne. 1986. "Notes toward a Politics of Location." In *Blood, Bread, and Poetry: Selected Prose, 1979-1985*, 210-31. New York: Norton.

Rivera Cusicanqui, Silvia. 2012. "*Ch'ixinakax utxiwa*: A Reflection on the Practices and Discourses of Decolonization." *South Atlantic Quarterly* 111 (1): 95-109.

Rivera Cusicanqui, Silvia. 2010. *Ch'ixinakax utxiwa: Una reflexión sobre prácticas y discursos descolonizadores*. Buenos Aires: Tinta Limón.

Rivera-Salgado, Gaspar. 2014a. "Pueblos Indígenas Transnacionales: The Intellectual Legacy of Michael Kearney." *Latin American Perspectives* 42: 26-46.

Rivera-Salgado, Gaspar. 2014b. "The Right to Stay Home: Equity and the Struggle of Migrant Indigenous Peoples." In *Development and Equity: An Interdisciplinary Exploration by Ten Scholars from Africa, Asia, and Latin America*, edited by Dick Foeken, Ton Dietz, Leo de Haan, and Linda Johnson, 87-104. Leiden, Netherlands: Brill.

Rivera-Salgado, Gaspar. 2006. "Mexican Migrant Organizations: An Overview." In *Invisible No More: Mexican Migrant Civic Participation in the United States*, edited by Xochitl Bada, Jonathan Fox, and Andrew Seeley, 31-33. Washington, DC: Woodrow Wilson International Center for Scholars: Mexico Institute.

Rivera-Salgado, Gaspar. 1999. "Mixtec Activism in Oaxacalifornia: Transborder Grassroots Political Strategies." *Acoustics, Speech, and Signal Processing Newsletter, IEEE* 42(9): 1439-58.

Rivera Zea, Tarcila, ed. 2015. *Nada sobre nosotras sin nosotras: Beijing +20 y las mujeres indígenas de las Américas: avances, vacíos y desafíos*. Lima, Peru: ECMIA.

Rivera Zea, Tarcila. 2008. "Mujeres Indígenas Americanas Luchando Por Sus Derechos." In *Descolonizando el Femenismo: Teorías y Prácticas Desde Los Márgenes*, edited by Liliana Suárez Navaz and Rosalva Aída Hernández Castillo, 331-50.
"The Road to Huairou and Beijing: Chronology, 1975-1995." 1996. *Women's Studies Quarterly* 24 (1-2): 16-17.
Robertson, Kimberly. 2012. "Rerighting the Historical Record: Violence against Native Women and the South Dakota Coalition against Domestic Violence and Sexual Assault." *Wicazo Sa Review* 27 (2): 21-47.
Robles Hernández, Sofía, and Rafael Cardoso Jiménez, eds. 2007. *Floriberto Díaz Escrito: Comunalidad, energía viva del penasamiento mixe Ajuujktsënää'yën - ayuujkwënmää'ny - ayuujk mëk'äjtën*. Mexico City: Universidad Nacional Autónoma de México.
Rocheleau, Dianne, and Robin Roth. 2007. "Rooted Networks, Relational Webs and Powers of Connection: Rethinking Human and Political Ecologies." *Geoforum* 38 (3): 433-37.
Rodriguez, Juana Maria. 2003. *Queer Latinidad: Identity Practices, Discursive Spaces*. Sexual Cultures. New York: New York University Press.
Romero Hernández, Odilia, Centolia Maldonado Vasquez, Rufino Domínguez-Santos, Maylei Blackwell, and Laura Velasco Ortiz. 2014. "'Género, Generación y Equidad: Los retos del liderazgo indígena binacional entre México y Estados Unidos en la experiencia del FIOB.'" In *Otros Saberes: Collaborative Research on Indigenous and Afro-Descendant Cultural Politics*, edited by Charles R. Hale and Lynn Stephen, 75-100. Santa Fe, NM: School for Advanced Research Press.
Rosaldo, Renato. 1994. "Cultural Citizenship in San Jose, California." *PoLAR: Political and Legal Anthropology Review* 17 (2): 57-63.
Rosenthal, Nicolas. 2012. *Reimagining Indian Country: Native American Migration and Identity in Twentieth-Century Los Angeles*. Chapel Hill: University of North Carolina Press.
Roth, Wendy. 2012. *Race Migrations: Latinos and the Cultural Transformation of Race*. Stanford, CA: Stanford University Press.
Rousseau, Stephanie, and Anahi Rosales Hudson, eds. 2018. *Indigenous Women's Movements in Latin America: Gender and Ethnicity in Peru, Mexico, and Bolivia*. New York: Macmillan.
Rousseau, Stephanie, and Anahi Rosales Hudson, eds. 2016. "Paths towards Autonomy in Indigenous Women's Movements: Mexico, Peru, Bolivia." *Journal of Latin American Studies* 48 (1): 33-60.
Rovira, Guiomar. 2000. *Women of Maize: Indigenous Women and the Zapatista Rebellion*. London: Practical Action Publishing.
Rubin, Jeffrey W. 2004. "Meanings and Mobilizations: A Cultural Politics Approach to Social Movements and States." *Latin American Research Review* 39 (3): 106-42.
Rubin, Jeffrey W. 1997. *Decentering the Regime: Ethnicity, Radicalism, and Democracy in Juchitán, Mexico*. Durham, NC: Duke University Press.
Saldaña-Portillo, María Josephina. 2016. *Indian Given: Racial Geographies across Mexico and the United States*. Durham, NC: Duke University Press.
Saldaña-Portillo, María Josephina. 2003. *The Revolutionary Imagination in the Americas and the Age of Development*. Durham, NC: Duke University Press.
Saldaña-Portillo, María Josephina. 2001. "Who's the Indian in Aztlan? Re-writing Mestizaje, Indianism, and Chicanismo from the Lacandon." In *The Latin American*

Subaltern Studies Reader, edited by Ileana Rodríguez, 402-23. Durham, NC: Duke University Press.

Sánchez-López, Luis. 2018. "Crafting the Mestizo State: Indigeneity, Customary Law, and Statecraft in Mexico." PhD diss., University of California, San Diego.

Sánchez-López, Luis. 2017. "Learning from the Paisanos: Coming to Consciousness in Zapotec LA." *Latino Studies* 15 (2): 242-46.

Sánchez Néstor, Martha. 2005. *La doble mirada: voces e historias de mujeres indígenas latinoamericanas*. Mexico City: UNIFEM/ILSB.

Sánchez Néstor, Martha, and Libni Iracma Dircio Chautla. 2010. "Un balance." In *La Coordinadora Guerrerense de Mujeres Indígenas: Construyendo la sequidad y la ciudadanía*, edited by Gisela Espinosa Damián, Libni lracema Dircio Chautla, and Martha Sánchez Néstor, 413-23. Mexico City: La Universidad Autónoma Metropolitana.

Sandoval, Chela. 2000. *Methodology of the Oppressed*. Minneapolis: University of Minnesota Press.

Sandoval, Chela. 1998. "Mestizaje as Method: Feminists-of-Color Challenge the Cannon." In *Living Chicana Theory*, edited by Carla Trujillo, 352-70. Berkeley, CA: Third Woman.

Sandoval, Chela. 1991. "U.S. Third World Feminism: The Theory and Method of Oppositional Consciousness in the Postmodern World." *Genders* 10: 1-24.

Santa Ana, Otto, Layza López, and Edgar Munguía. 2010. "Framing Peace as Violence: Television News Depictions of the 2007 Immigrant Rights Marchers in Los Angeles." *Aztlán: A Journal of Chicano Studies* 35 (1): 69-101.

Sassen, Saskia. 2002. *Global Networks, Linked Cities*. New York: Routledge.

Sassen, Saskia. 1991. *The Global City: New York, London, Tokyo*. Princeton, NJ: Princeton University Press.

Sault, Nicole L. 2001. "Godparenthood Ties Among Zapotec Women and the Effects of Protestant Conversion." In *Holy Saints and Fiery Preachers: The Anthropology of Protestantism in Mexico and Central America*, edited by James W. Dow and Alan R. Sandstrom, 117-46. Santa Barbara, CA: Prater.

Schaeffer, Felicity Amaya. 2022. *Unsettled Borders: The Militarized Science of Surveillance on Sacred Indigenous Land*. Durham, NC: Duke University Press.

Schild, Verónica. 2015. "Feminism and Neoliberalism in Latin America." *New Left Review* 96: 59-74.

Schild, Verónica. 2007. "Empowering Consumer Citizens or Governing Poor Female Subjects? The Institutionalization of 'Self-Development' in the Chilean Social Policy Field." *Journal of Consumer Culture* 7: 179-203.

Schild, Verónica. 2000a. "'Gender Equity' without Social Justice: Women's Rights in the Neoliberal Age." *NACLA Report on the Americas* 34 (1): 25-28.

Schild, Verónica. 2000b. "Neo-Liberalism's New Market Citizens: The Civilizing Dimension of Social Programs in Chile." *Citizenship Studies* 4: 275-305.

Schild, Verónica. 1997. "New Subjects of Rights? Gendered Citizenship and the Contradictory Legacies of Social Movements in Latin America." *Organization: The Interdisciplinary Journal of Organization, Theory and Society* 4: 604-19.

Schirmer, Jennifer. 1993. "The Seeking of Truth and the Gendering of Consciousness: The Comadres of El Salvador and the Conavigua Widows of Guatemala." In *'Viva'*:

Women and Popular Protest in Latin America, edited by Sarah A. Radcliffe and Sallie Westwood, 1–64. New York: Routledge.

Segura, Denise, and Pat Zavella, eds. 2007. *Women and Migration in the U.S.-Mexico Borderlands: A Reader*. Durham, NC: Duke University Press.

Sepulveda, Charles. 2018. "Our Sacred Waters: Theorizing Kuuyam as a Decolonial Possibility." *Decolonization: Indigeneity, Education and Society* 7 (1): 39–58.

Sieder, Rachel. 2008. "Entre la Multiculturalización y las Reivindicaciones Identitarias: Construyendo Ciudadanía étnica y Autoridad Indígena en Guatemala." In *El Multiculturalismo y el Futuro de Guatemala Comosociedad Multétnica*, edited by Santiago Bastos, 69–96. Guatemala City: FLACSO.

Sieder, Rachel. 2007. "The Judiciary and Indigenous Rights in Guatemala." *International Journal of Constitutional Law* 5 (2): 211–241.

Sieder, Rachel. 2006. "El Derecho Indígena y La Globalización Legal En La Posguerra Guatemalteca." *Alteridades* 16 (31): 23–37.

Sierra, María Teresa. 2021. "Women Defenders and the Fight for Gender Justice in Indigenous Territories." In *Indigenous Women and Violence: Feminist Activist Research in Heightened States*, edited by Lynn Stephen and Shannon Speed, 74–99. Tucson: University of Arizona Press.

Sierra, María Teresa. 2017a. "Guerrero Community Police Confront Macro-Violences." *NACLA Report of the America: North American Congress on Latin America* 49 (3): 366–69.

Sierra, María Teresa. 2017b. "Indigenous Autonomies and Gender Justice. Women Dispute Security and Rights in Guerrero México." In *Demanding Justice and Security: Indigenous Women and Legal Pluralities in Latin America*, edited by Rachel Sieder, 97–119. New Brunswick, NJ: Rutgers University Press.

Sierra, María Teresa. 2015. "Pueblos indígenas y usos contra-hegemónicos de la ley en la disputa por la justicia: Policía comunitaria de Guerrero." *Journal of Latin American and Caribbean Anthropology* 20: 135–55.

Sierra, María Teresa. 2012. "Indigenous Women Fight for Justice: Gender Rights and Legal Pluralism in Mexico." In *Gender Justice and Legal Pluralities: Latin American and African Perspectives*, edited by Rachel Sieder and John McNeish, 56–81. London: Routledge.

Sierra, María Teresa. 2010. "Indigenous Justice Faces the State: The Community Police Force in Guerrero, Mexico." *NACLA Report of the America: North American Congress on Latin America* 43 (5): 34–38.

Sierra, María Teresa. 2009. "Las mujeres indígenas ante la justicia comunitaria. Perspectivas desde la interculturalidad y los derechos." *Desacatos* 31: 73–88.

Sierra, María Teresa. 2007. "Justicia indígena y Estado: Retos desde la diversidad." In *Política, etnicidad e inclusión digital en los albores del milenio*, edited by Scott Robinson, Hector Tejera, and Laura Valladares Porrúa, 265–94. Mexico City: Miguel Ángel Porrúa.

Sierra, María Teresa. 2006. "Derecho indígena y acceso a la justicia en México: Perspectiva desde la interlegalidad." *Interamerican Institute of Human Rights Review* 41: 287–314.

Sierra, María Teresa. 2005. "The Revival of Indigenous Justice in Mexico: Challenges for Human Rights and the State." *PoLAR: Political and Legal Anthropology Review* 28: 52–72.

Sierra, María Teresa. 2004. "Derechos humanos, género y etnicidad: Reclamos legales y retos antropológicos." In *El Estado y los indígenas en los tiempos del PAN*, edited by Aída Hernández, Sarela Paz, and María Teresa Sierra. Mexico City: CIESAS—Miguel Angel Porrúa.

Sierra, Maria Teresa, and Shannon Speed. 2005. "Critical Perspectives on Human Rights and Multiculturalism in Neoliberal Latin America." *PoLAR: Political and Legal Anthropology Review* 28: 1–9.

Simpson, Audra. 2014. *Mohawk Interruptus: Political life across the Borders of Settler States*. Durham, NC: Duke University Press.

Simpson, Audra, and Andrea Smith, eds. 2014. *Theorizing Native Studies*. Durham, NC: Duke University Press.

Smith, Andrea. 2005. *Conquest: Sexual Violence and American Indian Genocide*. Durham, NC: Duke University Press.

Smith, Neil. 1992. "Geography, Difference and the Politics of Scale." In *Postmodernism and the Social Sciences*, edited by Joe Doherty, Elspeth Graham, and Mo Malek, 57–79. New York: St. Martin's.

Soja, Edward W. 1989. *Postmodern Geographies: The Reassertion of Space in Critical Social Theory*. New York: Verso.

Speed, Shannon. 2019. *Incarcerated Stories: Indigenous Women Migrants and Violence in the Settler-Capitalist State*. Chapel Hill: University of North Carolina Press.

Speed, Shannon. 2017. "Structures of Settler Capitalism in Abya Yala." *American Quarterly* 69: 783–90.

Speed, Shannon. 2008. *Rights in Rebellion: Indigenous Struggle and Human Rights in Chiapas*. Stanford, CA: Stanford University Press.

Speed, Shannon. 2006. "Rights at the Intersection: Gender and Ethnicity in Neoliberal Mexico." In *Dissident Women: Gender and Cultural Politics in Chiapas*, edited by Shannon Speed, R. Aída Hernandez Castillo, and Lynn M. Stephen, 203–21. Austin: University of Texas Press.

Speed, Shannon, Rosalva Aída Hernández Castillo, and Lynn Stephen. 2006. *Dissident Women: Gender and Cultural Politics in Chiapas*. Austin: University of Texas Press.

Speed, Shannon, Reyna Ramirez, Maylei Blackwell, Morna Macleod, Rosalva Aída Hernández Castillo, Rachel Sieder, María Teresa Sierra, Juan Herrera. 2009. "Remapping Gender, Justice, and Rights in the Indigenous Americas: Toward a Comparative Analysis and Collaborative Methodology." *Journal of Latin American and Caribbean Anthropology* 14: 300–331.

Speed, Shannon, and Lynn Stephen, eds. 2021. *Indigenous Women and Violence: Feminist Activist Research in Heightened States of Injustice*. Tucson: University of Arizona Press.

Spivak, Gayatri Chakravorty. 1993. "In a Word: Interview." In *Outside in the Thinking Machine*, 1–26. London: Routledge.

Staheli, Lynn A. 1994. "Empowering Political Struggle: Spaces and Scales of Resistance." *Political Geography* 13 (5): 387–91.

Stavenhagen, Rodolfo. 2001. "Indigenous Law Does Not Make Indigenous Right. A Look at Chiapas." *ReVista: Harvard Review of Latin America* 1 (1): 21–23.

Stephen, Lynn. 2021. "Confronting Gendered Embodied Structures of Violence: Mam Indigenous Women Seeking Justice in Guatemala and the U.S." In *Indigenous Women and Violence: Feminist Activist Research in Heightened States of Injustice*, edited by Lynn Stephen and Shannon Speed, 125–56. Tucson: University of Arizona Press.

Stephen, Lynn. 2014a. "Indigenous Transborder Citizenship: FIOB Los Angeles and the Oaxaca Social Movement of 2006." *Latin American and Caribbean Ethnic Studies* 9: 115-37.

Stephen, Lynn. 2014b. "Transborder/Transnational Citizenships: Migrants and Anthropologists." *Latin American Perspectives* 41: 47-53.

Stephen, Lynn. 2013. *We Are the Face of Oaxaca: Testimony and Social Movements.* Durham, NC: Duke University Press.

Stephen, Lynn. 2012. "Conceptualizing Transborder Communities." In *The Oxford Handbook of the Politics of International Migration*, edited by Marc R. Rosenblum and Daniel J. Tichenor, 456-77. New York: Oxford University Press.

Stephen, Lynn. 2011. "The Rights to Speak and to Be Heard: Women's Interpretations of Rights Discourses in the Oaxaca Social Movement." In *Gender and Culture at the Limits of Rights*, edited by Dorothy L. Hodgson, 161-79. Philadelphia: University of Pennsylvania Press.

Stephen, Lynn. 2009. "Women and Social Movements in Transborder Communities: Mexico and the United States." In *Rural Social Movements in Latin America: Organizing for Sustainable Livelihoods*, edited by Carmen Diana Deere and Frederick S. Royce, 291-320. Gainesville: University Press of Florida.

Stephen, Lynn. 2007. *Transborder Lives: Indigenous Oaxacans in Mexico, California, and Oregon.* Durham, NC: Duke University Press.

Stephen, Lynn. 2006. "Indigenous Women's Activism in Oaxaca and Chiapas." In *Dissident Women Gender and Cultural Politics in Chiapas*, edited by Shannon Speed, R. Aída Hernández Castillo, and Lynn M. Stephen, 157-74. Austin: University of Texas Press.

Stephen, Lynn. 2005. *Zapotec Women: Gender, Class, and Ethnicity in Globalized Oaxaca.* 2nd ed. Durham, NC: Duke University Press.

Stephen, Lynn. 2003. "Indigenous Autonomy in Mexico." In *At the Risk of Being Heard: Identity, Indigenous Rights, and Postcolonial States*, edited by Bartholomew Dean and Jerome M. Levi, 191-216. Ann Arbor: University of Michigan Press.

Stephen, Lynn. 2002. *Zapata Lives! Histories and Cultural Politics in Southern Mexico.* Berkeley: University of California Press.

Stephen, Lynn. 1998. "Genero y Democracia: Lecciones de Chiapas." In *Género y Cultura En América Latina*, edited by María Luisa Tarrés Barraza, 311-34. Mexico City: El Colegio de México.

Stephen, Lynn. 1997. *Women and Social Movements in Latin America: Power from Below.* Austin: University of Texas Press.

Stephen, Lynn. 1996. "The Creation and Re-Creation of Ethnicity: Lessons from the Zapotec and Mixtec of Oaxaca." *Latin American Perspectives* 23: 17-37.

Stephen, Lynn. 1991. *Zapotec Women.* Austin: University of Texas Press.

Swyngedouw, Erik. 1997. "Excluding the Other: The Production of Scale and Scaled Politics." In *Geographies of Economies*, edited by Roger Lee and Jane Wills, 167-76. London: Routledge.

Tamez, Margo. 2013. "Place and Perspective in the Shadow of the Wall: Recovering Nde' Knowledge and Self-Determination in Texas." *Aztlán: A Journal of Chicano Studies* 31: 165-88.

Taylor, Keeanga-Yamahtta. 2017. *How We Get Free: Black Feminism and the Combahee River Collective.* Chicago: Haymarket.

Tellez, Michelle. 2021. *Border Women and the Community of Maclovio Rojas Autonomy in the Spaces of Neoliberal Neglect*. Tucson: University of Arizona Press.

Tellez, Michelle. 2005. "Globalizing Resistance: Maclovio Rojas, a Mexican Community En Lucha." ProQuest Dissertations Publishing. https://search.proquest.com/docview/305006655?pq-origsite=primo.

Terven Salinas, Adriana. 2005. "Revitalización de la Costumbre Jurídica en el Juzgado Indígena de Cuetzalan, Retos desde el Estado." Master's thesis, CIESAS, Mexico City.

Thayer, Millie. 2001. "Transnational Feminism: Reading Joan Scott in the Brazilian Sertão." *Ethnography* 2 (2): 242–71.

Tsing, Anna Lowenhaupt. 2012. "On Nonscalability: The Living World Is Not Amenable to Precision-Nested Scales." *Common Knowledge* 18: 505–24.

Tsing, Anna Lowenhaupt. 2005. *Friction: An Ethnography of Global Connections*. Princeton, NJ: Princeton University Press.

Tsosie, Rebecca A. 1997. "Indigenous Peoples' Claims to Cultural Property: A Legal Perspective." *Museum Anthropology* 21 (3): 5–11.

Tuck, Eve, and K. Wayne Yang. 2012. "Decolonization Is Not a Metaphor." *Decolonization: Indigeneity, Education and Society* 1 (1): 1–40.

Tzul Tzul, Gladys. 2015. "Sistema de Gobierno Comunal Indígena: La organización de la reproducción de la vida." *El Apantle Revista de Estudios Comunitarios* no. 1: 125–40.

Urrieta, Luis. 2017. "Identity, Violence, and Authenticity: Challenging Static Conceptions of Indigeneity." *Latino Studies* 15: 254–61.

Vargas, Virginia. 1998. "Los Feminismos Latinoamericanos Construyendo los Espacios Transnacionales: La Experiencia de Beijing." Paper presented at the Conference on Transnational Organizing in the Americas, Santa Cruz, California, December 4–7.

Vásquez Vásquez, Juana. 2013. "La participación de las mujeres en la construcción de la comunalidad." *Cuaderno del Sur Revista de Ciencias Sociales*, 18 (34): 99–102.

Vázquez García, Verónica. 2011. *Usos y costumbres y ciudadanía femenina: Hablan las presidentas municipals de Oaxaca, 1996–2010*. Mexico City: Miguel Ángel Porrúa.

Velasco Ortiz, Laura. 2005. *Mixtec Transnational Identity*. Tucson: University of Arizona Press.

Velasco Ortiz, Laura. 2002. *El regreso de la comunidad: Migracion indígena y agentes etnicos (los mixtecos en la frontera Mexico-Estados Unidos)*. Tijuana, Baja California, Mexico: El Colegio de la Frontera Norte.

Velasco Ortiz, Laura, and Dolores París Pombo. 2014. "Indigenous Migration in Mexico and Central America: Interethnic Relations and Identity Transformations." *Latin American Perspectives* 41 (3): 5–25.

Velásquez, Maria Cristina. 2004. "Migrant Communities, Gender, and Political Power in Oaxaca." In *Indigenous Mexican Migrants in the United States*, edited by Jonathan Fox and Gaspar Rivera-Salgado, 483–94. San Diego: Center for U.S.-Mexican Studies and Center for Comparative Immigration Studies at the University of California.

Velásquez, Maria Cristina. 2003. "Discriminación por género y participación en los sistemas de gobierno indígena, contrastes y paradojas." In *Diagnostico de la discriminacion hacia las mujeres indígenas*, edited by Paloma Bonfil Sanchez and Elvia Rosa Martinez Medrando, 151–71. Mexico City: Comision Nacional para el Desarrollo de los Pueblos Indígenas.

Velásquez, Maria Cristina. 2000. *El nombramiento—Las elecciones por usos y costumbres en Oaxaca*. Oaxaca City: Instituto Estatal Electoral de Oaxaca.

Velásquez, María Cristina, and Araceli Burgete Cal y Mayor. 2012. *El Sello Indígena de La Institución Municipal En Chiapas y Oaxaca: Una aproximación a la Singularidad del territorio, la población y los sistemas normativos internos*. Programa de las Naciones Unidas para el Desarrollo (PNUD).

Ventura Luna, Silvia. 2010. "The Migration Experience as It Relates to Cargo Participation in San Miguel Cuevas, Oaxaca." *Migraciones Internacionales* 5: 41–70.

Veracini, Lorenzo. 2010. *Settler Colonialism: A Theoretical Overview*. New York: Palgrave Macmillan.

Vicenti Carpio, Myla. 2011. *Indigenous Albuquerque*. Plains Histories. Lubbock: Texas Tech University Press.

Volpp, Leti. 2015. "The Indigenous as Alien." *UC Irvine Legal Review* 289 (2): 289–326.

Wagua, Aiban. 2007. *Así lo vi y así me lo contaron: Datos de la revolución Kuna*. Panama City: Nan Garburba Oduloged Igar.

Wakida, Patricia, Luis Alfaro, Glen Creason, David Deis, and Leighton Kelly. 2015. *Latitudes: An Angeleno's Atlas*. Berkeley, CA: Heyday.

Wolfe, Patrick. 2006. "Settler Colonialism and the Elimination of the Native." *Journal of Genocide Research* 8: 387–409.

Wolfe, Patrick. 1999. *Settler Colonialism and the Transformation of Anthropology: The Politics and Poetics of an Ethnographic Event*. New York: Cassell.

Wood, Stephanie. 1997. "Matters of Life at Death: Nahuatl Testaments of Rural Women, 1589–1801." In *Indian Women of Early Mexico*, edited by Susan Schroeder, Stephanie Wood, and Robert Hasket, 165–84. Norman: University of Oklahoma Press.

Worthen, Holly. 2015. "Indigenous Women's Political Participation: Gendered Labor and Collective Rights Paradigms in Mexico." *Gender and Society* 29 (6): 914–36.

Worthen, Holly Michelle. 2021. "Rights to the Rescue? The Promotion of Indigenous Women's Political-Electoral Rights and the Rise of the Mexican Security State." *Political Geography*, 85: 1-11.

Yamashiro, Aiko, and Noelani Goodyear-Kaopua. 2014. *The Value of Hawai'i 2: Ancestral Roots, Oceanic Visions*. Honolulu: University of Hawai'i Press.

Yashar, Deborah J. 2007. "Resistance and Identity Politics in an Age of Globalization." *The Annals of the American Academy of Political and Social Science* 610 (1): 160–81.

Zavella, Patricia. 2011. *I'm Neither Here nor There: Mexicans' Quotidian Struggles with Migration and Poverty*. Durham, NC: Duke University Press.

Zavella, Patricia. 2000. "Engendering Transnationalism in Food Processing: Peripheral Vision on Both Sides of the U.S.-Mexico Border." In *Las Nuevas Fronteras del Siglo XXI: Dimensiones Culturales, Políticas y Socioeconómicas de las Relaciones México-Estados Unidos*, edited by Norma Klahn, Pedro Castillo, Alejandro Alvarez, and Federico Manchón, 397–424. Mexico City: La Jornada Ediciones, Centro de Investigaciones Colección, La Democracia en México.

Index

Note: Page numbers followed by *f* indicate figures

Abiayala, xix, 4, 15, 30, 96, 98–99, 102, 107–12, 141–42, 291–92; Indigenous organizing in, 4, 106; Indigenous weavings of, 116; spelling of, 297n1, 301n1, 302n7
Aguilar Gil, Yásnaya Elena, 150, 172–74, 307n13
Aikau, Hokulani, 30, 255
Altamirano-Jiménez, Isabel, 106, 109, 111, 182
altepetl, 9–10
Alvarez, Sonia, 110, 117, 292, 298n6, 302n16
Anzaldúa, Gloria, 36, 234
Article 4 (Mexican Constitution), 20–21, 67, 73, 269
Asamblea de Mujeres Indígenas de Oaxaca (Assembly of Indigenous Women of Oaxaca, AMIO), 186–88
Asamblea Nacional Indígena Plural por la Autonomía (National Plural Indigenous Assembly for Autonomy, ANIPA), 45, 51, 57, 68, 72, 121, 139, 300n17; Women's Commissions of, 67
Asamblea Popular de los Pueblos de Oaxaca (Oaxacan Popular People's Assembly, APPO), 187, 241–42, 307n18
Assembly of Zapotec-Chinaltec Authorities (AZACHIS), 163–65
autonomy, 42, 78, 298n1, 299n11, 301n23; comunalidad and, 151; feminist, 119; Guna, 302n9; Indigenous gendered political claims on, 30; Indigenous knowledges of, 293; Indigenous women and, 19, 24, 38, 41, 43–46, 54, 64–67, 70–72, 77, 80, 84, 101, 105, 116, 128, 145, 179, 189, 290, 298n3; legal understandings of, 94; pedagogies of, 44, 66, 154; regional and municipal, 175, 304n14; scales of, 19, 66, 87; spatial, 13; women's, 6, 57–59, 61; Zapatista philosophy of, 298n4. *See also* Indigenous autonomy

Barker, Joanne, 30, 132
Beijing process, 103–4, 118–19, 301n5
Bernadino, Monserrat, 54, 207, 220, 224, 250, 251*f*
Binational Center for Indigenous Development (Centro Binacional para el Desarollo Indígena, CBDIO), 248, 288
Boj Lopez, Floridalma, 17–18, 30, 116, 285–86, 310n12
borderlands, 34, 234; US-Mexico, 13, 223
Brady, Mary Pat, 9, 11, 19, 102
Brenner, Neil, 14, 297n4
Byrd, Jodi, 30, 34, 233, 255, 294

Calderón, Felipe, 25, 89, 190–91, 259
capitalism, 14, 32, 133, 179, 252, 260, 264, 267, 269; global, 294, 305n8; necrocapitalism, 90; neoliberal, 34
cargo system, 150–51, 157, 172, 236, 303n3, 304n9; civil, 175–76; religious, 175–76; women and, 177–78, 181, 186, 193–94, 209
Casa de Mujer Indígena (Indigenous Women's House, CAMI), 45, 53, 79, 162, 300n18
Chacón, Gloria, 30, 100–101, 136, 292
Chancoso, Blanca, 74, 132, 136
Chicano movement, 36, 256–57

citizenship, 6, 17, 104, 167, 187, 298n7; cultural, 33, 43; dual, 242; Indigenous, 174–75, 177, 229, 236 (*see also* cargo system); labor market and, 295; mestizo modernity and, 16; status, 7, 203, 226; women's labor and, 178

class, 6–8, 37, 50, 202–3, 226, 271, 308n28; bias, 129; borders, 35, 234; distinction, 212; exclusion based on, 118; exploitation, 295; gender and, 131; hierarchy, 196; identity, 119; Indigenous women and, 133, 185, 202, 205, 243; multiple colonialities and, 222; patriarchal power and, 126; power, 57, 98, 306n9; as vector of power, 94

Coalition for Humane Immigrant Rights of Los Angeles (CHIRLA), 240, 253

colonialism, 83, 99, 116, 133, 179, 202, 252, 260, 269, 308n28; gender and, 131, 215; geographies of difference and, 196; in Mexico, 126

coloniality of power, 9, 13, 34, 37, 196, 222–23, 257

colonial violence, 76, 90, 93–94, 215, 275

Comandanta Esther, 86, 261; speech at Mexican Congress, 1, 47, 81–82, 84–85, 301n20

Comandanta Ramona, 68–69, 261

Comité de Defensa de los Recursos Humanos y Culturales Mixes (Committee for the Defense of Mixe Human and Cultural Resources, CODREMI), 165–66, 304n9

Commission on Concordance and Pacification (COCOPA), 21, 60, 62; ANIPA and, 300n17; initiative, 21, 83, 85–86; law, 81, 85

Comunidades Indígenas en Liderazgo (Indigenous Communities in Leadership, CIELO), 261, 273, 275–76, 278–79, 281–82, 287

Comunitaria. *See* Coordinadora Regional de Autoridades Comunitarias-Policía Comunitaria (Regional Coordinator of Community Authorities-Communitarian Police, CRAC-PC)

COMANI (Coordinadora Nacional de Mujeres Indígenas/National Coordinator of Indigenous Women), 3, 28, 41, 44–47, 48f, 51–53, 66f, 67, 69–72, 76–79, 83, 85, 103–4, 112, 128–29, 139, 145, 155, 162, 260–64, 289–91; activists, 49–50, 74f, 87–88, 93, 135, 293, 298n8, 300n16, 300n18; AMIO and, 188; on feminicide, 91; members of, 3, 45, 68, 74, 126, 134–35, 287; networks and, 147, 152–53, 188. *See also* Coordinadora Guerrerense de Mu-

jeres Indígenas (CGMI); Hernández Cruz, Lizbeth; Gutiérrez, Margarita; Martínez Solano, Felicitas; Mendoza, Fabiola Del Jurado; Palomo, Nellys; Patricio, María de Jesús; Robles Hernández, Sofía; Sánchez Néstor, Martha

Confederación de Nacionalidades Indígenas del Ecuador (Confederation of Indigenous Nationalities of Ecuador, CONAIE), 1, 74

Congreso Nacional Indígena (National Indigenous Congress, CNI), 27, 45, 47, 51, 72–74, 139, 261, 264–67, 269, 271; ANIPA and, 300n17; drug trafficking cartels and, 90; formation of, 68; San Andrés Accords and, 24; Women's Commission of, 67, 69, 72, 82; women's session at third, 1, 61, 73–74. *See also* Consejo Indígena de Gobierno (Indigenous Governance Council, CIG); Patricio, María de Jesús (Marichuey)

conquest, 11, 99, 223, 283

Consejo Guerrerense 500 Años de Resistencia Indígena, 1, 70, 72, 103

Consejo Indígena de Gobierno (Indigenous Governance Council, CIG), 47, 90, 261–69, 311n3; presidential candidacy of, 271; role of women in, 31

consulta, 42, 57–59, 63–65, 67, 265, 269–70, 272, 290

Continental Encuentro of Indigenous Women, 103–4, 112

Continental Indigenous Women's Network, 1, 105

Convention 169 on Indigenous and Tribal Peoples, 20–21, 61, 99, 105, 299n12

Convention on the Elimination of All Forms of Discrimination against Women (CEDAW), 103, 138

co-option/co-optation, 22–25, 37; of gender, 22, 83–84, 87; Indigenous autonomy as resistance against, 44; of Indigenous knowledge, 115; of Indigenous rights, 22, 42; Indigenous women's movements and, 5, 65, 145; of women's rights discourse, 298n6

Coordinadora Guerrerense de Mujeres Indígenas (Guerreran Coordinator of Indigenous Women, CGMI), 155–57

Coordinadora Regional de Autoridades Comunitarias-Policía Comunitaria (Regional Coordinator of Community

Authorities-Communitarian Police, CRAC-PC), 158-62, 263
COVID-19, 88, 273, 278-79, 281, 285, 287, 289, 310n17
criminalization, 25-26, 43, 252; of migration, 253, 261; of protest, 261-62. *See also* war on drugs
Critical Latinx Indigeneities, 30, 35, 40, 232-34, 254, 256-57, 295, 309n4
cultural rights, 61, 81, 106; co-option of, 83; gender and, 177; of Indigenous peoples, 20-22; for Indigenous women, 272; state recognition of, 22, 24
Cumes, Aura, 30, 129, 134
Cunningham, Myrna, 131-32, 303n17

Dagnino, Evelina, 43, 298n5
Dalton, Margarita, 174, 177
deregulation, 20, 89, 259
diaspora, 306n10; Afro-Mexicans in, 272; Indigenous, 255; Indigenous belonging and, 19; Latin American Indigenous, 4, 30, 37, 40, 194, 227, 230-32, 234, 249-50, 254, 256, 275, 285, 294; Mayan, 17, 39, 203, 205, 216, 230, 284, 286; Mexican, 5, 18; Mexican Indigenous, 27, 88, 139, 205, 230, 269, 289; Mixtec, 34, 194; Oaxacan Indigenous, 39, 53, 241-42, 277-78, 284, 294
Díaz, Floriberto, 149-50, 173, 179, 304n9
Díaz, Maura, 208f, 213f, 305n2
differential consciousness, 18, 57, 100, 111, 117, 141, 289-90, 297n5
displacement, 93, 109, 266, 286; forced, 231, 255; globalization and, 306n10; Indigenous consciousness and, 226; of Indigenous people, 26, 230-31, 294; neoliberal reforms and, 20-21
dispossession, 25, 259, 261, 266, 270, 276; accumulation by, 26, 259-60; Indigenous, 26, 262, 283; territorial, 93-94, 232, 262, 283; war on drugs and, 13
doble mirada, 100-102, 111, 117, 130, 136, 292. *See also* Kab'awil
Domínguez-Santos, Rufino, 29, 32, 197, 306n5
Don Juan Pérez, Norma, 90, 92-93, 134-35, 262-263, 287-288
doubleweaving, 17-18, 101, 111, 185, 188, 192, 292
Driskill, Qwo-Li, 17-18, 30, 101, 185, 292. *See also* doubleweaving

ejido system, 11, 20, 175, 187, 259
Emergencia Comunitaria de Género (Gender Community Emergency, ECG), 91-93
encuentros, 304n15; continental, 38, 45, 96; feminist, 28, 117-18, 140-41, 302n16; Indigenous women and, 97, 119, 122, 126, 137, 141, 183; regional, 183, 186; statewide, 187
Enlace Continental de Mujeres Indígenas de Abya Yala (Continental Indigenous Women's Network, ECMIA), xix, 28, 38-39, 67, 74, 96-98, 100-105, 108-15, 133, 139-40, 146, 162, 291, 301n1, 303n2; as multiscalar network, 188; name change, 142; twentieth anniversary of, 129
epistemologies, 17, 30; Guna, 107; Indigenous women and, 100-101, 111-12, 130, 153, 260; interweaving of, 141, 146, 156, 192; Maya, 286; spatial, 98, 101; third space, 292. *See also* Indigenous epistemologies
erasure, 196, 256, 286; Indigenous, 11, 35-37, 98, 101, 231; of US third-world women, 297n5
Escobar, Arturo, 15, 28, 38, 145-46
ethnicity, 8, 133, 185
extraction: capitalist, 26; of gas and petroleum, 270; of labor, 94, 311n18; resource, 89, 103, 140, 252, 264
extractivism, 31, 43, 113, 126, 258, 261, 270, 283
EZLN (Ejército Zapatista de Liberación Nacional/Zapatista Army of National Liberation), caravan, 1, 21, 86; rebellion/uprising (1994), 2-4, 21, 23, 30-31, 37, 46-47, 57-58, 63, 82, 103-4, 143, 147, 189, 205, 290, 300n14; Women's Revolutionary Law, 23, 58, 147

feminicide, 89-94, 258, 262, 270, 291
feminism(s), 31, 117-18, 204, 214-15, 302n16; Chicana, 36, 256; exclusionary configuration of, 141; hegemonic, 98, 117, 130-31, 140, 150, 154, 292; Indigenous, 30, 111, 120-22, 128-29, 131-33, 136-40, 142, 149, 215, 292-93; Latin American and Caribbean, 112, 118-19, 133, 136; mestiza, 120, 126; transnational, 8; US, 297n5; Western, 134, 143, 148-49, 292
feminist movement, 22, 122, 129, 156; Indigenous people and, 93; Indigenous women's organizing and, 138-39; Latin American, 98, 104-5, 118-19, 126, 130, 292

feminists, 7, 91, 117-18, 122, 140, 300n15; autonomous, 119; Black, 118; Chicana, 257; Indigenous, 93, 126, 130, 132, 135, 283; Indigenous activists and, 124, 126, 129; Latin American, 110; Maya women and, 134; mestiza, 98, 100, 121, 136-37, 172, 301n23; native, 94; Oaxacan popular uprising and, 187; socialist, 177; women of color, 94, 297n5

Fourth World Congress on Women, 38, 67, 102-3, 105-6, 112, 141, 168

Fox, Jonathan, 242, 305n8

Frente Indígena de Organizaciones Binacionales (FIOB), 28-29, 33, 39, 152, 193-99, 201, 203-10, 212-20, 224-29, 234-35, 240-43, 247-50, 254, 261, 271-81, 284, 287-89, 294, 305n1; Women's Commission of, 39

gendered violence, 12, 75, 94, 130, 231, 262
gender hierarchies, 5, 133, 202, 215, 222
gender justice, 84, 96, 112, 129-31, 135, 149, 157, 161-62; FIOB and, 229
geographies, 242-43; colonial, 233, 250; of dissent, 240-41; gendered, 8, 196, 212, 253, 295; immigrant, 237-38; Indigenous, 42, 230, 232-35, 250, 253, 294; racial, 223, 227; racialized, 13, 259; of refusal, 18; sacred, 40, 116, 232, 243-44, 249-50, 254; social, 212, 253; spiritual, 232, 295; transregional, 252
geographies of difference, 6-8, 15, 18, 111, 142, 203-4, 213, 306n9; Critical Latinx Indigeneities and, 234, 295; differential consciousness and, 117; FIOB and, 215, 229; Indigenous, 35; Indigenous migrants and, 225; Indigenous women and, 44, 56, 97, 100, 192, 196, 202, 231, 289-91, 294; migrant organizers and, 222; transborder Indigenous activists and, 194-96, 226, 229
geographies of indigeneity, 4, 39, 203, 229, 231-32, 235-36
geography, 11, 13; conventional, 244; of difference, 7, 141, 194; of dissent, 240; gendered, 212; Indigenous, 17, 116; of Los Angeles, 235, 243, 253; Mesoamerican, 101; of remembrance, 242; of the sacred, 310n17; Tongva and Tatavium, 233
globalization, 8, 27-28, 115, 146, 196, 202, 298n8; of Indigenous rights, 159; neoliberal, 36, 100, 143, 306n10
Goeman, Mishuana, 11, 29, 311n19

governance, 26, 86, 176-77, 211, 259; colonial, 9-10, 99, 179, 188; Indigenous, 24, 37, 83, 94, 151, 153, 159, 170, 174-75, 182, 190, 264-65, 272, 303n3; Indigenous communal, 12, 151, 173; Indigenous women and, 5, 65, 82, 95; in Mexico, 13; neoliberal, 22-23, 83, 85, 106, 121, 298n6; in Oaxaca, 293; polity of Indigenous people and, 132; scales of, 167, 169, 235; settler colonial, 175. *See also* Indigenous self-governance
governmentality, 106, 286; gender as discourse of, 22-23, 44, 62, 83, 85, 143, 177, 182, 191; gendered, 23, 86; Indigenous normative systems as forms of, 148; neoliberal, 22, 43. *See also* multiculturalism: neoliberal
Grewal, Inderpal, 179, 225, 228
Guelaguetza (Oaxacan Heritage Month), 216, 235, 237-38, 276; restaurant, 240
Guna language, 107, 109, 301n1, 302n6
Guna people, 4, 96, 107; land struggle of, 302n9. *See also* Abiayala
Gutiérrez, Margarita, 50, 58-60, 62, 72, 99f, 103, 110, 127, 302n6; *Dualidad y Complementariedad*, 133, 287
Gutiérrez Nájera, Lourdes, 30, 237

Hale, Charles, 22-23
Harcourt, Wendy, 15, 145-46
Hernández Castillo, Aída, 13, 25-26, 31, 66, 94, 259-60, 294, 301n20, 310n14; on Indigenous women's organizing, 31, 131; *Multiple InJustices*, 25, 303n17; on the State Convention of Chiapanecan Women, 300n15; vernacularization, 153
Hernández Cruz, Lizbeth, 127, 135
Hernández Pérez, Laura, 88f, 135, 264, 288
HR 4437, 240, 310n11
HTAs (hometown associations), 33, 204, 220, 229, 235-37, 242, 247-48

immigrants, 22; backlash against, 254; Oaxacan Indigenous, 40; South Korean, 308n2; undocumented, 201, 310n11; US as country of, 32
imperialism, 179, 228, 230, 283
indigeneity, 4, 6, 8, 32, 35, 96, 120, 226, 294, 298n8; diasporas and, 232; gender and, 62, 81, 132, 196, 202, 209-10, 229, 235; geogra-

352 • INDEX

phies of difference and, 195–96; hegemonic discourses on, 31; indigenismo and, 256–57; Indigenous women's rights and, 215; jurisprudence and, 24; migration and, 222; mobile archives of, 17, 283–89; multiple colonialities and, 223, 231, 243, 254, 256, 294; neoliberalism and, 111; poverty and, 144; race and, 37, 81, 225; spatialization of, 236; state management of, 34, 36; as vector of power, 94, 126. *See also* geographies of indigeneity

indigenismo, 35–36, 108, 256–57

Indigenous archives, 10; mobile, 17, 283–289

Indigenous autonomy, 13, 19, 24, 31, 106, 155, 159, 176, 189, 219, 304n9; Ayuujk (Mixe) and, 167; CONAMI and, 45, 71; gendered demands for, 103; gendered meanings of, 113; Indigenous women and, 3, 6, 42, 47, 52, 57–58, 60, 65–67, 81, 94–95, 117, 147, 149, 290, 293; Law on Indigenous Rights and Cultures and, 168; in Mexico, 37, 41–42, 44, 62, 272; in Oaxaca, 174, 181; pedagogy of, 77; state's gendered logic of racism against, 82, 84, 86–87; state recognition of, 22; women's rights and, 23, 52, 54, 62, 65, 82, 153, 190; Zapatista call for, 163. *See also* consulta; EZLN

Indigenous belonging, 19, 33, 204, 232, 286

Indigenous cosmovisions, 1, 13, 17, 226, 231; colonial forms of governance and, 188; frames of resistance based on, 31; gender equality and, 138; Indigenous feminist consciousness and, 132; intersectional analysis and, 269

Indigenous customary law (usos y costumbres), 42, 64, 84, 154, 169–70, 179; autonomy and, 45, 101; critiques of, 301n20; elections and, 174–75; Indigenous rights and, 44; in Tlahuitoltepec, 180; women's rights and, 3, 24

Indigenous epistemologies, 10, 13, 17–18, 38, 107–8, 146, 149, 229, 292; alternative relationalities and, 106; comunalidad and, 151; ECMIA and, 114; Indigenous women's rights activists and, 133; scale and, 19, 42, 289; social movement networks and, 100

Indigenous knowledges, 17, 100, 108, 112, 115–17, 146–47, 185; academic research and, 283; of autonomy, 293; comunalidad and, 149, 151; Indigenous women's activism and, 292; MICA's preservation of, 289; unscalable elements of, 19

Indigenous languages, 61, 216–17, 248, 276, 278–79; in Los Angeles, 29, 39, 197, 216, 274–75, 282; loss of, 277; in Mexico, 20, 29, 274; repression and eradication of, 108; speakers of, 29, 39, 197, 205, 225, 235

Indigenous migrants, 3, 32, 34, 36–37, 222–23, 234, 244; cargo system and, 236; Central American, 273; diasporas and, 254; FIOB and, 204–5, 216; geographies of difference and, 35, 225; labor market and, 295; language access and, 225; mobile archives of indigeneity and, 286–89; multiple colonialities and, 228; Oaxacan, 33, 39, 201; organizing, 309n5; pan-Indian identities and, 256; place-making and, 235; settler colonial projects and, 255; spatial projects of, 232, 294; transborder geographies of indigeneity and, 203; transborder scales and, 15; transregions and, 203–4; weaving and, 17

Indigenous normative systems, 51, 58, 65, 71, 154, 170, 174–75; stewardship and, 116; women and, 82, 84, 148, 172, 178, 189–92

Indigenous rights, 21, 48, 52, 54, 59, 87, 145, 155, 299n11; Abiayala and, 109; consciousness of, 203, 227; discourse, 117; ECMIA and, 96; EZLN and, 147, 163; FIOB and, 205–6; gender and, 24, 46, 86, 126; Indigenous women and, 64, 84, 129–30; law and, 159; Mexican government and, 38, 42; MIEL and, 217; neoliberal governance and, 22; organizing, 147; usos y costumbres and, 44; women's rights and, 5, 81–82, 122, 128, 130–31, 179, 189, 293

Indigenous rights movement, 2–3, 43, 46, 53, 137, 224; activists, 81, 124; cooptation of demands of, 42; Indigenous women in, 37, 140, 168; international, 141; SER and, 304n10; women's rights and, 189

Indigenous rights organizations, 45–46, 51, 139, 152, 224

Indigenous self-determination, 24–25, 59, 99, 111, 190; communal, 304n9; decolonization and, 222; Indigenous women and, 65, 70, 138, 154; mestizaje and, 36; right to, 21, 24, 41–44, 168, 184, 299n12; scalar forms of, 12; struggles for, 163, 230, 311n18. *See also* Convention 169 on Indigenous and Tribal Peoples; Indigenous autonomy

Indigenous self-governance, 12, 23–24, 43, 45, 58, 62

Indigenous women's movement, 2, 5, 28, 41, 46, 59, 69, 95, 138, 168, 179, 211n287; Beijing NGO process and, 118; COMANI and, 70, 72, 81; ECMIA and, 103; scales and, 145, 159

Indigenous women's rights, 31, 61, 81; activists, 131, 133; COMANI and, 45, 85, 189; FIOB and, 215, 227; Indigenous autonomy and, 62; San Andrés Accords and, 44, 60, 67, 73, 127

intellectual property, 113; Indigenous, 115–17; law, 112, 115; rights, 71, 103, 111, 115–16

International Labor Organization (ILO), 20, 99, 105. *See also* Convention 169 on Indigenous and Tribal Peoples

internationalism, 34, 100

interweaving, 15, 25, 111–12, 115, 117, 153, 156, 168, 185, 188, 289, 292; transborder horizontal, 278

Jaminez Xum, Manuel, 216, 242–43, 274

Jiménez, Cándida, 51–52, 69, 72, 74, 76, 77*f*, 99*f*. *See also* COMANI

Juris, Jeffrey, 27–28

jurisprudence, 73; Indigenous, 24, 41, 45, 95, 170

justice, 27, 84, 96, 162, 299n11; access to, 92, 187; ancestral, 113, 115; communal, 100; communitarian, 159; Indigenous, 159; for Indigenous migrants, 222, 245; Indigenous women and, 271; lack of, 113, 280; language, 216, 273, 276, 279; seed, 283; social, 2, 7, 269, 286, 306n10; structures of, 99; struggles for, 31; women and, 91, 161. *See also* gender justice

Kab'awil, 100–101, 136, 292

Keme, Emil, 30, 107–8, 110, 302n8

Khasnabish, Alex, 27–28

K'inal Antsetik, 71, 79, 155, 300n18

kinship, 12, 173, 218, 229, 235

Kuna people. *See* Guna people

Kuuyam, 233–34, 254–56, 294

Latinidad, 232, 286; US, 37, 226, 254

Law on Indigenous Rights and Cultures, 22, 47, 155, 168

local, the, 8, 11, 130; COMANI and, 293; Indigenous women and, 13, 49, 144–45, 147, 182; REDMMI and, 185

localization, 15, 38, 153

Luna, Irma, 201, 289

Maceda, Oralia, 280–81, 289

Magaña, Maurice, 146–47

Maldonado, Centolia, 29, 197–98, 209

Mapping Indigenous LA Project, 29, 250, 310n17

maps, 10–11; language, 282; of Los Angeles, 230; scalar imaginary and, 9; story, 27, 29, 282

Martinez, Janet, 238*f*, 261, 273, 275–78, 281–82, 287; *Zapotecs: The Journey to Success*, 309n9. *See also* Comunidades Indígenas en Liderazgo (Indigenous Communities in Leadership, CIELO)

Martínez Luna, Jaime, 149–50, 304n9

Martinez Solano, Felicitas, 54–56, 147, 156–61, 221

Mayan Day Keeper Association, 244, 249

Mayans, 39, 99, 230, 232, 236, 249, 258

Mendoza, Fabiola del Jurado, 53, 88*f*, 90, 92–93, 135, 263, 287

meshworks, 15, 145–46, 156, 162, 167–68, 204, 292; interweaving and, 19, 146, 168, 185, 192

mestizaje, 35–36, 108, 256–57

Mexican Congress, 81, 271; EZLN and, 1, 21, 84–85 (*see also* Comandanta Esther)

Mexican Revolution, 20, 167, 175, 259

migration, 31, 37, 39, 207, 221–28, 235, 243–45, 254, 256; criminalization of, 253, 261, 305n7; crisis, 273; cross-border, 34; family separation as deterrent to, 258; gender arrangements and, 196–97; geographies of difference and, 196; Indigenous, 30, 32–33, 35–36, 40, 195, 203–4, 222, 231, 233, 236, 274, 293 (*see also* transregions); Indigenous women's activism and, 144, 210; internal, 209, 228; labor, 44, 49; mass, 222, 229, 306n10; Mayan, 255; neoliberal reforms and, 20–21, 259; settler colonial projects and, 35; transnational, 8, 33, 222

Mixtec language, 29, 194, 201

Mixtecs, 4, 10, 78, 151, 195, 249, 255

Mobile Indigenous Community Archive (MICA), 30, 283–89

mobility, 50, 144, 161, 195, 250, 259, 305n7; differentiated, 8; Indigenous, 39–40, 49, 231–33, 293; Indigenous consciousness and, 226; labor and, 232, 252–53; political organizing and, 197, 294

modernity, 31, 33, 83–84, 144; mestizo, 16; state projects of, 36

murder, 26, 78, 268; of Indigenous women, 90, 92, 113. *See also* feminicide; Jaminez Xum, Manuel
Muisca people, 133–34
Mujeres Indígenas en Liderazgo (Indigenous Women in Leadership, MIEL), 213–14, 216–21, 227, 250, 305n1, 308n26
multiculturalism, 179; neoliberal, 22, 37, 106, 190–91, 259; watered-down, 23, 25; women's rights and, 81
multiple colonialities, 32, 35–37; 196; geographies of difference and, 203, 222, 231; indigeneity and, 223, 231, 256, 294; Indigenous migrants and, 228; Latin American, 40; of Los Angeles, 233, 294–95; Tongva cartographies and, 230
multisited ethnography, 5, 27–28
mutual aid, 33, 134, 281

NAFTA (North American Free Trade Agreement), 20–21, 202
National Democratic Convention, 64, 67, 153; dissolution of, 300n17
National Movement of Maya Weavers, 18
national Indigenous movement in Mexico, 1, 57, 263; women and, 3, 6, 37, 50, 72–73, 94, 152, 269
nationalism: Indigenous, 131; mestizo, 120
neoliberalism, 89, 146; drug cartels and, 26; as form of governance, 106 (*see also* governance: neoliberal); indigeneity and, 111; Indigenous autonomy and, 22, 66, 298n4; Indigenous women's movements and, 6; Mexico and, 20; migration and, 294; multiculturalism and, 25 (*see also* multiculturalism: neoliberal); neocolonialism and, 252; NGOization of feminism and, 119; state responsibilities and, 21; Zapatistas as global force against, 5. *See also* deregulation; privatization
neoliberal multicriminalism, 26, 42, 259
neoliberal reforms, 20, 26, 259
Nicolás, Brenda, 30, 34, 210, 235–36, 309n5
nongovernmental organizations (NGOs), 6, 23, 104, 121, 168; ECMIA and, 146; feminism and, 119; feminist, 85, 98, 119–20; rights and, 153; State Convention of Chiapanecan Women and, 300n15
nonscalability, 101; theory, 110

Ong, Aihwa, 43–44, 204, 298n7
Oaxacalifornia, 33, 242, 278
oppression, 190, 228, 301n2; class, 202; colonial and capitalist, 151; economic, 196, 294; gender(ed), 8, 118, 132, 196, 226, 243; Indigenous, 118; Indigenous migrants and, 201; of Indigenous women, 61–62, 84, 133–34, 136, 185, 195, 202; migrant women and children and, 246; structural, 36; triple, 61–62, 185, 206; of women, 7
Organización Regional de Oaxaca (Regional Organization of Oaxaca, ORO), 33, 238
Ortiz Peña, Ernestina, 51, 72, 258, 261. *See also* CONAMI
Otros Saberes Initiative, 29, 197–98, 208f, 213, 216

Palomo, Nellys, 71, 85f, 138–39, 155
PAN (Partido Acción Nacional/National Action Party), 21, 190, 301n22. *See also* Calderón, Felipe
Patricio, María de Jesús (Marichuey), 47–49, 51, 68, 72, 77f, 82, 154–55, 186, 261, 264–71
Peña Nieto, Enrique, 267; administration of, 25
place-making, 231; Indigenous, 40, 232, 235–37, 239, 250, 294–95
plant medicines, 269, 283–84
political representation, 4, 14, 41, 59, 299n11
poverty, 21, 259, 270; feminization of, 22; indigeneity and, 144; Indigenous migrants and, 223, 227–28, 250; Indigenous peoples and, 89; Indigenous pueblos and, 109; in Oaxaca, 205
PRD (Partido de la Revolución Democrática/Party of Democratic Revolution), 59, 86, 280, 299n13; ANIPA and, 300n17
PRI (Partido Revolucionario Institucional/Institutional Revolutionary Party), 20, 84, 169, 301n22
privatization, 20, 89, 259, 270, 303n17

race, 6–8, 118, 120, 133, 226, 253, 308n8; cosmic, 36; domestic workers and, 271; gender and, 131, 196, 202; geographies of difference and, 195, 306n9; governmentalities of, 22; indigeneity and, 37, 81, 225; labor market and, 295; migration and, 222–23; patriarchal power and, 126; relations in Mexico, 228 racism, 21, 55, 118, 122, 124, 126, 187, 196, 201, 231, 234, 273, 291; cultural, 121, 301n22; of feminists, 85, 120, 129, 301n23; gendered forms of, 26, 81; gendered logic of, 22–24, 81–84, 86, 94, 121; Indigenous women's critique of, 130, 133; institutional, 274–75; of the institutional Left, 266; mestizo, 224, 301n23; in Mexican society, 268, 271; migration and, 223, 227, 246–47; nonstate belonging and, 43; structural, 191, 207; systemic, 269; as violence, 137

Radcliffe, Sarah, 13, 22

Ramirez, Reyna, 30, 233

Red de Mujeres Mixes (Network of Mixe Women, REDMMI), 149, 163, 167, 183–86, 188, 304n15

refugees, 26, 39, 258, 276, 285, 310n17

Regino Montes, Adelfo, 163, 179, 303n7

rights discourse, 24–25, 66, 95; human, 31, 117, 121; Indigenous, 117; practices of autonomy and, 6, 24, 37, 42; women's, 117, 298n6. *See also* Indigenous autonomy; Indigenous rights

Rivera Cusicanqui, Silvia, 16, 18, 30

Rivera-Salgado, Gaspar, 33, 215, 222, 238f, 242

Rivera Zea, Tarcila, 136–37

Robles Hernández, Sofía, 50, 72, 77f, 103–5, 147, 151, 163–71, 180–86, 189, 302n6, 303n2, 303-4nn8-9; MIEL and, 218, 307n22; scales of activism and, 15–16

Romero Hernández, Odilia, 28–29, 133, 197, 213, 238f, 241–42, 244–50, 261, 305n2, 310n14; *El Tequio* and, 273; Indigenous Interpreters program and, 273–76. *See also* Frente Indígena de Organizaciones Binacionales (FIOB); Mujeres Indígenas en Liderazgo (Indigenous Women in Leadership, MIEL)

Rosales Carreño, Ezequiel, 279–80

Rosa Luxemburg Foundation, 214–15

Ruiz, Ulises, 186, 240, 280, 307n18

Saldaña-Portillo, María Josefina, 13, 223

San Andrés Peace Accords, 3, 43–44, 46, 58, 67, 95, 151, 155, 168; COCOPA law and, 21–22, 81

Sánchez, Maria (Doña Mari), 218–20, 224–25, 227

Sánchez-López, Luis, 13, 30, 174–75, 217, 309n4

Sánchez Néstor, Martha, 1, 52, 72, 84–86, 103, 125f, 130, 139–41, 156–57, 159, 287, 289; on cultural racism within feminist discourse, 121; on abuse against Indigenous women, 76; on racism of mestiza feminists, 301n23. *See also* doble mirada

Sandoval, Chela, 18, 141, 192, 289, 297n5

Sandoval, Paty Torres, 53, 88f, 91

Sandoval, Tomasa, 1, 2f, 50, 74, 80–81, 85f, 127–28, 149, 179

scalability, 18, 101–2, 110. *See also* nonscalability; unscalability

scales of power, 4–6, 15, 27, 38, 57, 63, 96, 114, 290

self-determination. *See* Indigenous self-determination

Sepulveda, Charles, 233, 254–56

Servicios del Pueblo Mixe (Services of the Mixe Pueblo, SER), 45, 50, 70, 163, 166–67, 169, 188

settler colonialism, 17, 231–32, 254–57; logics of, 26, 37; in Mexico and Guatemala, 13; United States (US), 34, 230; violence and, 12

sexual assault, 25, 91, 93, 228

sexual harassment, 228, 279–80

sexuality, 7–8, 118, 212; colonial systems of, 30; decolonization of, 292; gender and, 131, 202; geographies of difference and, 195, 306n9

sexual violence, 26, 79, 93–94, 130, 244, 248, 259–60

Sierra, Teresa, 158–59, 161–62, 303n6

Simpson, Audra, 18, 30

social movements, 7, 31, 34, 305n8; criminalization of, 25–26; glocalities and, 146; Indigenous, 6, 20, 44, 65, 83, 304n14; in Latin America, 103, 298n6; scale and, 14, 98; success of, 62; transnational, 27, 32, 202–3, 298n6, 305-6nn8-10; women of color, 283

solidarity, 19, 38, 40, 93, 118, 233, 254, 257, 262; Abiayala and, 102, 107–9, 111, 141–42, 291; Chiapas uprising and, 104; cross-border, 96; difference and, 7; émigrés and, 306n10; FIOB and, 216, 241, 307n18; hemispheric, 3, 14; identity, 110–11, 113, 292; Indigenous, 6, 15, 98, 109, 204, 242, 256, 289; Indigenous women and, 103, 112, 124, 126, 130, 291; mestizos and, 224; Oaxaca teachers strike and, 240; spatial projects of, 101, 109

sovereignty, 36; data, 287; food, 113, 115, 283; state, 189, 232

Speed, Shannon, 13, 26, 30, 42, 175, 259, 294

Stephen, Lynn, 30–31, 33–35, 94, 167, 175–77, 182, 202, 234, 297n3, 306nn8-9; on autonomy, 298n2; on violence against Indigenous women, 26; on women's participation in Oaxacan popular uprising, 67, 211–12. *See also* transborder

Subcomandante Marcos, 58, 64
subjectivity, 294; collective, 43, 63, 96; feminism's political, 118; Indigenous, 23, 84, 121, 205; Indigenous women's political, 4, 46, 63–64, 96, 113; social, 203, 215

Tatavium people, 30, 250, 253
tequio (communal labor), 149–50, 174–75, 177, 189, 229, 304n9; cargo system and, 305n3
El Tequio, 216, 248, 273, 287–88
Teeter, Wendy, 29, 311n19
Tongva (Gabrielino/Gabrieleño) peoples, 4, 29–30, 39, 230, 233, 249–50, 253, 255. *See also* Kuuyam
tradition, 31, 33, 42, 58, 126, 175–76; gender-specific roles and, 235; Mexico's democratic, 24; patriarchal norms and, 148; sexist practices in the guise of, 101
transborder, 34–35, 234, 306n9
transborder organizing, 204, 216, 229, 234, 241, 306n10; Indigenous, 19, 36, 196
transindigeneity, 32, 109
transmigration, 27; scholars, 32
transnationalism, 32, 34, 109
transregions, 15, 32, 192, 203–4, 235; Indigenous, 236
Triqui language, 29, 197
Triqui people, 133, 198, 205, 255, 272, 274
Trump, Donald, 258, 273; immigration policies of, 229
Tsing, Anna, 18–19, 98, 101–2, 110–12
Turbicio, Hermalinda, 52–53, 78, 221
Tzul Tzul, Gladys, 12, 30, 151, 173–74

UN Declaration on the Rights of Indigenous People (UNDRIP), 99, 103, 107
Union of Indigenous Communities of the Northern Zone of the Isthmus (Unión de Comunidades Indígenas de la Zona Norte del Istmo, UCIZONI), 45, 70
unscalability, 110, 142

Vargas, Virginia, 104, 301n5
Velasco Ortiz, Laura, 29, 197–98, 204–5, 209, 223
Villa, Rufina, 50, 77

war on drugs, 13, 24–25, 43, 54, 89, 190, 259–60. *See also* Calderón, Felipe
weaving, 4, 16–19, 38, 102, 115, 141, 262, 290; collectives, 71; interscalar, 88, 143, 145, 168, 185, 260; technologies, 112. *See also* doubleweaving
women's leadership, 54, 157; FIOB and, 213–15, 220, 273, 305n1 (*see also* Mujeres Indígenas en Liderazgo [Indigenous Women in Leadership, MIEL]); Indigenous, 51, 261; visibility of, 46; workshops, 139, 219, 249
women's rights, 22, 73–74, 82, 84, 117, 139, 143, 148, 156, 161, 167, 182, 184–86, 188, 200; CONAMI and, 85f, 189; ECMIA and, 96; EZLN and, 82; Indigenous autonomy and, 23, 52, 54, 62, 65, 82, 153, 190 Indigenous customary law (usos y costumbres) and, 3, 24, 190; Indigenous rights and, 5, 81–82, 122, 128, 130–31, 179, 189, 293; Indigenous women and, 31, 272; multiculturalism and, 81. *See also* Indigenous women's rights
World Conference on Women, 98, 106, 112, 117, 168; Indigenous women activists' preparation for Fourth, 38, 67, 102–3, 105, 141, 168. *See also* Beijing process
Worthen, Holly, 24, 148, 150, 172, 174, 177–79, 182, 190–91

Xaam Të'ëxy, 166–67

Zapatista women, 1; political consciousness of, 49
Zapotec language, 29, 194, 197, 224, 246–47, 274
Zapotecs, 4, 151, 195, 209, 236–37, 249, 255

www.ingramcontent.com/pod-product-compliance
Lightning Source LLC
Chambersburg PA
CBHW021847230426
43671CB00006B/301